The King

Denis Law, hero of the Stretford End

by Brian Hughes MBE

EMPIRE
Publications

First published in 2003

EMPIRE PUBLICATIONS
1 Newton Street, Manchester M1 1HW
copyright Brian Hughes 2003

ISBN 1 901 746 35 6

Front cover photographs courtesy of the author
Back cover photographs courtesy of Harry Goodwin and the author
Jacket design: Ashley Shaw
Edited by Ashley Shaw and Stuart Fish

Front Cover - main picture: Denis Law wheels away in typical celebration. background picture: Denis produces a spectacular twisting header against Tottenham Hotspur at Old Trafford, 1967.
Back Cover: (clockwise from top left) Denis aged 10; his infamous backheel for Manchester City against United in 1974; lifting the 1967 League Championship; in action against Crystal Palace 1971; scoring against Manchester City in 1966; in jovial mood at a recent golf tournament; and celebrating Scotland's famous 3-2 victory over England at Wembley in 1967.

Printed in Great Britain by:
Biddles Book Manufacturers
Guildford, Surrey

I dedicate this book to my wife Rosemarie,
my sons Anthony, Damian and Christopher
and my daughter Rachel
- the best team a man could ever have

Contents

Illustrations

Picture Credits

*All photographs from the author's personal collection except 61 courtesy of Harry Goodwin;
Every effort has been made to trace copyright holders and we apologise in advance for any
unintentional omission. We would be pleased to insert the appropriate acknowledgement in any
subsequent edition.*

Acknowledgements

This book would not have been possible without the help of many people, not least Sean Kelly. Sean, a Manchester United fanatic, must posess the largest collection of Manchester United memorabilia - he was a great help and source of information and was always on hand to offer help and advice. Special thanks must also go to John Donohue for his invaluable contribution in securing dates and stories about the subject of this book. I would also like to thank Mr and Mrs Slingsby for their help in this enterprise, Colin Tasker for his unstinting technical assistance and Harry Goodwin, photograper to the stars, for the use of his excellent photographs.

Every effort has been made to trace the copyright owners for material used in this book but in most cases this has not been possible. I would also like to thank many others for articles loaned to me by several football supporters. Many people sent me unsolicited material such as newspaper cuttings and magazine articles and I would like to acknowledge with gratitude their help. I would also like to thank the people who sent me photographs for use in this book. A special thanks must also go to the fanzine *Red Issue*. David Meek has obliged me by allowing me to reprint his story about Denis Law which appeared in his 1989 book *Manchester United Greats*.

Finally, to anyone who I have failed to mention, my sincerest apologies - it has not been done for any malicious reason, purely through forgetfulness - please forgive me and enjoy the book.

Introduction

David Meek had the unenviable job of taking over from the well-respected, popular and experienced Tom Jackson as the feature journalist of Manchester United's fortunes for the Manchester Evening News. Dear old Tom had sadly perished at Munich. It was a mammoth task but David rose to the occasion and you could count on one hand the number of United's first team games he failed to report on from the late 50s until his retirement in the 1990s. Through his reports he told the story of the club's successes, scandals and failures. David didn't have an easy job, he was the man in the middle and walked a tightrope between being fair to the club and honest to his readers. He bridged that gap splendidly. He was there for all the club's signings, matches and controversies - both big and small. David, like I suspect many United followers, had a special affinity with Denis Law. In 1989 he wrote a book Manchester United Greats *in which he included Denis Law, and it is with his tribute that I would like to begin this book.*

*

Denis Law was the king and his subjects were the Stretford Enders. No player has commanded more allegiance from the terrace fans than the man who proved the most deadly marksman of all the famous players to perform on the Old Trafford stage. It wasn't just his prolific scoring that won their affection, it was his style and, I suspect, the streak of villainy that undoubtedly ran through his football. The lads at the Stretford End found it easy to identify with a player whose commitment and aggression were so obvious. He was slightly built, but there was a venom to his play which brought him into confrontation with opponents and referees. The crowd liked that; they love a man who brings not only skill to the game but a willingness to fly into the thick of the action with no holds barred. Denis Law was daring, cocky, impudent and abrasive; he could play a bit as well and the whole explosive mixture made him the supreme people's champion.

The famous litany of Charlton, Law and Best still trips easily off the tongue. Each was a star in his own right. Charlton was admired and Best fantastic, but Law was worshipped for the way he combined flair and fire. Few who watched Manchester United in the Sixties will forget the Law trademark as he signalled his goals to the crowd, punching the air and then running with one arm raised, finger pointing to the sky. The crowd would rise to his salute as a gladiator of old!

Goals are the name of the game of course and the Lawman got them more often than anyone. His scoring rate was phenomenal. Charlton was renowned for his cannonball shooting and he holds the club scoring record for his total of goals. Best was a wizard in front of goal and Dennis Viollet still holds the season's League record with 32 in 1959/60. Jack Rowley, Stan Pearson, Tommy Taylor, David Herd, Joe Jordan, Stuart Pearson and Mark Hughes are just a few of the other outstanding marksmen to have worn a red shirt, but Law reigns supreme because of his incredible ratio of goals to appearances, especially in Cup football.

In the League Denis scored 171 goals in 305 games for United, well over the usual strikers' target of a goal every two games. Bobby Charlton scored 198 times, but it took him 604 games to do it; and for all his scoring magic George Best's tally was a mere 137 goals from 361 appearances. I say 'only' for this is in comparison with the best in the business and when you turn to Cup competition, Law had an astonishing scoring rate. In Europe he scored 28 goals in 33 matches and in the FA Cup he hit 34 goals from 44 ties. When Wembley beckoned he was lethal. He once scored six for Manchester City against Luton only to see them wiped off the record when the game was abandoned because of a waterlogged pitch.

But of course the figures only tell half the story and certainly don't explain why he was so lionized by the crowd. What the fans loved so much was the way he scored them with his spectacular overhead and scissors kicks, and his whip-like headers. He jumped so high at times and seemed to hang there so long that it looked as if he had a sky-hook. He was lean and hungry with it, his courage never in question. Lightning over two or three yards, his reflexes were razor sharp. Yet few would have predicted such a glittering career looking at Denis Law as a youngster.

Born in Aberdeen the youngest of seven children, life was fairly hard. His father spent his working life on the trawlers fishing out of the port and there were few luxuries. His pal gave him his first pair of football boots so that he could play for the school Under 11 team. He remembers vividly his first new pair, bought on credit by his Mum when he was 13.

"I caught the tram and went down to the city centre on a cloud. I bought myself a pair of Hotspur boots - I can see them now, they had big ankle protectors and were as hard as a brick. I can remember when I got home sitting on the sink with my feet in a basin of water to soften the leather. I could hardly believe my luck," said Denis.

The boots were cleaned, dried, dubbined and cherished as young Denis graduated to play for Aberdeen Schoolboys, and was picked on one occasion as a reserve for the Scotland team. At top level he had a lot against him, for Denis had inherited a family affliction that caused him no end of misery as a youngster. From the age of five his right eye was badly crossed and he had to wear glasses to correct the squint. When he played football, though, he couldn't wear glasses so he adopted the technique of going through an entire match with his right eye tightly closed. He was in fact a one-eyed footballer, an experience that might well account for the competitive, abrasive streak that ran through his game.

Denis admits: "With a handicap you had to be harder and stand up and fight, and the only way I could fight was to go out on the pitch and play football." He attracted the attention of Archie Beattie, whose brother Andy was manager of Huddersfield Town and he was invited for a trial at the Leeds

Road club. "I couldn't really believe that Huddersfield Town were likely to be very impressed by me when they saw me. After all, I was only a skinny bit of a kid weighing little more than eight stone, and I still had my squint and my owl-like glasses, although by then I did have my name on a waiting list for an operation to correct the defect."

But Huddersfield liked what they saw and took him on to their ground staff. After a few months he went back home to Aberdeen for his operation which was a complete success, though right through his career the vision in his right eye was always blurred. The main thing, though, was that he could now play football without having to screw up one eye, and as Denis says: "I could now open both eyes without having to look in two directions at once. It was like a miracle. I've been told that I had a bit of a swagger on the football field. Well, that was the day it started. That operation completely changed my life. I strutted out of the hospital with my chest stuck out, no hurdle in life would be too great to climb from now on."

Bill Shankly, later Huddersfield's manager, but then in charge of the reserves, had not been too impressed by his first sighting of Law. "He looked like a skinned rabbit. My first reaction was to say get him on the next train home. But from the first moment I saw him play I realised that here was something special. There was never any danger that he wasn't going to make it," declared Shanks. Shankly soon had him playing in the reserves and on Christmas Eve, 1956, he was given his League debut at Notts County aged 16 years and 10 months. Shankly arranged for the café opposite the Huddersfield ground to feed him up on a special diet of steaks and milk. He was still as thin as a rake, but what he lacked in chunky muscle he made up for with his lightning speed off the mark, his instant reactions and of course his aggression. He oozed a natural arrogance that demanded a bigger stage. Matt Busby tried to give him one after Manchester United's youth team had played Huddersfield in the FA Youth Cup. He offered ten thousand pounds but it was turned down. Matt was obviously impressed and in October 1958, he gave Denis his first Scottish cap, making him the youngest since Bob McColl in 1899. Huddersfield were only a Second Division club at the time so it was a bold decision. Denis went on to play for Scotland 55 times, scoring 30 goals, a good enough record, though the player feels he might have done better for his country. "Injuries didn't help me very much in my international career. I played a few times when I wasn't fully fit. You can get away with it at club level but not in internationals. I'm very proud to have played for Scotland. There is nothing quite like pulling on a Scottish jersey, but I would like to have done more."

Back at Huddersfield it was clear he was going to move on, and Manchester City were the club who dug deep to find £56,000 for a player with only 81 League appearances to his name. Denis only stayed at Maine Road for two seasons before the chance of a big profit proved too much for City who would have found it extremely difficult anyway to stand in the way of a dream move to Italy. Denis had done his stuff for City with 21 League goals in 44 appearances, a scoring rate which brought Torino in with a £100,000 offer. It had been hard work, too, and had brought any number of clashes over training methods. "Apart from Bert Trautmann, only Ken Barnes and George Hannah could really play," says Denis, "I knew that if I stayed with City we faced the prospect of a continued fight against relegation. I wanted to go to Italy. There was a feeling that Italy was the place where it was all happening, that is was becoming the mecca of European football. John Charles had been with Juventus for four years, and now Gigi Peronace was back in England looking for more British talent."

Denis admits that lire was the lure. The kind of money on offer was a £5,000 signing-on fee plus bonuses of up to £200 for a win. It compared handsomely with the English maximum weekly wage of £20, though this was about to be scrapped, and in fact City offered Denis £80 a week to stay. But the financial dream became a nightmare; the money didn't turn out to be quite as good as promised and Italian football was a disaster. Although Torino had also signed Joe Baker from Hibs and they had each other for company, they were bored and lonely off the field, while on it they found Italian football an alien game. The fans and the Press made their lives unbearable and they were always in trouble and being fined by the club. Joe Baker so disliked being taken away into the mountains above Turin in preperation for matches that he went on a hunger strike and, much to the delight of the other players, the system was scrapped. Their most horrendous experience was when Joe turned his new car over going the wrong way round a roundabout and suffered head injuries with Denis fortunate to escape being crushed. The final nail in the coffin was when Denis was pulled off the pitch in a Cup-tie and accused of not trying because of a Scotland international that was coming up. Torino refused him permission to play in it and it proved the last straw for the Italian adventure.

Back in Scotland for the international, Denis contacted Matt Busby to tell him he wanted to come home and was delighted when the Manchester United manager intimated that if he was available he would be bidding. After a typical Italian complication when Torino attempted to sell him to rivals Juventus for £160,000, Gigi Peronace smoothed the way for him to return to Manchester for a record £115,000 fee with Denis a sadder but probably better player after his year abroad. Denis had been in a lot of trouble in Italy but he had still scored 10 goals in 27 League matches, a creditable effort when you consider that just four more goals would have made him top scorer in the whole Italian League.

To say he was glad to be back in English football is an understatement. He was ready to settle down and happy indeed to link up with the manager who had given him his first Scottish cap. His first season, 1962/63, was an eventful one, in which he was given a striker's role playing alongside David Herd. The team, still rebuilding after Munich, was nearly relegated but showed its potential by winning the FA Cup, beating Leicester City 3-1 in the final. Law remembers it well. "I can see Paddy Crerand now hitting me with a perfect ball from the left wing. I turned quickly and shot past Gordon

Banks' right hand. It was the first goal, and one I had always dreamed of scoring at Wembley. It was one of the greatest games I played for United."

Even though United finished 19th in the League, there was nothing wrong with the goal scoring. Denis got 23 from 38 League appearances while David Herd scored 19. Things came together better the following year with Law hitting a fabulous goal-a-game ratio of 30 from 30 appearances. Herd got his usual 20 and with the help of some tighter defence they finished runners-up for the championship. From there they launched a tremendous campaign to win the championship of 1964/65. There were 28 goals from Law, 20 from Herd, 15 by John Connelly and 10 apiece from Bobby Charlton and the fast-emerging George Best. They reached the semi-finals of the FA Cup three seasons in succession and repeated their championship success in 1966/67. Again Law was top scorer with 23 goals, well backed up by an all-star attack featuring Herd, Charlton and Best. The title win set them up for another crack at Europe, and this time of course they went all the way, beating Benfica in extra time at Wembley in 1968 to become the first English club to win the European Cup. Sadly for Denis he missed the final. A long battle with a knee injury ended with his admission to hospital three days before the big day at Wembley and the surgeon removed a piece of cartilage more than an inch long.

Some people had thought that Denis was imagining the pain in his knee because no one had been able to find anything really wrong. When the offending piece of gristle was located, Denis put it in a bottle and labelled it thus: "They said this was in my mind." Perhaps because he missed the final, Denis looks to the European Cup of 1965/66 for the highlight of his career in Europe, and he picks out the quarter-final second leg against Benfica in Lisbon as his most joyful experience. United had beaten the Portuguese 3-2 at Old Trafford in the first leg. The Benfica players had walked off smiling and not many other people considered a one-goal advantage would be enough to see the Reds through in Lisbon.

"Benfica in 1966 were the cream. They had been in three European Cup finals and had taken over from the legendary Real Madrid as top dogs," explains Denis. "Two years previously we had been beaten 5-0 in Lisbon in the Cup Winners Cup and when we went out, all the Portuguese fans were holding their hands with all five fingers up, giving us the salute. Sir Matt Busby had made tactical plans for a careful start because we could ill afford to give away an early goal, and see our slender advantage wiped out. To say we were keyed up would be an understatement, There was an 80,000 crowd packing the famous Stadium of Light, and I wasn't exactly pleased when Pat Crerand, kicking a ball about in the dressing room, banged it against the mirror. The glass shattered, and though no one said anything about seven years' bad luck, it certainly didn't help the mood, yet we went out and were three goals up in the first quarter of an hour.

"It was incredible and the best performance in my view from a United team in Europe. It was a beautiful experience and a joy to share in that splendid team effort. George Best, only 19 at the time, grabbed the headlines and no one begrudged him that; after all it was cheeky George who scored the first two goals and helped lay on the third for John Connelly. In the last quarter of an hour I put Pat Crerand in for a goal and Bobby Charlton waltzed through for the fifth. My name was missing from the scoresheet, but it was of no consequence because I knew I had played well, just like everyone else in the team. It was unusual for the three so-called stars, Charlton, Law and Best, all to turn it on in the same match, but we did that night. So did Nobby Stiles, Pat Crerand, John Connelly and the rest of them. Everything came off for us. By rights we should have gone on to win the European Cup that year but we played badly in the semi-final against Partizan Belgrade, losing 2-0 in Yugoslavia and winning only 1-0 back at Old Trafford. So we missed out on final glory. But Sir Matt Busby called our performance in Lisbon 'Our finest hour' and I think he summed it up well."

After recovering from his knee operation Denis came back

to make 30 League appearances in season 1968/69 and score 14 goals, but George Best had now taken over as the major goal scorer. Traumatic times also lay ahead as first Wilf McGuinness and then Frank O'Farrell took over as manager, trying to follow in the famous footsteps of Sir Matt Busby. Denis was still worth his place but his best years were over and when Tommy Docherty breezed in he greatly upset the Lawman by giving him a free transfer at the end of season 1972/73 after promising that there would be a job on the staff for him. The manner of the public announcement also riled the player who thought it had been agreed that his retirement should wait until his testimonial the following season. Instead to his horror he was home in Aberdeen when his picture was flashed on the television screen with the news that United had given him a free.

So that summer he moved back across the road for a final season with Manchester City which ended with the bizarre situation of scoring a goal which looked at the time to have sent United down to the Second Division. In fact United would have gone down anyway because their rivals in distress both won their games, but Denis wasn't to know that after almost casually back-heeling the ball past Alex Stepney for the only goal of the game. He walked back to the centre circle looking like a man who had just accidently stabbed his best friend in the back! Law's nine goals in 24 League appearances that season at Maine Road earned him a place in the 1974 Scottish World Cup squad for Germany and he played in their opening group game against Zaire. Scotland won 2-0, but Denis was then dropped in favour of Willie Morgan. He had played his last major game, and when he discovered at the start of the following season that Tony Book didn't have a first-team place for him, he retired.

It had been a stormy career at times with his aggression and short fuse always liable to see him in conflict with referees. He also seemed to have the knack of needling officialdom who twice suspended him for 28-day periods, draconian punishment for a player whose main offence was one of retaliation; the squint-eyed little boy was still always ready to fight. But the good times far outweighed the bad. Although his disciplinary record prevented him ever being voted Footballer of the Year by the English soccer writers, their Continental counterparts more readily appreciated pure talent and they voted him European Footballer of the Year in 1964, a well-deserved recognition.

Denis looks back fondly on his 11 seasons with Manchester United. "It was the Swinging Sixties in soccer as well as in the entertainment world with the Beatles, and I think we saw football at its best in that period. I was privileged to play in a great side. It was a beautiful team to play in with players like Pat Crerand, Bobby Charlton, Nobby Stiles, and George Best coming along. Over a period of five years it was a joy for the entertainment and goals. We always felt that if the opposition scored one, we could score two, and if they got two we could score three. It didn't always work out that way, but that was the feeling, and it was all very special for me."

Sir Matt fretted about his fiery nature but doesn't hesitate to put him in his team of all-time greats. He says: "Denis Law was the most expensive signing I ever made, but on achievement he turned out to be the cheapest. The Italians dragged me and my chairman all over Europe before we were able to complete the signing and at one time I was so angry at the way we were being treated that I almost pulled out of the deal. I'm extremely glad that I didn't. Once we had got Denis to Old Trafford I knew that we had the most exciting player in the game. He was the quickest-thinking player I ever saw, seconds quicker than anyone else. He had the most tremendous acceleration, and could leap to enormous heights to head the ball with almost unbelievable accuracy and often with the power of a shot. He had the courage to take on the biggest and most ferocious opponents and his passing was impeccable. He was one of the most unselfish players I have seen. If he was not in the best position to score he would give the ball to someone who was. When a chance was on for him, even only a half-chance, or in some cases no chance at all for anybody else but him, whether he had his back to goal, was sideways on, or the ball was on the deck or up to shoulder height, he would have it in the net with such power and acrobatic agility that colleagues and opponents alike could only stand and gasp. No other player scored as many miracle goals as Denis Law. Goals that looked simple only because Denis got himself into position so quickly that opponents just could not cope with him. He was the first British player to salute the crowd. Early on at Old Trafford the multitudes cheered him and he soon became what the crowd called him...The King. He is a good friend and a warm-hearted family man who is never less than cheerful."

Manchester is still home to Denis and his wife Diana with their five children. He works for a printing company, but is a familiar voice on radio and television with comments on football as perceptive and sharp as he was in opposition goalmouths.

Coronation Day

It is Saturday 25th May 1963, a full ten years after Elizabeth II's Coronation. Yet among the throng of Manchester United supporters at the vast, historic Wembley Stadium there is the buzz of loyal subjects awaiting the crowning of their new King. The Mecca for football supporters from all over England is bathed in brilliant sunshine - it is a really beautiful afternoon. The community singing is in full throttle. Everywhere you look on the way into the stadium and inside the ground is a mass of red and white scarves. For United supporters on this special May day there is a great feeling of anticipation - a turning point for their beloved club.

It had been precisely five years since United had last appeared in a Wembley FA Cup final. And what an emotional occasion that had been - less than four months after the terrible Munich disaster. The Reds lost that day 2-0 to Bolton. But hopes were high this time and the United optimists firmly believed that this was going to be a special occasion.

With over 100,000 spectators packed inside the ground, it appeared that 80 per cent of them were wearing the red and white of Manchester United. The noise was deafening long before the teams came out and it was all good humoured with not a sign of animosity or aggression nor foul language from either set of supporters.

The Mancunians were waiting with unbridled hope, enthusiasm and expectation. The chanting from the Reds supporters was like a tidal wave of noise: "United... United... United," they sang, then: "Law... Law... Law" in unrelenting unison. It made the hairs on the back of your head stand to attention. The 1950s United calypso was also being sung by the Mancunians intermingled with various other musical tributes to the Red Devils.

It had been five long years since the Munich disaster had brought the club to its knees. They had seen those fabulous, magical, famous Busby Babes decimated on the snowbound runway at Munich and the club almost go out of existence. Matt Busby's able and trustworthy assistant, Jimmy Murphy, had kept the club afloat almost single-handedly. And while optimists had hoped for an instant return to hegemony most realised that not even Matt Busby could rebuild a great football side overnight. It would take time and patience and United's success immediately following February 1958 was a little flattering.

The first couple of years, as they moved into the new decade of the 1960s, had been a mixture of elation and despair. The first season after Munich, the team quite unexpectedly finished the season runners-up to the eventual champions, Wolverhampton Wanderers. It was, however, a false dawn. The following two seasons saw the club struggle and following the acquisition of players such as Maurice Setters, David Herd and Noel Cantwell, Busby for the first time resorted to the quick fix of the transfer market.

Yet the seasons 1961/62 and 1962/63 were the worst under Busby's command. In 1962 they finished 15th and although they reached the FA Cup semi-final, they lost 3-1 to that wonderful Tottenham double-winning team. By the end of 1963 they were nearly relegated and eventually finished 19th.

Yet as disappointing as this was, United fans were no longer surprised. It was quite obvious that if United were to complete their recovery they would need a special type of player. A creative, entertaining player in the true Manchester United tradition who could generate huge excitement whenever he pulled on the famous red shirt.

Jimmy Murphy, Matt Busby's right-hand man and assistant manager of Manchester United, said that for two years following the Munich disaster Matt Busby was still having medical treatment for the injuries he suffered in the crash. And, added Jimmy, during this period Busby resigned his position as the manager of the Scottish international team in order to concentrate on United's restructuring and team building.

"It was clear to us that the club would have to go into the transfer market until our young players like Nobby Stiles, George Best, Tony Dunne and others in our youth system came through into first team contention," recalled Murphy of this particular era in United's history. "We had missed signing Dave Mackay, who was playing for Hearts at that time. He would have been a truly wonderful acquisition for us, but Matt was in hospital and Mackay moved to Tottenham before we knew about it. Of course we signed Albert Quixall, the golden boy from Sheffield Wednesday, Maurice Setters, a tough and uncompromising wing half, and Noel Cantwell. These players were experienced and helped strengthen our defence.

"We had also signed David Herd from Arsenal, but this was just the start. It soon became imperative that we signed someone with a big name, not just for the reputation, because we never went in for that sort of phoney policy at Old Trafford. It had to be a player with flair, character, drive and bags of enthusiasm. A forward to link up with Bobby Charlton. Bobby was already a world-class player, and a thoroughbred. It had to be someone with dynamism to lift the club out of the doldrums. To be perfectly honest we had searched the entire British Isles but truthfully, I don't think there were a dozen such players in the world, but there was one man who quickly became paramount in our plans."

The player Murphy was talking about was a slightly-built, golden-haired, ultra-confident and flamboyant inside-forward by the name of Denis Law. His fiery performances at inside-forward, allied to lightning reflexes and an unquenchable fighting spirit were just what United needed.

During the summer of 1962 Matt Busby and Harold Hardman, United's chairman, had closely monitored Law's situation very carefully. Denis had left Huddersfield Town and joined Manchester City before heading to Italian giants Torino after just one season at Maine Road.

Yet Italian football, in particular the internal politics and hysteria surrounding the sport in that country, was not to Denis's liking and he let it be known that he was far from happy.

Matt Busby was already a great admirer of Denis from the first time he had watched him play against United's youth team at just 16. Busby and Murphy knew that a player like Law could galvanise United and lead them on to further glory and honours.

So when, in July 1962, Law eventually signed for Manchester United, the pair felt a new era was in store for the Red Devils. Although quite how the coming decade would shape up was anyone's guess, United's prospects looked a good deal rosier.

*

Back at Wembley the community singing and chanting grew louder and more passionate with the anticipated arrival of Manchester United and Leicester City. In time the teams arrived - Matt Busby led United out to a rapturous reception, Noel Cantwell was the club captain. Wearing tracksuit tops over their club jerseys, the United players looked extremely confident, yet if the First Division table was a guide to the final destination of the Cup then most money would have been on Leicester City.

Coming into this final the Leicester team, managed by Matt Gillies, had enjoyed their most successful League season for many years and at one point they had been on course for the coveted double. However, their cup run interfered with their League form and they eventually finished fourth. Still, many regarded them as the team of the season.

This Wembley final represented the first ever cup meeting between the clubs. The Foxes had a hard-tackling defence in front of England goalkeeper Gordon Banks, while they boasted Frank McLintock at right half and Graham Cross and Ken Keyworth in a formidable line-up.

Yet right from the kick-off this was a rejuvenated Manchester United. It was a relief for the team that a week earlier they had beaten Leyton Orient to guarantee their First Division safety. Here at Wembley they expressed themselves and their new found confidence was evident in the way in which they sprayed the ball about on the beautifully manicured surface.

From front to back United looked winners from kick-off to final whistle. David Herd was ready, as always, to run through a brick wall in his eagerness to score goals for United. The wing-halves, Paddy Crerand and Maurice Setters, were in total command and the ever-dependable Bill Foulkes was masterful at the heart of defence, while Noel Cantwell played his captain's role to perfection and Shay Brennan was as neat and classy as a veteran.

Bobby Charlton out on the left wing looked the world class player he was, dictating play one minute, ready to pounce on the slightest Leicester mistake the next. He was dangerous every time he received the ball and his pace when running at the Leicester defence caused palpitations for the Midlands team. The Dublin-born Johnny Giles on the right wing was up and down his line; crossing, passing and running into open spaces to perfection, while golden boy Albert Quixall was enjoying perhaps his best ever game for the Red Devils. Those wide-open spaces at Wembley suited United's players perfectly and they thrived on the lush, green turf. The whole team synchronised and gelled together marvellously, they were a joy to watch but everyone agreed that although the whole United team played majestically, one player in particular stood out... Denis Law!

That early summer afternoon at Wembley, Law was in his element: centre stage before 100,000 soccer officiandos: he gave a bravura performance in the arts of inside-forward play. Even the Leicester City supporters applauded his five-star show and envied the Red Devils for having such a brilliant player in their team.

Denis was poetry in motion: his non-stop running, tackling, harassing, leaping for high balls directed at Gordon Banks' goal and passing was first class. Add to this a lightning velocity off the mark and the courage to absorb the buffeting of tough-as-teak defenders and you had a magnificent world-class forward - the equal of any in football.

That afternoon you sensed that Law's very presence gave confidence not only to his team-mates but to the United support. With flaxen hair blowing in the slight breeze, Law unveiled his full repertoire of skills and finishing.

Some Wembley finals have maintained a high pitch of excitement; the emotions of spectators continually aroused by the sway of the play. Other finals have been dour and hard fought, following a predictable course, only brought to life from monotony by the isolated stinging shot, flashing header or brilliant save. Still more, particularly those in the 50s and 60s, were spoilt by an injury to one side or the other in an era before substitutions.

However, this was one of those cup finals that would live long in the memory of all those who were fortunate enough to have watched it live. For in this showpiece game of the season, the Red Devils forgot the travails of a relegation-threatened season to give a scintillating, cohesive team performance.

*

Paddy Crerand masterminded United's attacks from midfield and sprayed the ball about with the deliberation of a snooker player looking to finish a frame. Bobby Charlton was making those powerful, unstoppable bursts down the left-hand side; delivering floating high balls and driving thunderous shots at Gordon Banks. Bobby, playing in a position he didn't like but putting the club's needs before his own views, provided a mixture of splendid and mediocre wing play but he was always thrilling and clearly had the Leicester defenders worried.

Albert Quixall, content to do the fetching and carrying, was in his element on the lush green turf, laying on the kind of service forwards dream of receiving. On the right wing John Giles was a 'Will-o-the-Wisp' using his trickery and accuracy to maintain a stream of crosses into the 18-yard box.

Law thrived on this kind of service. After getting into their rhythm, the Reds began to pile on the pressure and by the half hour they were in front. Gordon Banks had just made a good save from a typical Bobby Charlton howitzer when he hurriedly threw the ball to Davie Gibson, the Leicester inside-left. Crerand, reading Banks's intentions, moved forward and took the ball from Gibson, beat three players and squared a beautifully weighted pass across the penalty area to Denis the Menace. Law shielded the ball with his body, turned stunningly in a tight circle and before you could blink, moved to the right, across the Leicester goal. For a split second Banks wondered what he was going to do next. Yet just as Banks anticipated a shot to his left, Law suddenly and brilliantly placed a shot to his right. It was a goal fit for the occasion and for an instant the crowd fell silent in anticipation, before erupting.

All of a sudden the hitherto resolute Leicester defence didn't know what to do to contain the quicksilver king of Old Trafford. The United supporters puffed their chests out, they had undergone a thoroughly miserable season and now they sensed that this was the start of a glorious new era for the club. They realised instantly what Jimmy Murphy had been talking about with regard to 'that the special type of individual player' for here he was - Denis Law!

Minutes after scoring his spectacular goal Denis went on a brilliant dribble, played a one-two with David Herd and beat Banks, only for young Frank McLintock to clear off the goal line. Phew! That was a beautiful piece of football brilliance. Denis was so light on his feet that he looked like a ballet dancer: his poise and anticipation beating even the most determined tackler. United's fans responded to Denis' inspiration, chanting: "Law... Law... Law".

Later in the game, Denis once again brought the crowd to their feet when, following another gravity-defying leap, he gracefully flashed a header past a startled Banks. It struck the post. Banks looked on in disbelief and turned as if to watch the ball flying into his goal when to his great surprise and obvious delight, it landed back into his arms. As the oohs and aahs wailed out around the ground, Denis fell face first to the turf and thumped the grass in frustration. Only a player as great as he could have reached that ball in the first place yet Law was a perfectionist and his own chief critic. As the crowd rose to acclaim his outrageous attempt, Law could be seen embracing the famous Wembley turf in disappointment. The incident became Denis's trademark.

David Herd finally got the second goal United's glorious play deserved. In the 57th minute Johnny Giles delivered a lovely pass into Bobby Charlton's stride wide on the left and Bobby quickly set off toward the Leicester goal. Suddenly he let fly one of his famous thunderbolts. Gordon Banks stopped it but the shot was so powerful that he couldn't hold it and it ran free to Herd racing in. It looked all over. With the Mancunians in joyful mood, the singing and chanting became louder and louder. The Reds were rampant, yet Leicester hit back in the 80th minute when their centre-forward Ken Keyworth scored with a header that whisked past David Gaskell, United's young goalkeeper.

With 10 minutes of the game remaining it looked as though the Midland side could conceivably force extra-time against a United defence that had been conceding too many goals all season. Yet once United rediscovered their brilliant passing they quickly sealed the game. Johnny Giles centred immaculately from the right and Banks, who appeared surprisingly nervous, dropped the ball at Herd's feet in the six yard area. Herd made no mistake and United had ended their post-Munich trophy drought.

At the final whistle the Reds were worthy FA Cup winners and both sets of supporters applauded the teams. The United fans breathed a deep sigh of relief. They sensed their club was on the threshold of further greatness and in Denis Law they had a player who would fight tooth and nail for them.

As the final whistle blew, Denis, his shirt dripping wet, knew he had given the throngs of United fans the greatest gift he could bestow: every last ounce of his talent. The 1963 FA Cup final wasn't so much a game but a coronation for the new King of Old Trafford. At the whistle Matt Busby flung his arms around Denis as the jubilant players waited patiently for their invitation to the royal box to receive their medals. As they waited Matt Busby told them: "You've done it, boys! Now we are right back in the big time."

As United began their lap of honour around Wembley Stadium one player was missing... Denis Law. After the team had been presented with the FA Cup and received their winners medals, Denis rushed back to the dressing room and jumped into the shower. Jimmy Murphy had spotted Denis rushing from the pitch and followed him down the tunnel. Back in the dressing room Jimmy walked in, a huge smile across his face, and congratulated Denis on a masterful performance. Law, his face and body covered in soapsuds, popped his head from the shower and screwed his face, telling Jimmy that he should have been shot for missing with the header that had rattled the crossbar.

"That," said a gleaming Murphy later, "is Denis Law the perfectionist. He's given a rivetting 90 minute all-action, scintillating performance on that lush, green Wembley turf and here he was criticising his own performance. That's what makes him the very special type of player that he is."

Very quickly United's dressing room was packed solid with happy, relieved visitors after the game. Matt Busby, his face bathed in a big grin and with a bottle of champagne in his hand, was going from to player to player filling cups with bubbly. Twenty-five minutes after the final whistle Noel Cantwell walked into the room with the Cup, smiling. "I don't think we have played better all season," he said. David Herd, scorer of two goals, beamed broadly despite the fact that, at the time, Jack Crompton was busy bandaging his legs. "Just a little sore," he said, "nothing to worry about though. It was wonderful." Paddy Crerand, arguably the man of the match, wouldn't accept any personal praise for the victory. "It was a team effort," he said, "everybody played wonderfully well."

Cantwell, speaking about 'Wembley Nerves', said that on the eve of the Cup final, Maurice Setters had been feeling a little tense as the time seemed to drag while the team were in their hotel. So following his evening meal, Setters decided to go for a walk. He'd called into a pub and enjoyed a pint of ale and it helped him relax.

Setters hadn't been the only nervous United player - just before the teams were due to line up in the tunnel Busby had discovered that he was one short. Panic stations! A couple of minutes later Paddy Crerand casually strolled into the room. He told Busby that he had always wanted to hear the Wembley crowd sing 'Abide with Me'. "It's done me a world of good," Paddy told his team-mates. Denis and the other lads gave him a look of utter disbelief.

"It was 'Red Devil' Denis Law who took our FA Cup match against firm favourites, Leicester City - by the scruff of the neck," recalled Noel Cantwell. "It was Denis who scored that all-important goal when the match was only half an hour old. He did as he pleased for ninety tantalising minutes that I could tell it was sheer hell for the Leicester boys."

In his Wembley match report, Sam Leitch of the *Sunday Mirror* wrote: "I rate the Law solo performance almost as glittering as the historic Stan Matthews Final of 1953. Law was a probing puma in a number 10 shirt, scorer of the vital opening goal, the master man of soccer whom Leicester manager Matt Gillies admitted had wrecked his Final dreams." The sports reporter went on to congratulate the whole Manchester United team saying it was United's distinguished team blend that won the cup and gave a virtuoso performance.

The following morning United supporters eagerly lapped up the headlines: *'Wembley Super Show Gives United The Cup'*, *'Brilliant Denis Law Inspires 3-1 Win!'*, *'United's Cup - But It Was Law's Day!'*, *'United's Big Day - Law and Crerand'*, *'A Dash Of Scotch Makes It A Great Final!'*, *'Golden Boy Rocks Them!'*, *'Hail United - Wembley Wizards'*, *'Classy Crerand And Law Stars Of The Match!'*, *'Flying Scots Crerand And Law Serve Up A Banquet!'*, *'Law And Crerand Give United £170,000 Glitter!'*, *'Law The Master!'*, *'Colossal Law!'*, *'Law Genius Inspires United!'*, *'This Young Man Law!'*, *'The Rule Of Law!'*, *'And The Toast Is - Denis!'*

*

Gordon Banks was possibly England's finest-ever goalkeeper. He had joined Leicester City in 1959 from Chesterfield for £7,000. Talking about this game many years later he said: "Denis Law was magical at Wembley. I had appeared in a Wembley FA Cup final in 1961 against Tottenham, Danny Blanchflower's Super Spurs, who that year won the double of the First Division championship and the FA Cup. We were not too disappointed, though, we consoled ourselves with the fact that at least we had been part of a great occasion and our conquerors were one of the outstanding teams of all time. However, when we were beaten by Manchester United we were mortified. Denis was in spectacular match-winning form. I remember my team-mate Frank McLintock being close to tears as we came off with our losers' medals. 'I hate this place,' said Frank as he left Wembley."

Talking about the header from Law that rattled his crossbar, Gordon recalled: "That effort of Law's was the most staggering header I have seen from any player. It was such an awesome moment in football that I shall never forget it as long as I live. I was concentrating fully as United sent over a cross from the right. I decided against going for it as I could not sense any danger and, although Denis was in the penalty area, it seemed to be far too high for him to be expected to get it. Yet he made contact. With amazing reflex action and power of take-off he lifted himself what appeared to be at least three yards from the turf. I stood transfixed on my line. I was staggered that anyone could possibly leap so high. But he wasn't finished. He flashed in a header that I had absolutely no chance of saving and I could only sigh with genuine relief as the ball bounced off the post and flew straight into my waiting arms. I doubt if he had ever risen as high as he did for that cross. And, of course, the ironic twist about it from his point of view is that he failed to score. He was one of the game's greatest headers of the ball."

"People ask me about the goals I've scored," said Denis years later. "'Which is your best?' I am often asked. Well I don't like talking about my own play but the one goal that sticks out in my mind above all others wasn't a particularly spectacular affair. It was the one I scored against Leicester City in the 1963 FA Cup final. It was an important goal because we went on to win 3-1."

1. The Northern Lights

Although this is a book mainly about Denis Law's Manchester United career, it would be remiss of me if I didn't mention his roots and the genesis of his football career.

Denis Law was born on 24th February 1940 in a council flat, number 6 Printfield Terrace, in the Woodside district of Aberdeen. He was the youngest of seven children: three brothers George, Joseph and John, and three sisters Ruby, Frances and Georgina. The Laws were a typical loving, close-knit Scottish family; honest, hard working, poor but happy.

His father was a small, strong, quiet man. He was a trawlerman, which was a tough, demanding and low paid job. He would go to work on a Monday morning and wouldn't return home until Saturday morning. Mr Law had also served in the Army during the First World War and in the Navy during the Second World War. Denis' mother, also on the small side, was a hard-working housewife who made sure her children knew their manners, always had something to eat and she kept the house spotlessly clean.

The Laws, like most families in their neighbourhood, were poor and Mrs Law was a proud lady who had to use all her ingenuity in order to feed her family. Because of the food and clothing rationing during the war Denis had to make do with his brother's hand-me-down clothes. In later life he appreciated his humble and deprived childhood. As a youngster Denis went on his father's trawler on a brief trip out in the North Sea. He was appalled at the working conditions on board the boat and vowed that he would avoid it all costs.

Despite these difficulties however, Denis lived a simple life. During his schooldays there were no television sets and only a few families could afford even a wireless or radio as it was later called. It was football, football and more football for young Denis. He would practise day and night, kicking a tin can or, if he was fortunate enough, a ball against a wall. Many's the time he kicked a hole through the toecap of his shoe. He would play football on the way to school, during school at break time and dinnertime, then when he came home from school, his imagination would take over and he and his friends would make believe the cobblestone street they played on was the lush turf of Hampden Park.

So keen was young Law to practise his football skills that he even used his mother's clothes rack (this was hoisted up to the ceiling by a pulley) to practise his leaping and heading. In later life he averred that it was this practice with a ball during his childhood in Aberdeen that made him such an outstanding header of the ball.

Yet any football scout suggesting that this schoolboy represented the future of world soccer would have been laughed out of his job at the suggestion. The reason for this was not only that Denis was on the small side but he had a squint in his right eye and wore steel-rimmed school spectacles without which he would appear cross-eyed.

Denis was taunted unmercifully by other kids because of his looks and he consequently became very self-conscious. Nevertheless Denis would play football on the street wearing his glasses - sometimes they were broken and it would take weeks for new ones to be made. In the meantime the other kids made his life a nightmare.

During proper games he couldn't wear his glasses so he learned to keep his right eye closed throughout the entire match. Yet because of this affliction Denis became a fierce competitor on the field - it toughened him up. If anything it made him more determined to prove that he was the equal of any other player and he soon realised he had to fight harder than most.

He attended Kittybrewster School where a teacher named Mr Wright encouraged young Law in his football aspirations. Initially Denis played as a full back until Mr Wright moved him up to the inside-forward position. Academically he was quite bright at school and passed the school exam in order to go on to grammar school. None of the other Law children had gone to grammar school so it was a first for the family and they were very proud of his achievement. However, when Denis learned that the school did not have football teams, just rugby and cricket, that was the end of the matter. He decided he didn't want to go to a grammar school. Instead, he attended Powis Secondary Modern where another teacher, Mr Bill Durno, saw that though he was handicapped because of his eye, he was an enthusiastic and fierce competitor and encouraged the youngster.

"He was a natural," said Mr Durno, adding, "he thought twice as fast as other boys on the football field." With this encouragement Denis was soon selected for Aberdeen Boys under 12s team with whom he reached the final of a schoolboy cup competition against Motherwell and Wishaw. Disappointingly for Denis they lost on aggregate.

At 13 Denis played for Aberdeen Lads Club. This meant he was playing for his school on the Saturday morning and for the Lads Club in the afternoon yet he didn't own a pair of football boots until Christmas 1953, when his dear mother sacrificed enough to buy him his first pair. They were the old-fashioned hard type with big ankle protectors, but they were his pride and joy. He would clean and dubbin them every time he used them. He was selected for Aberdeen schoolboys under 15s team and teamed up with Alex Dawson, who would later join Manchester United after leaving school. Other lads in the Aberdeen schoolboy team were goalkeeper John 'Tubby' Ogston, later to play professionally for Aberdeen and Scotland's Under 23 team and another keeper, Adam Blacklaw, who went on to play for Burnley.

Also in this side was Gordon Low, who later followed Denis to Huddersfield and Joe Fleming, a right winger who played for Tottenham and Cardiff.

Much to his disappointment, Denis was never selected for the Scottish schoolboy international team - the nearest he came was as a reserve when Scotland travelled to play Northern Ireland. It was the first time he had ever travelled outside Scotland.

*

Just before Easter 1955 there was a gentle knock on the front door of the Law household in Printfield Terrace. Standing outside was a smartly dressed stranger. The Laws didn't know him from Adam, but he was invited inside, and the mild-mannered man introduced himself as Archie Beattie. He told Mrs Law that he was a scout for his brother, Andy, the former Preston North End and Scottish international full-back. Andy had retired from playing and was the manager of Huddersfield Town, a position he had held since April 1952. Archie told the Law family that he would like young Denis to go down to Huddersfield for trials.

"I don't send boys down to England if I don't think they have a chance," he told Mr and Mrs Law, with as much sincerity as he could muster, adding, "I would not be asking your son to go if I didn't think he had a chance of making the grade." And truthfully Archie wasn't giving the Law family the usual football scout's spiel, he really did believe that Denis had that something special. Denis was deliriously excited.

When the initial excitement died down he thought about his appearance and what the officials of Huddersfield Town would make of him. He was a skinny, awkward-looking schoolkid with owl-like glasses. He was, in fact, waiting to undergo an eye operation to correct the defect and was expecting to hear from the hospital any time. However, the family agreed he should make the journey to Huddersfield. "I thought I would be back home in Aberdeen within a month," remarked Denis many years later. Although legend has it that Huddersfield were the only club who showed an interest in Denis as a schoolboy, Sir Bobby Robson, the former England manager, said Denis was rejected by Birmingham City because they believed he was too small.

Denis left school at Easter and on the 3rd April 1955 he

made his way to England. His brothers, John and George, went with him to make sure everything was all right. "At that time," remarked Denis, "Huddersfield seemed like a million miles away from my home in Aberdeen."

As the Laws stepped from the train in Huddersfield they were met by Eddie Brennan, the assistant secretary of Huddersfield Town FC. "So this is the lad," said the smiling Mr Brennan, walking forward and placing his hand on George's shoulder. The Law brothers smiled. "You've got the wrong one," said John Law smiling, "this is our Denis," he said pointing to the gawky-looking youngster beneath a pair of school spectacles. The smile evaporated from Mr Brennan's face and he couldn't believe what he was looking at - young Denis measured 5ft 3ins, and weighed 8st 9lb. He gulped, looked again at young Denis, but being polite he didn't say anything, only a brief 'welcome' before taking the three Law brothers into Huddersfield's ground, Leeds Road and into Mr Beattie's office.

As they knocked on the door and entered, Andy was sitting behind his big oak desk, smoking his pipe. Denis stood blinking between his two brothers, who dwarfed him. He was holding an old attaché case that had a few sparse belongings inside. Never before has a less likely-looking player been paraded before a prospective manager. Beattie, a blunt speaking, no-nonsense type of manager, looked up at the brothers and seemed a little stunned and bewildered as he eyed the three brothers up and down, while giving Denis a look of absolute disbelief.

When the introductions were completed, he said: "Good God, the boy's a freak." It was understandable. Young Denis certainly did not look like a budding football star. It wouldn't have been unreasonable for the manager to have thought that his brother had made a terrible mistake by sending this boy, nor was it beyond the bounds of possibility that Archie was playing a practical joke on him.

Denis, from the top of his tousled fair hair to his toes didn't look strong enough to kick a caseball, let alone be able to stand up in a strong wind and withstand a hefty tackle. After the initial shock, the disappointment showed on Beattie's face. "I have never seen a less likely-looking football player," he told them. Archie Beattie had told his brother that this kid would become a huge star. What Andy didn't know was that despite Denis looking like a skeleton he was indeed a rare footballing prodigy and once on the field of play he became a different person.

His brothers told Denis to wait outside while they discussed a few details with the Huddersfield manager. After the discussions were completed the Law brothers were taken to a boarding house that the club used for their young players. It was named Pond House and run by a plumpish, friendly and jovial lady, Mrs Clark. Once the two older brothers saw Denis settled into his new home it was time for them to catch the train back to Aberdeen. All three walked to Huddersfield railway station and Denis was noticeably very quiet. He was already feeling homesick. Only those who have felt it can readily understand the feeling. As Denis watched his brothers board their train and saw it disappear from view he became even lonelier. Back at Pond House the diminutive young Aberdonian found himself sharing the 'digs' with sixteen other youngsters connected to Huddersfield Town, and to his surprise they were all English. Denis, up to this point in his life, had hardly ever had any association with English people and found it strange to say the least. The different accents of the other lads and Mrs Clark's deep Yorkshire vowels confused him, but he soon got over these little obstacles. Years later Denis said that he had gone to Huddersfield thinking that he wouldn't be there too long and he would be back home in Aberdeen in a matter of days if not weeks. However, after the initial shock of watching Denis in action, Andy Beattie revised his original opinion and gave him a job on the groundstaff at £5 a week, out of which he had to pay 47 shillings and 6 pence (£2.37) for his board and keep.

*

Just as today, in the 1950s hundreds of football scouts would roam the playing fields of the British Isles and, sooner or later, they would spot a lad who stood out as having greater control or fiercer determination than his peers. He's the natural, the kid who at 9 years of age is good enough to play for the 11-year-olds in school matches. He's the one who is easily picked out as being far in advance of all the others of his age. He is most probably the captain and in time receives higher honours, such as being selected for his city, town, county and country.

When they leave school, hundreds of these starry-eyed, potential footballers, would be signed by professional league clubs. Many kids and their parents were, and still are, under the false illusion that their lad has made it as a footballer at this point. Of course this is far from the truth. The fact remains that these kids have proved good enough to make it to the bottom of a very slippery pole. They would have to prove they were good enough to continue at that level and would have to improve all the time. It takes a special kind of human being to rise above the pitfalls and avoid joining the high percentage of those discarded. To become a great player and a legend took more than talent and physical advantage - in time Denis Law would prove to be one of this type of people.

Huddersfield Town Football Club is an historic club. Founded in 1908, it had been quite successful in its early years, winning the FA Cup in 1922 and a hat-trick of First Division championships between 1924 and 1926 under Herbert Chapman. However, since those glory days the club had fallen on lean times. Yet despite the club's standing there was never a shortage of starry-eyed youngsters willing to become groundstaff boys. In many ways it was a sad business because the fallout rate was horrific. The statistics showed that only one boy out of a couple of thousand ever made it to first team level and the odds on that lad becoming a world famous star were even larger.

Although he was terribly homesick and missed his family a great deal, the thought of playing football helped Denis come to terms with his problem. It was at this period that he came into contact with fellow Scotsman Bill Shankly. As a teenager Denis was still very conscious of his eyes. The other lads, as was their normal procedure, ribbed him unmercifully about his appearance. Needless to say the Law boy didn't take this mockery lying down and many was the time he would have a 'set-to' with the other kids in Pond House and Shankly or some other official would have to call and sort things out. On one occasion the landlady phoned the club after a fight between Denis and another Huddersfield Town youngster, a lad named Billy McDonald.

It seemed that McDonald called Denis names and Denis wasn't standing for that and belted him, bruising Billy's eye. Bill Shankly called round to the digs to find out what had happened. After listening to Mrs Clark, he called the two lads together and spoke sternly to them and warned them of the implications should it happen again. Denis told Shanks that if McDonald called him names again he would hit him again. Shankly admired the kid's pluck, but couldn't condone what had happened, saying: "Now we'll have no more of that sort of thing," before remarking to McDonald, "I hope you've learned your lesson."

Meanwhile life on the groundstaff was fairly humdrum. Denis cleaned the senior players' boots, swept up the cigarette and crisp packets, painted the perimeter fencing, cleaned the public toilets and swept the stands, beside a multitude of other jobs. He loved the afternoons, when all the chores were done and he could join in a training session.

The 1950s saw quite a few changes throughout the world. Here in the British Isles the post-war years were slowly being left behind as food rationing ended and consumer items were appearing in the shops. More fashionable clothing and exciting new types of entertainment were becoming increasingly common. Most households now had a radio while a few fortunate families were the proud owners of a 12-inch black-and-white television set. Some even had the luxury of a motor car. Yet while there was plenty of employment for everybody there remained a harshness about people's working lives that was hard and mundane.

Working class folk, especially the men, enjoyed their pint of ale and going to watch their favourite football team. It was their only real outlet and form of relaxation and it made them forget their problems for a few hours. The fifties also saw the start of teenage culture: the James Dean cult, Bill Haley and his kiss curl, and the exciting Elvis Presley and the dawn of the Rock and Roll years.

On Saturday Denis would usually play for one of Huddersfield's junior teams. He was a bundle of energy in those games, tearing all over the pitch. It was as if he had to play like this in order to show the doubters that he was a special kind of player, which indeed he was becoming. Away from football, Denis became quite happy at Pond House, although he still suffered from homesickness. Andy Beattie, who now had a different concept of Denis, noticed the lad's homesickness and had a chat with the youngster about the problem. After listening to Denis the result was that shortly afterwards Gordon Low, his friend from the Aberdeen Boys team, joined him at Huddersfield. This helped Denis to settle in Yorkshire much quicker and he and young Low became inseparable.

His only vice at this time, apart from his youthful exuberance of course, was smoking. He was a bundle of energy on and off the field and many of the older players thought he was a cocky youngster. One of the things Denis admired about Andy Beattie was the manager's insistence that all the youngsters on the club's books should maintain their education. This was something that pleased Denis, because as the manager often said to all the youngsters: "There are only so many who actually make it in football."

One day, a few weeks after his arrival in England, Denis received word from home that after a two-year wait he was to enter Aberdeen General Hospital for the eye operation he had been hoping and praying for. He was ecstatic at the news and couldn't wait to get back to Scotland and get it over with. He was in hospital for three weeks because he had picked up some kind of infection, his face swathed in bandages. Again one has to try and understand how the youngster felt at this moment. Ever since he could remember he had suffered with this affliction. He had been taunted and ridiculed. He had felt the heartbreak of kids teasing and laughing at his ungainly appearance and now he had gone through the operation and it was time to take off the bandages, clean away the blood and look in the mirror.

At first sight he thought the operation had failed and his heart sank as he saw his eye swollen and bloodshot, but within a few minutes he realised he could see properly with both eyes, without looking in two directions. The pupil was in the centre. He could go out without having to wear those horrid glasses. It was a bit like Clark Kent changing into Superman. After the operation, Denis, always confident on the football field, was now supremely confident in everyday situations and walked with a swagger. It was a new beginning for the lad from Aberdeen.

In 1956 Stan Liversedge, a friend of Matt Busby's and one of the top football writers of the era, travelled over the Pennines from Manchester to meet Huddersfield manager Andy Beattie. His purpose was to write a few articles for his Sunday newspaper - *The People.* The manager and journalist were coming out of the office heading for the car park as Denis was walking toward them. Mr Beattie turned to Stan and told him to get a good look at Law. "Believe me," he told the journalist, "that's Denis Law, and he's going to be a great player, but he's only 16." Realising Stan might include Denis in his article in the newspaper, Andy hurriedly asked him not to mention anything about him for a couple of weeks, Denis would then be 17 and could be signed as a professional by Huddersfield. Stan later said he wasn't impressed when looking at the frail, slim figure of Law. He certainly didn't look like anything special, thought Stan. However, once the journalist saw Denis play he knew Andy Beattie had been absolutely spot on with his prediction of greatness.

Another journalist to recognise the early promise of Denis was Harry Ditton of *The News of the World.* "Law was an exceptional footballer and personality," said Ditton, "I hope you don't think me immodest but after seeing Law for the first time when he was a mere 17 years of age I forecast he would play for Scotland within two years - and he did!"

Back in Huddersfield, Denis was coming on in leaps and bounds. Mrs Clark's helpings of her meat pudding speciality worked wonders for his physique and strength. He worked his way through to Huddersfield's youth team. Football equipment has changed considerably since the fifties, and the plastic balls used in modern day football are a million miles away from the old leather-panelled 'casey, with the laces', that was used in the 1950s. Those old leather balls used to soak up water and playing on the pitches of Denis Law's early days those balls became really heavy and a player had to have strength to kick them any distance. The fancy tricks such as delicate chips, lobs and juggling were almost impossible to perform. The hardest thing of all, though, was heading one of those cannon balls. One had to be a very brave player indeed to meet one of those old 'caseys', especially when it was soaking wet. Yet the British Isles produced world-class headers of the ball with the likes of Dixie Dean, Tommy Lawton, Nat Lofthouse, John Charles, and the great Tommy Taylor, to name but a few. However, the name of Denis Law would, over the proceeding years, be added to that exclusive club. On his own admission, Denis said he rarely headed the ball while training because of the danger of the laces ripping into his forehead and cutting him. He saved his heading strength for the actual matches.

Ray Wilson, a member of England's 1966 World Cup winning team, was a 20-year-old player at Huddersfield when Denis first joined the Yorkshire club. "I will never forget the first time I ever set eyes on Denis Law," smiled Wilson. "It was in 1955, in Pond House, run by Mrs Clark, where a number of Huddersfield's younger players were living. I was 20, just out of the army after serving in Egypt. My own home was in Mansfield. I had played a few games for Huddersfield's first team, but couldn't consider myself a regular at that time. I had been told that the club had signed a Scottish boy called Law from Aberdeen and when Denis and his two brothers called into Pond House I wondered which of the two older boys (both about my own age) was the budding footballer. The third brother, a tiny shrimp with glasses, had, I thought, been brought along just for the ride. I had to look twice when, during the conversation, it was mentioned that the little shrimp was the footballer. I couldn't honestly believe it, it was too fantastic to be true. He didn't look big enough to be a boy scout.

"But it didn't take long for everyone at Huddersfield to realise that he was an unforgettable footballer alright. From the very first time I saw him kicking the ball about I had no doubt that he was going to be something out of the ordinary, as a footballer and a person."

Ray mentioned that Denis's playing style was all-action, and said how talented he was and that what first struck him was Law's aggression, and how difficult he was to stop. "As a 15-year-old he wasn't in the least overawed by living with strangers in a town hundreds of miles away from his home in Aberdeen. He was very cocky and within a very short time he seemed to be running Pond House. He behaved the way he played - he wanted to be everywhere on the field. This is a good sign in a young boy, because laziness is worse than a wooden leg for ruining a football career." Ray went on to say that right from his first meeting with Denis he knew that the Aberdeen lad had his head screwed on about the whole business of being a professional footballer. Like others before him Wilson said the only doubts he had concerning Denis was whether he would be big enough or strong enough for League football. "Denis had no doubts. And he knew exactly where he was going - to the top!"

To make ends meet and earn a bit of extra pocket money Denis tried various spare-time jobs such as a painter and decorator. He also tried his hand as a joiner and for a spell worked in a garage but his overriding ambition was to make it to the top of the precarious football ladder of fame. He had no intention of going back home to Aberdeen as a failure. He was committed body and soul to becoming the best footballer in the whole world.

Roy Goodall, the Huddersfield trainer, worked with Denis and was delighted with the young Scottish kid's attitude and spent many hours out on the pitch with the young, budding genius. In Roy Goodall, Denis found a warm-hearted person who was steeped in football. Goodall, along with Sam Wadsworth, formed the legendary full-back partnership in the Huddersfield Town team that won the League Championship in three successive seasons between 1924-26.

The former Scottish international Bill Shankly was in charge of the Huddersfield reserve team and it wasn't long before Denis came under Shankly's wing. At the end of the 1955/56 season Huddersfield had been relegated into the Second Division. The first team was obviously not good enough and money was scarce so the club would have to depend on its young talent. Hence Denis, at 16, found himself in the reserves at Leeds Road, rather than where he had been playing with the juniors on those windswept mud baths around Yorkshire. In training Shankly was delighted with Law's attitude and progress, although still only slight and weighing no more than eight stone wet through, Denis would fly into tackles in order to win the ball.

In November 1956, Denis first clapped eyes on Matt Busby and Jimmy Murphy, the two men he would come to admire and respect in later years. Huddersfield had been drawn to play Manchester United's youth team in the second round of the FA Youth Cup at Heckmondwike, Yorkshire. The United youth system was the envy of every club in the league. Matt Busby and his right-hand man Jimmy Murphy had scoured the length and breadth of the British Isles looking for the right type of youngsters to groom into first team players. It was the period of the fabulous Busby Babes and Busby always attended these Youth Cup games. Alex Dawson, Denis's former Aberdeen Boys team-mate, was playing centre-forward for United's youngsters and he was a prolific goalscorer with head or feet. In the small changing room, Jimmy Murphy had lectured his team that he wanted a victory and wanted it in style.

Once the game started the little, wispy Huddersfield inside-forward with the tousled blond thatch of hair was chasing all over the pitch. He was a real terrier, he was here, there and everywhere. Matt puffed on his pipe and turned to Murphy and asked his lieutenant: "Who does that lad remind you of Jimmy?" Without a second's hesitation Murphy replied: "Peter Doherty." Doherty was a former Manchester City and Eire international inside-forward, a player rated as one of the greatest inside-forwards in the world. As the game progressed, Murphy was screaming out instructions to his players but it was to no avail because the Yorkshire team went two goals in front and it was all down to the blond-haired little scallywag.

"What's that boy's name?" Busby asked.

"Denis Law," came the reply.

In the 25th minute Law hassled the United defence and Huddersfield took the lead when he nipped in to score. Two minutes later the Yorkshire club went two goals up when Kevin McHale grabbed their second.

Although United pulled one back before half time, back in the dressing room Jimmy Murphy was giving his lads a roasting. "Get a grip of that little blond-haired kid," he screeched at his defenders. With their ears burning, the second half saw the stronger, classier Manchester United team move up a couple of gears and, although Denis was still working like a beaver, his old Aberdeen Boys colleague Alex Dawson scored twice and Kenny Morgans grabbed another. As the final whistle sounded, United's youngsters emerged as 4-2 victors. While Jimmy Murphy followed his team into the dressing room, Matt Busby shook hands with Bill Shankly and told him how impressed he had been with his young team, especially Denis Law.

A short while later, Busby spoke to Andy Beattie and offered him £10,000 for Law's signature. Denis said that after that game Matt Busby walked over to him and told him he had played well, but tried too hard by dropping back in defence.

"If you'd have kept harassing our defence, your team would have won," said Matt Busby. Had the Huddersfield manager accepted Matt Busby's offer, Denis might well have become one of the famous Busby Babes. Over the following years Jimmy Murphy never got bored when talking about Denis. "When I first saw him I knew he wouldn't have been out of place in our fabulous set-up," he often said. "We had wonderful young players in our first team, they were only kids but playing like seasoned professionals. And, the sad thing is, they were getting better with the experience they were gaining by playing in the European Cup. I envisaged young Law playing alongside big Duncan [Edwards], Tommy Taylor and Eddie Colman. But we had to wait. But the wait was well worth it as his record with us showed."

A month after his impressive performance in the junior team, Andy Beattie informed Denis that he would be playing in the first team. And so on Christmas Eve 1956, aged just 16 and still an amateur, Denis Law made his first team debut in a league game against Notts County at Meadow Lane. Denis was selected at inside-right and Kevin McHale, who was 17, played at outside-right. Eyebrows were raised throughout football circles at the youth of this right wing partnership, nevertheless Huddersfield won 2-1 and two days later, on Boxing Day, Denis made his home debut scoring the first of many Football League goals. He was on cloud nine and went on to play 13 times for the first team that season, scoring twice. Yet despite being in the first team, Law was certainly not earning a fortune. Players then were paid £12, £14 or £16 depending on their age, while the highest wage a player could earn was £20 a week.

Bill Shankly was a shrewd judge of young players. One day after training he was chatting to a local reporter and they got around to discussing Denis. "When I first saw him," said Shankly, "Denis looked anything but a world-class footballer in the making. But mark my words, he will become one. At times he looks so frail and you would think he might be bowled over by the wind. Go home and write your story but make sure you tell your readers that today you have seen a great player who

will play more than fifty times for Scotland." What a prophecy
to make!

Yet all was not well at Leeds Road. Andy Beattie was an old-
fashioned manager. He demanded to be addressed as Mr
Beattie by everyone, including the directors. He was a stickler
for discipline and he would not tolerate any kind of nonsense
from players or his staff. In many ways he wasn't really cut out
for the cut-throat business of football management, although it
was he who had organised the club's youth policy. Beattie had
been a great admirer of Manchester United's youth system and
the Busby-Murphy partnership. In 1955 he had told the
chairman, Bernard Newman, that he was fed up with the job as
manager of Huddersfield. The chairman persuaded him to stay
on but Beattie only agreed on condition that he could bring in
his old Preston clubmate and Scottish international colleague,
Bill Shankly. This was a strange request from Beattie, because
even as playing colleagues he and Shankly hadn't got on,
nevertheless Mr Newman agreed and in November 1955 Bill
Shankly arrived.

Shanks' job was to groom the youngsters at the club and
look after the reserves. However, it wasn't long before the two
men fell out. Toward the end of 1956 Beattie told his chairman
that he was tired and weary and felt it was now time for him to
leave the club. Although there was still a great deal of friction
between him and Shankly, Andy Beattie advised Mr Newman to
appoint Bill Shankly as the new manager, which he did. And so
in January 1957 Andy Beattie retired as manager of
Huddersfield Town and the enthusiastic, ambitious Bill
Shankly took over.

The rift between Beattie and Shankly healed in time. When
Shankly became manager of Liverpool he employed Beattie as
a scout. One of his greatest gifts to Shankly was discovering
Kevin Keegan and it was on Beattie's advice and
recommendation that Shankly signed the future England
captain and manager.

One of the first things Shankly did when he became
manager at Leeds Road was to sign Denis on professional

forms. Legally, young Law was free to join any club that he wanted. Shankly knew this and sent word to the Law household that he wished to speak to Denis' father in Huddersfield as soon as possible. Mr Law was whisked down to the George Hotel in Huddersfield where he spent the weekend at the club's expense and, as a sweetener, was given a fine cut of cloth from Mr Newman's mill. After Shankly enthralled Denis' father with how great his youngest child would become under his guidance, Denis signed as a professional with Huddersfield on 25th February 1957.

Denis had admired Andy Beattie and was sad to see him leave, but in Shankly he found a man full of zeal, ideas and to whom nothing else seemed to matter but football, football and more football. Shankly was an excitable man who spoke about the game passionately and animatedly during training. A keep-fit fanatic, Shankly believed footballers were a lot like boxers, his second favourite sport, and before matches insisted his players get a good steak down them. (This was the meal that great fighters like Jack Dempsey and Joe Louis ate.) He was so enthusiastic that it had to rub off on someone like Law.

In Law, Shankly saw that spark of genius that, with his teaching, would become a roaring flame on the field of play. He envisaged stoking that flame in Denis, helping him become a shining star in the football firmament. Shanks' intention was to turn Law into a football phenomenon. He loved his players to have a confidence and cockiness about their play but he certainly had no need to preach to Denis on that subject, the lad had it in abundance.

Yet, Shankly believed that the scrawny-looking Law, who weighed just under eight stone, needed to put a little weight on if he was not to be knocked off the ball by the ferocious tackling wing-halves of the period. So Shanks took Denis to a café near Pond House and told the proprietor to feed Denis big juicy steaks and milk whenever he came in for something to eat, which was nearly every day. "The great Jack Dempsey trained on steaks," roared Shankly, reinforcing the importance of diet. Denis must have wondered who the hell Jack Dempsey was. The Manassa Mauler was Shankly's hero, a former heavyweight champion of the world, while we must remember that even in the 1950s, lads like Law had hardly eaten meat because rationing and poverty had made it a luxury few could afford.

Under Bill Shankly the 17-year-old Law blossomed. "Denis has no fear, he flows straight over it," Bill was fond of telling people. Shankly liked his players to have bags of character and swagger beside a huge dollop of aggression. He preached this sermon to the Huddersfield players regularly. Denis, however, had no need to be told about these three requirements, because he already possessed them in huge quantities. He was literally going from strength to strength. He displayed a flair that the average player didn't have: his flamboyant style and ferocious enthusiasm was bringing him to the notice of other managers in the game. He had certainly brought a new excitement to Huddersfield's football.

In training Shankly made his players practise on their weak points. For example, if they were basically right-footed he would make them trap, control, pass, shoot and tackle with their left foot. All the players loved this new enthusiasm in their workouts. When they had completed their normal physical training he would have them playing three-a-side games on a full sized pitch. "He's football mad," Law told his friends.

Ray Wilson was a wing-half at the time before finding his true position as a world-class full-back. "Bill hated losing," he recalls, "he was so enthusiastic that it rubbed off on the players, especially the younger ones like myself and Denis."

In the following season, 1957/58, Denis played 18 times for the first team and scored five times. He was playing as an inside-forward, not an out-and-out striker as he would do later for Manchester United. He was more a scheming type of inside-forward. Denis would be all over the pitch, one minute trying to score a goal and the next back on his own goal line clearing the ball. Another one of Denis's strengths at this early stage of his career, and something that remained with him throughout his entire career, was his desire to fight for the ball against big, tough, robust defenders. This was something you didn't see inside-forwards do at the time. Many sceptics expressed doubts that he had the stamina for a lengthy career in the game because of his all-action style while Shankly feared that because of his style of play he would soon be plagued by leg and knee trouble.

In one game, against Sheffield United at Bramall Lane, Denis was tearing about all over the field as usual. On a few occasions he challenged Jimmy Hagan, the experienced Sheffield inside-forward, a little too robustly and Hagan admonished him about his tackling. Shankly said Denis was becoming a 'marked man' and he switched the youngster to outside-right.

At this time he was only known to Yorkshire folk as a potentially great player in the making. However, this was about to change. On a cold, freezing January, Denis appeared on black-and-white 12-inch Bush television sets throughout the land for the first time. Huddersfield played West Ham United in an FA Cup tie and the pitch was bone hard and covered in snow. Television was in its infancy then and very little football was shown, but the highlights were screened and on that lethally dangerous surface Law played a 'blinder' - all of a sudden other club managers took notice of this young man who seemed destined for greatness if he continued to improve.

"I remember the first time I saw Denis Law," smiled Sir Geoff Hurst, England's World Cup hat-trick hero. "It was a frosty January and Huddersfield were at Upton Park for an FA Cup replay against my team West Ham United. (Denis had scored Huddersfield's equaliser at Leeds Road to earn his club a third-round replay.) I sat shivering in the stand as I watched this pale, lightweight figure skipping across the bone-hard icy pitch. Although he didn't score in the replay, Huddersfield, then in the Second Division, beat us 5-1. Denis Law was my favourite. There were more prolific goalscorers, but Denis did more than simply score goals. He gave a theatrical performance in which, over the course of 90 minutes, he managed to be both villain and hero. He scored goals with an unmistakable flourish that sent a tremor through the opposition and then he would stand, with a single arm raised, above a distinctive mop of blond hair to salute the crowd."

In February 1958, upon reaching his 18th birthday, Denis would in previous years have been called up to do his two-year stint of National Service just as his club mate Ray Wilson had. This two-year stint in the armed services was a bind to many professional footballers as many believed it hindered their progress in the game. However, the previous year, conscription had been disbanded, much to the dismay of many older people. They believed, and still do to this day, that the ending of National Service signalled the beginning of the end of civilisation as they knew it as the country's youth subsided into bad behaviour and ill-discipline.

Bill Shankly, like his predecessor Andy Beattie, was a great admirer of the 'Busby Babes' team that Matt Busby and Jimmy Murphy had patiently moulded into a brilliant, exciting and awesome team. Shankly was forever talking to his players about how good they were both as a team and individually. Whenever he was in Matt Busby's company he would listen intently to everything the great man said. He, like Denis and everyone else connected with football, was devastated when hearing of United's fatal crash in February 1958. Busby had nearly lost his own life in the accident. Two weeks later, Denis and a friend travelled over the Pennines to watch the patched up United team take on Sheffield Wednesday in the fifth-round of the FA Cup at Old Trafford. "We paid eight times the usual price for a ticket at the scoreboard end," said Denis, adding, "but we just had to be there. It was only later that I realised, that if Huddersfield had accepted Matt Busby's £10,000 offer for me a couple of years before, I too might well have been on that plane in Munich."

2. The Hampden Roar

The following season Matt Busby, as we know, came back to manage his beloved United and also to manage the Scottish international team. I'm jumping ahead of the story but I will just digress again. During the 1958 World Cup in Sweden, Matt Busby was still having hospital treatment while the Scottish team had fared badly coming bottom of Group Two. It had been a woeful tournament for Scotland who had come in for a great deal of criticism. Scottish fans were hoping Busby could rejuvenate the team and put some much needed pride back. However, they were shocked at Busby's first selection against Jimmy Murphy's Welsh team in October 1958 at Ninian Park. Matt selected a five man forward line of players from the English League - this was unheard of at the time and resented by the biased Scottish press and the vast majority of their supporters who were of the opinion that Scottish-born players who played for English clubs were traitors.

The biggest shock of all though was Busby's choice of 18-year-old Denis Law, because of his age and the fact that he played for an English Second Division club. Law was the youngest player to be capped since Bob McColl in 1896. He had played in 12 successive league games before being selected for his country.

Denis learned of his call-up when, after training, Bill Shankly came rushing up to him excitedly. He clasped Denis by the hand and told him the great news that he had been selected for the Scottish team. Bill congratulated the lad and Ray Wilson and a few of the other players gathered round and added their congratulations. This was a great honour indeed for Denis and naturally he was overjoyed, as one would expect a patriotic, passionate Scot to be. It also showed how much

Busby believed in Denis's ability and character.

Yet, as mentioned, there were sceptical voices north of the border. "How can Busby select an unproven youngster like Law, who besides his age, has only had limited experience?" one Glasgow-based newspaper asked. Busby, however, took no notice of the criticism and stood by his selection. Denis never forgot this act of bravery by Busby, or the confidence he had placed in his ability. For his part, Denis was absolutely delighted at being selected for his country. He thanked Shankly for all his help and guidance although Shanks brushed this to one side telling Denis: "You deserve it son, if you have anyone to thank it is Matt Busby, he has always praised your ability."

Denis' mother and father attended the game in Cardiff. This was the first time they had watched their famous son, who always was and remains a proud and patriotic Scot. There was a tremendous atmosphere inside the ground as the teams filed out of the dressing rooms. The Welsh crowd were in fine voice singing 'Bread of Heaven' as Dave Mackay turned to Denis and remarked: "We are going to win this game, Denis lad. The fathers they are singing about can't help them today." There could have been no prouder Scot than Denis Law when he pulled that dark blue Scottish jersey over his slim frame, his heart was pumping ten to the dozen, and he felt ten feet tall.

On the surface Denis appears to have had a fantastic debut - Scotland beat Wales 3-0, Denis scored the first of 30 goals for his country. But to be perfectly honest, the goal was a complete fluke and Denis would be the first to agree that he knew very little about it. Welsh defender Dave Bowen booted a hasty clearance that smacked against the back of Law's blond head, stunning him but flying past world-class Welsh keeper Jack Kelsey and into the back of the Welsh net.

Denis played with some of Scotland's legends in this game, including Tommy Docherty, who would later become Law's manager at Old Trafford, and that brilliant wing-half and captain Dave Mackay. The full team was: Brown (Dundee); Grant (Hibernian), Caldow (Rangers); Mackay (Hearts),

Toner (Kilmarnock), Docherty (Arsenal); Leggatt (Fulham), Collins (Everton), Herd (Arsenal), Law (Huddersfield) and Henderson (Arsenal).

Denis was feeling on top of the world. However, the news that his mother and father had been involved in a serious car accident on their way back to Aberdeen soured the game for Denis. Their car was being driven by a family friend when it mounted the pavement and smashed into a lamp-post. Mr Law suffered cracked ribs while Mrs Law broke her leg. When they both recovered it was decided that this would be the first and last time they would ever watch Denis.

It was back to the hurly burly of Second Division football for Denis after the euphoria of mixing with characters such as Docherty, Mackay and Bobby Collins. Three weeks later, Matt Busby gave him his second cap when he was selected in the same team that had beaten Wales. This time the opposition was Northern Ireland, who had acquitted themselves brilliantly in the World Cup in Sweden. The match was played at Hampden Park. Ireland were captained by the majestic Danny Blanchflower, a supreme footballer and wing-half. Danny, a deep-thinking man, was more like a professor than a footballer. Football to him was a game to enjoy, where skill was paramount. He was revered throughout the football world. In the modern age he would undoubtedly have been given a knighthood.

Denis, meanwhile, was in raptures at the prospect of playing in front of Scottish supporters - it would be Law's first appearance in front of a Scottish crowd. Denis said after he had retired that although during his career he had played in some of the world's great stadiums for him there was nothing to compare with running out onto the pitch at Hampden Park. During his team talk before the game against Northern Ireland, Matt Busby emphasised the danger Danny Blanchflower posed if he was allowed to dictate the pattern of play by picking the ball up deep in his own half to re-distribute it to his forwards. Busby was a great admirer of the Irish captain, who incidentally reminded him of himself as a player.

Denis absorbed Busby's every word. "Denis, son," he said to Law, "I want you to stay close to Blanchflower. You will mark him closely. When he has the ball I want you to win it back." Denis nodded in agreement. He knew what was required.

When the game started there was Denis, clattering into the Irish captain. He took Busby at his word and marked him tightly, too tightly for the liking of Blanchflower and a number of newspaper reporters. Denis had kept Danny quiet and with the game almost finished Scotland were 2-0 in the lead, his future United colleague David Herd scoring and little Bobby Collins getting the second, when the young Law tired considerably. There were no substitutes allowed then, so he had to play on. As a consequence Blanchflower inspired his team forward. Northern Ireland equalised and nearly snatched a victory. After the game Denis was taken to task for his robust play against Danny Blanchflower by the press. Danny himself stated: "I was black and blue from this young player's attentions," adding "if he dashes about like he did in this game he will not last very long. And if he continues to play as he did against me he will get himself injured." With those back-handed compliments the legend of Law was well and truly cemented.

*

Toward the end of 1958 Denis received a very nasty injury. Playing against Charlton Athletic he twisted his knee. It was very painful but a few days later he turned out against Barnsley and injured the same knee. Huddersfield sent him to a specialist who diagnosed that Denis's cartilage was torn in three places. He was operated on and out of action for eight or nine weeks. Many believe it was this injury that caused him untold pain and heartbreak in the years to come. This was a serious blow for the youngster. In the 1950s medical care was nowhere near advanced as it is today and those kind of injuries could be career threatening. Denis was said to be injury-prone by certain newspaper reporters.

After getting over his injury it was May 1959 before he next played for Scotland. He went on tour, with the Scots winning 2-1 against Holland before a 1-0 defeat in Portugal. Denis played in both games. Before the year had ended he had helped Scotland beat Northern Ireland 4-0 in Belfast. Six weeks later he was in the team that drew 1-1 against Wales at Hampden Park.

Away from the international scene, other clubs were taking a fancy to Denis and scouts were regular visitors to Leeds Road with attendees often in double figures. Bill Shankly had worked hard and got a decent team together, with players such as Ray Wilson, who was now playing in his favoured left full-back position and Denis' pal Gordon Low at wing-half. There were also players like Les Massey, Kevin McHale and left winger Mike O'Grady to name but a few and Huddersfield were playing well enough to be quietly tipped for promotion to the First Division.

Yet behind the scenes Shankly had become disillusioned with the Huddersfield board for not giving him the money to buy other players. He had been eager to sign another forward. Brian Clough was making a big name for himself with Middlesbrough and Bill fancied him. Ian St John was another he wanted to buy and play alongside Law. He also wanted Ron Yeats, but the chairman told him that they could not afford the £25,000 fee for each player and he would have to rely on the club's youth system. Shanks frustration and ambition led him to quit Yorkshire for Liverpool.

Shankly had been inspirational for Denis and was a great motivator. He was the ideal person for grooming potentially good young players - if he told them to run through a brick wall they would attempt it. There is no doubt that the three years Denis spent with Bill Shankly at the start of his professional career in Huddersfield stood him in good stead for the remainder of his career in football.

"He oozed confidence," said Denis of Shanks, "it was he who helped me build up my own confidence, he was great." Only once did Shankly have to give a rollicking to Denis for lack of courage. It happened when Denis returned to the

Huddersfield team after missing a number of games through injury. After the first few minutes he did not seem to be trying and Shankly reproved him in the dressing room after the match. Shankly did not find out until some time later that Denis' injury had recurred and he could hardly walk after the game but Denis didn't complain either about his injury or Shankly's rebuke.

While with Huddersfield, Denis also appeared twice for Scotland Under 23s. He featured in a 1-1 draw against Wales and a 4-4 draw with England. He didn't score on either occasion but the recognition added to his transfer value. In all he played in four Under 23 internationals. In February 1961, in an unofficial international against the Army at Motherwell, the Scots won 3-2, Denis scoring twice. Three weeks later playing against England at Middlesbrough he scored the only goal to give Scotland a 1-0 victory.

Many believed that once Shankly established himself at Liverpool and knowing Huddersfield's financial position, he would soon be back to buy Denis. This however, was not possible. Years later, Bill told Denis that it was indeed something he had wanted to do, but couldn't because Liverpool, like Huddersfield, had no money. Liverpool were a Second Division team at the time and not the dominant force they were to become in later years.

Thus, with Shankly gone the Huddersfield team lost confidence and results started to go against them. Eddie Boot, who had been with the club for years, took over as the new manager. He was a quiet and sincere man but Denis had already decided to follow his mentor and find a much bigger club than Huddersfield. This was not being disrespectful to the club in any way but as an international Denis needed to improve his game and fighting for survival year in and year out with a club with little money was not for him. Who could blame him? A fee of £40,000 to £50,000 was quoted by the newspapers as the price Huddersfield had put on Law's head - an astronomical fee for a young Second Division player.

*

"At 15 Denis was much more mature than I was at 20," says Ray Wilson. "To me it was a great satisfaction to be playing at all. It took me several years to realise that there is very little future in football with a small club. When the day came when Denis wanted to move he told the club that he was going to leave and he went. Me? I asked Huddersfield Town for a transfer every season for six years! They told me I couldn't go and I accepted their decision and stayed, much as I wanted to play in the First Division." Ray was 29 before he got his big chance to join another club, Everton in 1964, for a £40,000 fee. He always maintained that he wished he'd had Law's determination and moved years before he eventually did.

Arsenal looked likely to win the bidding and sign Denis, and at the time he himself thought that was where he would be heading. It was said that one of the reasons Denis wanted to join Arsenal was because he wanted to play alongside his Scottish colleague Tommy Docherty. The Gunners offered David Herd, later to become Law's team-mate at Manchester United, as part of the deal plus cash. However, Manchester City also came into the equation and it was a straight fight between the two First Division clubs as to which one met Huddersfield's valuation. On Tuesday 15th March 1960, Denis was told to report to the ground after seven o'clock that night, and as he made his way there on the old trolley bus, he was visualising living in London and the glamour of playing First Division football for Arsenal. As he hurried inside the club offices he made his way into the games room and played table tennis unaware of the tense bidding taking place for his signature. He was extremely disappointed that there was no sight of George Swindin - Arsenal's manager. Ron Greenwood, the Arsenal coach, represented them, but he had no power of negotiation.

Les McDowall, the Manchester City manager, City chairman Alan Douglas, and a couple of City's directors were also at the club. Later, Mr McDowell told *Manchester Evening News* reporter Eric Thornton, that he had first set eyes on Law three years previously, after he had gone to Huddersfield to see if he could spot anything that might interest him. He said he had been immediately struck by Law's natural talent and he told Thornton 'This boy Law is going to be a great player.'

After talking things over with Mr McDowell and his directors Denis decided to sign for City. The fee was a new British transfer record - £55,000. To be honest, despite what Denis said on his arrival in Manchester the following day, he really did fancy going to London, but he felt that Arsenal had snubbed him by not turning up, so it was Manchester City for him.

Denis had been with Huddersfield for five years from April 1955. Denis himself said that he wasn't entitled to a share of the whopping transfer fee. However, manager Eddie Boot told him he would receive £300, yet never actually got a single penny from the deal. How times have changed. George Swindin told Huddersfield he was extremely disappointed at losing Denis and the £25,000 bid Huddersfield made for David Herd was rejected.

The following day the self-assured, bushy, fair-haired Law, with his alert features and intelligent eyes, arrived in the city in which he would play for the majority of his career. He carried an air of breezy aggression. He answered questions with a briskness and sense of humour. His bearing indicated complete belief in himself. The headline in the *Manchester Evening News* was 'Golden Boy Arrives - All Smiles'. The dusty old Exchange Station was given the Hollywood filmstar treatment to mark the arrival of Britain's newest golden footballer, £55,000 Denis Law. Flash bulbs popped and cameramen dodged in and out of barrier queues as Denis was almost swept out of the station by reporters. He shivered as he spoke to the newspapermen on platform 3. "I changed my mind about going to London," Denis told the reporters, adding, "after all, London might be a bit too big for a young fellow like me." He went on to say that he had friends in Manchester and said he had played in the city several times and had always received a good reception from the Manchester fans. When asked on his views about signing for Manchester City Denis replied: "All the fuss has put me into a bit of a daze, but I shall come out of it alright. I shall give my best every time and all the time."

At Maine Road there were even more television and newspaper cameramen. City manager Les McDowell and club captain Ken Barnes were on hand to welcome Denis. Smiling broadly, the City captain told Denis: "We are all glad you signed for us Denis, and you'll find there are some really good players here, and I'm sure you'll get on well with everybody." Denis moved into digs in Withington where City's former Scottish international inside forward Bobby Johnstone once lived. Manchester City decided to indemnify themselves with the signing of Denis by taking out three separate insurance policies for at least £50,000. The first would cover the ordinary week to week travelling risks, the second was to include all air flights, and the third was for match injuries.

There was a great deal of publicity in the newspapers about the size of the fee City had forked out to Huddersfield for a youngster barely three weeks out of his teens and Britain's costliest footballer. The fee was £10,000 more than the previous record. From the time Bryn Jones joined Arsenal, right up to Albert Quixall and Mel Charles, there had been a succession of players oppressed by having the millstone thrust upon them. Bill Shankly told the press: "There is only one player in Britain who can carry such a price tag on his back and that's Denis Law. He'll play his heart out on the field because he wants to prove that he is the best. He'll be worth £100,000 of any club's money in a year's time. He is the greatest thing in football." Shankly added that in his opinion Denis, in character, reminded him of Alex James. "He's confident to the point of brashness, assured and decisive."

Denis said that it was almost impossible not to think about the fee paid for his services, but it didn't worry him. "Both physically and mentally you have to establish your authority on the field. I feel I have the ability to do that."

Today, Fred Eyre is a self-made man. He experienced everything in football: groundstaff boy, apprentice professional (Manchester City's first-ever), full-time professional, part-time professional, non-contract player, player-manager, youth team manager, reserve team manager, scout and assistant manager. He is the author of best selling books, an astute businessman, a brilliant compere and after-dinner speaker, but in the 1950s, he was a gangling, ginger-haired groundstaff boy at Maine Road earning £4 a week, when Denis joined the Blues. Fred takes great pride in telling everyone how he used to clean and dubb the Lawman's boots.

"Denis was a great bloke," recalled Fred, "I remember one dark, rainy night City reserves were playing Huddersfield reserves at Maine Road. I was near the tunnel where the players ran out onto the pitch. When the game started I looked around and saw this blond-haired fellow in a debonair Italian styled suit with winkle-picker shoes. God, he looked a million dollars. You could tell that he was something special, something out of the ordinary as a person and young footballer. He was only about 18, but I thought to myself, 'That's how I'm going to look when I make it to the top of the football ladder.' And look where we both ended up? Denis went on to become a legend, while I was released by City and played for 20 clubs in 20 years! Played for 29 managers and 82 coaches! I remember his 21st birthday. Sackfulls of cards arrived at the ground for him and as he lapped the pitch with the senior players they stopped and tossed him up into the air."

Fred laughingly recalled an incident that happened years after both he and Denis had left Maine Road; Fred into Non-League football, and owning his own stationery business, while Denis became the undisputed King of the Stretford End. Fred was doing quite nicely in his new business venture and one day while delivering three desks, three chairs and a big filing cabinet to a Travel Agents on King Street in Manchester city centre Fred was faced with a problem. He did not think it was right to ask the owner of the travel agents, or his staff, to help him carry the stuff into his own shop. While he stood leaning on his van, scratching his head and wondering how he could get the furniture into the shop, from behind he heard the sound of a familiar Scottish accent.

"Hello, my son." Fred immediately recognised the voice as he turned to be greeted by, to use his own words "the greatest goal scorer in the world at that time," Denis Law. Fred said: "Denis looked the picture of health, his blond mane shining, his smile as broad as ever." The two men chatted and Fred mentioned the diverse nature of their respective football careers: "Denis's had rocketed skywards, while mine had plummeted to earth but I'll tell you this about Denis Law, whenever I saw him he was always affable, cheery and friendly. Even though he was a huge star he was a nice person." Upon hearing of Fred's dilemma, Denis told Fred to get one end of the desk while he took the other and they carried the desks into the shop. It was comical. Passers-by were amazed watching the most famous footballer in the world helping to carry the goods. Good natured banter was flowing.

"I always thought you'd end up working for a living," shouted one chap. "That's all you're fit for," shouted another, as they humped the gear into the shop and the eyes of the boss and his female staff nearly came out of their sockets at seeing the great Denis Law working as delivery boy. Later, when the goods were safely in the shop and Denis had gone on his way, the owner of the shop turned to Fred and said: "Good lord, I didn't know you had the great Denis Law working for you." Fred explained to the shop owner that Denis was merely helping him out of a quandary. The shop owner laughed and ordered more items. "I owe Denis a drink," said Fred laughing.

A few weeks after Denis had signed for Manchester City, he was coming out of the Midland Hotel in the centre of Manchester when who should be walking in but Matt Busby. They greeted one another like long lost relatives. Beaming, Busby shook Law's hand warmly and they chatted about Denis' move from Huddersfield. Matt smiled and told Denis: "I was contemplating making a bid for you. I thought it over very carefully. But we are playing very well at the moment." Busby then told Denis that Munich survivor Dennis Viollet was playing like his old self and scoring quite a few goals. He also mentioned that Albert Quixall, another inside forward, was starting to blossom, and that Law's old Aberdeen schoolboys chum Alex Dawson had also hit form. "Then," said the United manager, "I've also got Bobby Charlton. So I have an abundance of inside-forwards. That's why I finally decided not to make an approach for you." Then, with a twinkle in his eye and smiling Busby added: "But you never know what will happen in the future." With that the two men went their separate ways.

3. Citizen Law

The 1960s saw the dawn of a new era in British football. It became one of the most exciting decades in the history of football. From a game based on local support football suddenly entered the free market. The genesis of the sixties football revolution came in 1961, with the long-awaited abolition of the maximum wage, which then stood at £20 a week. Suddenly the clubs with the financial clout and larger support could offer higher wages and lure the big name players. This began the polarisation process in football. It is no conicidence that since the mid-sixties football has been dominated by large city clubs while smaller outfits such as Blackpool and Wolves have had hardly a sniff of glory since their 50s heyday.

Meanwhile on the pitch the majority of teams played attacking football and the fans lapped it up. Gone, or on its way out, were those old baggy shorts, replaced by the new lighter nylon type. The team jerseys also became lighter and more comfortable to wear. Boots and the caseball also changed and became lighter and waterproof. The boots had screw-in studs. Bladders were no longer inside the new lighter style ball, so prevalent in the old lace-up type. Games were played almost exclusively on Saturdays and few matches were filmed or televised, in fact it was 1964 before the BBC's Match of the Day appeared on our screens.

On the same day that Denis signed for City, Freddie Goodwin joined Leeds from Manchester United. Freddie, at 6ft 3, was a gifted wing-half. He had played regularly for the Reds since the Munich air disaster but had lost his first team place. In fact it had been ten weeks since Freddie had last played First Division football. Freddie would be making his debut against City in Denis' debut game at Elland Road the following

Saturday. Leeds' manager Jack Taylor told the press that when Leeds played City, Goodwin would mark Law. Poor old Freddie had walked into one of the hardest jobs of his career. On Saturday 19th March 1960, cars and coaches of all types jammed the 45-mile route from Manchester over the Pennines to Leeds as City fans went to see Law make his debut for the Blues at Elland Road.

The match ended with City being beaten 4-3 but Denis scored on his debut. The majority opinion in the newspapers was that Manchester City were a bad team and destined for demotion in the not too distant future. Even City's correspondent in the *Manchester Evening News*, Eric Thornton, said that the City players who said they would remain in the First Division were wearing rose-tinted glasses. But what did Freddie Goodwin think of the man he was told to mark?

"Denis Law is good...no, he's great," said Freddie, "I ought to know, because the first time I had ever seen him play was when I marked him at Elland Road." He said it was a pity that City didn't give him the support he deserved. "On the strength of one game it's hard for me to say he has any weaknesses - he certainly has a lot of good points. He shields the ball well and uses it cleverly. And he also positions himself shrewdly. He is obviously a natural player and you can see from the way he goes through a game that he has an instinctive knowledge of doing the right thing. He is fast and tricky and gets up to head the ball smartly, he is the sort of player you've got to watch carefully. He doesn't avoid the hard, unspectacular work. Unlike some inside-forwards, he doesn't leave you the room a wing-half would like. He challenged me continually and didn't allow me to get away with a thing. This is one of the jobs an inside-forward should do but often don't bother with. However, I don't think Law will save City from being relegated on his own."

Nevertheless Denis played in Manchester City's last seven games of the 1959/60 season helping them avoid relegation in the process. He scored twice but he soon learned that life was going to be no bowl of cherries at Maine Road. At this time City were a club in decline and destined for demotion to the Second Division. Denis knew when he joined them that the Blues were no longer one of football's elite, in truth they were struggling, but he believed things could change.

City still had some star names; Bert Trautmann, a former prisoner of war, was a world-class goalkeeper, little George Hannah, a lovely ball-playing inside forward, one of the best uncapped wing-halves in the British Isles, the elegant Ken Barnes and Roy Clarke, the Welsh left winger, were the other players of proven ability on City's books. However it wasn't long before Denis ran into problems. Playing was hard enough, but he had several fiery arguments with the City training staff, particularly Jimmy Meadows, the first team trainer. It wasn't that Denis didn't like training, that certainly was not the problem. In fact at Huddersfield under Bill Shankly he loved the five-a-sides, skill practices and sprints. Yet Meadows had him running full pelt up and down the stands, around the pitch and working on physical fitness. Denis was reported several times to manager Les McDowall for arguing with the trainer. Denis admitted himself that nothing ever came of these meetings with McDowall. The fact was City needed him to help them avoid relegation.

The following season Law played 37 times, scoring 19 goals. He also captained City for a spell when the regular skipper, Ken Barnes, was out injured. There was quite a bit of controversy when Les McDowall opted for someone as young as Denis to act as captain. Denis himself wasn't concerned one way or the other, as he told friends: "What's all the fuss about? I'm an international and I like to be a driving force wherever I play."

In January 1961, the Blues were looking very poor. It was thought that a good run in the cup competitions might bring a change of fortunes for the players and the club. The League Cup, a new competition that season, saw the Blues embarrassingly knocked out 2-0 by Second Division Portsmouth. In the FA Cup City were drawn against Cardiff City in the opening round and it took them three games before they overcame the Welsh side 2-0 in extra time at Highbury. Denis scored, along with Joe Hayes, to give the Blues their first victory in the FA Cup since they won the trophy against Birmingham City in 1956. In the fourth round they were drawn away to Luton Town at Kenilworth Road. For days before the tie the weather was shocking, it was raining non-stop and on the day of the tie it was even worse, making playing conditions atrocious. The pitch was like a quagmire and unplayable yet the referee announced that the game would be played but as he blew his whistle the rain fell heavier and the pitch cut up badly. After 18 minutes City were struggling as usual and already two goals down. It looked all over. Both sets of supporters were drenched to the bone. Obviously the Luton supporters wanted the game to continue, whereas City quite naturally wanted the game abandoned. The referee insisted the game must continue and it was at this point that Law decided that enough was enough.

Moving across the sticking, clinging mud like a hovercraft he plundered three goals, a hat-trick that had the Manchester fans shrieking with delight. At half time City were winning 3-2, the Blues followers wanted the game to continue, and who could blame them? Both sets of players were covered from head to toe in mud as they went in for a warm drink while the soaking wet spectators shivered in the queues for warm oxo and meat pies. On the resumption all the players had changed into clean, dry strips. Denis was on fire. He was like an electric eel on the atrocious surface of a pitch. He sprinted over the mud and struck his second hat-trick of the game, putting City 6-2 in front. He was ecstatic. What forward wouldn't have been after scoring two hat-tricks in one game? The Blues supporters were singing his praises from the top of their voices. He felt on top of the world! He had scored six goals in an FA Cup tie. Phew, six goals - what an achievement! But disappointment was in store, because with less than 20 minutes of the game remaining and the rain still pouring down as it had been throughout, the referee blew his whistle and announced he had abandoned the cup-tie, much to Denis' utter disdain and the disappointment of the fans.

The City team made their way back to Manchester and fans were saying that the team now had Luton's measure and the replay was a mere formality. This feeling however, was certainly not what Denis or his team-mates were thinking. As Denis himself confessed: "The pitch was terrible because it was raining all the time. But the annoying part of it was that it was even worse when the game was replayed! We had a feeling that we would lose the replay - and we did, 3-1. And I scored the one!"

Law had scored an amazing seven goals yet still ended up on the losing side. Most other players who had scored seven goals and seen six of them wiped out of the record books would have been heartbroken but Denis, although disappointed, merely shrugged his slight shoulders and carried on trying to help his club stay in the First Division.

Despite City's woes, Denis enjoyed himself in the short time he was at Maine Road. He made some good friends and enjoyed the 'mickey-taking' and company of the players. The Manchester City goalkeeper, Bert Trautmann, was world-class, there was no doubt about that assessment. He was one of the first goalkeepers who would throw the ball huge distances up the field to start a City attack. Denis, over the years, always praised Trautmann and Ken Barnes as great players and excellent colleagues. Bert, the big affable blond-haired German, was a great admirer of Denis.

"When Denis first came to Maine Road I remember training with him," said Trautmann. "He told me that he had joined City because he wanted to play First Division football. To be straight with you I thought he would have joined Arsenal or that the new Liverpool manager Bill Shankly would have signed him. It didn't take him long to realise that we were not a great team by any stretch of the imagination." Denis, Trautmann, Ken Barnes and Roy Paul became good friends. Denis and Ken Barnes are still great friends to this day. Trautmann, who had a short fuse of a temper, said that Ken Barnes and Roy Clarke would be constantly ribbing him.

"We're off to the pictures tonight Bert... it's a war film. You won't want to watch it because we hammer you again," they would say laughing and the other players would join in. Bert took it all in good fun but would get his own back at the appropriate time. Barnes was nicknamed 'Beakie' on account of his rather bony frame and long nose. "Denis had a rather long nose as well," added the goalkeeper, "and he got a lot of ribbing about it. But they took it all in good part." Bert was enthusiastic in his account of the 1960s version of Denis Law. "He was a cocky little fellow, very confident in his own ability. He knew he was good and wasn't afraid to flaunt it," recalled the City legend, "but he really did have tremendous ability. He stood out in our team, even at his tender age. You could see he would go on to become a big star."

In October 1960 the Football League broke with tradition and included Irish, Welsh and Scottish players in their representative teams. Denis was selected to play against the Irish League at Bloomfield Road, Blackpool. The team was Trautmann (Manchester City): Angus (Burnley), Armfield (Blackpool): Blanchflower (Tottenham), Adamson (Burnley), Mackay (Tottenham): Jones (Tottenham), White (Tottenham), Law (Manchester City), McIlroy (Burnley) and Connelly (Burnley). Denis' friend and club-mate Ken Barnes was selected as a reserve. Sadly, this would be Ken's only representative honour.

On paper it was a wonderful line-up but the Irish fought tooth and nail. The Football League eventually won 5-2 and Denis scored twice. In March 1961 Denis was once again selected for the Football League team, to play the Italian League in a game in Milan. Not surprising the Football League team lost 4-2. It was in this game that Denis got his first inclination of what Italian football was all about.

The cocky Scottish inside-forward soon ran into more problems when he announced that should City be relegated he would leave the club. There was uproar amongst City fans and officials. Making public statements was something Denis was not prone to do, but he had told a journalist his thoughts in all innocence and, as only a journalist would, he reported it in his newspaper. It was headline news in most of the newspapers. He was called arrogant, big-headed, disloyal and selfish. Denis was a young man now and he had served his apprenticeship with Huddersfield in the Second Division and he'd had more than his fill of the Second Division. He wanted to better himself and there was nothing wrong with that. Perhaps with hindsight he shouldn't have told the reporter his thoughts on the possibility that City would be relegated, but he was young, boisterous, with the football world at his feet. He certainly learned a valuable lesson which has stayed with him throughout his life, and that was to be more circumspect when talking to the press.

A good example of Law's reluctance to speak to the press came in the early sixties. The late Brian Moore was a broadcaster on the BBC's *Sports Report* programme. As Brian recalled: "Denis Law - need I remind you - was a remarkable footballer. What you wouldn't know, though, was that Denis was also a most reluctant broadcaster. Each time I tried to ask him questions for Sports Report he would ask me, 'Why would they want to hear from me?' and he always asked to be excused from giving an interview."

Smiling, Brian recalled that years later he finally cornered Denis in a Portuguese hillside village, of all places and persuaded Denis to face his microphone. "And very revealing it was too," added Brian. "As you probably know, Denis' quick-fire temperament had often got him in trouble with referees, opponents, and football authorities. He told me he had not enjoyed those skirmishes with officialdom, and was enjoying the game much more now that they were over. There was a lesson there for young players, when they felt like arguing on the pitch outside the laws. There was much more fun in the game when you played it straight."

There was another more serious incident that had far-reaching effects and which did not endear Denis to the Manchester City faithful. It ended in Denis being branded an upstart, a traitor and a disloyal brat to the cause of Manchester City. In April 1961 he was selected to play for Scotland against arch-enemies England at Wembley Stadium. The problem was that Manchester City had a vital League game on the same day, and their need was far greater than Scotland's.

Being full of youthful exuberance and a little brash, Denis didn't consider the implications of telling his manager, Les McDowall, that he wanted to play at Wembley for Scotland instead of turning out for his club. "I had never played at Wembley Stadium," said Law at the time, "I did not want to miss this wonderful opportunity." On the face of it this was a poor excuse. After all, City were paying his wages and Les McDowall should have insisted that Law play for his club rather than his country on this occasion. He didn't and Denis got his own way. He would, however, wish he had played for the Blues instead of Scotland, because England walloped the Scots 9-3, to win the Home International Championship outright. It was Scotland's worst-ever defeat, and Denis would lose his place in the Scottish team for the next game.

"It serves him right," said angry City supporters. Denis took some stick about this game against England but not as much as his Scottish colleague, goalkeeper Frank Haffey. The jokes about Scottish goalkeepers came thick and fast. "What's the time? Nearly 'Ten past Haffey'," was one of them. Another one doing the rounds in Sectarian Glasgow went: "Why didn't Celtic's Catholic goalkeeper want to touch the ball against England? Because it was orange." Poor Haffey later emigrated to Australia.

During the game against England, Denis and England's right-half, Bobby Robson, now Sir Bobby, clashed just under the royal box where Her Majesty the Queen was watching the game. Robson aimed a kick at Denis, who straight away booted him back. The England players were incensed and went in at Denis with extra fury, despite the fact that Denis and Bobby shook hands immediately after the incident. It's fair to say that Denis got his comeuppance.

And what of Manchester City? Well, they earned a credible 1-1 draw at West Ham that helped them survive another season in the First Division, but this was the beginning of the end of

Law's association with the Sky Blues - Italy was beckoning.

4. The Stormy Petrel

John Charles, Jimmy Greaves and Gerry Hitchens had been lured to the land of the lire. Denis was single and fancy free and set his sights on sampling what it would be like in Italian football. The money and weather was enticing. Then there was a lucrative signing-on fee, huge bonuses for winning and it all looked very glamorous compared to the restrictions of English football.

The maximum wage had only just been abolished in England and though he thought about his position with City he realised that even though they had survived, they would always be fighting against relegation. He liked the club and loved Manchester but he knew the team needed a new influx of players. He decided that he was going to Italy.

Denis received a great deal of criticism for speaking out on his plans if Manchester City were relegated. He was under fire from fans and supporters from all over the British Isles. The newspapers joined in the criticism as well. He was called big-headed, arrogant, abrasive, a know-all, over-priced at £55,000, and a difficult person for his team-mates to get along with. He was most certainly a 'stormy petrel'.

His pal, Dave Mackay, the Scottish wing-half, now playing for that wonderful Tottenham side of the early 1960s, spoke out in his friend's defence. "You can take it from me that Denis Law is neither a big-head nor a difficult character to get along with," said the barrel-chested Mackay, adding, "if I was a manager of a club interested in Denis Law, I would gladly have paid £75,000 for him, never mind the £55,000 Manchester City paid Huddersfield for him. Denis is a confident young man. Maybe it is his confidence that gives people the impression that he is 'cocky,' but I can assure you this is not the case. He's neither a big-head nor a difficult character to get along with. I know the boy well, and am proud to include him among my friends.

"For quite some time Scottish footballers have been in the shadows, but as a Scot I am delighted to see the likes of Scottish players like Denis Law, Jimmy Gabriel, Bobby Collins, Graham Leggatt and Bill Brown, who could walk into any Great Britain team." The Tottenham player went on to say that he would never dream of telling his manager at Spurs, Bill Nicholson, how he should build his team, saying that it wouldn't be right if he attempted to do that. However, he did say that in the spring of 1960, when Spurs were fighting hard to get among the honours, in his humble opinion he felt in his heart that had Tottenham signed Denis Law they might well have won the elusive League and FA Cup double.

"I firmly believe that the flaxen-haired Denis Law is among the greatest footballers in the world today, and with experience he will continue to improve. In my opinion, Denis Law should be chosen for Scotland before any other player, with the exception of John White," concluded Mackay. He compared Denis to John White. According to Mackay, Denis was always full of life, completely unreliable as far as time-keeping is concerned while White, on the other hand, lived his life according to a pre-arranged schedule. He was always on time, never a minute late, and as quiet as Denis was lively. "While Denis, by his tremendous zest for the game, is largely a goalscorer, John White is a goal maker. Two great players!"

Inter Milan were the first Italian club to show an interest in Law. He had meetings with a representative in Manchester's Midland Hotel. He was offered a £5,000 signing on fee, £100 a point and £200 win bonus; a massive amount of money when compared to what he was getting in England. It didn't take long for Law to agree terms and the Inter Milan representative said he would be back in touch with Denis within a few days. True to his word, the agent turned up at Denis's home with the appropriate forms for him to sign.

Foolishly, and naively Denis had not bothered to inform his manager, Les McDowell, or any officials at Maine Road, and he signed the forms. Of course, Manchester City and Inter Milan should have agreed on a transfer fee for Denis. However, Denis later received a visit from another Italian, Gigi Peronace, offering him the chance to join Torino, who had just completed the transfer of Joe Baker from Scottish club Hibs. Baker was born in England but his family moved to Scotland as a child. He had been capped for England, although he spoke with a strong Scottish accent.

Denis knew Baker and had, of course, played with his brother Gerry at Maine Road and this influenced his thinking on joining Torino. The deal on offer from Torino was exactly the same as the Inter Milan offer and Denis decided to sign for them. Inter Milan were furious and threats would follow once Denis arrived in Italy. A deal was done with Manchester City, by Gigi Peronace, for which City would receive a £110,000 transfer fee. It was by far the biggest fee ever paid by an Italian club for a British player.

So Manchester City made a huge profit on a player they had bought just over a year previously. Denis and Gigi, who spoke perfect English, remained close friends until Gigi's death a few years later. The Blues did not want to lose Law and by now the maximum wage had been abolished in England. Tommy Trinder, the Fulham chairman, offered to pay his star player Johnny Haynes £100 a week. Inter Milan had tried to sign Haynes but he had rejected their offer and remained at Fulham. In a further effort to keep Law at Maine Road, the City chairman, Alan Douglas, offered Denis £80 a week if he would stay a City player. This was a big increase from the paltry £20 a week Denis and all the other players had been earning under the old antiquated and unfair system. The Manchester City chairman tried hard to convince Denis that Italy was not all it was cracked up to be but the player thanked him for his offer and concern but he was determined that he was leaving to play in Italy. And so on the 6th June 1961 Denis signed an option to join Torino having played just 44 league games for the Blues, scoring 21 goals.

Before he left for Italy Leslie McDowell, Manchester City's

manager said: "I have no hesitation in naming Denis Law as one of the world's outstanding players, although he can become at times a stormy petrel. There are plenty of footballers with spirit and many players who are skilful, but it rarely happens that you get both qualities in the same man. Denis Law has both to an exceptional degree. He has a lot to learn but is young enough for that and I sincerely hope he will learn rapidly in Italy as I believe he would have done in this country. Let us keep our sense of proportion! One man can never make a football team and although I have talked so much about Denis Law, we have a lot of faith in the rest of our staff. Early last winter I was delighted with our form and I see no reason why we should not build another impressive side. The management are prepared to go all out for any new players we think will strengthen the team."

*

In June 1961 Denis flew to Torino with Manchester City, who as part of the transfer deal for Law had agreed to play a game against the Italians. Torino is situated near the Italian Alps and the city itself is full of beautifully clean, tree-lined boulevards. Their main industry was and remains the giant Fiat factory owned by the Agnelli brothers, then owners of Juventus.

In May 1949 Italian champions Torino were involved in a terrible air crash which claimed the lives of 18 of their players. Torino had been striving to get back to their former greatness ever since. Their main rivals and neighbours Juventus were now the top club in the region so there was a great deal of intense rivalry between the two clubs. However, that was of no immediate concern to Denis.

When the Manchester party arrived in Turin, Denis was treated like a film star. At the airport fans, directors and the Italian press were waiting in their hundreds to welcome him. He was besieged by autograph hunters and newspaper photographers and he lapped up the attention heaped upon his slim shoulders. But Denis soon discovered that the Italian press were completely different to English sports writers. The

Italians expected full, undivided co-operation from the players. While he was in Italy a huge argument was taking place between Inter Milan and Torino; Inter claimed that Denis was their player while Torino maintained he was theirs and although the argument was clearly political rather than serious Inter still threatened to have Law banned from football.

After the friendly, which had been abandoned in the second half due to torrential rain with City leading through a Law goal, the Manchester team flew back home while Denis remained in Italy to sort out accommodation and other matters connected to his transfer. Joe Baker had not arrived in the country at this point but Torino had booked both players into one of the top hotels in Turin. It was a luxurious place and they lapped it up (even though they were later shocked to discover that they would have to settle their own hotel bills).

Denis was idolised wherever he went. With his blond hair, smart tailored suits, upright stance, and cheery disposition, he stood out amongst the olive-skinned, dark-haired Italians. He did a few training sessions with his new team-mates and the first thing that hit him was the language barrier, because he didn't speak a word of Italian and only one or two of the Torino players spoke a little broken English. Gigi Peronace helped considerably. He acted as mediator and interpreter and during this time became a close friend to both Denis and Joe Baker. During the close season Denis travelled back to Scotland to visit his family to prepare himself mentally and physically for his new adventure in the land of the lire. It is true that both Denis and Joe Baker were thrilled about beginning their adventure in Italy. Nothing, however, could fully prepare them for what they were letting themselves in for when they eventually went back to play for Torino.

Denis had only met Joe Baker on a couple of occasions. He had of course played with Joe's brother, Gerry, at Maine Road. Joe Baker was known as England's 'Scottish' centre-forward. He must have been the first England player to call the caseball a 'fitba' in a rich Scottish accent. He became the first representative of a Scottish League club to play for England when he was in the team against Ireland at Wembley in 1959.

Born in Liverpool, Joe's family moved to Wishaw, near Motherwell in Scotland, when he was just two, while his brother Gerry was born in New York. Nevertheless Joe was Scottish through and through - in fact he had played for Scotland as a schoolboy international. When he was 15, he and his brother Gerry joined Chelsea. After a few weeks, however, Joe became homesick and Chelsea manager Ted Drake released him. Gerry stayed for a year, became a professional before he, too, felt the urge to return to Scotland. On his return Joe was snapped up by Hibernian and his career developed rapidly. In his first season as a professional he scored 30 goals. He was good with both feet and a wonderful header of the ball. Joe's reputation grew after a performance against Billy Wright, the Wolves and England captain, during a friendly between their club sides. Wright was suitably impressed with Joe and told Walter Winterbottom, the England manager.

There was an unwritten rule that the English Football Association would never go beyond the borders of England for an international representative, however well the English-born player might have been performing there. But England had just lost the great Manchester United centre-forward Tommy Taylor in the Munich disaster. Tommy had led the England attack with more verve and skill than anyone since the days of Tommy Lawton. After his death, England tried Nat Lofthouse again and even Tom Finney was given a run at centre-forward. Derek Kevan, Brian Clough and Bobby Charlton had been experimented with as leaders of the attack but none came up to expectation in the most exacting position on the field.

After two selectors, Sam Bolton of Leeds and Syd Collings of Sunderland, had been asked to watch Baker play for Hibs against Motherwell, where Joe had a fine game and scored twice, the pair returned with a glowing report. England had an Under 23 International against Poland in September 1958 and the selectors deemed this the ideal occasion to blood Baker.

For the match against Poland, Joe was meeting ten strangers. He was 18, but confident. He didn't score but his speed off the mark, enthusiasm and willingness to chase lost causes worried the Polish defence and helped create two goals apiece for Jimmy Greaves and Bobby Charlton. Three weeks later he played against Yugoslavia at Norwich. England won 3-0 with Greaves and Charlton again the goal scorers. Although he had not scored, Joe had impressed.

English First Division managers were now after him and the Hibs phone line was red hot with various offers. Wolves, Bolton, Sheffield Wednesday and Liverpool were all willing to pay a reported £50,000 fee. Joe made his full England debut against Ireland at Wembley. He had replaced Brian Clough, the Middlesbrough goal-scoring machine, who had a disappointing game in the last International against Sweden. Joe scored the opening goal for England against Ireland and enjoyed a splendid match, capped by a dash down the left wing in the dying seconds to centre for Ray Parry to score the winner in England's 2-1 victory. The bigger the occasion, the more Baker loved it. He soon became England's established centre-forward on the close season tour of Spain and Hungary. This, then, was the man who would join forces with Denis in Italy.

*

Although Denis was excited at the prospect of moving to Italy and playing a different type of football than that he was used to, he might well have heeded the danger signs by seeing what happened to the player with whom he was most often compared - Jimmy Greaves.

Greaves was an-out-and-out striker. A prolific goalscorer from the moment he started playing football as a schoolboy, Jimmy had joined Chelsea at 15 and was in the first team at 17, before he had even sampled reserve team football. He made his first team debut in August 1957 against Spurs in front of a 50,000 crowd and scored the equaliser in a 1-1 draw. He went on to score six times in his eight first team games, displaying his hallmark predatory goal scoring instincts. In his second season he got 32 and was the First Division's leading goalscorer. He netted 29 the following season and 41 in the 1960-61 season and was again the First Division's top marksman.

Selected for the England Under 23s Greaves scored a hat-trick against Bulgaria and the newspapers were saying he should be in the senior England team. Married at 18, Greaves was, like Law, hyper-active and very witty, a real 'Jack-the-Lad'. After scoring over 100 goals for Chelsea he asked for a move. He was now the father of a baby girl but the maximum wage remained in force in England and Greaves had heard of the astronomic amounts being offered to strikers to play in Italy, so that was were he wanted to go.

So in 1961, for a fee of £80,000, he signed for AC Milan. He was to receive a £10,000 signing-on fee, and a salary of £5,000 a year. Jimmy and his wife Irene knew this would be their hope for long-term security. "I only went to Italy for the money," Jimmy later admitted.

Yet once Greaves moved to Milan, he seemed to meet nothing but trouble. He didn't hit it off with Nero Rocca, the paunchy, miserable-looking Milan trainer. Jimmy hated the negative football the Italians played and after four months of arguments, Greaves had had more than enough of the place. He scored 9 goals in 14 games for Milan, which isn't a bad strike rate in a league where a premium is placed on goals. Nevertheless Jimmy soon left San Siro. In December 1961 Tottenham manager Bill Nicholson paid Milan £99,999. Nicholson said he didn't want to burden Greaves with a £100,000 price tag.

Once back on English soil Jimmy admitted he had not made a penny from his Italian adventure. His signing-on fee had been used to pay off his legal bills, tax and other expenses. Yet at Tottenham he blossomed and became an even better player than he had been at Chelsea. He was neat and precise, possessed lightning speed, beautiful skill, anticipation and bags of flair. In eight seasons with Spurs he scored 220 times, and was the leading goal scorer in the First Division on four occasions.

Football writers loved nothing better than to compare Greaves with the Law Man. Both Denis and Jimmy had a mutual admiration and respect for each other's scoring ability. It is fair to say that the general consensus of opinion was that both were truly great goal scorers. Jimmy was a born and bred goal poacher whereas Denis only became an out-and-out striker when Matt Busby moved him up front. Indeed, wearing Huddersfield Town's colours in 91 games Law had managed just 16 goals, while with City he hit just 23 goals in 48 League and FA Cup games. Yet it is true to say that while the Englishman was clinical, accurate and thoughtful, the Scot was instinctive, dynamic and thrilling.

For six weeks before their first league match of the new season, Torino took their team to Frabosa Soprana, a training camp 3,000 feet above sea level in the Alps to prepare. This certainly wasn't to Denis' liking. In his first game for Torino in August, Denis found the weather boiling hot. They played Sampdoria, in Genoa, and lost 2-0. Not the start he would have liked. Denis found the heat and bonehard ground a problem. He also quickly discovered that Italian defenders took no prisoners. Poor Joe Baker, as a centre-forward, was forced to stay right up front and take the punishment of the ruthless defenders.

After the defeat the team were changing in the dressing room and Denis couldn't help but notice the change in attitude of the Torino management. Petty incidents accrued that made Denis realise it all depended on the result of the game. That, to the Torino board, was imperative. If they won, he could have almost anything he wished. However, a loss meant long faces and an acceptance of the implications.

He got a further example of this in his first home game against Lanerossi, in which Joe Baker scored a brace of goals and Torino went into a 3-0 lead a short while later. They were cruising to victory when Baker got sent off after retaliating against one of the opposition players who tried to gouge his eyes out. In the end the result was a 3-3 draw. Denis went to great pains to tell people that Joe had been provoked and was simply defending himself. The Torino officials were not best pleased! Both he and Denis usually had two giant defenders marking them tightly. Denis, being an inside-forward, wasn't stationed in one spot. He could roam about. But he, too, felt the full brunt of the 'hatchet' men. The shirt pulling was annoying but the kicking, sly punches, elbowing and spitting was something they had to get used to very quickly indeed. Denis later admitted that he had gone mainly for the money, but he also wanted to improve himself as a player, yet the defences he came across practised nothing more than unlicensed violence.

In the return fixture with Lanerossi, Denis fell foul of the referee. He was blatantly hacked down by one of their defenders, Fusato, who was known throughout Italy as a spiteful defender. As Law got to his feet and brushed himself down he trod on the big defender's ankle. We have all witnessed the hystrionics of the Continental players when feigning injury and this fellow was no exception. The outcome was a £10 fine, a week's suspension by the Italian league and, because the suspension meant he missed Torino's next game against Inter Milan, he was fined £200 by his club!

As a consequence Denis, single and impetuous, rebelled against the rigid discipline that was part and parcel of the Italian football structure. He was becoming bored by the lack of familiar entertainment, the constant pestering of the press and his manipulation by his Italian masters.

After a few weeks the novelty of playing in a foreign country was wearing a little thin. When Torino won, the players would be treated like royalty and rewarded with bonuses. Yet Denis was shocked after one away defeat to see the home supporters hurling stones and bottles at the Torino coach as it left the ground. While playing Palermo in Sicily, the pitch was like a mud bath and the Sicilian fans were ferociously hostile and abusive to the Torino players. As Denis took a throw-in he was pelted with oranges, broken bottles and spectators spat in his face.

There seemed to be incidents concerning Denis and Joe every week in the newspapers as stories about their exploits became headline news. Denis was accused of doing everything short of murder. The club's supporters in Italy, unlike their counterparts in Britain, ruled the roost. There were many rich supporters among them, people who employed perhaps hundreds of fans and the owner would supply the transport for away games. After one game Denis and Joe had arranged for an Italian they had befriended to meet them at the airport in Turin when they returned from an away game. The man was there with his car but as Denis and Joe got in the vehicle, all of a sudden, holy murder broke out. Their pal was arguing furiously with the president of the Torino supporters club and suddenly the two men started fighting. Denis and Joe were flabbergasted - what was it all about?

Well nothing really. Denis' friend, whose car he and Joe Baker were seated in, just happened to be a Juventus supporter. The president of the Torino supporters club shouted at the two players to get out of the car immediately and join the rest of the team. Both were told that they must have nothing whatsoever to do with him again. All because he supported Juventus!

Italy was turning into a nightmare for both players. On another occasion, while strolling along the bank of the Grand Canal in Venice before a game, they were besieged by a horde of photographers. After taking plenty of pictures one fellow in particular continued to follow them even though he had been asked very politely by Denis to leave them in peace. A scuffle ensued between Joe Baker and the photographer, resulting in the Italian receiving a punch. All hell let loose and the incident caused the two players considerable notoriety throughout Italy while Joe received a hefty fine from the club. Poor old Gigi Peronance was virtually at their beck and call day and night, he was in the middle of it. It was he who had to sort out all the questions and information from both players, while telling them what they were expected to do and where to report for the club officials.

As explained, for the first few months in Italy Denis and Joe Baker shared a room in a high-class Turin hotel. At first this was great but the two lads soon become bored with the monotony of everyday life in Turin. A typical day consisted of little more than breakfast in their room, followed by a journey by taxi to Torino's ground where the trainer would check that all his players were still in the city. Then Denis and Joe would travel back to their hotel where they would sit and read the English newspapers. At 2pm they returned to the ground for nearly three hours' training. Both players loved this. In fact, it was the best part of their day. Back at the hotel they would have dinner and go to bed. They were not allowed out to socialise in any respect.

Three days before a game they would join the rest of the team in another hotel, one that the club had chosen. The monotony of their existence would drive any high spirited young men to despair. Let's face it, they were two young, unmarried men, highly popular with the ladies and like all young fellows they enjoyed a drink and a dance but if they ventured outside their confines then it would appear in every Italian newspaper. And how they would embellish it - if Denis and Joe had done only a quarter of what the Italian scribes reported they had been up to, then they would have been supermen.

Eventually Torino put the two players in separate flats in a beautiful hill setting overlooking the city. The flats had all mod cons and were absolutely exquisite. However, living in these palaces on their own soon bored the pair to tears. Their only solace was on Sunday, the day the games were played, and even this soon descended into a familiar battle of wits against physical aggression. Playing against an eight-man defence felt like they were banging their heads against a brick wall and it wasn't long before Baker was dismissed from the field and suspended. Denis was booked and fined several times.

It was bad for Denis but at least he retained a cheeky chappie swagger. Yet poor Joe Baker had never been away from home before and he was feeling down in the dumps more often than Denis. It was completely the opposite of what they had expected, although it must be stressed that before Denis left England for Italy there were many sceptics of the opinion that he personally was not cut out for the Italian lifestyle and

most certainly not their way of playing football and
'entertaining' the paying spectators.

There were a few things Denis did enjoy about Italy and that
was the diet and their method of training. The coach was an
Argentine, Beniamino Santos, a former player for Torino.
Denis said there was no comparison between the English way
of training and the method he saw in Italy. In a typical session
the first team squad would line up in pairs, nobody was allowed
to talk. Santos would direct the session with a whistle. The
players would do a little light jogging and when Santos blew his
whistle they would stop and do exercises. On another blast of
the whistle the players would jog to another part of the pitch
and do more exercises. They would work on fast sprints and
ball control while the goalkeepers trained together. The
forwards worked on short, sharp runs and each player would
work with a ball. Each player had a training programme suited
to his specific needs. This was just what Denis loved doing. It
was much better than the stamina and long distance work that
his former club Manchester City had favoured.

Yet despite the benefits to his game, Denis' social life ceased
to exist and a serious incident brought the beginning of the
end of his stay in Italian football. Denis' brother Joe paid them
a visit and stayed on for a few days. On the Sunday, Torino had
won a game and later that night Denis and his brother Joe,
along with Joe Baker, were invited to a restaurant for a meal
with some of Torino's rich supporters. The restaurant was
outside the city. After the meal the three of them decided to go
into the city to a dance. They travelled in Joe Baker's brand
new Alfa Romeo. Driving quite sensibly at a safe speed but not
quite used to driving on the right hand side of the road, he
took a roundabout, then a loud bang was heard as one of the
wheels hit a kerb and in a split second they crashed. The next
thing Denis recalled was waking up in hospital. He blinked his
eyes, looked across the room and saw Joe Baker in another bed.
Joe looked dreadful. His jaw and nose was broken, his palate
split, and one of his eyes was severely swollen and damaged. Joe
Law had escaped unscathed but was shaken up.

As if to make matters worse, a newspaper photographer suddenly appeared and proceeded to take pictures of Joe from his bedside. Poor Joe lay helplessly on his bed in terrible pain and the nurses and doctors were not in the least bothered as this man quite callously continued taking his photographs. Denis wanted to get off his bed and belt this insensitive fellow, and he shouted to the man to stop taking pictures and get out immediately or accept the consequences.

Naturally the Italian newspapers played up the accident for all it was worth. They even suggested that the accident happened because of a drunken orgy. The truth was the two players had consumed just two lagers each, yet because of the accident Joe would be out of action for quite some time. If anything the incident made Denis' mind up for him. He was thoroughly fed up with the whole Italian adventure and would have made his feelings known quite forcibly had it not been for the language barrier. Denis had started to learn Italian but was not yet fluent enough to give the Torino officials a piece of his mind. He was annoyed and intended to fulfil his contract to the best of his ability but both he and Joe Baker vowed to leave the country at the earliest opportunity. Indeed so keen were they to now get out, that Joe struck a bet that he would sign for an English club first.

*

As I mentioned earlier, while Torino were winning, everything was hunky-dory, but once they lost, things became very unpleasant. At this time Torino were far from a good, solid championship team. Apart from Denis and Joe and perhaps two or three others, the team was quite average. It was a virtual impossibility for a team like this to mount a serious challenge for honours. The final straw for Denis came during a cup-tie against Napoli. A few days previously Denis had sent a letter to club president, Signor Filliponi, requesting a transfer. He was determined to go back to England and he dearly wanted to get away from the cynicism and brutality of Italian defensive play.

The Torino-Napoli game was Joe Baker's first game back

since his car accident. The weather was boiling hot, much too hot for football and in a poor game with few highlights the score was 0-0 when, in the second-half, the ball went out of play and Denis dashed to retrieve the ball. He was about to take a throw-in when he saw his team-mates and the referee move over to him. The ball was hastily snatched from his hands by one of his own team-mates and before Denis knew what was happening the Torino coach, Beniamino Santos, was on the touchline screaming obscenities in Italian at Denis and the next moment the referee ordered Denis off the field.

Denis was understandably completely baffled with this whole shoddy affair, but somehow he had been sent off. The crowd hooted, whistled and started booing. Gigi Peronance rushed over to Denis and took him back to the dressing room. Gigi explained to Denis that Santos, the coach, told the referee to dismiss him from the game because he disobeyed the coach's orders not to take throw-ins. This was pathetic! To make matters worse, with only ten players, Torino not surprisingly lost 2-0. Afterwards an angry Denis had a few choice words with Signor Fillipone, and rushed out of the ground never to return. Denis was later to learn that there were more shenanigans going on behind his back. The Torino officials were behind his sending off. This kind of plotting and conniving was quite common in Italy. He was suspended for two weeks, fined and told he must not go anywhere near the ground.

Geoffrey Green, writing in his book *There's Only One United,* the official Centenary history of Manchester United explains: "In the case of Denis Law, there was a certain James Bond element in the way he returned to England from Italy." Denis told Mr Green that he had become disillusioned with Italian football. Yet he tacitly accepted the rigid discipline, the way the team were taken to a mountain retreat to prepare for matches and all the other things Torino insisted upon but ultimately he found it boring and he was just not enjoying his football.

Gigi Peronace, talking about Denis's period in Italy, saw things a little differently. He said that matters between Denis,

Joe Baker and the Torino officials came to a head after the car crash that saw Joe out of action for a few months. He said that before the Torino versus Napoli cup match, being the passionate Scot that he was, Denis wanted to play for his country in an important match at Hampden Park a few days later. He asked for a release to play in this game. When this request wasn't forthcoming and he didn't receive written permission to play for Scotland, he didn't put in any effort in the cup-tie. Gigi recalled sitting on the bench when Santos shouted the Torino captain, Enzo Bearzot, over to him and ordered him to tell Denis to leave the field. The captain refused, so Santos did the necessary. Following that incident Denis vowed that he was finished with Torino.

5. Lawmania

Two weeks after his sending off Denis was told to travel to Lausanne in Switzerland where Torino were due to play a Friendship Cup match. However Denis was not sent to play but to meet Matt Busby with a view to him joining Manchester United. Denis' joy cannot be described - he was as happy as a sandboy for this was what he had been hoping and praying for, a return to English football and an opportunity to play for the manager for whom he had the greatest respect. Yet despite the deal appearing to be a foregone conclusion things were not quite so straightforward.

The United manager, chairman Harold Hardman and Louis Edwards, conducted themselves impeccably during discussions with their opposite numbers from Torino yet Denis wasn't allowed into the meeting. Yes, that's correct, the player the Italians were trying to sell for thousands of pounds was not allowed to sit in and listen to these men discussing his career. This might seem unbelievable now when players and their agents appear to be all-powerful but this was reality in the early sixties in Italy.

"Don't worry, Denis," Matt Busby told his prospective signing during a break in the meeting, "everything is more or less settled." Little did Busby or Law realise what lay in store for them over the next few heart-wrenching weeks. Denis was told to travel back to Italy while the transfer was sorted out but once back in Turin Denis was eager for negotiations to be hurried along so he could head home. Imagine his anger, dismay and shock then when he was told by Torino president Signor Filliponi that they had sold him to Juventus for £160,000. "You have to do what you are told in Italy," Denis was informed by officials.

After his initial anger, during which Denis issued an earful of expletives to his employers, he returned to his flat, packed his case and with the help of Gigi Peronace, who paid for his taxi to the airport and airfare back to England, Denis was gone!

David Miller, the author of *Father of Football*, the story of Sir Matt Busby, tells a slightly different story. In his account of the Law transfer he claims that George Sturrup, Real Madrid's agent in London, had received a phone call from Emil Oesterricher, the technical director of Torino and former manager of Real Madrid. Oesterricher told Mr Sturrup that he was absolutely fed up with both Law and Baker and wanted to transfer them and asked him if he knew a British club who were interested. Real Madrid and Manchester United had a good relationship and Matt Busby was highly respected by the Madrid hierarchy. Mr Sturrup phoned Busby and, after the usual friendly formalities, asked Matt if he would be interested in buying two players who he thought might interest him. The United manager, never one to show his excitement, asked the names of the two players.

"Joe Baker," he was told. Busby did not think Baker would fit into his plans at that time.

"Who is the other?" Matt asked casually.

"Denis Law," replied Sturrup, smiling to himself. There was almost an explosion at the other end of the telephone. Matt told him not to say anything to anyone or move anywhere until he arrived at his home. Matt jumped on the first train and arrived at Sturrup's house in South London. Once there, arrangements were made to meet Torino officials.

However according to other sources the seeds of this transfer saga had been sowed long before, in November 1961, when the Football League played the Italian League in a match at Old Trafford. Denis was included in the Italian team and when Denis met Matt Busby at the ground they had a long conversation during which Law told the United manager he was unhappy in Italy. Busby listened intently and gave Denis a few words of encouragement but both men had to be a little guarded in what they said - nevertheless the die had been cast.

A few months later at Hampden Park, when Scotland played England, Denis and Matt met again. Denis told Busby the situation with Torino had deteriorated and he wanted to come back to play in England. The United manager assured Denis that if he should be made available, then Manchester United would be in touch with Torino immediately. This pleased Law greatly and he felt reassured about his future.

While all these shenanigans were taking place the sports pages were full of the possibility of Denis Law's return to British football. Throughout the summer Manchester United followers were hoping and praying that Matt Busby could pull off the coup and bring the Law man to Old Trafford. As the saga appeared almost daily on the back pages the highs and lows of the situation had the fans moaning and groaning in despair. They, like Matt Busby and Jimmy Murphy, knew in their hearts that before United could become a great team again they needed a magnetic player like Law. When the news in the papers was favourable supporters would be beaming with the prospects of what Denis could do for the team yet for long periods it seemed that the Italians were intent on putting up obstacles to Denis' transfer.

On 3rd May 1962 Real Madrid played Benfica in the European Cup Final in Amsterdam. Matt Busby was at the game and later he and a couple of Manchester United's officials held a secret meeting with Torino officials. Then, on 22nd May Busby, Harold Hardman and Louis Edwards went to Italy for further discussions but after being messed about by the Torino officials, the three United officials walked out in disgust the following day. It was immediately announced that Denis Law would not now be joining United. Apparently the Torino president had attempted to impose new terms on the transfer and the United delegation refused to be shunted around and promptly flew back to Manchester.

Later, as an act of diplomacy, or perhaps out of desperation to see the deal concluded, Torino put Gigi Peronace in charge of the transfer negotiations and finally on the glorious 12th July, Denis became a Manchester United player. He cost United a record £115,000 and immediately became the most expensive player in English football history and the first to be valued at over £100,000. One newspaper wrote that the British record fee made Denis worth £48 an ounce. It had also pushed his total transfer cost to an astronomical £300,000 and Denis was still only 22.

It had been a long hard road for Matt and Denis but over the coming years it would prove to be worth it. Denis signed a two-year contract on a salary of £100 a week. The Bondesque saga was now over and Denis could settle down and thrill the Mancunian public with his special brand of magnetic football skills.

Denis recalled his end of the transfer saga: "After the meeting between Matt Busby and the Torino officials broke down a few weeks passed, then I received a message from Gigi Peronace. He told me he had the authority to sell me to Manchester United. Of course I was delighted. When I actually signed for Manchester United, the club I had always wanted, it was like signing a peace treaty after a long hard battle. Matt Busby seemed as pleased as I was."

And what of Joe Baker? Well he lost his wager with Denis that he would be transferred first. However, it was a close call because four days after Denis signed on the dotted line to become a Manchester United player, Billy Wright, the legendary Wolves and England centre-half now managing Arsenal, flew to Italy to clinch Joe's signature for a £70,000 fee.

As a guide to how well Denis performed for Torino one must bear in mind that in the season before he and Joe had joined, Torino had avoided relegation by the skin of their teeth and, despite all the trouble and problems Denis encountered, the fact remained that during the season they were there the club finished 7th in Serie A, their best finish for several years - Denis scoring 10 times in 27 games. It was little wonder the Torino fans idolised him and were heartbroken at his departure.

*

John Charles had been the first British player to make a big impression in Italian football. On 2nd August 1962 the Gentle Giant left Juventus and rejoined Leeds United for £53,000. Charles had been idolised in Italy and is arguably Wales' greatest-ever footballer. He was equally brilliant as the leader of the forward line, at centre-forward or as the pivot of the team at centre-half. When Leeds first sold him to Juventus in 1957 they received a £65,000 fee. John stayed in Turin for five years. In 155 appearances he scored 93 goals and figured in the top three in the European player of the year polls for 1958 and 1959. After his return to Leeds he later returned to Italy in a £70,000 move, this time joining Roma. Sadly, the magic had gone and Charles returned to Cardiff City in 1963.

Yet even to this day the giant Welshman is remembered in Italy with affection. Speaking about the problems Denis and Joe Baker faced during their short time in Italy, John said that it was Baker who never really settled in Italy. "The trouble was that both Denis and Joe were young and single," he said, "Eddie Firmani, Gerry Hitchens and myself had our wives and families with us in Italy. Denis and Joe were boisterous, happy-go-lucky youngsters who were on their own, and that didn't help them to settle down. They were two young, single, good-looking boyos, and a perfect target for the scandalmongers of Italy.

"Denis settled much better than Baker did because he had, after all, been away from his Aberdeen home since he was 15. He had also lived in Huddersfield and in Manchester, so he wasn't such an easy prey for homesickness, which can be heartbreaking." John said that Denis was the sort of footballer who could have settled in Italy: "He soon picked up the language, and he was an immaculate ball-player, he could score goals and believe me he could look after himself on the field against those vicious, cynical, hard defenders that were built like Praetorian Guards."

John said that Denis picked up all the gestures. "I remember seeing a film of him on an Italian television sports programme. He had just scored a goal and he turned round, stood perfectly still and raised both arms above his head in a gesture of

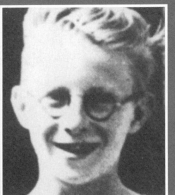

The Boy

The Lawman later admitted that as a child he seemed the most implausible footballer but the skinny lad with the National Health glasses and hand-me-down clothes possessed a will of iron capable of overcoming apparently insurmountable disadvantages - a belief he also took onto the football field.

The Professional

Denis' arrival in Huddersfield in 1956 brought raised eyebrows from his manager Andy Beattie but life changed for the scrawny Aberdonian, first with an operation to correct his squint and later when Shankly force-fed him steak and milk to build up his strength.

Here he signs professional forms on 25th February 1957 watched by manager and mentor Bill Shankly.

The Player

Denis made his league debut for Huddersfield Town on Christmas Eve 1956 against Notts County and scored his first goal two days later in the return fixture. With the Yorkshire club strapped for cash their reliance on youth meant early opportunities for Law and his fellow lodgers at Pond House.

Favourite Son
A Shankly favourite from
the moment he became
embroiled in a scrap at
his Pond House digs, the
future Liverpool manager
had this opinion of young
Law:
'Right from the start Denis
stood out with his
enthusiasm and will to
win - nastiness, if you like.
He would have died to
have won. He had a tem-
per, and was a terror - a
bloody terror, with ability.'

Above: Denis (fifth from
right) takes heed of Shanks'
advice and (right) in
post-match mode circa
1958.

Rise to Fame
*Denis' reputation grew
with a memorable
performance in a
televised cup replay
against West Ham in
January 1958.
From that moment he
drew envious glances
from the nation's
larger clubs.*

*Denis' rise to football fame was 'capped' with his
selection for Scotland in October 1958. Matt Busby,
back in charge of the national team following
Munich, had no hesitation in picking 18 year-
old Law.* **(Right)** *he challenges Welsh legend John
Charles during a debut in which he also scored.*

*With the football world aware
that Huddersfield were prepared
to sell Denis, the battle for his
signature was hard-fought. In
the event Denis joined
Manchester City for a new
British record £55,000.
(Above) Ken Barnes welcomes
Denis to Maine Road; (top right)
Denis signs on watched by City
manager Les McDowall and
directors. His debut the following
Saturday was a taste of things to
come as* **(right)** *Law scores
during a 3-4 defeat to Leeds.*

Citizen Law

Denis quickly settled down in Manchester. Staying in digs in Withington, he soon warmed to the people of his adopted city. Yet he faced problems on the pitch, not least City's poor form and constant fight to stay in the First Division.

Denis proved an important asset to City as he joined their annual battle to avoid relegation. (Above) Denis in typical poacher's form against Chelsea.

Denis' most famous match in his first spell as a City player will not be found in the record books. In a fourth round FA Cup-tie against Luton Town in 1961, Denis scored 6 (six) times before the match was abandoned after 69 minutes. Almost inevitably City lost the re-arranged fixture in what proved to be Denis' last cup-tie for the Blues for 23 years. (Above) Law scores his first and second goals in a downpour at Kenilworth Road.

Appetite for Success

With City showing no sign of improvement Denis outraged many Blues by accepting a lucrative offer from Torino. Here he tucks into the national dish alongside Gigi Peronace who brokered the deal on behalf of the Italians and went on to become a close friend during Denis' stay in Turin.

Too Many Cooks

Denis joined Joe Baker at Torino and the pair became inseparable. Denis later admitted that, though certain aspects of his Italian experience had been terrible, the lifestyle suited him down to the ground. Yet young, free, single footballers came under much more attention than their married counterparts and the pair soon became daily tabloid fodder.

Two Man Attack
Above: *Denis* **(front row, far left)** *lines up alongside*
Joe Baker **(back row, third from right)** *for Torino in April 1962.*
The Italian style of play did not suit the British pair,
with Italian sides adopting an ultra-defensive policy.

Despite the handicap of
playing against cynical
Italian defences Denis
still managed 10 goals
in his season in Serie A,
just four goals behind
the league's top scorer.
Meanwhile he adopted
an acrobatic style of play
that made him a player
every defence feared

Turin Brakes

Denis and Joe Baker's car crash (above) proved a catalyst for their return to England in the summer of 1962. Joe crashed his brand new Alfa Romeo as he returned from a dinner at a supporter's restaurant. **Inset:** Denis attempts to raise spirits following Joe's release from hospital.

Right: Matt Busby had been chasing Denis Law since he was a teenager while Denis openly admitted Busby's influence. The two men seemed destined to be paired but it wasn't until July 12th 1962 that the pair were finally united after a tortuous transfer negotiation that was nearly scuppered by the Italians.

Mirror Sport

British transfer record goes

UNITED LAND LAW—AT £115,000

By BILL HOLDEN

MANCHESTER United yesterday signed Denis Law, Scottish International forward, from Torino for a fee of £115,000.

But Torino, who signed Law from Manchester City for a similar fee in June last year, receive only £75,000.

For they still owed City £40,000, and United had to hand City a cheque for that amount before Torino could clear the transfer with the Italian and English Football Associations.

When Torino signed Law, they paid a deposit on the fee and agreed to pay the remainder in instalments over a short period.

Afterwards, they claimed they could not meet the payments within the time limit.

The sum United are now giving for Law, 22—the son of an Aberdeen trawlerman —is a record payment by a British club.

It makes the player worth about £48 an ounce.

Previous highest fee was the £99,999 Spurs handed over to Milan to buy Jimmy Greaves.

Law, delighted at joining United, said: "It has always been my ambition to play for this club."

He has also won a £5 side-bet with Torino clubmate Joe Baker that he would be first to re-sign for a British club.

Baker, whom Arsenal hope to sign, will visit Highbury on Monday for a medical check-up and further discussions.

United at last!
(above) Denis signs
on watched by Busby,
Jimmy Murphy and
Gigi Peronace following
protracted negotiations
with Torino officials.
(right) Busby and Law
greet each other outside
the North British hotel in
Edinburgh following his
return to Britain. Few
doubted that the strong
personal ties between the
pair were crucial in Denis
deciding to join United.

triumph. The Italians loved it, they really lapped it up, the way he stood like a Roman Gladiator accepting the cheers of the crowd, the newspapers were full of stories and photographs about this blond-haired Scots kid. They have no time for the cold British attitude of running back to the centre line with players giving nothing more than a few handshakes or pats on the head. Law would have succeeded in Italy. Not only was he deadly near goal, but he was a general and a character as well. Nothing upsets him, so if things are going wrong he gives the impression that he is having a great game.

"He could command the middle of the field which is a difficult job, especially in Italy. He could tackle hard and when he had possession he had the skill to draw a packed defence out of position. If the defence retreated Law could slow the game down, hold the ball and then either create a gap for himself or, if his colleagues moved quickly to make space, make the final, killing pass with deadly accuracy. Yes, they loved Denis in Italy."

Another little story that reveals how much the Italians thought of Law is told by Brian Glanville, the well-known sports journalist. In 1963 Brian worked in Rome for an Italian sports magazine and over the proceeding years got to know the Italian scene well. He devised and wrote a BBC television film entitled *European Centre Forward*. The hero of the film was the England centre-forward Gerry Hitchens, who was playing in Italian football at the time. Gerry was transferred to Torino and the television crew located themselves there to film Hitchens. Obviously comparisons were made of Gerry Hitchens and some of his predecessors from Britain, mainly Denis Law. Brian said that Denis and Joe Baker detested it in Turin.

"Once in the dressing-room, at half time in a match, Law threw his jersey into a corner in disgust, while Baker knocked down an over-persistent photographer by a Venetian canal. Eventually they ran their car into a road island in Turin in the small hours of the morning. None of this prevented the blond, wiry, infinitely versatile Law from making a colossal impact in Turin. Indeed, when we were making the film and I spoke to an

elderly Torino fan outside the Stadio Filadelfia, he told me that
Law was the finest-inside forward the club had ever had. 'Even
better than Valentino Mazzola?' (The former captain of Torino
and Italy) I asked. 'Yes,' was his reply."

*

The newspapers were full of Law's return to English football. It
was incredible! There seemed to be non-stop coverage and his
image appeared on television screens throughout the British
Isles with constant updates about his whereabouts and
movements. In Manchester, especially in the red half, they
couldn't get enough of Denis Law. Articles appeared in the
local newspapers and various magazines. He was discussed and
his ability dissected in the hundreds of pubs and clubs
throughout the city and surrounding areas. He was the main
topic of conversation. It was Lawmania.

Denis appeared to have the strongest influence of any
footballer in this period and for the next few years that never
really diminished. If anything, it grew. Even today, young fans
who weren't even alive in this period are influenced by his
legend. That was the power of Denis Law. With Law in your
team anything seemed possible - he was a genius whose time
had come.

Upon his return to Manchester Denis moved back to the
digs he used when he was a City player - 23 Goulden Road,
Withington. He was very fond of Mrs Atkins, his warm-hearted
landlady. Above everything else he adored the beautiful meals
she prepared for him. The old cheerfulness returned, his smile
was broader and the swagger in his walk became more
pronounced. In short, the old Denis Law was back on the scene
and everything looked wonderful.

"He's a pioneer, a trailblazer and an unforgettable figure,"
remarked Jimmy Murphy, adding, "what you notice is his
poise." There was a special buzz around Manchester. The Reds
supporters were wishing their lives away waiting for the new
season to begin. The newspapers were full of stories expressing
opinions on the kind of influence Denis would have on

Manchester United. Yet, in an echo of the signing of Eric Cantona, there were many sceptics who prophesied that Law would be a destructive influence at Old Trafford and it wouldn't be too long before there was conflict between him and other United players because of his arrogant and cocky nature. They also pointed out that because of his frail physique he would miss games through injury. Yet nothing could have been further from the truth.

Nevertheless reporters and many away fans saw him as a very aggressive young player who, if he did not get his own way, would be off to pastures new. Yet, as Jimmy Murphy remarked: "He was just the opposite to the way the critics perceived him. A lovely, quiet lad, who liked a bit of fun but was serious about his football and away from football remained a private person."

There was one player in particular who was delighted to see Denis back in English football and that was his close friend Dave Mackay. "I've read stories that Denis is frail and injury prone, what a load of nonsense," said the Scottish powerhouse, "Denis is well built and as hard as teak. Denis can tackle accurately and with great power, while he can also take a tackle. He never allows the opposing wing-half to take any liberties. By that I mean that Law is always around to try and put the brake on a wing-half who attempts to break through." Pointing out that this was something the great inside-forward, Raich Carter, was famed for doing during his illustrious playing career, Mackay added: "As the left-half behind Denis in the Scottish team I can fully appreciate just what such service means, not only to me but to the team as a whole."

It has been said that Law's fortunes changed for the better after he had surgery in 1956 to correct the squint in his eye and straighten it, and that his confidence (which he had never been short on) and ego grew from that moment. It became clear that if Denis was Clark Kent before his operation he was Superman on the field afterwards, his swagger became more pronounced and his mode of dress more conspicuous. That might well be true, yet what is certain is that on his return to English football after a season in Italy Denis was a changed person, both as a player and a person.

If it was possible he was even more assured and cocksure and many reporters quickly pointed this out. Many believed he was 'big-headed' and arrogant. Yet having successfully adjusted to the uncompromising attentions of Italian markers, he now found the clumsy, one-dimensional British defenders quite easy to play against. Denis could drop deep into his own half to win the ball and his awareness of where to deliver it was uncanny. His dribbling ability saw him leave opponents in his wake. He could play with his back to goal, or move forward, keeping the ball at his feet as he flew past defenders while his acceleration away from a marker never ceased to amaze people. In effect his season in Italy had improved his all-round game immeasurably - one thing was abundantly clear, he would be a vital part of Manchester United's return to glory.

In Denis' first training session with his new club-mates, the media were also allowed to watch. Jimmy Murphy and Matt Busby were walking round the pitch as trainer Jack Crompton put the United players through their paces. After about an hour, when the physical training had been completed, the players were split up into groups for a five-a-side game. Matt and Jimmy watched quietly and a reporter, named Don Hardisty, standing close by the two United officials heard Murphy turn to Busby and say: "Denis could be even better than Pele!" The reporter moved a little closer as Busby, puffing on his pipe, nodded his head in agreement with Murphy's sentiments. Mr Hardisty knew that Murphy was well qualified to judge and make such a statement because, as the Welsh international manager he had had first-hand knowledge and experience of the Brazilian supremo. Mr Hardisty turned to Busby's assistant and asked him to explain exactly what he meant. Jimmy, warming to the task, told him that, while he agreed that Pele was indeed a master footballer in one half of the field, Law was the complete inside-forward because he spread his talents in both halves. Busby added: "I think Denis can help everybody in the side to cut out the aimless stuff which crept into our play last season."

United's management team were quite honestly overjoyed with their new acquisition. Along with Bobby Charlton they knew they had two truly brilliant world-class forwards. They loved their teams to attack and entertain spectators. With each passing day Matt and Jimmy knew in their hearts that Denis Law was the kind of player who was made for Manchester United. As Jimmy said: "Even at £115,000 we bought a blue chip. Matt and I had watched his progress from that Youth Cup game we played against Huddersfield in 1956. He reminded us both of a young Peter Doherty. Once he settles into our system he will become a far better player. He is what we call an intelligent player."

To Denis, Matt Busby and Jimmy Murphy were steeped in football knowledge. They allowed their players to go onto the pitch, express themselves and entertain the public. The United followers believed they were two geniuses. Matt would say something to his players and without question they believed he was right. Denis was really charmed by him. He was a real gentleman. So nice, and quiet, and the way he treated players always seemed fair. Denis said Matt hardly ever had to raise his voice to anyone. He would talk to his players, one-on-one, in a civilised way. He would also help you personally and not just concentrate on what you did on the pitch.

Jimmy on the other hand was very passionate. The real secret ingredient was their belief that you, one of their players, were the best. Jimmy in particular was funny, smart and completely convincing. As John Aston senior put it: "He made players believe that anything was possible. If you didn't know Jimmy you couldn't appreciate the quality of his magic. He was the type of person who could make older women feel young again. He could convince players to play way above themselves. Denis Law thought a great deal of Jimmy."

Noel Cantwell had joined United in November 1960 from West Ham United where he had spent eight years, winning a Second Division championship medal with them in the 1957/58 season and making 248 League appearances. Capped by Eire on several occasions he was known as the 'Professor' by his colleagues at Old Trafford because he was a deep thinker about the game and was forever discussing tactics and different ideas. Indeed, it was believed that when Sir Matt Busby retired, Cantwell would be his successor. Noel stood slightly over 6 feet tall and was a cool, cultured left full-back in the Johnny Carey and Roger Byrne mould. He became the Manchester United captain for a while. He was immensely impressed when United signed Denis and looked forward to training and playing in the team alongside him. They soon became close friends, going out for meals and enjoying a quiet drink with their families.

Cantwell's admiration for his team mate was boundless: "The trouble with Denis, if you like, is that his natural reflexes are supernaturally quick. He seems to think faster, move quicker and react more smartly than most players. And, equally, he could react just as swiftly the wrong way. In Matt Dillon's day I suppose he would have been the fastest gun in the West."

Noel certainly had first hand knowledge concerning Denis' reflexes. In a five-a-side practice game, the two men clashed! There they were - Britain's highest-priced footballer at just under 5ft 10 and the 6ft plus superbly-built full-back, just a fraction away from a full-scale punch up. It happened as the five-a-side got going, the game became really competitive and within seconds there was a clash between the two and with a characteristic speed of movement Denis squared up to him. Fortunately, both players quickly realised the implications and came to their senses and the whole thing ended as rapidly as it began. "Naturally," said Cantwell, "we were above silly feuds at Old Trafford and of course Denis and I were even firmer pals than ever."

Denis would have a Saturday night meal and drink with Noel Cantwell, Maurice Setters and later Paddy Crerand. They, along with their wives, were often in the Midland Hotel, one of the city's more old-fashioned institutions. It was considered too 'upmarket' and expensive for the ordinary working class fan to frequent and this exclusivity made it a favoured watering hole for the sporting and show business celebrities appearing in

Manchester. It was here that the players could relax, have a meal and a drink in complete privacy, without being constantly pestered for autographs and photographs.

Setters, with his crew-cut short hairstyle and his bandy legs, was a ferocious competitor and rather outspoken. He, along with loyal clubman Bill Foulkes, gave United that little bit of 'steel' in defence. Meanwhile Cantwell, a wonderful, friendly, bubbling personality like Denis, enjoyed a laugh and a joke. They also played golf together. Maurice Setters would probably never feature in anyone's team of all-time greats but when he first joined the Reds he was just the type of player the club badly needed. A friend of Bobby Charlton's from their army days, he strutted about the field with the air of a sergeant major on the parade ground. He was bombastic and loud and stood just 5 feet 8 inches tall. Yet despite his lack of inches he was excellent in the air and tackled with the force of an uncontrolled steamroller. He read the game superbly and above all he was a dominant character in the heart of defence.

This then was the Manchester United that Law walked into for pre-season training in 1962. A mix of colourful and loyal characters struggling to find the right blend to counter the dominant teams of the era - most notably Tottenham Hotspur.

*

Denis Law's debut in United's colours was in a game for the 'Glasgow Charity Cup' played at his beloved Hampden Park before an expectant crowd of 82,564. Manchester United faced a Glasgow Select team, which was virtually the Scottish international team. The United line-up for his debut read: Gaskell; Brennan, Dunne; Stiles, Foulkes, Setters; Giles, Quixall, Herd, Law and Moir. The Scottish team: Niven (Partick); Mackay (Celtic), Caldow (Rangers); Crerand (Celtic), McNeill (Celtic), Baxter (Rangers); Henderson (Rangers), McMillan (Rangers), Hughes (Rangers), Divers (Rangers) and Wilson (Rangers)

The crowd waited with baited breath for Denis to justify his £115,000 price tag and they were more than a little disappointed as Denis failed to stamp his authroity on the game. Then, in the 75th minute, with United 2-1 down and looking a beaten team, Law proved the catalyst during a 14-minute spell that turned the game in United's favour.

First he picked up a loose ball, jerked into one of those famous electrifying zig-zag runs and released the ball with perfect timing for left-half Maurice Setters to crack it into the Scottish net. Five minutes later Denis set off again, weaved his way through a ruck of defenders and sent a pile-driven shot that rebounded off the bar and was pushed out for a corner from which David Herd rose magnificently to score. Ian Moir, playing on the left wing in Bobby Charlton's absence, scored twice while David Gaskell saved an Eric Caldow penalty. So within that short spell, Denis' debut for his new club was followed by headlines in the newspapers such as, '*Law's Magic Touch Winner*', '*Stinker - Then Law Lights Up Glasgow*', '*Brilliant Law Hushes Hampden*', and '*A £115,000 Flop Then Law Sets Game Alight*'.

United's first match of the 1962/63 season and Denis' League debut was at Old Trafford against West Bromwich Albion on 18th August 1962. Bobby Charlton was out of action, having undergone a hernia operation following his involvement in England's unsuccessful World Cup campaign in Chile.

On the day of his debut Manchester was bathed in beautiful sunshine as Denis made his way from his digs to Davyhulme Golf Club. This is where the first team assembled before all their home games. They had lunch there and the players could have a game of cards or snooker. Denis was feeling a little nervous as he got out of his car and made his way into the club, hurriedly signing autograph books from the horde of schoolkids awaiting his arrival. After lunch the team was taken to Old Trafford to get ready for the match. In the dressing room Denis was still a little edgy, it seemed as if his confidence had deserted him as he nervously laughed and joked with his new colleagues. He felt at home when he heard Ian Moir's Aberdeen tones as they were changing into their playing strip.

Moir was 18, a truly gifted and brilliant winger at times but baffling and inconsistent at others. His dribbling ability reminded old-timers of the great Stanley Matthews and on form he had everything a great footballer requires. For this game he was deputising for Bobby Charlton on the left wing. Maurice Setters and Denis engaged in some light-hearted banter as Matt Busby walked into the dressing room. Busby nodded at Denis and gave him a reassuring smile. Matt had a quiet word with one or two of his players before wishing them all good luck and telling them to enjoy the game.

Outside the ground there were hordes of photographers waiting for Denis' arrival before his appearance in the famous red shirt. As the team ran out of the tunnel onto the pitch a wall of sound erupted, the photographers clicking away as the chanting and singing reached a crescendo. As soon as he kicked the ball the confidence returned to Denis' body, the swaggering genius was now in full flow, he lapped it up, and the United supporters were blissfully happy and jubilant at the sight of their new signing.

The last time the fans had felt this confident about their team's prospects was before Munich. They had great expectations for the coming season and their optimism seemed justified when, after a mere five minutes, big David Herd put the Reds in the lead with a powerful shot. In those opening minutes, Denis had been moving up and down the field looking for the ball, feeling his way into the game and Herd's goal seemed to lift a weight from his shoulders because despite looking extremely confident, Denis was more than a little apprehensive following the hysteria after his signing.

Yet the huge Old Trafford crowd was willing him to succeed and you sensed they were desperate that he score on his debut. A couple of minutes after David Herd's goal it happened, and in a manner that those present will remember some forty years later.

The ball came to Giles on the right wing, he looked up and centred a high ball towards the West Brom penalty area. If anything, it seemed a little too high for one of the United players to reach but all of a sudden Denis leaped skywards and hung in the air. Then he came out of the clouds and whoosh, his forehead connected perfectly with the centre of the ball and it went whistling into the back of the net. The Lawman had made his entrance and pandemonium ensued. You would have thought a winning cup final goal had been scored from the volume created by the faithful. As he fell to the ground, a big grin across his face, Law was surrounded by his joyous team-mates in congratulation. Then the chants began, and Manchester United had a new folk hero, 'The King' had found his subjects.

Few players had experienced this kind of adulation after just one goal for the Reds. There was no way to describe accurately the feeling of being at the centre of that kind of frenzy. Or, as many older supporters would say, words can't express. Over the coming years the louder the fans screamed and sang his name, the more Denis wanted to please them. It was thrilling.

The relationship between crowd and performer was unique in football at the time - he loved it as much as they did. Indeed Law savoured it. It made him feel like a king, appeared to invest him with superhuman powers. And as intense as it was, he wanted more. Louder. Bigger. More. Perhaps Denis didn't understand quite how powerful his influence was, which was perhaps why United fans gave him their unquestioned loyalty throughout a career that would later involve a hand in the team's relegation. For while other players of his era may have had more influence, been capable of more soccer wizardry on their day, none could lay claim to the title 'The King' - for the Stretford End the others were courtiers at the knee of their master.

As if to underline the impact of Law's arrival, fans would wait outside the players' entrance for hours, knowing that they wouldn't get an autograph, but just hoping to get a glimpse of him as he rushed to his car and drove home. And, despite the fact that in this particular game West Bromwich fought back to earn a deserved 2-2 draw the supporters didn't honestly care, as the talk in the pubs and clubs that night focussed on Law's brilliant headed goal - the legend had begun.

Nonetheless, as the season progressed, fans soon pondered the prospect of relegation. The simple fact was that although the Reds drew huge crowds home and away through their exciting, attacking outlook they were leaking goals. With players such as Maurice Setters, Noel Cantwell and Bill Foulkes in defence the Reds looked quite solid on paper but Matt Busby put their defensive frailty down to a lack of confidence and a settling down period among their new acquisitions.

Bobby Charlton was missed in the opening games, there was no doubt about that. During the summer, Bobby had played in the World Cup for England and had been highly impressive. Barcelona, the Spanish giants, made an offer of £300,000 for his services, although Matt Busby turned down their approach. Then again there were doubts whether Bobby would have left anyway. He was Manchester United through and through and came from a famous football family - the Milburns. His mother was the sister of Jack, George and Jimmy Milburn, of Leicester City fame. Part of the same family was Jackie Milburn, the Newcastle United star centre-forward of the 1950s, while Bobby's brother Jackie was playing centre-half for Leeds United.

Bobby was a lovely, quiet, well-respected player who hated the limelight. This unspoiled and shy young man received more fan mail than any other player in Britain, (this was long before George Best came on the scene.) His cannonball shooting and sporting demeanour made Bobby a crowd puller in the Matthews-Finney-Lawton class. As one of the least injured of the Munich air tragedy in 1958, he had the task of welding the new Manchester United together. He had filled almost every attacking role and, in fact, had played for England at centre-forward, inside-forward and on the left wing. His hobby at this time was music and in January 1959, almost a year after he had survived the dreadful Munich air crash in which many of his friends had perished, he won a £1,000 prize in a television contest for his knowledge on pop music and records. The programme was ITV's hit quiz show *Double Your Money*, the show hosted by the well-know show business personality, Hughie Green.

Denis was delighted when he heard the familiar sounds of an Aberdeen dialect at the Cliff training ground. The voice belonged to United's latest signing, 16-year-old John Fitzpatrick from Aberdeen. 'Fitz', like Denis, was another fiery tempered all-action player but was a year behind schedule because he had broken his leg the previous season. He had been working as an apprentice welder while his leg healed. Obviously he had worried throughout the year as he anxiously waited to see if there would be any further setbacks. The injury could have spoilt his dream of joining Manchester United before it ever got started. His journey to England followed closely on the heels of Denis Law. They both came from Aberdeen, both played for the town team and both were inside forwards, (although John was converted into an influential wing-half) and they both left home soon after leaving school to seek football fame. By another remarkable coincidence, Fitzpatrick was spotted by the same scout who first discovered Denis and set him on the stairway to stardom. Denis was delighted to hear another familiar voice and along with Ian Moir they got along fine. In February 1965, John made the first of 141 first team appearances.

After the opening game against West Brom it was a further seven games before Denis got on the score sheet again. Playing against his old club Manchester City at Old Trafford, in September, Denis grabbed two goals in a 3-2 derby defeat. The following week, at home to Burnley, the Reds were thrashed 5-2 - Denis and Nobby Stiles getting United's goals. In the opening ten games played that season United managed only three victories, which wasn't good at all. However, despite United's faltering league position Denis was certainly doing the business for them.

Before joining the Reds, he had played an orthodox inside-forward role; roaming about the field he would be up front trying to score one moment, then in the half-back line playing as a wing-half the next. He would also drop deeper into his own defence to clear the ball. One day Matt Busby pulled him to one side and explained that he didn't want him tearing about all over the field but told him to concentrate on staying up field in the opposition's penalty area and going for the other team's goal. And so from then on the hitherto ubiquitous Denis was to stick in the front line trenches. In other words, to use a modern parlance, he was now a striker!

After Blackburn Rovers thrashed the Reds at Old Trafford (0-3) United visited Tottenham Hotspur at White Hart Lane. The London-based critics were not slow to claim that Denis and the rest of the United team would find it more like 'White Hot Lane'. There was a great deal of silly talk that Denis wasn't doing the business for his new club. This of course was utter rubbish. However, their proclamation that United would get hammered was correct, the Reds lost by 6 goals to 2!

One reporter wrote: "From fiery Italian flourish to Manchester United, a team trapped by its own talent at the bottom of the First Division. That's the sad tale of Denis Law." The writer compared Denis with Jimmy Greaves in the Spurs match. "Contrast the mood and success of Greaves to Denis Law. I watched them clash as Spurs thrashed Manchester United 6-2. It was a startling comparison." The writer went on to say that Denis looked a fidgety, talented fellow, who was lacking the kind of support Greaves enjoyed at Tottenham.

"Denis seems infected with a total lack of confidence that has shackled half a million pounds worth of Red Devils. Arrows mark their path to the Second Division." He then posed the question: "Is Law getting the best out of United? Or, are United getting the best out of Law?" Matt Busby, the reporter said, was not one to dwell on self-pity or bravado, even in the club's present crisis state. "He paid £115,000 for Law, one of the world's best inside-forwards." He then wrote that Matt Busby knew that when Denis pulled the blue jersey of Scotland over his wiry Aberdeen shoulders he was flashy and flamboyant, and as dangerous as any one single forward in the world. "Law himself maintains his international majesty, yet all his former clubs - Huddersfield Town, Manchester City, Torino and,

Manchester United have all had to struggle when he was playing with them." While true at the time, this would prove to be a wrong analysis of Denis Law, as we shall see.

Another journalist wrote that United were not exploiting Denis' remarkable talents. He said that some of Denis' colleagues looked as if they resented him swooping down on them from all over the field. If Matt Busby could afford to have patience at the foot of the league table he should apply it in the case of Denis. He suggested that the team should be built around Law and use his spring-heeled energies to the full. He gave some blunt impressions of Denis from, he claimed, a Scottish player who once played alongside and shared digs with him. "On the field he's not an easy fellow to get on with. At first his style takes a lot of getting used to, as his habit of wanting to do your job as well as his own. I reckon a club has to have Denis at least six months before either he or the team benefits. By that time the boys have to get over their 'Give-it-to-Denis complex'." This, said the journalist, was realistic advice from a man who knew Denis.

Yet Denis was typically bullish about his team's disappointing start to the season: "Frankly, what the man in the crowd and the Press have to say about me never causes me a moment's worry. The only place I can prove myself is on the field and there, quite naturally, I have my good and bad days. It's not possible to play like a £250,000 footballer every week. If I worried about it I would only play worse. Once I've done my best, I can accept praise or adverse criticism with indifference. I see no call to complain or explain."

What were his views on his Old Trafford colleagues? Well, his opinion was that although they had the basis of a decent team, they needed a top quality winger and, like most supporters, he felt there was a weakness in midfield. This however, was rectified the following season, with Paddy Crerand playing an attacking role at right-half (it was an old saying but perfectly true, that when Crerand played well, United played well.) Later, Nobby Stiles won a regular place in the first team in his favoured wing-half position. He was used as a left-half, but his job was as a sweeper, alongside Bill Foulkes. Besides this role, Nobby also broke up the opposition attacks and countered beautifully by feeding the forwards. Playing this way Nobby would go on to be selected for England and help them win the highest honour, a World Cup, but I am running ahead of the story. Back to 1962.

In October of that year, at home to West Ham in pouring rain, Denis followed Busby's instructions to the letter. Instead of being the head cook and bottle washer he remained up field in West Ham's area. Albert Quixall was left to do the scheming and he did it masterfully, scoring twice. Then 12 minutes from time Denis beat two defenders and scored himself. It was no coincidence that United won their first game for weeks.

On 7th November, Denis gave one of the finest exhibitions of soccer brilliance ever seen at Hampden Park in an international against Northern Ireland. It turned out to be, without any doubt whatsoever, one of his greatest-ever games for his country. Scotland; clever, cultured and lightning fast, played the brave Irish into the ground but they might never have had a goal to show for their superiority without the tremendous, tireless Law.

Straight from the opening blast of the referee's whistle, Denis gave a display of outstanding skill and tremendous power, worth every penny of his £115,000 price tag. It's true to say that had Law not been playing for Scotland they would have almost certainly struggled to contain a lively Irish team who opened the scoring in the 8th minute through Billy Bingham. The 60,000 exasperated Scots in attendance were groaning in dismay as the Irish team then proceeded to erect a solid defensive wall of green that, it seemed, the Scottish forwards couldn't break down. The Irish defended resolutely and went in at half time with the score 1-1. Denis had scored Scotland's goal. In the dressing room Danny Blanchflower urged his men to go out and attack and sure enough the Irish team, feeling buoyant, took Blanchflower's advice and went all out for victory.

Yet this attacking outlook proved to be their downfall,

because the Irish were annihilated, not so much by Scotland, but the Lawman. He was simply incredible! He had been switched from inside-left to inside-right in order to partner little Willie Henderson, and oppose his Old Trafford team-mate Jimmy Nicholson. Together they ran riot. In the 64th minute Denis scored a second goal. He had the main feature role and was here, there and everywhere. In the 77th minute Scotland scored twice, Denis got his hat-trick and Henderson also got on the score sheet. With only five minutes remaining Denis made it a night to remember when he shot Scotland into a 5-1 lead. Man for man, the Scots were not four goals the better team, but Scotland had Law. Bobby Irvine saved the Irish from a far greater embarrassment. Denis, although jubilant at scoring four goals, felt a little sadness when it was learned that his performance against the Irish might cost Jimmy Nicholson his international place.

Just after midnight an Irish reporter walked up to a newspaper stand in Glasgow to buy a morning paper. "What a player that Law is," said the vendor, who wore a Scottish international jersey, "I wish we had him at Ibrox." The following morning, at Renfrew Airport, even the BEA baggage staff were talking about the blond bombshell, now unquestionably the greatest inside-forward in Britain, and one of the top three in the world. In fact, Law was the centre of soccer conversation, not only in Scotland, but also by the thousands of Ulster people who saw the match live on their television screens. They were mesmerised by his whiplash goal poaching and hunger for the game.

Harry Gregg, Law's team-mate at Manchester United, said that Bertie Peacock, Northern Ireland's new team manager, need not despair too much after the 5-1 drubbing they received from the Scots. "After all," said Gregg, "Northern Ireland were up against the greatest inside-forward in Europe!" Harry said that Northern Ireland had worried Scotland when Billy Bingham scored first and Scotland were hard pressed to stay on level terms. "That was," beamed Harry, "before a human-dynamo called Denis Law turned on his own special brand of soccer witchcraft. From what I have heard, it seems Northern Ireland were defeated not by Scotland, but by the fair-haired genius who hammered four goals into their net."

Gregg went on to say that the £115,000 fee was certainly not extravagant. He was also of the opinion that during United's slide down the league table Denis was perhaps trying too hard. "Maybe Denis does take a little too much on his shoulders," added Gregg, "but to me that's no crime. Denis Law is cast in the mould of men for whom I have the greatest admiration and respect, players such as the great Peter Doherty, Danny Blanchflower and Bertie Peacock. These four men have a great deal in common - and that is that they believe you must give everything you have when you go out on the field of play."

Gregg said that he had seen Peter Doherty dripping in sweat, almost too exhausted to stand up, yet driving himself forward and inspiring his team-mates to do the same. Harry said that Denis Law was cast in the same mould - no quarter asked or given. Every ounce of energy expended in doing the job to the best of his considerable ability. "I don't believe you can shackle a player like Denis and demand that he should play to a set pattern. All right, maybe you can instruct him to play more upfield, in attack, where you can make the most of his flair for carving defences wide open but you cannot be dogmatic and say that he must never move back to help his defence. Denis believes that when you go out there you should throw yourself heart-and-soul into the business of trying to win. You should hate to lose - and you should refuse to accept defeat until the final whistle has gone. Against the Irish boys, the Scots were coming in for criticism from their own fans - many of whom had expected a slaughter of the innocents. Denis took the game by the scruff of the neck and made it go Scotland's way. Even the experience of Danny Blanchflower, who so successfully directed tactics for a large part of the match, had to concede best to the electric Scot. Without Denis Law Scotland might well have run into trouble and one consolation for the Irish boys is that they won't come up against Denis regularly. Denis Law joins my list of great players!"

There had been a discussion on television, carried through onto the radio sports programmes and into the newspapers, about players' wages since the abolition of the maximum wage a short time before. The spotlight fell on players such as Johnny Haynes of Fulham, who was believed to be the first British player to get £100 a week, Jimmy Greaves and of course Denis Law. Many of the commentators, viewers and listeners were of the opinion that because these 'star' players were earning much more than their team-mates, this resulted in unrest and unfairness.

"I don't exactly know what Denis Law earns at Old Trafford," said Noel Cantwell, United's captain, "I have no doubt that he is quite a comfortably-off young man." Noel said he expected Denis would be picking up £100 a week in wages but, he added: "We don't discuss wages between ourselves. That is a personal matter between ourselves and Matt Busby." He went on to say that the other players were big enough to accept that another player might be worth more than themselves.

"There is none of this nonsense of running to Mr Busby complaining that Law or anyone else was getting £80, when I am only on £40 or £50, whatever that figure might be." Noel said this kind of talk was voiced by lots of people when Denis first joined United. He stated that this kind of talk appeared in any profession. "Yet," he said, "at Old Trafford they take an intelligent view of the situation. Denis is a more accomplished player than most. His ability and goals help to win us matches." He pointed out that with Denis in the team gates were vastly improved. "It really wouldn't worry me a jot if Denis Law was earning £1,000 a week. We all get rewarded for that elusive success. And, believe me, Mr Law is Mister Success."

So why were Manchester United struggling with the players they had at their disposal? That was the question everyone was asking as the season unravelled. The Reds at this time had an abundance of players in all positions. For example the forwards consisted of: Albert Quixall, Bobby Charlton, Mark Pearson, David Herd, Nobby Lawton, who could play inside-forward or at wing-half, Sammy McMillan, Ian Moir, Phil Chisnall and

John Giles. At wing-half they had Maurice Setters, Nobby Stiles, Jimmy Nicholson and Willie Donaldson. The full-backs included Noel Cantwell, Shay Brennan and Tony Dunne, and the goalkeepers Harry Gregg, David Gaskell and Ronnie Briggs. This, on paper, was as good a squad of players as one could wish for. These were all talented players in their own right.

Denis was impressed by little Nobby Stiles, the Collyhurst kid. He admired Nobby's indestructible 100 per cent style, and the way he demanded the same from the players around him, no matter who they were or what kind of reputation they had. He was unmerciful with his tongue on anybody he thought was slacking in the cause of the team.

After their victory over West Ham, on November 3rd the Reds were away to the surprising First Division champions Ipswich Town. The critics were having a field day because of United's inconsistent form. There were more snide remarks that Denis wasn't doing the business for his new club which was, of course, nonsense and Matt Busby and Jimmy Murphy were extremely angry at these silly accusations. The critics said Ipswich would hammer United, forcing them further down the league table. As it turned out Denis and his colleagues went out and showed the guttersnipes how wrong they were in the best possible way.

The weather was absolutely dreadful and threatened to sabotage the match. However, the referee made his decision that the game was playable and so it went ahead, and it was a classic. Both teams went all out for victory and it was played in a Cup final atmosphere, with the Ipswich fans yelling themselves hoarse and the United supporters doing their best to out-shout them. United got off to an explosive start when they took an early lead, after two minutes to be exact, when Stiles, Quixall and Law combined, and Law finished from an acute angle. In the 9th minute Crawford equalised for Ipswich. The cry went up: "Here we go again!" The moans and groans could be heard back in Manchester. It was Crawford's 150th goal for the club. After 15 minutes David Herd pulled the ball back for Denis to score his second goal. He completed his hat-trick in the 21st minute after a brilliant run down the middle by Johnny Giles. Both sets of supporters were by now hysterical with excitement and Denis was naturally delighted with three goals but desperately wanted his team to win the game. That, he said, was more important. He was aggressive, tackling as if his life depended upon the result.

Although the Reds were leading 3-1 they were still going for more goals and it came as no surprise when David Herd put them further in the lead. Ipswich pulled another goal back after half time, when Blackwood headed a great goal. A few minutes later, the same player made the score 4-3 and the home fans were screaming for the equaliser when, in the 85th minute, the Ipswich goalkeeper parried a shot from Stiles to Denis to score his fourth. He was mobbed by his team-mates. United had to thank Denis for this victory, he was in a mood of aggressiveness all afternoon. Having a stern talking to from the referee didn't curb his spirit - he had been superb throughout the 90 minutes.

Matt Busby promptly rejected an approach by Arsenal for the transfer of 20-year-old Jimmy Nicholson, the Irish international wing-half, who was at the time playing in United's reserve team and was considered the deputy for club captain, Maurice Setters. Matt explained his reasoning: "When Arsenal manager Billy Wright made the inquiry he wondered whether there was any possibility of our releasing Jimmy, in view of his recent appearances in our Central League side. I told him straight away that there was no chance of a deal. We simply could not allow a player of Nicholson's ability to leave, and recognise just as much as anyone that he has a fine future. Jimmy has done quite well in the first team this season but he understands that with three other players competing for the wing-half position [Nobby Stiles, Nobby Lawton and Maurice Setters] appearances for some will be limited. He is quite happy at Old Trafford and we are happy to keep him."

After a 3-3 draw with Liverpool, in which Denis didn't score, he was back on the goal chart when United travelled to the

Midlands to face Wolverhampton Wanderers at their Molineux ground. And what a wonderful game it turned out to be. It was one of the greatest games ever between these two famous clubs. Wolves went two goals in front after forty minutes' play, both scored by Barry Stobart, the forward who wanted to leave the Wolves. 2-0 down at half time, you could have had 10 to 1 on the Red Devils' chances of coming back at Molineux. But what a fightback by United and what a brilliant piece of goal snatching by the golden boy Law and what a shock the 25,000 fans had after the interval.

Like a team hell-bent on victory, in the space of 30 minutes the Reds turned that two-nil deficit into a 3-2 lead. It was tremendous. Giles started the recovery when he set up Herd for the first goal and then Law took over. Setters hit a power-packed shot which Fred Davies, the Wolves goalkeeper, could only parry, Denis nipped in and tapped home the equaliser. The final, killer blow for Wolves came in the 73rd minute when the £115,000 star crowned it with a wonderful individual effort. He dispossessed Stobart and beat three men to score the greatest goal of five wonderful efforts. Denis was also on the scoresheet when United beat Nottingham Forest 5-1 at Old Trafford in early December. Forest had not beaten the Reds at Old Trafford since they had returned to the First Division seven seasons earlier and they never looked likely to improve on that record in this game. David Herd netted twice while Charlton scored a spectacular individual goal that brought the crowd to their feet. Giles got the fourth and Law stabbed home the fifth in injury time. Albert Quixall was voted man-of the-match with Giles, Charlton, Herd and Nobby Lawton signalled out as being outstanding. Three days later, Denis Law was a married man.

6. Law, Love and Marriage

In early December 1962 Denis announced that he would be getting married on the 11th of that month. His wife to be was Diana Rosemary Leith Thomson. Diana was born in Glasgow but worked in a solicitor's office in Law's hometown, Aberdeen. The couple had met in a dance hall in Aberdeen. During the season, after every game, home or away, Denis would fly back to Aberdeen to see her. Matt Busby gave Denis his permission. The United manager liked to see his senior players settled down and not gallivanting all over the place at weekends.

However there was an element of controversy to Denis' nuptials. His father, George, told a reporter named Stanley Shivas that he thought it would be a good idea if Denis waited a year before getting married, or until the close season. His mother added: "We have met Denis's fiancée, Diana, and we think she's a nice girl but we believe he should have waited for some time, after all, he has a great future ahead of him." His father said that he and Denis's mother were probably the last to know about the engagement. "I am very hurt that he didn't consult us about getting married, and I will have a thing or two to tell him when he comes home again."

Denis, speaking from his digs in Goulden Road, Withington, was shocked when the reporter told him about his mother and father's comments. "I am shocked that my parents should have said such things. It's the first I have heard about it. They were certainly not the last people to know I was planning to get married. I told them immediately I popped the question. It's true that I haven't talked this matter over with them but I don't see that it has got anything to do with anyone else. It took me a long time to make up my mind about marrying in December.

I didn't rush into it with my eyes closed but I am sure Diana is going to help me in my career. At my age (22) I expect to make all my own decisions." For the record, Denis's mother and father became proud of Denis and Diana and also delighted grandparents when Denis and Diana married and presented them with five beautiful grandchildren.

Diana, then 23, speaking from her home in Great Western Road in Aberdeen, said: "I know Denis's parents did not expect him to get engaged so soon but I don't think we are rushing into anything. I know we shall be very happy, and I don't agree that we should wait to get wed." Denis and Diana were planning to buy a house and settle down in Manchester. On Tuesday 11th December 1962, they were married in Aberdeen. They were a devoted couple and eventually had five children - Gary, Andrew, Robert, Iain, and Diana. The Laws are still living happily in Manchester.

"I'm marrying a girl - not a game of football. For all the rubbish you hear about me," he said quietly, "you would think she was going to be the other woman in my life instead of a bride. It's been suggested that I'm already married - to a goddess called football."

At 22 Denis, with broad shoulders tapering to slightly pigeoned-toed size eights, had already fetched a total of £268,000 in transfer fees. His travels from Huddersfield to Manchester City to Italy and Manchester United put £10,000 worth of signing-on fees in his bank balance. It was reported that Denis could be set to earn more than £1 a minute under the New Deal pay scheme for English footballers. He was earning more money in a month than his father had earned in the best years of his life as a deep-sea trawlerman. It was also reported that he was paid to endorse football equipment and was collecting royalties on his autobiography at an age when most people have just begun to live. It all added up to an overwhelming dowry if Law was really tempted to marry the game.

"But there are other things in life than kicking a ball about," he said, "nobody should get so involved in a game that there is no room to find a wife, raise a family and so on." Diana provided the link between the world beyond a football field. She was the reason he said: "By the time I'm about thirty something, I'll be going to a football match only to sit in the stand and watch. I've no ambition to stay in football for ever and ever."

Before he actually married Diana, Denis told Matt Busby he was bringing her to Manchester so she could look around the city. Matt was extremely worried about how she would react to the huge press coverage to which she would be subjected. Peter Slingsby, a friend of Denis Law's from his Manchester City days, now a journalist for the old *Manchester Evening Chronicle* and contributor to the Manchester United official programme, was at Old Trafford when he bumped into the United manager. After exchanging pleasantries and other matters Busby told Peter of his concern about Denis' prospective wife.

"I don't know what hotel I should book the young lady into," said Matt adding, "the press will give the girl no peace at all. I don't want her upset or bothered by reporters and photographers." Busby went onto tell Peter that he thought the newspapers would have every hotel sussed out before he said: "Peter, would you let her stay at your house? They wouldn't suspect for a minute that the girl would be staying with you." Peter readily agreed so, when Diana came to Manchester and the press pack were searching high and low for her - she was comfortable in the Slingsby household.

Freda, Peter's wife, has fond memories of Denis. She said that the phone rang constantly with Peter's press colleagues asking if he [Peter] had any idea where Denis's future wife was staying. Freda was gushing in her praise for Denis. Their young son Paul was ill in Booth Hall Children's hospital. "Denis was brilliant," said Freda. "He used to visit Paul regularly and you should have seen the expression on all the faces of the nursing staff, it was a picture. All the children were excited and overjoyed at seeing Denis. He also took some of his club-mates to visit Paul and the other children. He really was lovely, the kindness and consideration he showed. He was a pillar of strength to us. A beautiful, warm-hearted human being."

Denis said over the next eight years he aimed to build up some kind of business so that he could step out of the game while he was still in his prime. "Maybe it's wrong to say this, but while I love playing football I'm not fanatical about it. I've got other interests too," he said whimsically, adding that he spent money mainly on his clothes. And he said he had just bought a new bright red MG saloon, before quickly adding: "I don't do a lot of chasing about and living it up." He said that after the game on Saturday he would go with his club-mates for a few drinks, but most other evenings he stayed home and watched the television. "I switch it on at six, switch it off at eleven and go to bed," he said.

One sports columnist suggested that Denis preferred to come back to Manchester instead of signing for a big London club because the huge transfer fee made him the King of Manchester, whereas in London he would have just been another big name. "What a load of rubbish," was Law's comment on that idea, "I just wanted to get back to England. United paid the fee and I signed for them. As simple as that."

Nobody could say he lived like royalty in Manchester - he lived in the same house in a quiet street in Withington with the same landlady as when he first came to Manchester from Huddersfield. "Italy was different," said Denis. "Now that was the nearest to living like a king I'll ever get. They rigged us out, Joe Baker and me, with a flat the size of a football pitch, a car, a servant and all that jazz, and although we didn't do half the things the Italian press said we did, we did have a good time."

He said he might have stayed in Italy, but the rules and regulations they imposed on him proved too much. "It all started after our famous car crash (both Denis and Joe Baker were injured and later fined for this after-curfew spree.) That's when the going got tough out there." Denis, laughing, said that it wasn't much of a crash, Baker was driving, doing about 30 but he was in reverse at the time. "No driver, that Baker," he said.

Wasn't Manchester an anti-climax after sunny Italy, where it was reputed the hardest work he did was to carry his wages away from the stadium? "Not a bit of it," shot back Denis, "I'm happier here in Manchester playing for United. They let you use your own loaf and don't try to tie you down all the time. The thing I'm grateful to Italy for is that my one season there improved me as a player a whole lot."

There was no doubting the fact that Denis returned as Britain's most expensive player. Yes his season in Italy had added a new edge, a new dimension to his game, creating the unparalleled fusion of thought and movement that made Denis so prodigal a player when he was fit and well. He was also now displaying a unique combination of two of football's most valuable gifts. He had stamina and could work like a demented Trojan for every second of the game and he had skill - so great that it become a magical quality to dominate twenty-one other players, to shape the course of a game.

After the great Alfredo Di Stefano, he was possibly the finest striker in European football, able to make an immense contribution to attack and defence should the need arise. As a spearhead he possessed formidable powers - exquisite ball control, rapid acceleration, marvellous accuracy, the ability to move faster and to jump higher than an opponent at any given moment. That goddess of football could not have been more lavish in her efforts to win this Golden Boy for herself. Yet he refused to be dazzled. When Denis Law, footballer extraordinary, talked about his future it meant only one thing - the life he was planning with Diana Thomson.

What an eventful week this was for Denis. After United's superb 5-1 victory over Nottingham Forest it looked as if the Reds had turned their season around. Denis had married Diana, but was back on duty the following Saturday when United were away at West Bromwich Albion, the team against whom Denis had made his league debut. United were simply woeful against West Brom, with the immaculate Don Howe at full-back directing events. The pitch was very heavy and West Brom did all the foraging. However it was the Reds who almost took the lead in those early minutes. Denis was all over the field, giving the Albion defence some anxious moments and

Ian Moir hit the post. West Brom went on to win 3-0 and inflict United's first defeat in seven matches.

Yet during the game Denis complained that the referee, Gilbert Pullin, made a number of derogatory remarks about him and his background in football, and threatened him with disciplinary action within seconds of the game commencing. At half time Denis told Matt Busby about the referee's strange behaviour. Matt frowned but didn't want to make an issue of it and he told Denis to put it out of his mind and get on with the game. However, there was no let up in the second half and Mr Pullin continued with his uncalled for remarks to Denis. At the end of the match Denis and other players had further words with the United manager. After discussing it with the United Board it was decided to send a written complaint about the alleged misconduct to the Football Association.

The 46-year-old Pullin, a GPO technician, had been a League referee for eight years. It was learned that only 62 days before, on the 17th October, he had been cleared by a special FA commission on similar charges made by Oxford United players, who protested about alleged remarks made to them. It was said that Mr Pullin was accused of making a threat to the Oxford centre-forward Bud Haughton during a league match at Torquay. Six Oxford players, as well as referee Pullin, were called to give evidence in this historic case, the first of its kind in the 99 years of the Football Association.

After hearing all the evidence the Commission said: "We are not satisfied he made the statement alleged by the Oxford player." The FA would obviously have to appoint a new Commission to investigate the fresh allegations from Law and his Manchester United team mates. It was understood that the West Bromwich players had informed Manchester United that they were willing to make statements. At his home in Bristol Mr Pullin protested: "I am amazed that Denis Law had any complaint about Saturday's game." He said he couldn't recall the incident as described by Law. "Of course a referee speaks to players in the course of every game but I can recall no disparaging remarks of any kind. I did not threaten Law with any disciplinary action."

Matt Busby said: "The directors discussed the complaints made by the players regarding remarks made by the referee during the game against West Bromwich Albion last Saturday and decided that a strong protest be made to the Football Association and the Football League." Later Busby said that this was the first protest of this nature to be made during all the years he had been with the club. He said that he had spoken to Denis and Albert Quixall about the alleged remarks made and admitted that a distressed Law complained to him at half time and again at full time. It was regarded as something of a test case. In recent weeks protests had been made from the Professional Footballers' Association about the manner in which referees were applying stricter rules that season. PFA secretary Cliff Lloyd had met with the FA the previous week in an effort to straighten out many matters which the Association felt were unfair and left a player at the mercy of the referee without the right of appeal.

Denis said of the matter: "I would rather leave it in the hands of the club for now. I have seen the boss about what happened on Saturday and all I can say is that it was a most unusual experience and one I have never had before in my football career."

In later years, while discussing this incident, Denis said reporting Gilbert Pullin was one of the biggest mistakes of his life. Denis said he did not know Mr Pullin before the game against West Bromwich Albion but through the match the referee was making remarks to him. If, for example, Denis had a shot at the goal and missed, Mr Pullin would run near him and make a snide remark. Denis said this baiting by the referee continued throughout the second half of the match and quite genuinely put him off his game. He wasn't saying that this caused United to lose the game 3-0, not at all, because West Brom on the day, were by far the better team.

After being called to a hearing in London in front of a disciplinary committee and, after hearing all the evidence, they severely censured Mr Pullin. The referee was extremely upset at the outcome and announced his retirement from refereeing. Denis said he felt sorry for the official but didn't realise the full consequence and the effect it would have on his own career. From now on he would be a marked man.

*

Denis and Diana soon settled into their club house in the Chorlton-cum-Hardy district of south Manchester. God only knows what Diana must have thought as she left home for the first time in her life. The house had no central heating or carpets. Compare this to the luxury modern mansions present day players live in and you realise how tough and uncomfortable conditions were for the newly-married Laws.

To add to their discomfort, within three weeks of the married couple settling into their new home the country was under heavy snow and freezing cold weather, the worst in living memory. After the infamous West Bromwich game the Reds managed only one more game, against Fulham at Craven Cottage, where they won 1-0 with a Bobby Charlton goal, before the deep freeze halted all Football League games for seven weeks. During this break Matt Busby and Jimmy Murphy tried everything they could to adjust the pattern of team play. They had hour upon hour of conversation, trying to get the right balance for the team. It was terribly frustrating for them but because of the weather conditions, they couldn't try out their various permutations. They needed competitive games, even friendly matches, to try out their ideas. The players trained, of course - they managed running, although this had to be done carefully, a few weights and physical exercises. There was talk of Albert Quixall being transferred but Matt Busby said this was mere speculation.

Desperate for a game, United accepted an invitation to play a friendly against Jimmy Hill's Third Division team Coventry City in Dublin. The weather wasn't as bad in Ireland and the hosts were delighted with the opportunity to watch their favourite team. The Milltown ground was packed to its 20,000 capacity crowd, plus thousands more who 'jibbed' their way in

somehow or other. There was a carnival atmosphere with
spectators delighted to be able to watch the likes of Harry
Gregg, Bobby Charlton, Noel Cantwell and Denis. The United
players were cheered and mobbed wherever they went. The
scenes of adulation had to be seen to be believed.

Coventry, favourites for promotion to Division Two, were
unbeaten in 14 games and Jimmy Hill had put a good side
together. A heavy overnight frost had left the pitch quite tricky
in places and quite naturally the players were told to be extra
careful and not take chances. United went into the lead
through Albert Quixall, but Coventry struck back and went
into a 2-1 lead. Bobby Charlton scored the equaliser and chaos
ensued as fans mobbed him. There were amazing scenes as
hundreds of Irish supporters invaded the pitch and it took
several minutes before it was cleared. The match ended in a
2-2 draw.

The Reds had at least managed a game, which was the only
bonus, but Busby and Murphy were far from happy. The team
was still spluttering along, the wonderful flowing rhythm wasn't
there. A few days later, back at Old Trafford, Matt and Jimmy
were talking about who they might sign, who could bring the
team together, give the forwards the kind of service they
thrived on Glasgow Rangers' brilliant attacking wing-half Jim
Baxter was mentioned. Baxter, besides being a tremendous
player, was also a 'character' loved and adored in Scotland by
'Gers fans.

At one point Noel Cantwell walked in and joined in the
conversation and mentioned Paddy Crerand. Crerand, a
Glasgow Celtic player, was also a Scottish international wing-
half. What's more, he was on the transfer list. Denis was asked
his opinion on the two players concerned, and he was
instrumental in persuading Busby to buy Crerand for United.

On a day of memories, 6th February 1963, Paddy Crerand
signed for Manchester United. It was five years to the day since
the Munich disaster. Manchester United's red-and-white flag
flew at half mast over the main stand at Old Trafford as down
below in the club office Paddy, in the company of Jimmy

Murphy, joined the Red Devils. It took Busby just 20 minutes to persuade the 23-year-old Scottish international to join the club. It was a transfer that cost United £56,000. Matt told the waiting press that he had just signed the best wing-half in Britain: "Some people say he's the best in Europe!" added Busby.

Crerand, the Gorbals boy, was the idol of half of Glasgow. His departure from Celtic had split the city. Paddy was a centre-forward with St Luke's school in the Gorbals before moving on to Holyrood Senior Secondary School. It was from this school that a letter arrived, signed by over 100 boys, in an almost tearful appeal begging him not leave Celtic. Older, hardened football fans were saying that Celtic had sold half their team. When Crerand had first asked for a transfer a week before United signed him, people were stopping him in the street, writing to him, telephoning him, all with the same massage: "Please Stay." It was a situation he could never have imagined when Celtic signed him, as a lanky boy from Duntocher Hibs in 1957. Within 18 months he was in Celtic's first team and when English scouts began whispering his name he always said, simply: "I'm Celtic daft. I always have been." But football clubs, even Celtic, have to be ruthless to stay in business. The golden boy of Parkhead was left out of the first team for two matches a month earlier and Paddy asked for a transfer.

It was too soon to say that, in the five years since the Munich Air disaster, Busby and Murphy had completely rebuilt the team he lost in Germany. However it had been pointed out by the press ten months before, following Spurs' defeat of United in the FA Cup semi-final, that Busby would have to buy a world-class inside-forward and a first class wing-half before the club would be a power again. Denis had arrived a few months earlier and Crerand had now been signed. These two were not merely first-class but world-class players. This pair, along with Bobby Charlton, gave United three great players in three vital positions. After the signing of Crerand, Busby said he hoped to play him as soon as possible. The present side could stay together until after the third round FA Cup tie against Denis' old club Huddersfield Town, which had been postponed several times already because of the bad weather. United asked the FA for a special ruling on Crerand's availability for the cup. Under the '14 day' rule he would be ineligible for the original fifth round date, 16th February, but qualified for the new date a week later.

"My pal Denis Law and his wife Diana have been very good to Noreen and me on our short visit to Manchester and I'm now looking forward to meeting the rest of the lads at Old Trafford. I'll be very keen to see how Mr Busby wants me to fit into the team. Scotland usually play me in a defensive role, but Celtic let me move around the park. I'm happy either way," Crerand said.

A few days after the Reds signed Paddy Crerand, Matt Busby announced that Ronnie Briggs, the big red-headed goalkeeper, had been put on the transfer list. Eighteen months before, Ronnie had played his only full international game. With David Gaskell and Harry Gregg holding down the first and second team positions, there were few opportunities for Briggs at Old Traffiord. During his five seasons at the club, the Belfast youngster had made only nine First Division and two FA Cup appearances for the club and besides his full cap against Wales the previous season, he had also played for Ireland's under-23 team. Briggs, a former schoolboy international, was only 17 when he made his League debut against Leicester in January 1961. He had a disastrous start, conceding six goals in his first game and then another eight in the following two matches which included a Cup-tie defeat by Sheffield Wednesday - United were only asking for a small fee. Matt Busby also listed another Belfast lad, wing-half Willie Donaldson. Donaldson had not played in the first team but had been a regular in the Central League team.

With League fixtures still postponed because of the bad weather, United decided to launch Paddy Crerand into their first team in another friendly game, this time against Cork City in Ireland. Three First Division teams with a total value of over £1,000,000 flew from Manchester over to Dublin as Bolton Wanderers and Stoke City joined United in search of football.

All three were hoping to get in some practice on the frost-free pitches of Ireland.

The top attraction was United playing Bolton in front of a 20,000 plus crowd in Cork. It was a limb-loosener for the players and an escape from the boredom of training, but still not truly competitive action. Bill Ridding, the Bolton manager, said that when he told his team about the trip to Ireland and the game against United they were as pleased as if they had won the cup. "I am grateful for the co-operation of Manchester United and the Cork club," said the Bolton boss. "The team? That's easy. In case you have forgotten let me remind you that in our last game we beat Tottenham! Same team!" The two teams flew to Dublin together, stayed in the same Dublin hotel, shared the same compartment on the train from Dublin down to Cork.

Yet the game at Cork Hibernians' Flower Lodge ground was played in farcical conditions, the very thing they had flown from Ringway to avoid. It poured down with rain and Matt Busby, Jimmy Murphy and Bill Ridding were saturated by the relentless downpour that continued throughout the match. At half time, former England goalkeeper Eddie Hopkinson couldn't leave the pitch. He had become cemented into the deep mud. Had it been a normal English League match it would most definitely have been abandoned at half time, but both teams made a magnificent game of it. Happiest of all, after the most fantastic debut he could ever have imagined, was Paddy Crerand, who celebrated with a goal. Eighteen-year-old Francis Lee played on the wing for Bolton and scored the opening goal after 15 minutes. Crerand equalised with a 20-yard rocket while Denis Law and Albert Quixall overcame the conditions and played superbly. Albert scored a penalty, but the goal of the game came from the Law Man himself. He made the crowd forget they were shivering and drenched to the skin with a brilliant piece of football. He beat three Bolton defenders before waltzing round big Roy Hartle, the Bolton full-back, and slammed the ball into the net from 18 yards. Crerand brought Freddie Hill down in the box and 'Lee One

Pen', Francis Lee, scored the penalty. Johnny Giles lobbed a lovely goal to give the Reds a 4-2 victory. Dennis Walker, a young black player, made his debut for United on the left wing.

Finally, on 23rd February 1963, United resumed their League fixtures, drawing 1-1 with Blackpool at Old Trafford, David Herd getting the goal. The following match, away against Blackburn Rovers, turned out to be a wonderful attacking display of exciting football from both teams. It was thrill-a-minute stuff and the Ewood Park ground was a wall of ear-bashing noise. The match ended in a 2-2 draw after Bobby Charlton had scored with a typical strike for the first. Byron equalised and Fred Pickering put Rovers in front before Denis hit the post after a brilliant run through the Blackburn defence, then netted the equaliser.

The Manchester United faithful were wondering what on earth was wrong with their beloved club. It had been five years since the terrible Munich disaster and they had not seen any trophies arrive at Old Trafford. Bill Foulkes and Bobby Charlton were the only players remaining from that team. Shay Brennan, Johnny Giles and Nobby Stiles were home-grown players and Busby had broken the transfer record when he paid Sheffield Wednesday £45,000 to bring Albert Quixall to Old Trafford. Maurice Setters, David Herd and Noel Cantwell had also been signed for huge fees. Then, at the start of the 1962/63 season, he broke the transfer record again and signed Law, followed a few months later with another massive fee to secure Crerand. Still the team had not blended and, on recent evidence, did not look like potential winners of anything.

The case of Albert Quixall in particular seemed to perplex everyone connected to Old Trafford. Since crossing the Pennines five years previously to great fanfares, he had failed to stamp his authority at Old Trafford. 'Quickie,' the nickname by which he was known by all his team-mates, was quite popular because of his easy going, laugh-a-minute manner. He could juggle the ball for ages and amazed fans with his dexterity. He was also an accomplished cricketer and golfer yet while he was happily married and settled in Manchester with two sons and a daughter, many supporters thought it was about time that Albert started showing his true ability, and his undoubted class. It was said that in the tough games, Albert went missing. Meaning that he didn't relish the hard tackling and fight for victory. Yet when the team clicked and played well he came into his own and it was this coming season when the Old Trafford faithful would see the very best of 'Quickie'.

The FA Cup was the supporters' sole hope for glory. So on Monday night, 4th March 1963, United played their seven times postponed Third Round tie with Law's old club Huddersfield Town in front of 47,703 at Old Trafford. As the teams ran out of the tunnel, the biggest cheer was reserved for Ray Wood, United's former goalkeeper, now playing for Huddersfield. The United players looked much more relaxed for this game than they seemed in their League games. Denis was particularly bubbly and sharp. Within three minutes, the Reds scored when Denis picked up a long kick from Harry Gregg, gave an exquisite pass for Quixall to run onto and score from point-blank range. Eight minutes later it was 2-0 and the Stretford Enders were gloriously happy. Law latched onto a lovely ball following a move between Herd and Setters, and blasted his shot into the roof of the net. The tension seemed to lift from the players and fans and the relief could be seen clearly on Matt Busby's face. This kind of scoring was what was needed.

Johnny Giles got a third for United when what appeared to be a simple centre sailed into the net. But although there was a hint of fortune about the third, United were playing vintage football; the inter-changing and one-two movement a joy to watch. Huddersfield tried hard but they were being overrun in every department. In the 29th minute Denis scored a goal to savour as he accepted the ball from Herd and twisted his way through the jittery Yorkshire defence. Ray Wood spotted the danger, raced off his line like a whippet, but Law feinted a miskick before ramming the ball into the net. Two minutes from time he completed his hat-trick after Charlton's electrifying run and beautifully floated centre was met by a spring-heeled Law who headed violently past Wood. The ground was a sea of red and white scarves as they rose to acclaim the King of the Stretford End.

Ray Wood, the former United and Huddersfield man sadly passed away on 9th July 2002. However a few years ago I was priveleged enough to interview him about his career in general and his association with Denis in particular. I started by asking about the cup-tie just described.

"In that match Denis Law was phenomenal." Smiling as he recalled the cup-tie he added: "If there was a loose ball in the area he would be on to it in the blink of an eye. His speed and reflexes were fantastic. He fought for every little half chance, he never let up, no cause was lost when he was around. Denis could do the lot on the football field. Shoot, pass, head the ball, control the ball, tackle and he had that special gift of incredible speed of the mark, you name it and he could do it. He also had that unbelievable confidence to try the most amazing feats on the field of play, something which we in the British Isles thought only the South Americans could do. They talk about 'hard' players today and I have to laugh, because none came tougher or harder than Denis. What people forget was that he was only a slightly-built fellow."

Wood had joined Huddersfield in December 1958, and had been on hand to watch the teenage Law develop. "When I first went to Huddersfield it was a big step down from life with Manchester United. Not that Huddersfield were a bad club, they were a nice homely club. However, I soon adapted to life in Yorkshire, although I stayed friendly with Dennis Viollet and a few other mates at Old Trafford. All the talk in Huddersfield was about this 18-year-old wonder boy, Denis Law! You have to remember that I was at Old Trafford at the beginning of the great 'Busby Babes' era; I had watched, trained and played with extraordinary, breathtaking young players such as Dennis Viollet, Liam Whelan, Bobby Charlton and the greatest of them all...Duncan Edwards! So to my way of thinking this lad Law would really have to be something special to impress me.

"Well quite honestly, when I spotted him he stood out from

the other players. He seemed to have a mischievous grin on his face all the time. It never seemed to leave him until he put his kit on and started playing. He seemed to strut about, always in a hurry or so it seemed. 'Hyperactive' was the word used to describe him in those days, oh yes, he was very cocky and confident. With his mop of blond hair you couldn't help but notice him. Even when relaxing, playing billiards or snooker, he wanted to win. He was very sharp-tongued and quick-witted. As a player he was of average height and slim but because of this unbelievable skill it was hard to knock him off the ball. And those defenders who did would find themselves being tackled and challenged by this robust youngster.

"After playing in practice games with and against him, then playing in Huddersfield's first team with him, I was impressed. He had this wonderful knack of awareness. He had amazing ability in his play and he had this aura about him. Other players and officials were in complete awe of him, that's for sure. Another thing that impressed me about Denis was that he was absolutely fearless for such a slight player. He would mix it with seasoned defenders. Nobody took liberties with him and got away with it. He seemed to enjoy the physical side of the game. A couple of the senior Huddersfield players told me that Denis could jump from a standing position and land on top of a snooker table. I personally never saw him do this but it would not have surprised me in the least. I certainly appreciated Denis Law.

"Recently a friend was talking about the transfer fees for modern day players such as the £15 million Newcastle paid for Alan Shearer and similar deals. My pal asked me, without being nostalgic, if there were any players in my time who would be worth that kind of money. I smiled at him and mentioned players that I had personally played with like Dennis Viollet, Liam Whelan, Tommy Taylor, Bobby Charlton, Duncan Edwards (who could play anywhere) and going back to the sixties, I named Denis Law, George Best. But I could have told him about John Charles and Jimmy Greaves just to name two from other clubs. Quite truthfully, though there were really several great players in every team in the 1950s and 1960s, Denis Law would have been great in any era."

Ray Wood expressed the view that Denis was always a Manchester United type of player and was destined to eventually join the Reds. Ray said that Denis came across to people who didn't know him as an egotistical and conceited kind of person. He had a mind of his own and knew even while only a teenager that he would move to a much bigger club than Huddersfield Town. In those days clubs had players under their thumb, so to speak. The maximum wage was still in force and consequently players were tied to their clubs for as long as the clubs pleased. Ray pointed out the case of Tom Finney, now Sir Tom, at Preston. Tom was a superstar of the highest order. He was offered a small fortune to move to Italy but was told by Preston's chairman, a blunt-speaking Lancashire man: "Thee will play for Preston Tom, or thee will not play at all." And so Tom ended his playing days with the club he joined from school. Ray also mentioned the Huddersfield and England full-back, Ray Wilson. "Ray was about 30 when he finally left Huddersfield and joined Everton," commented Ray, "Denis was different, he was determined that when the time was right he was leaving and he did."

Wood said that although Denis signed for Manchester City after deciding to leave Huddersfield, then after a short stay at Maine Road moved to Italy, he believed that Denis was destined for the Red Devils. "I know that Matt Busby and Jimmy Murphy watched Denis whenever possible but the time wasn't right for him to go to United. United had some fair old forwards around that period. Jimmy Murphy was always raving about a young player named Mark 'Pancho' Pearson, who was an inside-forward. What a hard lad he was. He could play as well. A lovely passer of the ball and he tackled like a Nobby Stiles. They also had Albert Quixall who they paid a lot of money for. Then there was Dennis Viollet, who was an exceptional player and very underrated and Alex Dawson, who scored for fun. Then they had the jewel in the crown in Bobby Charlton and youngsters like Lawton, Giles and Stiles, who could also play inside-forward. However, by 1962, things at Old Trafford were different and Busby moved every obstacle to get him.

"I worked under both Shankly and Murphy and both were steeped in football, they talked about it morning, noon and night. Fearsome coaches the pair of them and Denis was their type of player. Murphy loved him, thought the way he ran back to tackle those big full-backs and half-backs was brilliant. He was very friendly with a journalist named Len Noad and Jimmy used to ask Len about Denis quite a lot. When Denis signed for United, Jimmy Murphy was the happiest man in the world."

In March 1963 United parted company with Nobby Lawton. Nobby had joined the Reds in 1956 as an amateur. He had played for Manchester and Lancashire Schoolboys as an inside forward. Nobby, hailing from the Newton Heath area of Manchester, was a sensible lad who knew he had a mountain to climb if he was to progress during the Busby Babes era. Nonetheless he was a brave-hearted, talented player who never knew when he was beaten. During his United career he fought back after a serious illness and later a broken leg. After the Munich crash he turned professional and went on to appear in 44 first team games, scoring six goals. Before Matt Busby signed Paddy Crerand, Nobby had been used as an inside-forward and a wing-half. He never let Manchester United down but knew it was time to move on. His close pal Alex Dawson had joined Preston North End in October, 1961 and Nobby followed him to Deepdale, playing so well that he became their captain and helped them reach the 1964 FA Cup final where they were unluckily beaten 3-2 by West Ham United.

Meanwhile, the United followers were feeling a little prouder after their team's wonderful execution of Huddersfield. They reasoned that better things were to follow. However a few days later the Reds were at home to mighty Tottenham Hotspur. A crowd of 53,416 packed into Old Trafford looking for revenge for the 6-2 drubbing Spurs had inflicted upon them earlier in the season. The Huddersfield victory had given them false hope. What a huge disappointment was in store! United had 26 excellent scoring chances to only seven for Spurs but it was the London team that won the day 2-0, Cliff Jones and Frank Saul getting their goals. In the League, United continue to falter losing their next three games but sandwiched in between was a 1-0 home FA Cup victory over Aston Villa, who were managed by the genial Joe Mercer, in front of a whopping crowd of 52,265. Albert Quixall got the only goal in a very ill-tempered match. Nobby Stiles was being bedded into United's first team during this cup run, although in the League Paddy Crerand returned to the side. This was great experience for the little Collyhurst lad and he took it all in his stride.

Five days later, in the fifth round of the FA Cup, played once again at Old Trafford, the Reds tackled Tommy Docherty's young Chelsea side. The Chelsea inside-left Sorrell was detailed to man-mark Denis. Future England manager Terry Venables played at right-half for the 'Pensioners' and looked a mature player. However it was golden boy Albert Quixall, having a wonderful spell for the Reds, who made the opening for Denis to score the opener after 16 minutes. Chelsea looked the better balanced team, but it was Quixall who put United further into the lead when he scored from a delightful pass from Setters. Chelsea pulled a goal back through Sorrell but United progressed to the sixth round.

They were drawn to play Third Division Coventry City at Highfield Road on 30th March. Two days before, United had lost 1-0 at home to Ipswich Town. The players knew that it was the cup or nothing for them but remained nervous at the club's perilous position in the league, yet they put their league woes to one side before facing Jimmy Hill's team. United captain Noel Cantwell was out injured and Tony Dunne replaced him at full-back while Denis donned the captain's armband. But while it was a proud moment for Denis to be made captain, the question vexing the faithful was whether Albert Quixall could continue his scoring streak in the cup. Another change saw Nobby Stiles stepping down for Paddy Crerand, who had been cup-tied in the previous rounds. What a shock, though, for United when after just five minutes Terry

Bly, the Sky Blues' tall centre-forward, sent the Highfield Road crowd into hysterics by scoring the opener. An upset looked a definite possibility as the well-organised Sky Blues threatened to overrun an out-of-sorts United. But home hopes faded once Bobby Charlton took over, almost single-handedly dragging his team back into contention. He made some telling, dynamic runs towards the home goal and was finally rewarded with the equaliser, then almost instantly put the Reds in the lead. The Midlands team seemed frightened every time he received the ball now and Quixall continued his scoring streak with another goal to send the Reds through to the semi-final 3-1.

Although delighted at United's FA Cup run and his own form, Denis was disappointed at the club's League position. Since scoring against Blackburn Rovers on the 2nd March he had now gone six games without a goal in the League. United had lost five and drawn two in that period, with a solitary win against Aston Villa, a game which Denis missed. This was relegation form. Despite the gloom, Matt Busby reassured his players that they were playing the right way and just needed a bit of luck here and there.

An example of United's topsy-turvy form came during Easter 1963. The Reds played high-flying Leicester City at Old Trafford and United touched the heights, playing beautifully during a 2-2 draw. The newspapers were glowing in their praise for the Old Trafford team. '*Busby Jewels Dazzle Leicester*', '*Busby Men Hit Cup Stride*', and '*This Is Just The Cup, United*' were just a few of the headlines from the morning papers.

After this performance the return at Filbert Street the next day took some believing. Two hat-tricks were scored by Leicester's Ken Keyworth and Denis Law and no one in the 37,002 crowd could have complained about the entertainment as the teams traded goals. Leicester took the lead through Terry Heath only for Denis to equalise after a brilliant Quixall-Crerand-Stiles move opened up the Leicester defence. In the second half the game exploded with four goals. In the 50th minute Keyworth scored the first of his five-minute hat trick - before United could catch their breath they were 4-1 down. Yet from this parlous position the Reds fought back - Denis scored a stylish goal that had the Leicester fans clapping and cheering him: Stiles delivered a beautiful ball forward and with a tele-style, acrobatic overhead kick, Law flashed the ball past a startled Gordon Banks. This was indeed a majestic piece of athletic improvisation from Law. "The goal of the game," wrote reporter Brian James, "Stiles passed forward, Law trapped it in mid-air and then flipped backwards like a seal to score with an overhead kick that left Banks gazing in reluctant wonder."

Now the home side came under pressure - every time Denis had the ball it looked dangerous and Denis made sure he saw plenty of it. In the 70th minute he scored again, again from a pass from Stiles - it was now 4-3 and Leicester were heading for a worrying, slithering finale. In the closing stages David Herd should have equalised: he was set up with several chances but squandered them all. Mind you, David often won vital games for United with his goals. Nevertheless as the final whistle sounded Busby must have despaired at the five minutes of madness that sank his team. The following day's headlines eulogised about both teams' attractive approach to the game: *'Law Genius Highlights Goal Gala'*, *'The Fabulous Trailer - To Wembley of Course'*, *'Law Strikes Peak Form In Vain'*.

For the supporters heading back to Manchester, the talk on the trains and coaches was of the ensuing relegation struggle. Was Busby right to claim that results like those against Leicester could be put down to sheer bad luck or were United heading for relegation?

*

What was Denis really like once the game had ended, or the training finished? Many people were asking this question because, as we have described, at this time Denis was a huge star who was perceived as a 'Jekyll and Hyde' character. The Manchester United supporters could see no wrong in him. They worshipped the ground he walked on and idolised him. Yet supporters of other clubs reckoned he was a dirty player, a big-headed so-and-so and self-opinionated.

His professional colleagues had a rather different view. John Aston senior, who was a coach at Old Trafford, said that Denis was a very private person. "My first impression of Denis was what a humble person he was," recalled John, "he was extremely friendly towards everybody at Old Trafford and he got on well with all the other players, and even the staff, not just the coaching staff either, I mean the office staff and the ladies who cleaned at the club and the tea ladies. He always seemed to have a sunny disposition and would chat to anyone. He would do his training and afterwards, while other players would perhaps hang around talking football or whatever, Denis would be showered and changed and off home.

"During training he would join in the banter and 'mickey-taking'. We never heard any scandal or received phone calls to the club from people claiming they had seen him out boozing or such-like - never. He hurried into Old Trafford or the Cliff, did his training and hurried off to where ever he was going. A lovely, friendly, affable fellow."

Harry Gregg maintained that people got the wrong impression of Denis Law. They saw this bubbly, hyperactive player on the field, and thought that he was the same Denis Law off the field. They couldn't have been more wrong. Harry added that at the various functions they attended Denis would come across as the man who was constantly on the move, walking from table to table, laughing and joking but, he concluded, this was all an act. Denis, said Harry, was a genuine, likeable fellow, extremely quiet and reserved and... shy.

Noel Cantwell's opinion of Denis was that the Lawman was an intelligent and shrewd person. "You wouldn't often find him appearing on television," said Noel, who went on to say that it was strange that Denis thrilled millions of people, was a genius and a showman, but had an independent spirit. The other United players used to tell him he could earn a lot of money by appearing on television, but he would never do it. Cantwell concurs with Gregg's assessment that Denis was basically a shy lad at heart.

Denis' close pal, Paddy Crerand, said that Law made few

public appearances and would rather have his privacy than the fees he could have earned. Paddy also said that Denis avoided public places where he would be quickly recognised. "He was a lone wolf," he said. Denis would patiently sign autographs for young fans, but he couldn't understand what an adult would want with his autograph. This of course was in the days before the memorabilia trade.

John Aston senior had played in United's brilliant 1948 team and was there at the start of the Busby Babes era in the 1950s. He had seen all the great players and characters at Old Trafford but when he discussed Denis Law his eyes brightened up and a gentle smile crossed his face. "A remarkable player, truly remarkable," he said, "what amazed me about him was the transformation that took place once he ran onto the pitch. He became a different person entirely. Playing football saw him become larger than life, a genuine genius. He was flamboyant, determined, aggressive, and with energy to burn. He was an exciting showman who could play up to the biggest audiences. It was here that his star illuminated the game and his qualities came to the fore.

"And those amazing goals he scored were pure magic. If you didn't actually see him score them then you'd find it hard to believe. He loved playing and scoring goals and his enthusiasm rubbed off on the rest of the team. Another of Denis' great assets was the way he found space. United played a type of football that could not be coped with by the methods teams employed during the sixties. The trio of Charlton-Best-Law was a joy to watch and I know from the other players who were in the team they thought it a joy to play in. Jimmy [Murphy] always said that when Denis was in the team we could beat anybody."

Before the first round draw for the FA Cup, Matt Busby had picked four teams who he believed would feature in the Cup final. They were Burnley, Aston Villa, Liverpool and Manchester United. Two had survived to the semi-final stage: Liverpool and United. "Two of my selections were eliminated by my two survivors," said Matt Busby, "I stick to my selection for an all-Lancashire Cup Final between Liverpool and, of course, Manchester United." Busby said he was delighted United had drawn Southampton and avoided the Merseysiders in the semi-final and said this wasn't because he didn't think his team would lack confidence. "Common sense dictates that when two teams are playing as well as Liverpool and Leicester are this season it is best to avoid them for as long as possible."

Asked why United were doing well in the Cup and so poorly in the League, Matt told them that results were misleading. "Losing matches doesn't worry me so much when the lads are playing well because I know our turn will come. We have played really well in a number of games but been unlucky. This isn't complacency and I'm not suggesting I'm happy with our League form, not at all, but I am not depressed either. Manchester United have the right players now. What we have to do is strike a consistent rhythm and form."

The date for the FA Cup semi-final was set for Saturday 27th April. Denis was bristling because on April 4th he helped Scotland defeat England 2-1 at Wembley (Jim Baxter scoring twice) - the middle match of a three game winning streak that a patriotic Law enjoyed against the Auld Enemy.

Before the semi-final at Villa Park, there were two vitally important League matches to be fitted in. The first saw Sheffield United at Old Trafford but the fans' hopes that the team would suddenly click proved unfounded as United looked and played like a disjointed, dejected team. Their form was anything but that expected from a side with one eye on Wembley and they went in at half time a goal down.

Nevertheless in the 55th minute Graham Shaw, the Sheffield United left-back, brought Quixall down for a penalty. The Reds' supporters' glee soon turned to bewilderment as they witnessed their players' reluctance to take the spot kick. The tensions in the team were surfacing in this vital game and at a vital moment. What on earth was going on? Unsurprisingly when Bobby Charlton stepped up take the kick, his right-foot shot was easily saved by Blades' keeper Hodgkinson. Nobby Stiles, playing at inside-right with Albert Quixall on the right wing in place of Johnny Giles, was the player driving United forward. However his 'never-say-die' spirit seemed to be falling on deaf ears until Law grabbed a priceless equaliser nine minutes from time. Stiles robbed Richardson, the Sheffield right-half, passed to Charlton, who fed Quixall and his tantalising centre was met by Denis' neat, well-placed header. A point closer to safety.

Next United faced Wolves at home on the Monday before the semi-final. They had not won a League match at Old Trafford since 8th December and they looked such a listless and lethargic team that Southampton were being tipped to cause a huge upset. The newspapers were full of stories that the United players were falling out with each other and relations were clearly strained.

In the event Matt Busby's stern words following the Sheffield United fiasco seemed to have done the trick as United delighted the home support by securing a home win for the first time in four and a half months. David Herd, back to his best, was a constant threat and it came as no surprise when he opened the scoring with a header after five minutes. The defence went jittery again, though, and poor Tony Dunne's back pass ended up in the net. But United regrouped and Denis scored the winner to give the Reds victory and a huge boost before for the semi-final against Southampton. Don Hardisty, a respected journalist, wrote: "Just as important as the victory for United, which slightly eases their relegation burden, was the fact that they are at last growing up. United avoided the internal bickering which has marred their teamwork for so long."

7. From Blunderland to Wonderland

In the days leading up to the semi-final speculation was rife that Harry Gregg, Noel Cantwell and Johnny Giles would be omitted from United's team. This was mere newspaper talk and Matt Busby didn't divulge his team until nearer the game but doubts persisted about United's form. The boss explained: "I thought we were just beginning to knit before the long break after Christmas, welding established players who have learned their game elsewhere into a team takes time, sometimes 12 to 18 months. You have to be patient. We are now beginning to make the openings, a sign that we are playing better."

Busby was also asked about his extravagance in the transfer market, explaining: "We had our disappointments with some of our youth players. Perhaps we expected too much too quickly. So we had to buy irrespective of cost. Our fans demanded it. We are still pursuing our youth policy as hard as ever. The present side still has a few of our home-grown players: Shay Brennan, Billy Foulkes, Johnny Giles and Bobby Charlton in the first team, and Nobby Stiles, Phil Chisnall, Jimmy Nicholson and Tony Dunne are on the verge. I think we can face the immediate future with some confidence." Of his team's prospects in the forthcoming semi Busby said: "Yes, I think we'll make it."

The eventual team to face Southampton read: Gaskell; Dunne, Cantwell; Crerand, Foulkes, Setters; Giles, Stiles, Herd, Law and Charlton, while Southampton lined up: Reynolds; Williams, Traynor; Wilmshurst, Knapp, Huxford; Paine, O'Brien, Kirby, Burnside and Sydenham.

Terrence Elliot, writing in the *Daily Express* said: "It's Law's Turn To Dazzle! Bobby Charlton and Denis Law, more than any other Manchester United players, hold the Wembley destiny of their club in the semi-final. While United should, man for man, defeat Second Division Southampton at Villa Park, it is to Charlton and Law that I look to for the brilliant flashes that will shoot them into the Cup Final."

Harry Gregg believed that United would most certainly not be relegated to the Second Division. "Win or lose against Southampton, the Manchester United players know they have a tough job on their hands fighting for our First Division survival," he said, "everybody at Old Trafford is conscious of the fact that the danger of relegation is very real. But likewise, everybody connected with the club is confident that we won't go down."

Noel Cantwell said that United's Cup and League form were so different. "Some irate United supporters have suggested to me," said the United captain, "that we may complete an unwanted 'double' by winning the Cup and going into the Second Division. The second part of that double has never ever been considered by the players at Old Trafford."

Meanwhile Ted Bates, the Southampton manager, was very confident that his team could cause an upset by toppling the Reds. He said that ever since he knew who his opponents were he had had them watched. "We must be the best briefed team in the country," added Bates, who had gone to extraordinary lengths to 'spy' on United. He called his entire nationwide scouting staff, sending them all to watch the Old Trafford men's recent games. The spies sat in different parts of the ground. They did not compare notes or discuss their views but afterwards each sent an individual report to Bates.

Yet, after all the talk was finished and before a crowd of 68,312, there was no giant-killing ding-dong from Southampton at Villa Park. The game was fought out between two defences that were at times jittery and attacks which tended toward the disappointing. United, in an all-white strip, won because two of the Red aces in Matt Busby's pack of stars came up trumps at the vital moment. Denis and Paddy Crerand were singled out as the players who gave them the edge over the Second Division side. Denis got the all-important goal, the winning one as it happened. It had a touch of luck about it. In the 22nd minute Herd, out on the right wing, took a pass from Giles, looked up and lashed the ball forward into the Southampton penalty area. Denis misheaded it and a second of fatal hesitation by the Southampton defence cost them a most important goal. Instead of going to meet the ball Reynolds, the Saints goalkeeper, stayed rigid on his line, Denis, on one knee after falling to the ground following his mis-directed header, reacted first to the loose ball and prodded it home. "I was lucky to get it," said Law afterwards, "I completely misheaded the ball but it fell at my feet and luckily I got a second bite of the cherry. Being a Scot, I couldn't miss that!"

It was certainly not a classic match, not by any stretch of the imagination. Semi-final nerves spoilt the game, but as far as the United following were concerned they were joyously happy at the end result. On the positive side, United's half-back line of Crerand-Foulkes-Setters quietened the Saints' forwards. Crerand played a 'blinder' in the last 20 minutes of the game as some of the other United players seemed to be rather hesitant. Joe Mercer, the Aston Villa manager watching from the stand said: "It was nearly as bad a semi-final as the one Villa played against Wolves."

One man who everybody agreed had quite definitely played himself right into Wembley on this showing was goalkeeper David Gaskell. He gave a performance of calm skill while his save from the lunging solo blaze of Terry Paine was a classic display of agility and safe handling. United supporters were even happier that Leicester would be their opponents at Wembley. The Foxes had beaten Liverpool 1-0 at Hillsborough despite the Merseysiders laying siege to the Leicester goal for long periods. Gordon Banks, playing one of the greatest games of his career, saved an incredible 34 goal attempts by Shankly's men.

Of the other semi-final, prominent journalist Maurice Smith, said: "In 40-odd years of watching football I have never seen a more unpromising semi-final victory. Villa Park authorities proudly told me this was the biggest-ever pay-day for their famous pitch. Receipts of £28,499, seven shillings and six pence. To me, no fault of Villa's of course, it looked more like a £28,000 highway robbery so far as the standard of football was concerned. I salute United only because they were slightly the better of the two sides who never settled down and for taking one chance."

"If our Easter games with Leicester are anything to go on," said Denis looking forward to the final, "we must be in with a good chance." The following day's headlines underlined the fortunate nature of United's victory, '*Law's Ace, Brilliant Denis Law Snaps Up An Early Goal Chance*', '*He's Scored!, Now For Wembley - The Goal By Law Of Course Takes United To The Final*', '*Double-decker - Law Stages A Sit-Down Strike*', '*A Bit Of Law And A lot Of Luck*', '*Law's Goal Did The Trick*', '*Law Goal Slays Killers*', '*Flying Scot Sinks Saints*'.

Matt Busby was overjoyed at the result. He promised that everything would be different at Wembley. "Our semi-final against Southampton was not a great game, I agree," he said, "but I feel that is what you have to expect. To play in a Cup Final at Wembley is something every player dreams about; one slip can end all those dreams. Now we are through and United players, I know, will feel free to play their normal, natural football. I remember the two matches over Easter between us and Leicester City, both games were full of good football. I can see this being one of the great footballing finals."

Harry Gregg, who lost his semi-final place to David Gaskell, said that the hardest 90 minutes work he ever did in his life was at Villa Park during the semi-final, doing precisely nothing. "They say you can't have your cake and eat it - but I found out that you can be part of something and yet be completely out of it," said Gregg, "any player knows when he is not playing well, and I don't kid myself that things have gone 100 per cent right for me over the past few weeks. At the same time I felt the breaks must surely start to go for the team and when that time comes, we will all be back on song. If I said I wasn't disappointed about being out of the team at such a stage of the season, with the club fighting for League survival and Cup glory, I wouldn't expect anyone to believe me. Of course I'm disappointed!"

A few days after their semi-final victory, United were back battling for much needed points for First Division survival. At Old Trafford United faced Sheffield Wednesday where fans faced more doom and gloom as the Reds surrendered 3-1. The situation was now becoming quite desperate. Fans were upset and rightly so, they couldn't fathom out what was wrong. Here you had great players and yet the team was playing in fits and starts. They were in a crisis, like it or not. Three days after defeat to Wednesday, Manchester United travelled to Turf Moor, the home ground of their bitter Lancashire rivals Burnley, in search of two vital points. If ever United needed a miracle, a huge piece of luck, or a special person to rescue them then this was the occasion.

Cometh the Hour - Cometh the Man! Denis Law was that man! He changed the course of Manchester United's history when, in the 69th minute, his tousled blond head popped up to guide a golden goal into the Burnley net. Law's goal was one of few memorable moments in the match as Albert Quixall centred a high ball and in a flash Denis rose up to the heavens, arched himself and sent the ball flashing past goalkeeper Adam Blacklaw into the net with his forehead.

The sky over Old Trafford looked a lot clearer after the Burnley victory, but their last five games of the season turned out to be nail biting. Following Burnley, the Reds played Arsenal at Old Trafford where they lost a great game of exciting football 3-2, Denis scoring both United's goals, one of them a superb overhead hook into the net.

The next game against Birmingham City saw another loss, this time 2-1, Denis scored again, meaning that with three games of the season left, United had 31 points and were in grave danger of relegation. To add to the tension United's next game was a derby at Maine Road against fellow strugglers City. The Blues had just beaten Spurs 1-0 to move within a point of United, a defeat for either team would probably mean the drop for sure.

This proved to be one humdinger of a relegation derby. The teams line-ups were - United: Gaskell; Dunne, Cantwell; Crerand, Foulkes, Stiles; Quixall, Giles, Herd, Law, Charlton. City: Dowd; Kennedy, Sear; Oakes, Leivers, Gray; Young, Dobing, Harley, Hayes, Wagstaffe. The atmosphere inside and outside the ground was red hot, the Cup Final by comparison would seem pretty tame fare to the Reds after their reception they ran into at Maine Road. With 52,424 packed into the ground the atmosphere was electric. It was almost a certainty that either City or United would be consigned to the Second Division following the outcome of this game - it was without a doubt the most vital of the 74 Derby matches so far between the two clubs.

A spotter plane circling overhead and mounted police both inside and outside the ground all added to the tension of the occasion. And when City centre-forward Alex Harley, who had already scored 31 times for the Sky Blues that season, gave the match an explosive and sensational start by putting City in front after just 9 minutes, United looked done for. Maine Road shook and the cheering from the City followers could be heard in Old Trafford.

The tension was rising by the second and both sets of players were squabbling and feuding, as tempers were quickly lost in this battle for survival. Harley was booked by referee George McCabe of Sheffield for a foul on David Herd which ripped Herd's stocking to his ankle and cut his shin. Mr McCabe pointed threateningly to the tunnel as he lectured Harley. There was more controversy in the 30th minute when Harley appeared to have doubled City's lead with a thunderbolt, only for the referee to rule it offside. Phew! The tension was unbearable.

After this incident the tackling got fiercer and Wagstaffe and Crerand argued and tussled constantly. Harley and Stiles both went violently in for a loose ball - two more names were jotted down by the busy referee, then Crerand and Wagstaffe became embroiled in a tussle near the grandstand. The press later claimed that as the players left the pitch at half time, Wagstaffe was knocked to the ground by an unnamed United assailant. For most of the game Denis had been very ineffective and quiet against his old club, but in the 84th minute all that changed as he became the key figure in one of the most hotly-contested decisions in Manchester derby history.

It all started when David Wagstaffe, always a central figure in this game, was pressured a good 30 yards away from his goal. Suddenly he attempted what proved to be an absolutely suicidal back pass. Law, out of the game for so long, suddenly seized his chance and raced into the Blues penalty area chasing down the ball but appeared to be felled by Dowd, the City keeper.

Harry Dowd himself takes up the story: "I went down at Law's feet and pushed the ball away for a corner. After the ball had gone I was kicked on the temple and knocked out. When I recovered I was staggered to be told it was a penalty." For Law's part he maintained that the referee got it right: "It was a penalty; the goalkeeper had hold of my legs - but I would never have scored! I was going away from the goal and had lost the ball. It was a lucky break for us". With the decision all hell broke loose and tempers flared again. The referee consulted his linesman before Albert Quixall scored from the spot. The game ended 1-1. The Reds now needed just one more point from their two remaining fixtures, while City were surely doomed.

In the vital home game against Leyton Orient, United gained the 3-1 win that ensured safety. Yet the London team took the lead when Dunmore scored after nine minutes and it wasn't until the 54th minute that the Reds scored and even then it was an own goal. Ten minutes from the end Charlton robbed Langley and Denis nipped in to finish with a left foot shot. Bobby got the third after Denis set him up. To be perfectly honest this was another forgettable game. Charlton, Setters and Crerand put United's victory down to the Reds new 4-2-4 formation. Matt Busby said the team had used this system before but perhaps it had not looked so pronounced. "It looked very effective," commented Busby. The last League match of a forgettable league campaign was at Nottingham Forest. Denis was suffering with a bruised thigh, didn't play and United lost 3-2 - Giles and Herd scoring. By the way Manchester City needed two points from their final away game of the season at West Ham but were thrashed 6-1 and consequently relegated.

Everybody at Old Trafford felt a deep sense of relief that this dreadful season was over at last. And although it was now all systems go for Wembley there had been casualties amid the relegation scramble: Bobby Charlton had incurred a nasty ankle injury while Bill Foulkes complained of a bruised hip; Maurice Setters, who had missed three of the last four League matches, was also struggling again with an injured right ankle. He, along with Charlton and Law, continued to receive treatment from United's physio Ted Dalton while Nobby Stiles, who had played against Forest, had a groin strain.

Law's impact on his new club had been substantial to say the least. From a goals point of view he had scored 29 in 44 League and Cup games and had had a big say in keeping the club in the First Division. The number of vital goals he had scored and contributed to, almost certainly prevented United's descent into the Second Division, while he had also tipped the balance in terms of his club reaching Wembley, a great achievement by any reckoning.

The Manchester United fans were in little doubt as to the importance of his contribution to the team. Matt Busby and Jimmy Murphy were, needless to say, convinced that once the team settled down into a rhythm, then Denis would be a big bonus for the club.

Of his first season at United Denis commented: "I'm glad to be back in British football. I never really settled down in Italy, it was a different way of life and not to my kind of liking but there was something about the football that appealed to my instincts. Italian footballers have great technique. If they were allowed to play as they would like to, they would probably be better to watch than the Brazilians. They used to excite me because they were never afraid to indulge in spectacular attempts at goal. I liked that."

The Reds' faithful now had first-hand knowledge of Denis' unorthodox abilty to score goals, be they tap-ins, ferocious shots, side-footers, thrilling headers or acrobatic overhead kicks - his performances had Stretford Enders gushing with praise. Since returning from Italy Denis had harnessed that unorthodoxy to unusual courage and an ability to do the impossible. The combination proved deadly. He was loved at Old Trafford and by the Stretford End in particular. They had already proclaimed him 'The King'. Whenever he launched himself into an extravagant horizontal position for an overhead kick, the entire Stretford End would hold its breath in amazement at the audacity of it all - whether his attempt went in or not. It was this skill that appealed most because of its unfamiliarity. Few British players had the confidence to attempt the bicycle kick and managers brought up with a belief in more orthodox principles rarely encouraged it. In Europe and South America it was a regular feature of play yet United fans were the first in the country to witness this sort of spectacular football.

Once it became obvious that Harry Gregg would miss out on Wembley, there was a great deal of speculation concerning his future. It was reported that Gregg had talked things over with Matt Busby at United's pre-Cup final headquarters at Weybridge, giving further emphasis to the whispers that Gregg might leave Old Trafford for a new club in the close season. Harry had been unlucky with injuries and personal misfortune over the last two-and-a-half years and now he had lost his first team place and the chance of a Cup winners' medal.

Five weeks before, 22-year-old David Gaskell, his understudy since 1959, had taken over for the semi-final against Southampton. Bitterly upset and disappointed when he could not regain his place, Harry told the pre-Cup Final press: "I'm giving some thought to my future with Manchester United but don't want to say anything more about it at this stage. However, I would like to put the record straight as far as Wembley is concerned. I am not out of the team because I am unfit. The stitches I had in my hand while playing for the reserves at West Bromwich are out and apart from feeling a little sore, I am perfectly fine." Matt Busby replied: "I can understand and appreciate Harry's disappointment, but on the whole he has taken the decision to play Gaskell quite well." Stoke had been watching Gregg play for the Central League team and had been very impressed.

*

Denis' outstanding display in that classic final has already been described and, following United's 3-1 success, the entire staff, including tea ladies, cleaners, coaches, players and directors, were invited to a pink champagne celebration at the Savoy Hotel. Of the 360 guests, including officials from some Continental clubs, the toast of the celebration was the mercurial Denis himself. Everyone there to honour the 3-1 victors over gallant Leicester City sang the praises of Denis, the £115,000 wizard from Scotland.

Maurice Setters put everyone's thoughts into words: "Denis was fabulous. Once we saw him play like the ace he is, it was a pushover." It had been Law's opening goal that sealed the fate of Leicester and carved his name indelibly in Manchester United's hall of fame but the Red Devils had that optimism which made 11 players into a Cup-winning formation. Setters continued: "I never had any doubt of the result. In fact I gave £200-to-£1 two weeks ago that we would win."

And Matt Busby thought the same as three security guards watched over the Cup: "I knew we could do it. We always rise to the occasion." Speaking about the players he continued: "I never single out any player because it is team work, but Denis Law pulled out all the stops. He played brilliantly." A smiling, jovial Jimmy Murphy was in raptures over the way the team had played. After giving praise to the unlucky Harry Gregg, Shay Brennan and Nobby Stiles, he simply oozed praise and was delighted when describing the victory: "Wasn't Denis something special? He showed all the doubters what a sensational player he is. A perfectionist is Denis. The whole team functioned brilliantly. Myself and Matt were confident they could play in that manner. Forget our League form this season, it was too bad to be true. All the lads put 100 per cent effort in, Bobby made some telling runs on the left and always looked dangerous. David Herd received his just rewards with his two well-taken goals. Paddy and Albert Quixall commanded the midfield, but what a player Law is, wouldn't you agree?"

There is no doubt whatsoever that this 1963 FA Cup victory was the start of Matt Busby's third great team's success. Since his arrival at Old Trafford in 1945 he had revamped the 1948 Cup-winning team, replaced that wonderful, exciting squad with the fabulous, never-to-be-forgotten Busby Babes team and now his post-Munich team of which he had three world-class stars: Bobby Charlton, Denis Law and a short while later, the incomparable George Best. Yes, the club had emerged from those dark, despairing bleak days of Munich.

Over in the losers' hotel, Leicester City chairman Syd Needham set the tone for the defeated team's dinner when he said: "We were well beaten by a better side. If you can't lose gracefully it's no good playing the game at all. We all intend to have a good time." Meanwhile jubilant United supporters thronged into the West End, filling the bars, restaurants and clubs enjoying themselves in a good-natured fashion. In Trafalgar Square, 34-year-old Donald McWilliams, of Foxton Road, Disley, dressed in a scarlet top hat and tails, led a victory sing-song while back in Manchester plans were in operation for a 'Welcome Home' United would never forget.

Later that night, Busby's eyes twinkled as he talked about the challenge ahead for next season - the European Cup Winners' Cup. "We are back in the act," he said, "and from what I saw from our players today, I am confident we can make our mark in European football again." That was the burning question now that United had clicked: would they stay in that confident, masterful mood? Crerand agreed with his manager and said the team and players had been nervous during the season. He said that if they lost an early goal or things didn't go right straight away they would go to pieces. "But," added Paddy, "we all believed that there would come a day and this was it. All we needed was the proof and there'll be no looking back."

The Sunday after the Cup Final was a beautiful sunny day. Denis was leisurely strolling back to his hotel. He was returning from a London pub with his club blazer tucked underneath his arm and a big smile on his face that matched the sunshine. In the hotel he came face to face with Desmond Hackett, the Daily Express sports journalist famed for wearing a brown bowler hat, who had predicted United's 3-1 win. The journalist had described Denis, much to Denis's embarrassment as: "The glory boy of Manchester United, the mercurial, majestic, master of Soccer. This young man Law, who can command the admiration of the greatest Soccer crowds on earth, off-field he is a charmer, a modest, willing signer of small boys' autograph books."

They chatted about Denis's Italian adventures. Denis told him that he was glad that it was all behind him, but he was still glad he went to Italy: "You got the money all right but it was like being in prison and who wants money in a prison?" Law told him. Discussing his goal in the final Denis said: "I felt the first team to score would win and I'm proud I was the man who did the scoring but I still feel that header that hit the post and the time the shot was scraped off the line would have been better value." On his scuffles with referee Ken Aston, Law told him that when playing he gave everything and he couldn't hold himself back. He told Mr Hackett that when he watched some of his antics on the screen afterwards he was astonished and a little embarrassed. Denis told the journalist that he was happily married, played golf badly and that with having to play football twice a week he just didn't have time to get up to any mischief. Hackett said Denis was likeable and friendly, and a genius on the great occasion. "That is Denis Law," he commented.

As Denis and Mr Hackett chatted the irrepressible Pat Crerand who, to use the journalist's words, was "the co-star who got a Cup winners' medal in his first season with Manchester United," was living up to his title 'The Joker.' This young, husky Scottish wing-half with bow legs that were not designed for a kilt, was doing a Cassius Clay impression insisting: "That was my greatest game, I was great, just great." Crerand, who found it difficult to fit into a defensive role with Manchester United, was told to go out at Wembley and just play wherever the game took him.

"And what he thought added up to a half-back presentation of purring excellence," said the journalist, who added, "but then every man in this United side became a hero possessed of unforgettable splendour, glowing in brilliance until they looked good enough to beat those Continental sparkling men of football: European Cup duellists Milan and Benfica. They brought back the old lustre to soccer played the English way and this in the same month that Tottenham had been applauded as an 'English team fit to send anywhere with pride.' Alas, poor Leicester. For ten minutes they had Manchester United tottering and uncertain." He was of the opinion that Leicester were desperately unlucky not to score when Noel Cantwell caught the ball with his studs and that United were within a programme width of a crippling own goal. And again when Maurice Setters, on this day precise, calming and great, sent David Gaskell into a back-crinkling slide with a header that spun the wrong way. After which Leicester did not smile again - well, only thinly and briefly."

Mr Hackett said that Manchester United, with rich artistry, had written their fame on the noble turf of Wembley: "It was a matter of poets and peasants with these rare men from Manchester finally composing the greatest team show I have ever seen in a Wembley final. It flowed grandly from that half-hour goal of which the architect was this so accurate, sweet-moving man Crerand and it was scored by Law with a shot that was majestic in the taking. It was a goal which had Law standing erect, arms flung into the blue, sun-blessed sky to embrace the cheers that poured down upon him. And there was one final moving scene as the whole audience rose to the manager of United, Matt Busby. As the salute sounded out, this loveable man straightened his back, held high his beaming face and moved proudly from the scene of one of his club's most

magnificent achievements. Now Matt Busby will be off down
the golden trail of European cup tournaments. If his team play
as they did at Wembley they will journey with pride."

Later that day, at St Pancras station, came the unusual
announcement: "The train now leaving platform 4 is the
Champagne Special bound for Manchester," and as the
jubilant team, their wives and officials stepped aboard they
were clapped and cheered by hundreds of supporters. As
captain Noel Cantwell leaned from the window holding the
trophy, the fans went wild with delight. The joyous journey
back home started. On board the train were 100 bottles of the
best champagne, and several hundred bottles of beer, fruit
juices and 200 lamb cutlets. It was a sight similar to a royal
progress as the train left the station and carnival time began as
hundreds of Red supporters started singing and dancing as
they waved their heroes off. As United's jubilant Cup winning
team left London by special train a woman's voice over the
station loudspeaker asked loudly: "Three cheers for the
Manchester United team!" Immediately a roar hit the air that
was absolutely deafening.

The official club party numbered 250, this included the
players' wives, who had arrived at the station from the Savoy
Hotel where many had been up until 1am and several all night
celebrating. There were many tired, bleary-eyed people but
they were simultaneously happy and raring to celebrate again.
The FA Cup that had been kept in a London strongroom
during Saturday night had been handed to skipper Noel
Cantwell at the station.

Matt Busby was mobbed by hundreds of fans seeking
autographs and he had been the last to board the train. "It was
a great, great day," said a beaming Busby, "it was a day I have
waited a long time for. Yes, the bottles will be cracked open and
the lads deserve it." Half an hour earlier from this same
platform the beaten Leicester team had departed. There had
been about a dozen people standing on the platform and they
cheered them. A couple of men said: "We are Manchester
United supporters but we thought we would give the losers a

cheer. They took defeat in a very sporting fashion." What would football do for that kind of sportsmanship today? The station master, Mr J G Handley, who saw both parties off, changed his buttonhole between the departure of the Leicester team and the arrival of the United party. For Leicester he had worn a buttonhole of blue forget-me-nots but he was wearing a buttonhole of red and white flowers when the Manchester United team arrived!

Manchester United and the FA Cup came home in the late evening to a tumultuous welcome from thousands of fans thronging the streets. For hours before the team arrived in the city, crowds were gathering along the route to the Town Hall. This was a day when the city began to believe in its heroes again. The day when triumph at Wembley kicked the bitter disappointment of the team's League failure down the back streets. As the team coach reached the Town Hall in Albert Square for a civic reception at 8.20pm, two of United's youngsters were discreetly situated, completely anonymously, at a wonderful vantage point - George Best and John Fitzpatrick, stars of future homecoming parades.

The United party were welcomed and congratulated by the Lord Mayor and Lady Mayoress, Alderman and Mrs R C Rogers. The Police Band played, but the vast crowds drowned them out as they gave the team a hysterical welcome and swept away the barriers. It was estimated that more than 300,000 people had converged on Albert Square and the vicinity. Young Best and Fitzpatrick left where they were standing, joined the team and waved back at the crowd as if they had played in the final. The police linked arms in an effort to hold the throng back and erected double crash barriers. The corridors of the Town Hall looked like a front-line casualty station as victims of the crush were treated on stretchers. Officials of the Red Cross and the St John's Ambulance Brigade estimated that at least 350 people were treated, but only eight were admitted to hospital. Thankfully, they were not detained. An official of the Red Cross commented: "I've been in a lot of crowds and seen a lot of street affairs, but I really got frightened when I went out onto the steps. If the police had not been so strong, I don't know what would have happened."

Before they had arrived at the Town Hall, the team bus had paraded the Cup winners on a tour of the city to thousands of happy, jubilant fans. Noel Cantwell and his team-mates held the trophy aloft to deafening cheers. Yet there had been a hitch on the journey home. The team that had steam-rollered Leicester City ran out of steam on the train journey from London... at Leicester! A very embarrassed British Railways spokesman explained: "The engine ran out of steam just before reaching Leicester and we had to put a diesel on the front to bring the train back to Manchester." At the Town Hall reception Mr Harold Hardman, United's elderly chairman, joked: "This is our biggest gate of the season," while Matt Busby added: "I have never seen such a wonderful demonstration by so many people. We have brought this Cup back to Manchester and we did it so wonderfully well."

To many who did not know him Manchester United's longest-serving player, Bill Foulkes, was thought of as someone who kept himself to himself, some even described him as dour. Foulkes prided himself in keeping in top physical condition and Denis often said that Bill was one of the fittest players he had ever seen. Bill was not one for giving out opinions, especially about his club colleagues. After Denis Law's first season with the Reds, Bill was asked what he thought of Denis as a player and a person. "Since he joined us from Italy he has been a revelation," said Bill, "Denis was responsible for me breaking my run of bad luck in Wembley FA Cup finals, something I will never forget. I had been to Wembley in 1957 with the Busby Babes team. On that occasion we were beaten by Aston Villa after Ray Wood, our keeper, had been badly injured. And then of course I was there again after Munich in 1958. So it was with a little trepidation that I prepared for my third visit in 1963. And don't forget Leicester were hot favourites. They had been going for the double at one time while we had a terrible season - almost getting relegated. But I had no need to worry because Denis made the difference to our team. To be fair all the team played excellently but he scored that all-important first goal. That settled us down and I at last got my winner's medal. He was a predator, one of the sharpest. His goals saved us on many occasions. Beside being a phenomenal goalscorer, he was a lovely distributor of the ball. He would control the ball in a second, turn his body sideways, and send the perfect pass to a team-mate. He must have been exciting to watch for spectators, because he was brilliant to his club-mates. As a person I found him very, very private. He would lark about with the lads in training or on away trips, but once business was complete he would head home. You never heard any scandal about Denis. A great, truly great player, and a wonderful, friendly person."

A week after their scintillating Wembley performance, the Reds jetted out of Ringway airport bound for Italy where they took part in a two-match, ten-day tour. Harry Gregg received some heartening news that cheered him up no end. Harry was told to pack his bag, check his passport and report with the rest of the team. David Gaskell, the man who replaced Harry at Wembley, had gone into hospital for a nose operation, so Gregg, who thought he would be spending the summer back home in Ireland, was now back in favour. The first game on tour was against Juventus, who had finished runners up in the Italian League. The match was played in heavy rain in Turin and 21-year-old Sammy McMillan, a stand-in for the injured Albert Quixall, scored the only goal of the game, but it was Foulkes and Crerand who were praised by the Italians for their performances. But the one player who wanted to do well, Denis Law, had a stinker! He had been feted by thousands on his arrival back in the city where he had starred for Torino. During the match he got a finger-wagging from the referee and in the second half he was booed incessantly by Juventus fans.

The following game, against Roma, was tough; Denis and Sammy McMillan were United's goal scorers, with an own goal also going their way. The match was played on the emerald green turf of the Flaminia Stadium. There were thrills, spills and tough tackling amid terrific excitement. And spectators caught the unusual sight of big John Charles losing his temper. Charles had a mixed game and was out of favour with his club. What surprised Jimmy Murphy and Matt Busby most was that big John, the Gentle Giant, was responsible for the 60th minute incident that could have detonated the match. Bill Foulkes brought Charles down. Foulkes also fell and Charles appeared to kick him in retaliation while also waving his arms in anger. Charles said: "I did not kick Foulkes. I was annoyed but my foot was pinned under him." Bill Foulkes, upon hearing this, replied: "I said to John, 'what do you expect me to do? I have to go for the ball.' And he said. 'Yes, but you don't have to do it like that.'" Denis was booed again. He went to a Roman hospital for treatment to a calf injury before flying out of Italy to join up with the Scottish international party.

So after a season of gloom, everything had suddenly gone right in a wondrous week for the club and players. After beating Juventus 1-0 and Roma 3-2, the Reds found themselves the talk of Italian football. The Italian press were unanimous that the Reds had introduced a style in advance of anything seen from an English club for quite some time. This was sweet music to Matt Busby's ears. He loved his teams to be praised. After the victory he told his players: "I'm very proud of every one of you, and I'm sure that the people back in Manchester will be delighted."

While the United team and officials were in Rome, the newspapers were full of the possibility of a massive bonus for United's players following their cup triumph. Busby had said that because of all the travelling and preparations for the FA Cup final there had not been time to go into details about the players' reward for winning the Cup but "there will be wage increases," he told the press.

The players had also been contemplating the extent to which the club would reward them for winning the FA Cup. Various players were saying just how much money they were expecting to receive. Some were expecting a rather large bonus. The maximum wage had been abolished less than two years before and it was known that Burnley, who had been beaten at Wembley the year before, received £1,000 a man. It was also said that the Leicester players were getting £1,000 apiece. Imagine the United players' disappointment when, following a couple of days in Italy, Matt Busby told them that their Cup final reward was £20 each! Some of the players thought he was joking. When they realised that he wasn't, a few of the more senior players met the manager to discuss the miserly sum they had been given. Matt Busby told them there was nothing he could do about the situation because the team had struggled in the League. Like it or lump it, that would be the only extra money they were getting. It was no understatement to say that the entire team felt let down and embarrassed about the size of the bonus for winning the world-famous trophy.

After listening to the complaints about money, in which he had no interest whatsoever, Jimmy Murphy, still buoyant at United's cup final victory and the manner in which the team played told the press: "Money is the root of all evil." When he was asked what he thought of the derisory payment made to United's players for winning the FA Cup Jimmy replied: "That does not concern me. That's up to Matt and the directors."

But Jimmy was a very happy man, he wasn't concerned about the wrangling over money, he was more concerned that his beloved club had achieved honours. He told reporters that it was a pity that the English season had ended because there was no doubt in his mind that United had now found the correct pattern of play. "These matches in Italy have given the boys experience of playing against Continental opposition," said Jimmy. Of United's entry into the European Cup Winners' Cup Murphy said: "We have drummed into them that in this type of football they must try to keep possession of the ball. That is one of the ingredients of success against Continental opposition."

Meanwhile Denis was back in Scotland pulling on his dark blue Scottish jersey for the international match against Austria at Hampden Park. Denis was again in scintillating form as the Austrians were defeated 4-1, scoring twice and a few days later he and Scotland embarked on an ill-fated trip to Norway for a friendly in Bergen. Norway's amateur footballers pulled off their biggest upset for many years when they beat the Scots 4-3, having trailed 2-1 at half time. Denis was the only Scottish player who didn't lose his reputation amid this pathetic shambles of a game. The Scottish captain Dave Mackay, suffering from muscle trouble, went off in the 76th minute to be replaced by Frank McLintock, who had been in opposition to Denis in the Cup Final. Denis scored a hat-trick in the 13th, 22nd, and 76th minute.

"I played my first game for Scotland in this match in Bergen," recalled Arsenal's future double-winning captain McLintock, "I was one of the track-suited reserves sitting on the touchline. There were only 21,000 people inside the ground and we believed we would win convincingly, and the Scottish newspapers wrote that we would have a runaway victory. Perhaps we all expected it to be a walkover because we never clicked as a team. As I stepped onto the field to replace Dave Mackay, we were winning 3-2 with just 15 minutes left. Norway equalised straight after my substitution. I hardly got a kick of the ball before they scored their winner. I felt dejected at the final whistle. Denis Law had more cause to be disappointed because he had scored all three goals, a hat-trick, and he finished on the losing side."

More disappointment was in store for Denis and his Scottish colleagues because five days later they met Eire at Dublin's Dalymount Park. The Scots once again thought they would gain a victory here but they were wrong. The Irish, roared on by a fervent support, secured a 1-0 victory. Feeling a little down in the dumps after their two defeats, the Scottish party were booked to leave London on a flight bound for Madrid for a friendly against Spain. While sitting on their plane waiting for take-off, Denis and the other passengers received a nasty fright. A shrill message came over the tannoy telling all passengers to leave their seats and calmly make an orderly exit from the aircraft. It was reported a bomb had been placed in the luggage hold by an anti-Franco political party. A three-hour delay followed while the baggage was searched and when the police found nothing sucspious, the flight was allowed to depart for Madrid.

Yet despite this set-back, and just four days after their defeat in Ireland, Scotland shattered the Spanish in the Bernebeu. They were forecast to get a hammering but turned the tables by beating the hosts 6-2: Denis opened the scoring after 15 minutes while Gibson (16) McLintock (24) Wilson (33) Henderson (51) and St John (83) rained in the goals in front of 40,000 shocked Spaniards. These four post-season Internationals underlined the schizophrenic nature of the Scottish team - they had scored 13 goals, conceded eight, beaten one of the better teams in Europe and lost to two of the lesser lights yet throughout Law kept finding the net. If only the team could find some consistency in defence, Scottish fans pleaded, qualification for the next World Cup in England in 1966 might not be beyond them.

*

During the early sixties the atmosphere at Old Trafford changed considerably. In keeping with the dawning of a new era there was an inevitable influx of talent while many of the old hands and the remainder of the Busby Babes slipped quietly away to other clubs. Paddy McGrath, a close friend of Matt Busby, recalls the atmosphere at the club during this period: "Before Munich, Manchester United was the nearest thing you could get to a family club. It was wonderful. Matt, Jimmy Murphy, Joe Armstrong, Bert Whalley, and the other backroom staff were lovely, intelligent, caring people. They were extremely knowledgeable in football matters and had the right formula for developing brilliant young footballers. Yes, these people were steeped in football. The fans also felt part and parcel of the club. You could sense that we were all part of something very special indeed. Over the proceeding years I have heard various players and managers of other clubs talk about 'spirit'. Believe me they don't know the true meaning of the word. United had it, and had it in abundance.

"After the crash it was different. Matt and Jimmy were busy

beavering away with the club and players but the whole system had come off the rails because of the disaster. New players were brought to the club and of course they didn't know how Matt operated the team. He had a simply philosophy about how teams should play. Get eleven of your best players out on the pitch and let them play football. It was only to be expected that the new players coming to Old Trafford might have expected the types of training and coaching schedules that they had received at their former clubs. But Matt believed in simplicity and his players were free to express themselves on the field. He managed the team and, after Munich, Jack Crompton became the first team trainer. Of the players Matt brought to the club after Munich it was Denis Law who gave the club and team the biggest boost, that something special that United were famous for. He was a great player!"

There was no doubting that after the new players settled in to their new environment they began questioning the running of the club, criticising the type of training they were given and the preparation for games. They couldn't understand why they hardly saw Matt Busby and complained at the absence of tactical discussions.

Eamon Dunphy was a young player with United at this time and he later wrote an excellent biography of Busby entitled *A Strange Kind of Glory*. In it he wrote: "Noel Cantwell thought the place was a joke. One afternoon after training he started chatting to me. 'Is that it?' he asked after the training routine finished. I told him it was." To be fair, the majority of clubs had very basic ideas on how players should train. It was usually the same for everyone, lapping the perimeter of the pitch, sprinting to the top of the stands, circuits, head-tennis, and five-a-sides with perhaps a few other physical exercises thrown in for good measure. At Old Trafford small cliques formed, something unheard of before Munich but as Leo McKinstry writes in his book *Jack and Bobby*, "a harmonious dressing-room is not always a pre-requisite for success." He mentioned the unfriendly nature of Teddy Sheringham and Andy Cole in the 1990s and the same was true of United in the 1960s. It was true that Denis, in his early years at Old Trafford, never joined the cliques or voiced an opinion about the other players' complaints. He kept himself to himself, as did Bobby Charlton. Later, however, there was a degree of friction between Denis, Bobby, and George Best. Yet in fairness to both Denis Law and Bobby Charlton it should be stressed that though they might not have seen eye to eye with each other at that period, they never publicly aired their differences.

8. Hero of the Stretford End

Before United met First Division champions Everton in the Charity Shield game at Goodison Park at the start of the following season, Matt Busby told the press that if the team played as they did in the Cup final he wouldn't fear any opposition: "Sometimes they give it to me and sometimes they don't. It could be that one or two need shaking up." That last comment was delivered with a smile, but there was no mistaking the velvet covered threat. He was determined not to tolerate some of the fifth-rate performances of the previous season.

Yet in a pitiful and gutless display, the Reds were thrashed 4-0 by the champions. The United fans were wondering if they were in for another season of misery like the previous one while Matt Busby was seething. The axe fell on the Cup-winning team before the first League game of the new season. "We've played three pre-season games," said Busby. "Glasgow, Frankfurt, and at Goodison Park, and that's why changes have been made. Everyone must play for their places all the time." So out went Albert Quixall, Johnny Giles and David Herd. David Gaskell was also dropped through injury as Ian Moir took Giles' place on the right wing, Phil Chisnall replaced Quixall at inside-right and 17-year-old David Sadler replaced Herd. Sadler a 6ft, 12st Maidstone boy United had snapped up the previous season, when every club in the country was chasing him, would make his League debut straight from youth football, leap-frogging the formality of reserve team experience. Quixall and Giles immediately asked for transfers. Herd, although disappointed at being dropped, said he would fight for his place.

The United team coach had barely left Goodison Park after

United's humbling at the hands of Everton before the critics were saying that Denis would also have to accept a large share of the blame. There was irresponsible talk of enmity between Denis and his Old Trafford club-mates. It was said that he was only a 'big match player' and that Matt Busby should boot him out of the senior side.

It was left to Tom Finney to stick up for the blond-haired Scot: "I used to laugh, but I could have cried at the ignorance shown by the comments about Denis Law. Denis is for my money one of the finest inside-forwards in world soccer today. I would not dream of trying to offer him one bit of advice on his play. It would be an insult to his astounding ability. But Denis is like the rest of us in one respect. He cannot be held responsible for the failure of an entire team. And that's what too many misguided football-watching folk are trying to do to him. It's the penalty of a genius."

Tom Finney continued: "Denis, like any other player, has faults. His habit of roaming all over the field instead of staying up front, where he is most deadly and dangerous and often the match-winner is one but I believe that he has curbed this tendency. I also regret Denis' occasional outburst of temperament on the field. I know he himself has put it down to enthusiasm, but enthusiasm must go along with intelligent appreciation that enthusiasm must be controlled. Certainly in this he is no worse than many other players. But in natural ability he's streets ahead of most players in Britain.

"After last May's Cup Final most Old Trafford fans would have said the same. If Stan Matthews earned the Freedom of Stoke, they felt Denis should have been given Manchester, lock, stock and barrel. What a difference it makes when your team has just suffered a crushing defeat as United have against Everton in that Charity Shield match. It's easy to forget the Cup run, which a somewhat fortunate United won because of Law's skill and sharp-shooting. Or those vital end-of-season League games, when, but for Law, United might have been in the Second Division. Law has already paid back a large chunk of that £115,000 transfer fee and he'll pay the remainder back, with a high rate of interest, before long. But not by being dropped!

"Scotland sees him play well because he's playing with other top-grade internationals. The men picking the World team to play England think he'll play well for them, with other world-class players. Are both Scotland and the World soccer experts wrong and the dissenters right? I can not see it."

A few days after the disastrous Charity Shield match, Matt Busby announced that the Manchester United board of directors had agreed to the transfer requests of Quixall and Giles. There was considerable surprise among supporters that Giles in particular should be allowed to leave. John Giles had joined United in July 1956 from the famous Stella Maris Boys and Home Farm clubs in Dublin. John's best position was inside-forward but Matt Busby had used him as an outside-right in the first team. Although only a youngster, Giles was certainly not frightened or in awe of the United manager. If he thought something was wrong he would speak out.

"Matt Busby considered me as being 'cheeky,'" remarked John when discussing his career at Old Trafford in a BBC television documentary on Matt Busby. "It was common knowledge around the Old Trafford dressing room that when he was going to drop you from the first team, he would call you into his office and ask: 'How do you think you played?' referring to the last match. If, like most young players, you said 'not bad', or 'so, so', he would then say 'Yes, I agree, so I'll give you a rest this week.' But when he asked me that question, I'd turn it around and ask him how he thought I'd played. He didn't like that. I also asked him for more money than what he told me I was going to receive in my wage packet. That didn't go down well either."

When Leeds' Don Revie signed Giles for £35,000, the negotiations took only minutes to finalise. Leeds, then in the Second Division, should have been arrested for highway robbery. "I've been happy with United," said Giles at the time, "but if you join somewhere as the office boy, you never seem to get out of being an office boy in the eyes of the employers.

They are not conscious of this. You are. I asked for a move not just because I'd been dropped. I've been unsettled for some time, even before the Cup final. I thought I was sort of taken for granted. Then, of course, as a married man, there was the financial angle." It was a complete surprise to the followers of United, who believed Johnny was a Manchester United player forever. At Leeds, Giles became one of the best, toughest and most influential inside-forwards in Europe. For United he had played 114 first team games scoring 13 goals, for Leeds he went on to play 528 games during an 11-year career, scoring 115 goals and winning two championships and an FA Cup for the Yorkshire club.

United's first game of the season, away at Sheffield Wednesday, ended in a 3-3 draw but not before Denis received his second booking in eight days. The Reds started badly and were two goals down after just 13 minutes. Yet Ian Moir, who gave away a penalty, more than made up for it with some breathtaking football. Throughout the game Setters and Law were loudly booed by the Hillsborough crowd for their aggressive play. Nevertheless Bobby Charlton had a superb match getting two goals and almost completing a hat-trick, while Moir hit the bar twice and Sadler skimmed another off the woodwork. Whatever anyone said, this was a fighting display from the Red Devils and if they continued to show this kind of grit and determination throughout the season the United followers would not complain. The three youngsters (Chisnall, Sadler and Moir) played well and would keep their places in the team, yet the following day's newspapers concentrated on the petulance of certain players, Denis being one of the names mentioned.

A straightforward 2-0 win in a midweek game against Ipswich Town at Old Trafford was purely an appetiser for the game the senior professionals of United's first team wanted badly... the opportunity for revenge at home to Everton the following Saturday. Nearly 63,000 spectators crammed into Old Trafford for this fascinating Lancashire derby, packed with eventful and entertaining football. In a spectacular exhibition of everything that was great about football, Manchester United humbled the League champions 5-1 - it was a footballing feast! Everton full-back and Scottish International Alex Parker was breathless after the game. "I feel four inches shorter than I was a couple of hours ago," he said as United's new attack tore the Merseysiders apart, Phil Chisnall (2), David Sadler and Denis (2) on the scoresheet. Moir was brilliant again as United massacred the Evertonians out of sight. Nevertheless the visitors took the lead through Roy Vernon before Denis scored two magnificent goals to start a heart-warming team performance of the highest calibre. Jimmy Gabriel, Everton's wing-half and Scottish International, commented: "That young right winger Ian Moir was a revelation. What speed! What talent!"

Denis was overjoyed. Four goals in three games made for a great start to his season. It was especially sweet because after the Charity Shield game the 'knockers' had come out in full force, sniping about United in general and him in particular.

After the pulsating victory over Everton, United travelled to Ipswich Town for a midweek League game. This would be a test of their character. The team was the same that had annihilated the champions with the three youngsters keeping their places. What a difference a fortnight made for the Red Devils. Against Everton in the Charity Shield they were a punchless parade of mixed-up personalities yet in hammering Ipswich 7-2 they were suddenly top of the First Division table with seven points and 17 goals from just four games - Manchester United were indeed on their way back!

United's magnificent seven began when Denis rolled a ball into David Sadler's path for the first in the 6th minute. Then, in the 34th, Denis controlled a cross from a rampaging Bobby Charlton to score his first goal of the game. Maurice Setters scored the third with a header and was later booked by referee Peter Bye for arguing. Ipswich pulled a goal back through Moran before Phillips missed a penalty for the home team. Ian Moir, having another storming game, got the Reds' fourth before Denis showed how easy penalty taking could be by hitting his spot kick high into the net after Sadler had been fouled. Then Moran pulled another goal back for the home team before the Reds completed the rout with a goal from Chisnall and another from Law, which completed his hat-trick and ended a night of terror for Ipswich. The last time an away team had managed seven goals in the First Division had been back in 1960 when West Brom had mauled local rivals Birmingham City 7-1.

Despite scoring his riveting hat-trick it wasn't Denis who received the following morning's plaudits but Ian Moir. "Ian looks as if he has arrived at last," said Matt Busby, "but I'm keeping my fingers crossed because, like a lot of lads, Ian has a lot of downs to balance the ups." Moir came to Old Trafford at 15 and although his talent was obvious and he had played in the first team at 17 he had had to wait two years for his next senior game, against a Glasgow Select XI. He was acclaimed in Scotland, where they don't go overboard after just one glance and looked well set but his form had taken a dip, as had his confidence. At one stage Aberdeen manager Tommy Pearson, knowing Moir was a local, had asked Matt Busby if he was for sale, yet Busby decided to give the youngster a bit longer to show his true form. "I'm glad I did," said Matt. Moir's time finally arrived at the start of the 1963/64 season when he was picked ahead of Johnny Giles. His debut against Sheffield Wednesday was always going to be tough against experienced, no-nonsense defender Don Megson. But after the game Megson had no doubts that Ian Moir was a rare talent. He had speed, a tremendous shot in either foot, skill with the ball, an ability to centre it accurately at the right time, and equally important, a large heart. This was something he needed because Moir looked a little willowy although at 5 feet 10 and 11 stone he could take some battering. Moir's performances against current champions Everton and 1962 champions Ipswich had repaid Busby's faith in him and though he wouldn't be brilliant in every game, the fans believed that he had arrived.

The Reds' next game, at St Andrews saw them held 1-1

before they returned to Old Trafford with a resounding 3-0 home win over Blackpool during which Bobby Charlton bagged a brace and Denis weighed in with a goal.

Law missed the following two games, one of which saw the debut of George Best against West Bromwich Albion at Old Trafford in front of a 51,000 crowd. It was a game everyone was looking forward to: United the League leaders, against a classy West Brom side in second place. Still just 17, Best came in for the injured Moir. He hadn't originally been selected to play but just before the game Busby sent for George. "You're playing," he told the youngster who showed few signs of nerves or fear. The young Irishman had a quiet first half but in the second he switched wings with Bobby Charlton and came into his own, while David Sadler scored the only goal of the game. Yet disappointment followed as the Reds lost the return fixture with Blackpool 1-0, before Denis' return against Arsenal at Highbury.

Fans flocked to the Arsenal Stadium by car, tube, bus, and on foot to see soccer royalty when United played Arsenal - they even stopped the traffic for Manchester United and Denis Law. And what a bloodcurdler of a game they saw. Butterflies swarmed in the stomach and hearts pounded like pumps. If not great football, this was great theatre. One moment almost poetic in its delicate pattern of passes; the next exploding into violence with all the finality of a bayonet thrust. Right from the third minute when Laurie Brown forced Harry Gregg to make a daring one-handed save, the electric entertainment was on. Denis made a goal for David Herd to score against his former club. Bobby Charlton almost broke the crossbar with one of his cannonball shots. Setters gave away a penalty which George Eastham converted. Denis fizzed and popped and exploded all over the field and had his name taken by the referee for fouling Eastham. Nine minutes from time Denis' friend Joe Baker scored the winner for the Gunners. United made three classic attempts to save a game they did not deserve to lose through Setters, Charlton and Law but it was not to be as they left Highbury empty-handed.

On 25th September 1963 the Reds travelled to Rotterdam for the first leg of the European Cup Winners' Cup to play Dutch Cup winners, Willem II of Tilburg who were lying seventh in the Dutch Second Division. In the end United gained a creditable 1-1 draw. Denis had been suffering with a knee injury but was passed fit to play as David Herd scored for the Reds. However after this game Law missed a further three matches because of the same injury. He returned to first team duty on 15th October for the second leg of the tie and helped United to a 6-1 win at Old Trafford (before a moderate 42,672 crowd) with a brilliant hat-trick. Although the first leg of the tie was mediocre, the return saw the Reds hit top form. Denis was at his elusive and arrogant best. The Dutch team played much too slowly and besides Denis having a great game, two other players could feel proud of their performances: youngster Phil Chisnall, who went to school less than 200 yards from Old Trafford, and David Sadler.

Someone once said that some men were born great while others had greatness thrust upon them. "Whoever said that was definitely not involved in football," said Denis. "In football you have to be born great. You don't become a 'great' by being regimented into a set pattern, making your play a replica of the other players in our team. You need the flair to do something that little bit differently, that little bit more excitingly, indeed, that little bit better." Denis said the player he admired most of all was the great Real Madrid centre-forward Alfredo Di Stefano. He said he did not have the pleasure of seeing Sir Stanley Matthews at his peak; nor had he played against many of the South American maestros, notably Pele. "If either of those two is, or has been, better than Alfredo Di Stefano I find it hard to believe. Alfredo is the most regal player I have ever seen. He looks like a king when he is playing. Nothing short of majestic in all he does." Denis said that Di Stefano had no need for coaching manuals because he was one-footed. But added that Di Stefano was better with one foot than most players were with two. He said that Alfredo was the complete footballer and he could play in any position, even full-back, "and he would star in that position!" said Denis. He spoke about how one minute Alfredo was helping out his defence and the next he would be up in the opposition's area shooting at goal. "When he runs from defence you can see another hallmark of his greatness, because he can still accelerate. The really great forward must be an Olympic-class sprinter over four or five yards." Over the years, Denis never tired of talking about the virtues of Alfredo Di Stefano but he was about to find out what it was like to actually play alongside the great man.

*

The 23rd October 1963 is a date that Denis will never likely forget. He was thrilled and honoured to be selected for an important and prestigious game - The Rest of the World versus England at Wembley Stadium. It was billed as the 'Match of the Century' and was organised to mark the 100th anniversary of the formation of the Football Association. On hand to witness this historic football showpiece were 100,000 spectators, who paid £90,000 in gate receipts, every penny of it handed over gladly. And though it often happens that the quality of a game of this magnitude fails to match up to the importance of the occasion, there was no such disappointment on this momentous afternoon.

"England will do well to make a fight of it," was the general consensus of opinion by the supporters and newspaper reporters. It was a logical one, bearing in mind the scintillating array of talent parading for the Rest of the World team. Denis was chuffed to bits as well he might be because it was a momentous occasion for him. At last he would have the chance to judge himself against the world's greatest footballers. He couldn't wait. The added bonus for him was the chance to score against England. The great Brazilian, Pele, expressed a wish to play in the match but unfortunately he was injured and obviously in the circumstances unavailable but a glance at the names of his team-mates would have delighted Denis.

There was Djalma Santos (Brazil), Ferenc Puskas (Hungary), Raymond Kopa (France) and to Law's absolute delight the one and only Alfredo Di Stefano who was born and once played for Argentina but was now a naturalised Spaniard.

The full team read: Lev Yashin (Russia); Djalma Santos (Brazil), Karl Heinz Schnellinger (West Germany); Svatopluk Pluskal, Jan Popluhar, Josef Masopust (all Czechoslovakia); Raymond Kopa (France), Denis Law (Scotland), Alfredo Di Stefano (Spain), Eusebio (Portugal) and Francisco Gento (Spain). What a team! That was not all, because in the second half it was arranged that there would be several changes made in order that spectators could enjoy as many world class players as possible, and so Soskic of Yugoslavia, Eyzaguirre of Chile, Jim Baxter of Scotland, Uwe Seeler of West Germany and Ferenc Puskas would play in the second-half. Names like these betokened opposition of the very highest order.

To all intents and purposes, this was nothing more than an exhibition match, although it must be stressed that the England manager, Alf Ramsey, and his England players desperately wanted to win this prestigious game and consequently took it a lot more seriously. However, Denis had the same commitment as always and he thrived in the company of these wonderful and brilliant world-class players. Prince Philip and the Duke of Gloucester were the guests of honour but, like the huge crowd, they had come to admire the skill and subtlety of players that they might never have the chance to see again. They were not disappointed. The game had hardly started before it became clear that England were up for it. The referee, Mr R H Davidson of Scotland, blew his whistle to start the game and twice in the opening minutes Yashin, Russia's ace goalkeeper, had to be at his brilliant best to prevent his team falling behind. Each time the threat came from the dynamic feet of Jimmy Greaves.

Before half time, Yashin was called on to make more world-class saves, this time Bobby Smith, the burly England and Tottenham centre-forward, was the danger man. The match was scoreless at the interval. The Rest of the World side had started the game playing at a leisurely pace, letting the ball do the work. They stroked it around on that lovely lush, green turf. They did some wonderful, magical juggling with the ball, displaying their immaculate control of the ball and performing their neat little flicks and volleys - this really was football played with a smile. They were at Wembley to put on a show, and they did it, without neglecting to defend their reputations. Denis had been quite lively and presented Di Stefano with an open goal that the great man missed.

Indeed Denis was in his element, he looked as good as any of his team-mates and he gained immense pleasure from his performance. He had proved, if ever he had to, that as far as talent was concerned he was most certainly on the same level as these other world-class players. Not only that but playing alongside them rubbed off on him and it would be seen in the future. He was never known as a shrinking violet, he was always cocky and confident on the football field and this game gave him even more confidence and belief in his own ability.

In the second half the Rest of the World team, now with the great Puskas in their forward line, found a new resolve. With their prestige at stake they had found commitment yet it was England who took the lead through Terry Paine, their right-winger. Fifteen minutes later Denis struck as Di Stefano and Puskas combined in a move with the flaxen-haired Law that was reminiscent of Real Madrid's best days - Denis taking an immaculately judged pass from Puskas to equalise. His joy at scoring was incredible to watch. One could be forgiven for thinking he had scored the winning goal in the World Cup final itself. His joy turned to misery when, with just three minutes remaining, the mercurial Jimmy Greaves scored to give England a deserved 2-1 victory. However, it had been a fascinating game of football and a game Denis would remember with fondness. If there is as entertaining a match in 2063, when the FA celebrate their second centenary, they will do well.

In early November, three days before United's match against Tottenham, Denis played for Scotland at Hampden Park against Norway. Because of dense fog on the night, the match had to be postponed at enormous inconvenience for 24 hours.

This was Scotland's chance for revenge following the defeat in Bergen that summer. Denis made this a personal vendetta, scoring four times in Scotland's 6-1 victory, while giving an impressive display of skill and marksmanship. His pal Dave Mackay scored the other two. Yet despite the one-sided scoreline, this was far from an impressive victory by the Scots and the press were unanimous in their view that it might have been better if some other Scottish players had left the field earlier with their reputations intact. The Norwegians, all amateurs getting leave from their jobs, could not live with the Scots for stamina and speed but they scored first on eight minutes through Kristoffersen. The Scottish defence found themselves under extreme pressure with only Ian Ure outstanding but with Law, Scotland had the decisive factor. The Norwegians were complete novices within ten yards of goal, an area in which the fair-haired destroyer was at his most ferocious.

Many in the 35,000 crowd thought that two of Law's goals were offside but judging Denis' true position as the ball was played was often too hard for a middle-aged official 30 yards from play. Many errors were made as Law moved with such sudden and stunning pace that it was easy to think he had been offside when in reality he was no such thing. Denis and the late John White were at the hub of everything that was positive about Scotland's performance. For his third goal Denis dummied the Norwegian goalkeeper and rounded him to put the ball into the net. Alan Gilzean, the former Dundee and Tottenham striker, made his international debut in this game and recalled: "I was selected at centre-forward instead of my usual spot at inside-left but it was the wearer of the number 10 shirt who emerged as the hero of the game. A certain Denis Law who scored four of our goals. What a player!" said Gilzean. After the game Denis had to travel back to Manchester on the overnight sleeper in readiness for the big game against Spurs - many reporters claimed that he would suffer from fatigue.

On 9th November United were at home to Tottenham before 57,413 spectators with a new face in attack. Graham

Moore was a blond-haired, 22-year-old Welsh International centre-forward bought from Chelsea. In December 1961 he had joined Tommy Docherty's side from Cardiff City for £35,000. Although he stood slightly over 6ft and tipped the scales at a solid 13st 2lbs, the ideal build for a goal-scoring, swashbuckling centre-forward, Moore preferred to play as a deep-lying centre-forward. When Matt Busby brought him in for this game he told him that he wanted him to play as a midfield linkman in order to release Law and satisfy the obvious need for more goals at Old Trafford. Graham was the club's first Welsh International since Colin Webster had departed for Swansea five years before. With a friendly smile and a softly spoken Welsh lilt, Moore was a rugby lover and avid cinema goer. Graham had met his wife Rita at his local swimming baths in their home town of Bargoed and the couple had a 17-month old daughter, Deborah.

In a whirlwind transfer, Moore met his team mates on the Friday and went straight into the first team. And what a debut he had! The match against Tottenham rated as the Reds' most important of the season so far, for Spurs were one of the greatest teams in Europe and certainly among the favourites for the League title. Without a win in three games, Phil Chisnall and Ian Moir were dropped as Albert Quixall went on the right wing with Moore taking his place at inside-right.

Yet it was Denis the irrepressible who gave Spurs a roasting that put significant doubts on their ability to challenge for honours. Law created mayhem in the Tottenham rearguard with a scintillating performance and scored another hat-trick to take his tally to seven goals in three days! New signing Moore gave exquisite service to Herd and Law and his vision was excellent - he looked a world-class player on this performance. United won 4-1 and the comparison the press made about the two main marksmen, Law and Tottenham's Jimmy Greaves, was won unanimously by the Lawman! Greaves never even got the satisfaction of adding his name to the solitary Spurs goal as Harry Gregg was later credited with an own goal. In the 40th minute Denis collected the ball on the halfway line and set off on a brilliant solo run - he hit a rocket of a shot that Bill Brown, the Spurs goalkeeper, could only parry and Denis headed into the net. The crowd were still cheering as another great Law sprint down the middle saw him set up David Herd for goal number two. Later, Dave Mackay passed back to Brown and like a whippet Denis intercepted the pass and flashed it into the net. Three minutes later, from a similar move, he made it 4-1. This was a really majestic performance from Denis; it was almost mystic. He seemed to move faster than the eye could see - and in a flash... it was a goal. He helped the whole team play well. In this mood he looked the most electrifying and exciting goalscorer in the world - United fans believed he was heading for immortality and, indeed, was already on the doorstep.

In the United dressing room after the match the superlatives didn't end... "I know I've said it many times before but he's the greatest footballer in the world - and that includes Pele and Puskas," said Jimmy Murphy. The subject was of course Law who had just completed a near single-handed demolition of one of Europe's best teams.

The press found it hard to disagree with Murphy's assessment. "I've seen some dazzling displays from Law," wrote David Jack, "but I cannot remember any game where he so terrorised a defence, or looked so much like a man playing with boys." Denis wouldn't confirm this was his finest display, instead he was more concerned at telling reporters about how well Graham Moore had played: "I thought Graham was fabulous. What a debut!" said Denis. The papers were in agreement that there wasn't a single weakness in the whole Manchester United team but they singled out the man who not only hit a hat-trick but had two other goals disallowed on tight offside decisions. He emerged head and shoulders above everyone - on this form he was stolen from Torino for £115,000!

Denis had been called a great player but then in his time he had been called quite a few other things such as talented, temperamental, niggly, nonchalant, hot-headed, exhibitionistic, cocky and confident. He had been simultaneously described as the most dangerous player in Britain and the most overrated. For example in the same week that he was selected for the World team, his critics recommended he be dropped by Manchester United.

"Take a public opinion poll about his claim to greatness and you won't get a single 'Don't know'. You would certainly get a firm 'Yes' from me," wrote Frank McGhee, who added: "But lately I have wondered if Denis Law, the man who dares to be different in an age of anonymous footballers, is getting a fair deal from referees, fans and critics. His reaction, as it is to almost everything off the field - is a big grin."

"'Referees picking on me?' said a smiling Law, 'Never. Referees have got to be unbiased and I think they are. Maybe they make mistakes sometimes but don't we all?' Unfair fans? 'I haven't noticed anything, but they are entitled to give you some stick if they feel like it. They've paid to get in.' When he scores a goal he stands transfixed, one arm raised as if in a salute to himself. It doesn't exactly endear him to friends and enemies. 'That's what this game is all about,' says Denis, 'you train all week to do that one thing really, put the ball in someone's goal. You've got to give people something to look at or laugh at; a bit of the old fanny.' Is his style unnecessarily hard? 'If someone kicks me I might have a go back at him. I'm only human. You've got to go in meaning to get the ball. Things happen quickly in this game and some things look worse than they are.' However it is when you ask Denis Law whether he feels he ought to change some of his ways that you get the most revealing reaction. An amazed stare; the thought has not occurred to him because he can't, won't and doesn't want to change."

*

How fickle is football adulation? After the Spurs demolition the Reds went to Villa Park and Denis, the hat-trick hero of United's sensational 4-1 victory, was ordered off in the 33rd minute. He was involved in an incident with Villa's England

Under 23 wing-half Alan Deakin. In the 1960s it was a rare occasion for a referee to send a player off. Villa had their best gate of the season for this clash with the Reds; 40,000 plus had turned out to see United and their star Law in particular and in a great opening spell Villa shocked the championship challengers with two goals in the first 17 minutes. Hateley put them into the lead after just 35 seconds before in the 17th minute, Deakin scored a second. Later, Denis and the Villa midfielder clashed several times and it was clear that Deakin had been instructed to mark Law tightly as they went at each other hammer and tongs. In the 33rd minute there was a tremendous fracas in the Reds penalty area in which Gregg and the Villa centre-forward Hateley were involved. With the crowd shouting and booing loudly, Deakin went down as if poleaxed, holding his face after a clash with Law in midfield. Villa Park erupted and the ground was in complete uproar as referee Jim Carr sprinted towards Law and pulled out his notebook as players from both sides rushed toward the scene, squaring up to each other. Even Harry Gregg dashed upfield to join in the argument. While the Villa trainer was treating Deakin, chants of 'Off, Off, Off, Off' rang around the ground, Denis eventually emerged from the melée having received his marching orders. As he walked towards the dressing room grim-faced, the Villa fans shouted disparaging remarks at Denis and pelted him with orange peel, apple cores and bits of paper, until he disappeared up the tunnel. After the interval, Hateley scored with a diving header and Burrows completed the scoring in a 4-0 rout.

Later, Denis refused to comment. He could have mentioned the known fact that some opposition players were told to provoke him during the game, but he refused to say anything. Having already been booked three times that season Law now faced suspension: bookings in the Charity Shield game against Everton, a week later against Sheffield Wednesday and at Arsenal had conspired to seal his fate. After the game Denis was booked again, this time on a flight to Scotland for a midweek international. Matt Busby had given Denis permission to fly from the Midlands and spend the weekend in Aberdeen with his girlfriend before meeting up with his Scottish team-mates.

By coincidence, on the coach taking the team to Villa Park, Denis had been busy making plans for a speedy exit from the ground to catch his flight as his team-mates laughingly teased him by betting that he wouldn't make the airport in time. "Perhaps I'll get sent off," Law had said to his team-mates. Had he been tempting fate? The next day's headlines predictably made much of his misfortune, '*Law Sent Off at Villa Park*', '*Denis Law Sent Off, Marching Orders in the 33rd Minute*'.

Any aspirations toward the championship were recediing quickly as United proceeded to lose their next home game against Liverpool 1-0. Seconds before half time the game had flared into a frenzy of excitement when goalkeeper Harry Gregg was taken off with a fractured right collar-bone and Maurice Setters was knocked out trying to clear a corner from Liverpool left-winger Peter Thompson. As Gregg walked off with his arm held across his body, David Herd took over in goal. The Reds tried hard and were on level terms until big Ron Yeats headed the only goal late in the game. Denis was more than a little subdued, understandably given the circumstances, but most agreed that United were terribly unlucky not to have had at least a share of the points.

The following match saw United visit Bramall Lane, Sheffield. United needed a boost - the injury to the brave-hearted Gregg had floored the entire team. David Gaskell had to take the plaster cast from his injured thumb in order to help the club in a desperate situation. When the chips were down Denis could be counted on - although he had a disciplinary hearing hanging over him he put all these concerns to one side and got on with helping United earn two valuable points. It was Denis and Bobby Charlton who pulverised the Sheffield team. After 19 minutes Law and Charlton linked up beautifully for Denis to race through like a flash of lightning and shoot past the Blades' keeper Thompson. Bobby Charlton also had a hand in the second goal, although the final pass was delivered by Graham Moore for Denis to convert. This was a day when spectators could watch in admiration as Denis, playing like a perfect gentleman, inspired attacks like a master tactician and fell back unsparingly when his defence needed him. In this mood he must be classed as one of the greatest inside-forwards of all time. David Gaskell, having his first game of the new season, played confidently in a fine victory for United. *'Fine Law Double Turns Tables'*, *' 2-Goal Denis Lays Down The Law'*, *'Law At His Greatest'*, *'Law Double Sinks Blades'* and *'Law Strikes As Defence Slips Up'*.

*

Courage is an immeasurable quality and, as we all know, it reveals itself in many ways from the stark heroism of the battlefield to the mere ringing of the dentist's bell that tells you it's your turn. Every one of us has to show courage and fortitude sometime or other in life. It went without saying that Denis Law had it in abundance. However, Denis marvelled at the courage of his club-mate, Harry Gregg. The Northern Ireland goalkeeper had been in the Munich air crash. As the wreckage of the plane lay on the snow-covered airfield and with shouts to evacuate the area in his ears Gregg had gone back into the wreckage to rescue a baby girl before continually re-visiting the plane to help other injured people.

In 1962 Harry's attractive young wife Mavis, the mother of their two baby girls Karen and Linda, became incurably ill and sadly died a short time later. Harry appeared to his club-mates to be the same happy-go-lucky man they'd always known yet he was desperate - grieving and wondering what the future now held in store for him. Playing for United against Tottenham a couple of seasons before his right shoulder had popped out of its joint. He endured more dislocations, eight in total. Each brought extra agony and frustration for the hero of Munich. On away trips Denis often roomed with Harry and they laughed and joked a great deal. Denis was full of admiration for Harry's attitude toward his career-threatening injuries and more so for the plight and distress of his wife's illness.

On 23rd November 1963, with the world still in shock following the assassination of President Kennedy, Gregg was playing against Liverpool at Old Trafford, when he broke his right collar-bone just before half time and had to be helped from the field. In the second half, fans were staggered by his show of courage as he returned to the field and played on the right wing.

On the 3rd December the Reds played the European Cup Winners' Cup holders Tottenham Hotspur at White Hart Lane in the first leg of their second round European Cup Winners' Cup tie. David Gaskell kept his place in goal - he had to because 20-year-old Ronnie Briggs and 15-year-old Jimmy Rimmer were the only other fit goalkeepers on the books. There had been talk that Matt Busby would buy Eddie Hopkinson, the former England keeper who was still doing a good job for Bolton Wanderers, while Stockport County's Graham Beighton had also been mentioned, along with Everton's Gordon West, Hartlepool's Norman Oakley and Jimmy O'Neill of Stoke.

Meanwhile at White Hart Lane, before 57,447 spectators, United lost 2-0 with Spurs skipper Dave Mackay and Dyson on the scoresheet. United would have it all to do in the return leg at Old Trafford. On this display Tottenham looked the more likely victors - as mentioned Spurs were a wonderful team in those days, having won the double in 1961 by playing exciting, attractive football and had followed it a year later by winning the FA Cup and in 1963 became the first British team to win a European trophy by winning the Cup Winners' Cup, a trophy they now intended to defend.

Three days later Matt Busby called Denis into his office at Old Trafford. Busby informed Denis that notification had been received from the FA regarding his punishment for the sending off at Villa Park and, after a 15-minute chat, Law emerged looking rather like an errant schoolboy who had endured a fearful wigging from his headmaster. His face was flushed, his lips pursed, his hands behind his back. He nodded to people but avoided any questions, going straight into the physiotherapy room for treatment from the genial, ever-smiling Ted Dalton on his pulled muscle. Five minutes later a solemn-faced, stern-looking Matt Busby appeared in front of reporters and said simply: "Denis Law has been suspended for 28 days from Monday. Neither the club nor the player have anything further to say."

The day that the FA Disciplinary Committee announced Law's suspension was tinged with irony at Old Trafford. The post that brought news of the sentence also brought two Christmas cards, one for the club and one for Denis, which showed a picture of Law in his Torino colours. The cards came from Gigi Peronace, the Italian agent who negotiated Law's big money moves to and from Italy. There was more irony an hour after the bad news arrived when Denis passed a fitness test for the game against Stoke. He had suffered an injury in the midweek loss at Tottenham and it was announced that Denis would play his last game of 1963 for Manchester United against Stoke City at Old Trafford on Saturday the 7th of December.

Denis was staggered at the harshness of his 28-day ban by the FA. He had expected to be punished but not this severely. It had never been known before for a player to receive such a long suspension. Perhaps the FA had decided to make an example of the high-profile Law. In those days a player under suspension lost his wages and was not allowed anywhere near his club and even by sixties standards this seemed an antiquated rule. Nevertheless rules were rules. After the Stoke game the next time Denis could turn out for United was in the new year. By then United might be out of the European Cup Winners' Cup and too far behind in the League championship race. There was also a grave risk that United might make an early exit from their defence of the FA Cup. His suspension was to begin on Monday 9th December.

Many journalists, after the shock reaction to his ban, calculated Denis' personal losses (including wages and bonuses) at £481. Could you imagine one of today's stars going for a month without wages? There would surely be a revolt! Nevertheless in 1963 this kind of treatment of professionals was commonplace - even if in this case the sentence handed down was a little extreme. Meanwhile the fans pondered the cost to the club. United appeared to be paying an extremely high price for one rash moment. The loss of Law's match-winning skills for a total of nine hours of competitive football at one of the most crucial stages of the season led to United falling out of contention in the league.

Denis would not only miss the second leg of the European Cup Winners' Cup, but he would also miss vital championship games against Sheffield Wednesday, Everton and Burnley twice. He would also miss the FA Cup third round tie. His club-mates were stunned by the severity of the ban. "We all think it's savage," said Bill Foulkes, "they seem to be getting at the club. Of course the boys will have a whip-round for Denis." David Herd said: "It's ridiculous. What I'm thinking is unprintable." Club captain Noel Cantwell added: "I think the suspension seems a bit severe, but we have got to accept it." Meanwhile Jimmy Murphy was seething: "The Law sentence is one of the stiffest handed out by the FA for years." Jimmy went on to say that those people who accuse Denis of being a hard player should see his legs after a match to appreciate the punishment he takes from unscrupulous defenders. "One of the longest post-war suspensions was imposed on the present Doncaster Rovers manager Oscar Hold, who was given six weeks after being sent off when playing for Norwich in 1947," said an irate Murphy. The only bright note amid the gloom was that the FA revealed that they would not be taking any action against David Herd after his sending-off in the European Cup Winners' Cup first-round tie against Willem II in September.

With Law gone many believed that Bobby Charlton must now take on Denis's mantle as match-winner. The enigmatic, almost shy Charlton was going to have to be Matt Busby's major hope of winning a prize for the Reds that season. "With Denis Law suspended for 28 days Busby must rely on his other world-class forward to break some of England's most powerful defences," wrote Derek Hodgson. Other observers reckoned that Bobby had allowed himself to be overshadowed by the firecracker personality of Law. This of course was ridiculous,

Bobby was feeling his way back to form after a hernia operation in the days before a fast-track healing process. Many reporters were advising the United manager to move Bobby into an inside-forward position and utilise his vast repertoire of skills, pace, stamina and shooting power.

Although Denis did not comment on his 28-day suspension, it came as a huge blow to him. Indeed Denis told some of his team-mates that he now intended to 'put his feet up and rest for a time' but having expected no more than a 21-day suspension and really expecting a 14-day absence, to receive nearly a 4 week ban shook him rigid. Denis needed to hit back. Not verbally, because he remained tactfully silent to newspapers and everyone outside Old Trafford but where better to do it than in front of the Old Trafford faithful against Stoke City before his suspension kicked in. And what a treat awaited those lucky enough to have been present. There were almost 53,000 spectators inside Old Trafford as the Reds ran out of the tunnel and the cheers echoed around Trafford Park. Stoke City manager Tony Waddington had told the newspapers that his team had come to Old Trafford to win, not draw and certainly not to lose. "Stanley Matthews will be at outside-right for us," said the Stoke manager, adding, "we are not fielding the sort of team that could play defensively. We shall attack and will be playing for a victory." The United fans were in a festive mood for this game was akin to a valedictory Sinatra appearance.

And what an occasion it proved to be as Denis bade farewell to football for a month by scoring four times! In the fourth minute it was Law's persistence that caused absolute panic in the Stoke defence as Herd blasted in an unstoppable shot from close range. Five minutes later the huge crowd saw the true magnificence of this man Law. Bobby Charlton dispossessed Stoke's right-half George Kinnell and stroked the ball to the lurking Law. He seemed to lose control of the ball but within a split second he regained it and from 18 yards let fly with a terrific right-footed shot that fairly whistled past Lawrie Leslie, the Stoke goalkeeper and the crowd erupted into sustained applause that rocked Old Trafford to its foundations. Just before half time, with United playing brilliantly, Maurice Setters was injured. After treatment he was a passenger on the right wing because substitutes were not allowed. The second half saw Stoke come more into the game. The injury to Setters had upset United's rhythm and John Ritchie reduced the arrears for them. It was then that the dynamic Law took a hand, completing his hat-trick with two goals in the space of two action-packed minutes. In the 76th he streaked into the penalty area, nodded down a ball from Crerand and smashed it past Leslie almost in one movement. The crowd had scarcely got their breath back and recovered from that breathtaking goal before Denis scored again from a David Herd pass - gliding the ball into the net. Peter Dobing pulled back another for Stoke but with less than a minute to go Bobby Charlton, who'd had a wonderful game, out-stripped the Stoke defence in a breathtaking run and played the ball to Denis who materialised from nowhere to nonchalantly tap the ball into the net. A few seconds later the final whistle brought the game to its conclusion and with the players and crowd applauding him, Denis retired for his enforced midwinter break. He had nothing to say of course. He had said it all...out on the field.

United's former captain, Dennis Viollet, was the first to shake Law's hand. Viollet, who still holds United's goalscoring record of 32 League goals in a season, was full of praise for his successor: "What a brilliant way to say goodbye to football for a month," said a smiling Viollet, "he is a world-class player and showed it today. I believe that Denis Law, in this merciless four goal mood, would have savaged any team." Derek Wallis, a *Daily Mirror* journalist commented: "Since his suspension, Denis Law has said nothing of any significance publicly. The attempt to keep himself to himself had to break down some time. When it happened it was more eloquent than all the words in his vocabulary. If this is the new Denis Law, the ruthless, but even-tempered footballer, then the end of his suspension cannot come quickly enough."

Three days after Denis' breathtaking four-goal farewell,

United faced Tottenham at Old Trafford in the second leg of the European Cup Winners' Cup with a two-goal deficit to overcome. Before the game Frank McGhee interviewed Bobby Charlton who in McGhee's opinion now held the key to the Cup clash. McGhee said that a study of United's statistics provided pessimistic proof that this season Bobby and every other forward on the club's books had leant far too heavily on Denis. "In League games Law has hit 17 - only six below the total achieved by seven other attackers," he wrote, "of this Charlton's share is a meagre four. Yet to me, Charlton is the only United forward available who has the basic flair, magic and brilliance to burst through or batter down Spurs' barricade."

He went on to say that Bobby was quieter, steadier and less flamboyant off the field and in contrast to Denis couldn't turn it on to order. Yet Charlton understood his responsibilities saying: "Everybody in our team, not just me, feels that we have got to pull out something extra and special to make up for Denis. I certainly feel it myself. It is a big handicap being without him. But not too big." Mr McGhee then put it to Bobby that it was up to him primarily to go out against Tottenham in an 'I'll show 'em' mood, to prove that Law alone didn't make the team. Bobby refused to go along with that theory. "The idea that the team depend on Denis has been built up, understandably, by you sportswriters. But I don't want to give the idea that any of the lads resents this. Why should we? He is doing it for us, not for himself! Denis deserves all the credit that he gets but I'll just say that the team definitely don't think that without him we are finished." Mr McGhee ended by saying that he couldn't see United beating Spurs - unless "Charlton proves me wrong and proves his own right to be ranked as a match winner the equal of Law," he said.

The Reds' re-entry into competitive football at European level had rekindled mixed memories for their fans. The coming Cup Winners' Cup game against Spurs was United's 20th competitive match in Europe since that wonderful night in 1956 when the Busby Babes beat the Belgian champions

Anderlecht 2-0 in Belgium. So you can imagine the excitement from the Reds fans. Although the sight of Tottenham was a little more commonplace than some potential European opponents, they were nevertheless one of the most attractive and crowd-pulling teams of the era. Three times in post-war football they had scored 100 League goals or more; in 1962-63 they had scored 111 and seemed well on their way to repeating that feat this season. Their two strikers, Jimmy Greaves and big, burly Bobby Smith created havoc in penalty areas. Smith had already netted over 200 League and Cup goals while Greaves had also reached his double century following a prolific start to his career at Chelsea. Was it any wonder that United supporters were feeling concerned that their star finisher would be missing?

The great Tom Finney claimed that: "Manchester United are virtually out of the European Cup Winners' Cup. Their second-leg match with Spurs now seems a sad formality. The absence of Denis Law makes all the difference." Tom explained that Jimmy Greaves and Denis were both world-class players but that United would miss Denis much more than Tottenham would miss Greaves. "Under the present circumstances he is the more vital to his club's success and I'd have to give the honour to Law." He went on to say that both Greaves and Law were in a class of their own as goalscorers. Greaves, he said, had hit the headlines more often than Denis in the field of scoring goals, but this was because Greaves got greater opportunities. He mentioned that John White supplied him with opportunities, as did Dave Mackay, whereas Denis had to act as a link-man himself, going in search of the ball.

"United, kicking off two goals behind from the first leg, desperately needed the genius of Law to help them back on level terms. I believe with Law they would have won, without him I fear they have no chance." Yet remarkably United beat Tottenham and moved on to the quarter-final against Sporting Club Lisbon; Bobby scored two great and remarkable goals with David Herd also netting twice. Sadly, after a collision with United's Noel Cantwell, the brave-hearted Dave Mackay suffered a broken leg and was rushed to hospital. Denis and his club-mates visited Mackay in hospital.

Talking later about the game Denis re-iterated his admiration for his Scottish international colleague, Dave Mackay. Denis said that what made Mackay such a 'great' was his fanatical determination to win and, said Denis, this was what also made him the best captain he had personally played under. "He makes you want to win no matter how ferocious the battle on the field," said Denis, adding, "he is the only player I tremble to play against. I feared him that much that for a split second when he was hurt during the game I was glad." Don't get the wrong impression from this statement. Denis would never wish anyone to get hurt, certainly not as serious as Mackay's broken leg. What he meant was that if someone had to get hurt in the game between United and Spurs, he preferred it to have been Dave Mackay for the simple reason that he was always such a danger. "As soon as I realised he had broken his leg I felt ashamed for having such a thought. Football cannot afford to lose such a man."

Nobby Stiles, United's ebullient little utility man, was bitterly disappointed at being left out of the team to play Spurs. Nobby, the young stand-in for the stars, had played in the first leg at Tottenham and there was no disputing that he had, as always, done a good practical job against Spurs. But he wasn't selected for the return even though the Reds were without Law. Like any other self-respecting young man, Nobby had ambition. He wanted to play League football regularly and quite a few First Division clubs were poised to dash to Old Trafford if there was the slightest chance of Matt Busby letting him go. It was pointed out that in the last year or so Nobby had seen other United reserves meet with immediate success after leaving Old Trafford. Nobby Lawton, Alex Dawson, Frank Haydock and his brother-in-law Johnny Giles were all enjoying the prominence that went with playing for a League club, even though it may be in a lower division. Nobby had a heart-to-heart chat with Matt Busby. Bill Fryer, a wonderful sports journalist, spoke to Matt Busby about Stiles and the United manager told him that

Nobby had asked for a transfer. However, Busby said, he would have to wait for an answer until the New Year because there was no directors' meeting until then. Wolves and Leeds were in the hunt for young Stiles but Busby's prevarication was surely a sign that he intended to give him more appearances in the near future.

Peter Slingsby, a prominent journalist for the *Sunday Mirror* and contributor to the United's programme *United Review,* said that he expected Denis to break the goalscoring record for Scotland. "Denis seems likely to finish his second season at Old Trafford as their top marksman. At this stage of the season he has scored 24 goals from 21 League and Cup matches and is also within striking distance of the Scottish scoring record," wrote Mr Slingsby - the record was 24 goals in 38 games by Lawrie Reilly - "On current form, Denis should top that figure before too long. If he does, United would then have two players with an international scoring record to their credit" - Bobby Charlton had scored 31 goals in 48 games for England.

In the four League matches Denis missed through suspension United won two (3-1 against Sheffield Wenesday and 5-1 against Burnley at Old Trafford) and lost two (1-6 at Burnley and 0-4 at Everton). How damaging this run proved is open to discussion, but there was little doubt that a Law-less United struggled in this period.

The two Christmas games against Burnley provided dramatic proof of United's inconsistency without Law. They lost 6-1 at Turf Moor where Paddy Crerand was sent off, the fifth United player to receive his marching orders that season. The other four players to head for an early bath were David Herd, Albert Quixall, Noel Cantwell and Law. Yet remarkably United won the return fixture 5-1 at Old Trafford with George Best scoring his first League goal. Willie Anderson, another teenager, made his debut on the other wing.

Denis also missed the epic third round FA Cup tie at Southampton. It was a fascinating game that saw the Reds fall two goals behind only to pull it back and grab a late winner in the 85th minute. The scorers were Moore, Herd and Crerand.

Law's first United line-up, August 1962
Back row, l-r: Maurice Setters, Jimmy Nicholson, David Gaskell,
Shay Brennan, Mark Pearson, Noel Cantwell.
Middle row: manager Matt Busby, Bill Foulkes, Sammy McMillan,
Tony Dunne, Nobby Stiles, Nobby Lawton, trainer Jack Crompton
Front row: Johnny Giles, Albert Quixall, David Herd,
Denis Law, Bobby Charlton

Well Done, Son
Denis' return to Britain was a welcome sight for his family.
Yet Mr and Mrs Law watched their son play just once, on his
full Scottish debut in 1958. But following a car crash on
their return from Cardiff, they vowed never to watch him again.

Law and Marriage

In December 1962 Denis married Diana Thomson much to the surprise of his parents. Denis claimed he was never 'married to football' and remained sanguine about reports that his parents had been kept in the dark. They are pictured here on their wedding day and with Di, first son Gary and newborn Andrew.

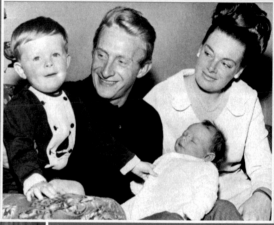

Despite the money, glamour and fame of football stardom Denis clearly preferred the quiet life of his family. His marriage to Di survived the usual tabloid tales while his family continued to grow until, in his own words, he 'declared at five'.
(Left) Di and Denis celebrate Christmas 1964 in typically high-spirited fashion.

A Taste of Glory - 1963 FA Cup Final
(Above) Law beats Banks for the second time in the 1963 FA Cup Final
- unfortunately Frank McLintock (out of picture) was on the goal line to
clear the ball.

*In the second half Law continued to keep Banks busy, this time **(below)***
he slumps to the Wembley turf in frustration following a brilliant header
that beat the England legend but hit the bar. Nevertheless Denis and
United were triumphant, beating Leicester City 3-1.

Best in the World

In October 1963 Denis was honoured by selection for the Rest of the World XI to play England at Wembley in a game to commemorate the centenary of the FA. Law gave more than a good account of himself in a stellar team that lined-up as follows: (back row, l-r) Ferenc Puskas, Djalmar Santos, Svatopluk Pluskal, Lev Yashin, Jan Popluhar, Karl-Heinz Schnellinger, Milutin Soskic, Josef Masopust, Eyzaguire, Jim Baxter (front row, l-r) Raymond Kopa, Denis, Alfredo di Stefano, Eusebio, Francisco Gento.

In the game itself, Denis scored following an astute pass from Puskas yet England ran out 2-1 winners. Later (above) he fired over from a good position as England's defenders appealed for offside in vain.

Two Early Baths
Denis landed himself in hot water on more than
one occasion in his heyday.
Inset: *Playing Aston Villa in November 1963 he*
was dismissed following a fracas
with Alan Deakin at Villa Park.
Main pic: *He makes an early exit following a*
clash with Alan Ball at Bloomfield Road,
Blackpool exactly a year later.

Law admitted his part in the first incident but
denied referee Peter Rhodes' claim that he had
sworn at the official in the second. Nevertheless both
dismissals cost Denis 28-day suspensions during
which he was denied his wages.

European Law

Denis made his European debut in 1963. Yet United's first European season since the Munich Air Disaster ended in calamity when they travelled to Porto holding a 4-1 advantage only to crash to a 5-0 defeat. (Above) Denis slots home the first of his first-leg hat-trick on 26th February 1964.

The Greatest!

Denis rounds Aston Villa goalkeeper Geoff Sidebottom to complete his hat-trick. Law took his personal tally to four on the day as United hit seven without reply against a shaken Villa outfit on Saturday October 24th 1964.

**Back with a Bang!
United v. Nott'm Forest
Saturday, January 16th
1965**
Denis returned following
a 28-day suspension
incurred after his
dismissal against
Blackpool in mid-
November. Typically
Denis scored within
minutes of his comeback,
celebrating here with a
joyous salute to United's
travelling army.

Great Scot!
Denis loved playing for Scotland and there's little doubt that this goal from
the 1965 fixture against England was among his personal favourites:
a scorching 30-yarder that beat Gordon Banks. Denis was so far away
from goal he's out of picture in the main shot but celebrates with United
colleague Pat Crerand (inset). Denis and colleagues went on to draw 2-2.

Grudge Match - United v Leeds - FA Cup Semi-Final - March 27th 1965
The hairy tale of Jack Charlton's little black book, in which he kept the
names of opponents he intended to 'sort out', lit up the sixties.
Many believed Denis was the first name on Jack's list but the future Eire
manager claimed he was 'a great pal of mine'. Nevertheless the pair seemed
to relish their regular confrontations - this one eventually went Jack's way -
Leeds winning the replay 1-0.

It was around this time that Bobby Charlton was brought to inside-forward from his left-wing position. Bobby hated being stuck out on the wing, although he had stayed there for almost three-and-a-half years because the club lacked a quality left-winger. This was when Bobby showed his true loyalty to United's cause. Of course, he played so well there that he was capped several times by England at outside-left and Denis always believed that it was as a left-winger that Bobby was at his very best. But Bobby's move infield had been facilitated by the arrival of a new talent who was to make the number eleven jersey his own - George Best.

Thus it was with some relief that Matt Busby announced Denis' return to United's line-up for the visit of Birmingham City on Saturday 11th January 1964. The *Daily Mirror's* Frank McGhee asked Denis what it had been like sitting out the past 28 days. "Murder, absolutely murder," came Law's reply. "I'm not really nervous though. Maybe a wee bit but no more than I am say, at the start of a new season." The journalist then asked Denis if he felt there was an increased danger that opponents would deliberately set out to test his temper, rough him up, destroy his concentration and spark the sort of electrically angry reaction that had resulted in his suspension? Denis laughed: "This has always happened to me. I don't expect things to be any different. I am a professional and I have to remember that." Denis then told him that his New Year's resolution was to learn to count to ten: "I haven't tried this out yet but I hope I can hold my temper - I think I can."

Mr McGhee said he wondered if Denis had learned any other lessons in the five weeks he had been out of football. Five weeks watching, waiting, training and thinking. "I've learned this," Denis told him, "I'll never make a manager. I can't stand watching my own team. I tried it against Spurs and had to leave. I tried it again against Southampton and only lasted the first half. It's hard to describe, I'm not exactly nervous. It's just that I can't just sit there and not be involved in the game." Surely, said Mr McGhee, you've been out of action for spells before your suspension? "Only with injuries and that's not the same because then you know there is nothing you can do anyway. This other business has been terrible but I'll be practising my counting."

The following day, as he ran out onto the pitch at Old Trafford, there were dozens of press photographers snapping at his entrance and almost 45,000 spectators roaring a welcome back. Despite Denis working tremendously hard and being unlucky not to score even Law couldn't save United going down 2-1 to a determined Birmingham outfit.

There were some who claimed that Denis would be a bit stale on his return, but he wasn't. He was the same old Denis, with the same skill and the same darting speed in practice games. He hadn't done much training during his month away from action and many expected him to carry a few extra pounds after spending Christmas and Hogmanay back home in Aberdeen. Mind you, as Noel Cantwell said: "It was perhaps a good thing Denis didn't have to put in any extra lapwork or exercises, because the Law Man simply hates training. That is, the old routine stuff. He considers it a bit useless." Denis liked juggling the ball, shooting and dribbling just as long as he was training with a ball. Denis believed that because of his slight build, he did not need the power training that his former mentor Bill Shankly and other United players advocated. Although it would be wrong to get the impression that he did not like training, he did believe in fitness yet depended more on his reflexes and speed off the mark that he naturally worked into his training. Even during the summer months, if not touring with club or country, he would go home to Aberdeen and maintain his condition. He would usually meet his old Huddersfield mate Gordon Low who had since joined Bristol City and together they would train either on the beach or at the local gym. During this period Denis also acquired a liking for golf.

On the Saturday following Law's return the Reds were away to West Bromwich Albion at the Hawthorns. It was a match that many sceptics believed United would be fortunate to emerge from with a point. Denis, however, was like an eager beaver after his break and wanted to get back on the scoresheet while Maurice Setters was also anxious to get a result against his old club-mates. Before the game Maurice wandered into the West Brom dressing-room showing off his new, expensive, Continental-style football boots. He told his former colleagues that all the other United players had the same boots and claimed they were perfect for the tricky, frost-bound turf. Yet despite Setters' pschyological trick it was Albion who made all the headway from the start, and were it not for Foulkes, at the heart of United's defence, having a stormer against the dangerous West Brom centre-forward John Kaye, Albion could easily have been ahead. Instead on 20 minutes the Reds took the lead; Crerand pushed the ball to Herd on the right wing, his cross found Charlton whose missile-like shot flew into the net. Then five minutes before half time came a flurry of goals; first Simpson levelled with a rasping 35-yard drive that beat Gaskell before Denis delivered a beautiful ball for Best to blast into the West Brom net.

Charlton, now playing a deep-lying centre-forward role, was the architect of the Reds' resurgence. Afterwards he said: "I'm happy playing in the middle, there's never a dull moment and I can really get into the game at centre-forward." The whole United team provided a standard of entertainment one would have thought impossible in the conditions. United should have had two penalties. The second penalty incident emphasised how much Denis was trying to discipline himself. He was pushed quite forcibly off the ball just when he looked certain to score. It was the sort of moment that had made Denis explode in the past but, true to his New Year's Resolution he picked himself up and counted to ten. In any case he had the last laugh as United scored two late goals for a deserved 4-1 victory.

The fourth round of the FA Cup was the next game at Old Trafford. The Reds were drawn against Third Division Bristol Rovers but there proved to be no chance of glory for the underdog when a player like Denis Law has his eye fixed on another day out at Wembley in May. Denis; lurking, stalking, and menacing, rammed three brilliant goals past the brave Rovers with the arrogance and power of a player at the top of his game. This was a Law even his worst critics could not find fault with. There were no signs of the tantrums and temperament his critics had formerly used to beat him with. Gone was the fouling and he even light-heartedly played up to the crowd in spite of the Cup fever that gripped both sets of supporters. Noel Cantwell was injured and a passenger out on the wing after straining his back after 16 minutes yet Bobby and Denis, United's two blond bombshells, destroyed Bristol.

United took an 11th minute lead after Paddy Crerand had ripped in a tremendous 25-yard drive that Hall in the Bristol goal failed to collect. Denis turned poacher and banged the ball triumphantly past the goalkeeper. After half an hour Herd made it 2-0 and in the 62nd minute Denis made it three but the plaudits went to Bobby Charlton. He sprinted around two defenders, looked up and spotted Law's run - his perfectly flighted centre was meat and drink to the Scot who rose to nod home. Denis celebrated by swinging on the crossbar and completed his hat-trick in the 83rd minute after another run downfield that would have done credit to an Olympic sprinter. Herd got to the ball first only to see Bristol keeper Hall palm his effort to the far post. There was no need to guess which red-shirted player took off for the leaping header.

Denis' hat-trick was his third of the season that also included two four-goal outings already and, when a reporter pointed this out to him Denis, looking rather sheepish, said: "Och, we were terrible." He set himself and United, a high standard, but he seemed a bit hard on himself to be included in this criticism. He lurked as only he can to score his first and last goals while his second, with the aid of his world-class colleague, was a thing of sheer speed, artistry, economy, and efficiency. Bobby Charlton, describing Denis explained: "The word 'electric' sums up Denis Law because sparks certainly fly whenever he plays. He creates problems for defenders and if goalkeepers drop the ball, even six inches, he's in like greased lightning."

The following Saturday United faced Arsenal at Old

Trafford. During the kickabout before the game, Denis and his old pal Joe Baker managed a short chat and a laugh before Mr Holland of Barnsley blew his whistle to start the game. The Reds' attacking formation had spluttered at West Brom and in the cup against Bristol Rovers - there were complaints that young Graham Moore and the newly re-positioned Bobby Charlton were a little slow to supply Denis and former Gunner David Herd. Billy Wright, the former England captain and manager of Arsenal, claimed his team were really up for this match and intended completing a double over United. Thus the entertainment was of the highest standard. Denis captained the Reds in the absence of Noel Cantwell and like an old soldier at a tenderfoots' tea party, he set out to win with an adventurous flourish. After four minutes of shrill expectancy he threw in a thrill to behold: a devastating flick from Law laid on the opening goal of a splendid game as David Herd cut inside like a tailor's knife across broad green felt, collected the ball and crashed it past Jim Furnell in the Arsenal goal. Law had pounced and the 50,000 crowd bayed for more. Yet the Londoners made the Reds work hard and sure enough Arsenal equalised after 16 minutes through left-back McCullough. The crowd encouraged United forward again and it fell to Law to galvanise his team but he and Ian Ure, the Arsenal centre-half, were having a rare old tussle. It wasn't until the 77th minute that United finally broke through, Setters scoring with a power-packed header. With seven minutes of the game remaining Denis struck himself. All the confidence flowed back as he latched on to a long ball from Charlton and cheekily tucked it past Furnell - Arsenal's faint hopes evaporating with Law's touch of magic.

Denis' phenomenal heading ability was now a regular topic for reporters on radio and television. They were amazed at just how high he could leap to head the ball. Noel Cantwell said that during some matches he worried that Denis ran the risk of injuring himself the way he went up for the ball near goal. "He soars up as gracefully as Nureyev and he seems to miss the crossbar with his head by inches before falling into the netting."

Jimmy Murphy described Denis as one of the best headers of the ball in the history of football. "Devastating pace helped make Denis a world-class player," said Jimmy, "but it was courage and athleticism which made him such a great goalscorer. Although he was just 5 feet 9 inches tall, Denis could outjump almost anyone, no matter how big or powerful. He was a constant danger when coming in at the far post and he had a fearlessness that took him into goal scoring positions that were scorned by others who were not as brave. Denis and Cliff Jones (Wales and Tottenham left-winger) got goals out of nothing because they were always looking to make things happen. These two were classic examples of what players can achieve if they combine courage with skill. There have been few better in the air." When asked to elaborate on Law's skill in the heading stakes Murphy added: "Considering his lack of inches he was phenomenal." Jimmy said that Denis had not been particularly outstanding in the air at Manchester City yet "hours of practice and a fearless approach led to him becoming as respected as any of the great far-post forwards. Denis would fight his way upwards. In a crowded goalmouth his blond head would suddenly wriggle free to get the vital touch. He was exceptional because of this prodigious leaping power."

Another great admirer of Law's heading ability was Jimmy Greaves. Greaves said that although he himself was only an inch shorter than Law his own aerial power was nothing to boast about. "I have always recognised the importance of strong, accurate heading," said Greaves, adding that was especially so in the British game, "and I am happy that I was able to nod in the odd decisive goal now and again." Jimmy went on to say that all the outstanding headers of the ball took care to head it squarely with the front of their forehead. "Although some of the best, like Denis Law for example, flicked the head sideways at the last moment to get extra impetus and steer the ball away towards the corner of the goal. Denis used a salmon-like leap which gave him an extra hitch in mid-air and took him above much taller men to balls that seemed well out of his reach. He exemplifies another important characteristic of successful heading - an unflinching determination to meet the ball and strike it firmly. Denis really was phenomenal when it came to heading goals."

In 2000 the late Sir Stanley Matthews, writing in his riveting autobiography *The Way It Was* described his friend and former team-mate Stan Mortensen thus: "Once airborne, it was if the thumb and first finger of the right hand of the good Lord had reached down, nipped the shirt on his back and held him there because Morty seemed to defy gravity and hang in the air for ages. Denis Law in his heyday with Manchester United in the sixties is the only other player I've seen do that."

Despite Law, United's form remained inconsistent. At Filbert Street they could consider themselves extremely unfortunate to lose 3-2 and as Maurice Smith, of *The People* wrote: "The 35,538 crowd saw a match in a thousand, the game I'm personally rating as the best I've been lucky enough to see all season. It was 90 minutes of thrust and counter, art and craftsmanship, all carried out at racetrack speed." Denis opened the scoring after only two minutes when he headed a corner just inside the far post. Leicester equalised and went ahead in the second half with two goals from Hodgson, their right-winger. David Herd pulled a goal back and two minutes from time it looked like the Reds had earned a point when George Best headed the ball into the Leicester goal only to see referee Burns of Dudley disallow the goal for offside against Denis.

"It was a stupid decision," said an angry Law later, "when George headed the ball into the net I was standing behind him and I raced into the goalmouth just to follow the ball home. In actual fact goalkeeper Gordon Banks touched the ball over the line. I just couldn't understand why the linesman waved his flag and I was given offside when I didn't start to move until the ball was played. Like I said, I ran through to make certain but the ball had already crossed the line when I touched it, so how could I be offside?" Gordon Banks chipped in: "Law was standing offside when the ball came towards him." From the stand it looked as if both the referee and the Leicester defenders had been fooled by Law's quickness because he ran past three players. By most people's reckoning it was a perfectly good goal. Denis left Leicester wondering whether it paid to have just about the speediest pair of feet in British soccer.

The fifth round of the FA Cup saw United drawn away at Barnsley's Oakwell. The Barnsley fans are still talking about an Englishman, an Irishman, and a Scotsman in the pubs and clubs: for it was Irish wonder-boy, 17-year-old George Best, Scottish genius Denis Law and Manchester's own Nobby Stiles who ended their team's hopes. On these big occasions Denis was in his element. He thrived on the expectation and pressure. His magic moments were the highlights of this tough battle from which the Yorkshire team emerged beaten but with credit. Electric Law scored twice and laid on goals for Herd and Best by thinking and moving twice as quickly as anyone else on the field. Best was also superb, scoring the first goal following a one-two with Law. George proceeded to give right-back Hopper a torrid time. David Herd's goal followed a typical piece of inspiration from Law - Denis burst onto a pass from Charlton and though it looked like a defender's ball Denis moved up another gear, rounded the keeper, realised he was at an impossible angle and pulled the ball back for his Scottish team-mate. Denis later added a brace and United sailed through to the next round.

The Reds had been drawn against 'crack' Portuguese outfit Sporting Club Lisbon, in the quarter-final of the European Cup Winners' Cup, the first leg to be played at Old Trafford on 26th February 1964. These were exciting times for United and their supporters and the game was discussed at work, in the social clubs, pubs and almost anywhere that United followers frequented. However, Matt Busby still had aspirations of winning the prestigious First Division championship once again.

After the Leicester match, United played Lancashire neighbours Bolton Wanderers at Old Trafford and it was a massacre as the Red Devils ran out 5-0 winners. Surprisingly

Denis was not on the scoresheet and he even missed a penalty, the goal glory going to George Best and David Herd who got two apiece, with Bobby Charlton getting the other. Then came another all-Lancashire clash with Blackburn Rovers at Ewood Park. For some reason United were the team Blackburn fans loved to hate. They were up for it and ready to play their hearts out. On the way to the ground a Rovers supporter commented: "People are sick of hearing about Denis Law. You'd think he was the only player in United's team." Needless to say, the man didn't surface afterwards, because Denis broke their hearts.

The Reds were watched by two representatives from Lisbon among the 40,000 spectators and their reports might have made for uncomfortable reading back in Portugal as United strolled through the game. Anselmo Fernandez, the Sporting Club manager, said: "I am going to telephone Lisbon and ask for four policemen to come to Manchester with the team…one for each leg and arm of Denis Law. What a player!" The manager's anxiety was well-founded as Denis alone won this game for the Reds, their last in the League title race before two vital Cup games in Europe and at home. Law provided the dynamite that exploded Blackburn's hopes of victory - he began by blasting a ferocious shot that Fred Else parried for Phil Chisnall to screw the rebound into the net. Fred Pickering then levelled for Rovers before Denis struck. He picked up the ball in his own half, swivelled past a defender and let fly with a rocket of a shot from 25 yards that fairly whizzed past Else in the Rovers goal. Later, Denis ran on to a clever Crerand pass for his second and United's third. The Rovers fan who had complained about Law would, no doubt, have dashed back into town to spread the gospel.

*

George Best was now receiving rave reports from the newspapers and radio and television broadcasters but what did his older club-mates think of the youngster? "George Best is a boy who is most definitely star material," enthused fellow Ulsterman Harry Gregg, "it's been a long time since I was impressed by a young forward. I had, of course, spoken about George to people a few months ago but I make no apology for bringing up the subject again. I had predicted soccer stardom for him. I first noticed him when I played in a five-a-side game against him at the Cliff. This dark-haired slip of a lad brought the ball up to me. I leaned one way and dived the other - a move which was almost a certainty to kid young, inexperienced players but I found I was diving at thin air while this kid was calmly slipping the ball past me on the other side. 'Fair enough,' I thought, 'perhaps I had made an error of judgement or, more likely the kid was having beginner's luck.' But a few minutes later I was really taking notice because the kid was sending me the wrong way again. Twice in one match, against me, a man who was supposed to be an experienced goalkeeper. I made sure I found out his name then!"

When Harry learned Best was from Belfast he was all the more interested in him and he made it his business to watch him in action as often as he could. George soon broke into the first team and held on to his place on merit, winning headline notices. An old player pulled Harry up after watching George play and said: "This lad is like Bryan Douglas. He shows the ball to defenders, makes a monkey out of them and pushes through the shrewdest of passes. He's not only an accomplished footballer - he's an entertainer."

"The one thing I was wondering was would we see George as a successor to Tom Finney and Stanley Matthews or would we see him emerge as an inside-forward of the calibre of Denis Law?" Harry added.

After the win over Blackburn Rovers Matt Busby took his team to Blackpool in preparation for the important game against the classy Portuguese that Wednesday. It was estimated that over 130,000 spectators would watch the two cup ties over the next three days. The last of the tickets for the European game had been sold days earlier while the remaining tickets for the Reds' sixth round FA cup tie against Sunderland at Old Trafford on the Saturday were almost sold out. Les Olive, United's secretary, was in no doubt that it would be a complete sell-out. When the Lisbon team arrived in Manchester it was raining heavily. They looked like superbly fit footballers and the coach took them straight to Old Trafford where they were moved by the plaque over the entrance commemorating the tragedy of Munich. They stood in silence to pay their respects; a touching, symbolic gesture.

The match that night turned out to be a thrilling tussle with the Reds roared on to victory by a highly emotional 60,000 crowd. Denis certainly lived up to his post-match headline 'Lion-tamer Law' because on this night he most certainly tamed the lions of Lisbon. In the opening minutes he was so quick off the mark that he deceived the linesmen into thinking he was offside when he clearly wasn't. Yet the Reds took a big step towards the semi-final when, after 22 minutes, Denis put them in the lead. Charlton delivered an exquisite pass through the middle, Denis darted through, side-stepped two lunging heavy-footed defenders and sidefooted the ball past Carvalho in the Lisbon goal. Then Charlton broke away and scored another and with Law's constant pestering of the Portuguese defence there was no let-up for the visitors. Seven minutes before the interval he got his second goal, this time from the penalty spot. Silva pulled a goal back for the Portuguese but in the 74th minute Denis scored another penalty. Interestingly the two spot-kicks that Denis scored were a little bit special. His first, an unstoppable shot, went to the right of the goalkeeper while his second was different - running up to the ball Denis sent Carvalho the wrong way with a little body swerve and neatly placed the ball to the left of the diving keeper. Despite the apparent ease of the 4-1 scoreline United were guilty of rank bad finishing. Nevertheless, the predictions of Lisbon's manager had been accurate - Denis' speed of movement proved too much for the Portuguese.

*

The training at Old Trafford was very basic indeed. Most of the other clubs did practically the same thing: running, a few exercises, a bit of head tennis and perhaps one or two other things. After this preparation the highlight of any session would be a game. If they were training at Old Trafford the players would go around the back near the Stretford End to play six or seven-a-side-games. This was a very dangerous place for so many highly priced players to play and it was a wonder that nobody was seriously injured in these highly competitive games that often turned into full-blooded battles as players crashed into each other without a care in the world. In a typical example of the ferocity of these 'training' games George Best recalled an incident just after he broke into the senior side: "I remember one day when big Bill Foulkes knocked Denis to the ground and Denis jumped up and punched him. Bill hit him back and the next thing, everyone was piling in." Nevertheless the balance and control required simply to survive these training games cannot be underestimated - some have said that it was Busby's secret weapon.

Indeed these games proved to be ideal preparation for United's next fixture - a home Cup-tie with Sunderland in front of an expectant capacity Old Trafford crowd. The game ended in a 3-3 draw and United could count themselves extremely fortunate to have a second crack at the Wearsiders for the visitors were by far the better team on the day. Whether it was because the Reds were weary after their mid-week European Cup game only the players knew but with five minutes of the game left the home fans were resigned to defeat as they watched their heroes trail 3-1. Denis had been strangely subdued for far too much of this game. Charlie Hurley, Sunderland's expensive centre-half, otherwise having a sensational match had scored United's only goal while Johnny Crossan had scored twice and George Mulhall got the Rokerites' other goal. Thankfully late goals from Best and Charlton rescued a replay and spared United's blushes.

Although the United players were delighted to be still involved in the FA Cup they could certainly have done without the added burden of a replay. The midweek return with Sunderland a few days later at Roker Park saw another highly charged game end in a 2-2 draw after extra time - Denis and

Bobby Charlton getting United's goals. On the following Saturday United, missing both Law and Charlton through injury, beat West Ham 2-0 at Upton Park with goals from Herd and Sadler. Yet both stars returned for the second replay of the FA Cup tie with Sunderland, played this time at Denis' old stamping ground Leeds Road, Huddersfield. And what an occasion. With the roars of the Reds' fans hitting the night air like claps of thunder, the incomparable, irrepressible Law returned to Huddersfield and set his old town alight with a wonderful hat-trick (his eighth of the season) to blast Sunderland out of the Cup. "It was like a home from home for me," said Denis, playing under the 'Denis Law Lights', the name given to Huddersfield's floodlights bought with the proceeds of his transfer to Manchester City four years earlier. In a spectacular game that had the 55,000 fans in a frenzy of excitement, United won 5-1 to set up a semi-final clash with West Ham at Hillsborough on Saturday 14th March.

Having beaten West Ham 2-0 in London just a week previously without Law and Charlton, Busby was quite confident of a repeat performance against Bobby Moore's team. Yet the weather leading up to the match was atrocious. Torrential rain on the morning of the game left the pitch like a cow field, with puddles of water all over and the mud ankle deep. As the decision was being made to play or not, Paddy Crerand went out to look at the pitch - it was still pouring down as the referee threw a ball down to see if it bounced. It splashed into the mud and stayed there. Paddy told the referee the game couldn't possibly be played under such conditions.

"It's the same for both teams," he was told. "It's not," replied Crerand, "if you put a cab-horse and a race-horse at one end of this pitch and ask them to race to the other end, the cab-horse has got as good a chance as the race-horse." He wasn't belittling West Ham in any way, but said Paddy: "It does make a big difference." But the referee's decision was final and over 65,000 fans were soaked to the skin and shivering as they watched the game. True to Crerand's predictions West Ham adapted the better and deservedly won the game 3-1 despite

Denis scoring United's consolation with a brilliant header.

Four days after that semi-final defeat the Reds travelled to Lisbon for the second leg of their European Cup Winners' Cup tie against Sporting Lisbon. The team, by now drained following two replays against Sunderland and the heavy going encountered against West Ham, nevertheless held a 4-1 lead from the first leg and the newspapers tipped them to advance to the semi-finals. 'A mere formality' seemed to be the received wisdom. Imagine their bitter disappointment then when they were hammered 5-0, losing 6-4 on aggregate. The strain of playing for three trophies; League, FA Cup and Cup Winners' Cup had proved too big an obstacle. The less said about this game the better. Matt Busby, for the only time during his managerial career, lost his temper with his team and laid into them good and proper after the game. He accused his players of lacking effort and hinted he would drop some and fine others. The only thing left for United now was the First Division Championship and they would have to pull themselves together and raise their game because three days after the disaster in Lisbon they were due at White Hart Lane to face a Spurs team thirsting for revenge after League and Cup Winners' Cup defeats at the hands of the Reds already that season.

One thing was for certain, Spurs would hit back with a breathtaking display of classy, exciting and cultured football. Yet Paddy Crerand, with a grim-faced Denis nodding in agreement, was able to tell the assembled press afterwards: "We were lashed in Lisbon, and we didn't like it. So we decided to show the critics how wrong they were when they said we were finished. We are an angry team." United humiliated Spurs with a rampant team display full of the vigour missing from the two semi-final defeats. Ace destroyers Charlton and Law were in full flow - in a twelve-minute spell in the first half United scored three goals. First, receiving a beautifully angled pass from Best, Law headed for goal with big Maurice Norman, the Spurs centre-half, hacking away at him yet still Denis lashed a right footed sizzler into the net. Graham Moore and Bobby Charlton got United's other goals while Jimmy Greaves, from the penalty spot, and Brown were Spurs' scorers. This was a brilliant team effort from United. "We didn't need telling how badly we played in Lisbon," said Denis in the dressing room, "it was unfair when people tried to make out that just because we lost two games we never had been a good team and never would be one."

Later that night the United team received a police escort to a reception at the House of Commons. The club had been invited by Leslie Lever, the well-known MP for Ardwick. The Minister of Transport, Ernest Marples, represented the Government at a dinner laid on for the team and officials. Mr Marples told a story about his boyhood days when he watched Manchester United. He gave the team line of forwards and half-backs with no mention of the full-backs or goalkeeper. Hugh Delargy, the Labour MP for Thurrock, shouted out: "What about the rest of the team?" which started everyone laughing.

Many of United's senior players marvelled not only at their young Irish team-mate George Best's skill, they were amazed at how he never seemed to suffer with nerves before a game. It didn't seem to bother George how important the game was, he just got on with it. Most players admit to suffering from nervousness before running out onto the pitch. They all have their own little quirks and rituals, that often become superstitions. When Best first got into the first team he avoided the chit-chat and leg-pulling in the dressing-room and when the older players spoke to him he would be much too shy to answer. But from being a shy, quiet kid Best was now answering the older players back. He would willingly have played seven days a week if he could.

His thoughts before games were so concentrated on the pleasure of getting a ball at his feet that there was no room for butterflies: "I was really fortunate in that before my 18th birthday I was not only a regular member of one of the world's greatest clubs, Manchester United, I was partnering that world star Denis Law," said George years later. "I was also playing for my country, Northern Ireland, and I was earning the sort of money many a person twice my age would call a little 'goldmine' and I was getting sackfulls of fan letters a week. Yes, there I was, a raw youngster being partnered by the one-and-only Denis Law. Why should I worry? In all honesty how could I go wrong?"

George said that there was a mistaken impression about Manchester United. People thought because there were so many top stars and individuals there was little team spirit. "In fact, the opposite was true," Best explained, "because the team spirit was terrific." He said that when he first broke through, everyone from Denis downwards went out of their way to make him feel like 'one of the boys' and the Old Trafford team gelled together instantly both on and off the field. Talking specifically about Denis, he said that they were different characters. He pointed out that Denis was older than him, and a married man. He also said Denis was always well groomed and smartly dressed in expensive suits, whereas he was still a teenager wearing the modern clothes of that period.

"Denis was always livelier, always rushing. What surprised me about him was that although he was a massive star with bags of experience, he used to get nervous before a game. Quite honestly, I never used to suffer in this respect about football. The game is all the same to me whether it is a League game, an important Cup match or just a kickabout. Denis, though, couldn't watch United if he was not actually playing. He would go and sit in the dressing room because he got so wound up wanting his team-mates to do well."

George was inundated with requests from friends and fans asking him what it was like playing in the same forward line as Denis. "The simple answer is 'fabulous.' I thoroughly enjoyed it, really. He thinks and reacts twice as fast as other players. He delivers the ball perfectly, straight to your feet. I am also asked why he got into so much trouble on the field - well it is his razor-sharp reflexes that land him in bother. He loves being the showman on the field and gets quite embarrassed when he sees himself on the television or his picture in the newspapers, he cannot believe he has done things he sees. He is deadly serious about football and likes to win, even playing cards, head tennis or some other game he has to win. He is competitive and hates losing. What a player to have in the team. What a great, great player he is though. Some of his goals are out of this world."

George went on to explain that the team spirit was prevalent before matches. He said the long wait before the kick-off got on the nerves of the most experienced players. "Denis and his pal Pat Crerand are a comical pair. They sit on the coach or in the dressing room ribbing each other unmercifully. Momentarily, the game is forgotten and the tension soon disappears. They have arguments about things such as 'Who's the ugliest footballer?' Both claim that the other is the leading contender." He said that at times he couldn't believe his good fortune to be playing alongside Denis and concluded by saying that both Denis and himself had one thing in common - that neither of them looked much like footballers when they left school. Denis' story is told earlier in this book but George said that two Irish clubs had decided he was too small to play for them during scouting missions to George's Cregah Youth Club in Belfast.

After the wonderful, uplifting victory over Tottenham, the Reds' championship ambitions were permanently derailed as they drew the next three games: at Chelsea (1-1) in which Denis scored, Fulham (2-2), Denis and David Herd scoring and finally at Wolves (2-2), Bobby Charlton and David Herd the scorers. Denis missed this last game through injury but was back for a 3-0 win over Fulham with Crerand, Foulkes and Herd the goalscorers. Then came a walloping at Anfield where champions-elect Liverpool thrashed the Reds 3-0. Denis spent most of the game helping out in defence and had to run the cruel gauntlet of thousands of Merseysiders delighting in his failure. The volatile Law was booked for a foul on his close friend Ian St John. It was a game he and his colleagues wanted to forget.

In the last five games of the season the wheels truly came off the United wagon. From these five fixtures Denis got four goals while missing the game at Stoke. United won three, drew one and lost one before the last League game of the season against Nottingham Forest at Old Trafford. Just as the season started for United, so it had ended with the priceless Denis Law the chief entertainer, the chief executioner, a soccer sorcerer and as ever the golden hero. In the ninth minute Charlton took a corner, Moore headed toward the Forest goal when suddenly Denis did a corkscrew and scored a great headed goal. That was it, his seal was on the game, his genius had it by the throat. However he injured his thigh just before the interval and afterwards went on the wing although playing at less than half pace. Moore scored the Reds' second goal while Hinton got one back for Forest. In the 55th minute Best delivered a perfect pass for Denis to rifle a right-footer past Forest keeper Peter Grummitt. At the final whistle the crowd rose to applaud him and hundreds of youngsters, eager to embrace their heroes, invaded the pitch.

Denis was obviously disappointed that the team hadn't won the Championship and could only finish runners-up to Liverpool who had 57 points to United's 53. Law's own personal record read: League - 30 games, 30 goals; FA Cup - 6 games, 10 goals; European Cup Winners' Cup - 5 games, 6 goals - a phenomenal record. Forty goals in all competitions was something to be proud of and United's achievement in finishing runners up in the League, semi-finalists in the FA Cup and quarter-finalists in the Cup Winners' Cup was a definite all-round improvement on their desperate showing the previous season. On a personal note, Denis' standing in the world game could be measured by the fact that he was voted third best player in Europe in 1963 behind Russia's Lev Yashin and Italy's Gianni Rivera.

In April 1964, Matt Busby paid Burnley a fee of £60,000 (some say it was only £40,000) for the speedy, dynamic right-winger John Connelly. This was a shrewd signing by the United manager. Connelly had won a First Division Championship medal with Burnley in 1960 and two years later an FA Cup runners-up medal. He had been capped by England and although there were several rumours that he was past his best this proved unfounded as his spell with the Red Devils would prove. Half an hour after the deal had been completed, United recouped £30,000 when they surprisingly sold Young England inside-forward Phil Chisnall to League champions Liverpool. This raised a few eyebrows, but Busby knew exactly what he was doing. The Connelly deal was done at Turf Moor only a few hours after Matt Busby had watched Connelly play against Liverpool and put his offer to Burnley chairman Bob Lord.

Connelly was overjoyed at the move. "I am very happy about this move," he told the press, "my wife and I gave it a lot of thought. It will be grand to play with a team of United's quality and I am looking forward to playing with men like Bobby Charlton and Denis Law...who wouldn't?" He also said that he had been very happy at Burnley and it was a friendly club, "but let's face it. I'm not getting any younger, and I think a change of clubs will give me a new start. Of course I'll miss the players at Burnley but I believe the set-up at Old Trafford is a very happy one and I know one or two of the players quite well." Connelly was still only 25 and had won 10 caps for England.

Denis had a great deal of time for Connelly and would come to relish the service he provided during his two-year stay at Old Trafford. A St Helens lad, John had joined Burnley at 18, from St Helens Town. He was an inside-forward but Burnley converted him into a skilful, dashing, goalscoring winger. Having helped Burnley win the First Division Championship in 1960 and reach an FA Cup final he was their top scorer. His record with Burnley was impressive - in 265 League and Cup matches he had scored 105 goals - a staggering rate for a winger. John was at home on either flank and unlucky in his seven-season international career that he had only gained 20 caps. This low number had as much to do with the 10 other outstanding wingers battling for the same England position as Connelly's undoubted ability. Joining United rejuvenated the quietly spoken Lancashire lad and he was held in great esteem by United supporters for the impact he made at the club. Always well groomed, with his hair slicked back with brylcream, he helped tear opposition defences apart. With his acquisition Busby was able to pick a forward line of Connelly, Charlton, Herd, Law and Best - over the next few seasons this would prove a fearsome combination for opposition defences.

9. A Champion at Last

Despite the glittering testimonials showering his performances Denis was yet to earn significant honours. In his seven-year professional career so far he had just one FA Cup medal in his collection. And although, in fairness, Denis had spent a large part of his career at clubs with little prospect of honours, now at Manchester United there was a feeling that potential must be turned into prizes and the League championship (and with it a place in the coveted European Cup) remained top priority for everyone connected with the club.

Thus on the eve of a potentially prosperous season, United embarked on one of their most successful pre-season tours. Indeed, the team's games in Hamburg, Dublin and the several private practice matches at Old Trafford resulted in a fully fit, ultra-confident first team. During their 3-1 defeat of Hamburg they looked classy - the Germans had been unbeaten on their own ground the previous season and had just defeated Dukla Prague, a team United played in the European Cup a few seasons previously, in a friendly. John Connelly scored his first two goals for the Reds and laid on the third for David Herd. Denis and Herd inter-changed throughout the game and all the forwards played up to scratch. Later, in Dublin, United played Shamrock Rovers and Charlton, Best and Herd (2) led United to a well-deserved 4-2 victory.

Matt Busby and Jimmy Murphy believed that with the signing of John Connelly, United now had the nucleus of a Championship winning team. Both believed that two wingers were essential for all great teams. Now with Connelly and young George Best on opposing wings, Bobby Charlton as the deep-lying centre-forward and Denis and the much criticised but highly respected David Herd they had the forward line they wanted. With Harry Gregg still struggling with a shoulder injury they had started with goalkeeper David Gaskell but after just five games he was replaced by Pat Dunne (no relation to Tony) who had been signed back in May 1964 for £10,000 Shamrock Rovers. The full-back pairing would prove to be the bedrock for the entire season. Shay Brennan and Tony Dunne played such commanding roles that club captain Noel Cantwell managed just one appearance. The half-back line was Paddy Crerand, Bill Foulkes, and little Nobby Stiles, who had replaced Maurice Setters. Setters would also struggle for selection, managing just five first team appearances before a transfer to Stoke City. Ian Moir played just once before he, too, was transferred to Blackpool in February 1965. Meanwhile David Sadler, John Fitzpatrick and John Aston junior remained on the fringes of the first team.

Yet in the minds of Busby and Murphy these players would merely provide defensive cover the fantastic forward line the Reds now called upon: Connelly - Herd - Charlton - Law - Best! All these players could be almost guaranteed to score double figures: it was a football fan's dream. Supporters would set off early to get to Old Trafford so that they wouldn't get locked out. In those days fans turned up and paid at the turnstiles and it was mostly standing. Thousands would climb the concrete steps onto the Stretford End, while others made their way behind the Scoreboard and still more for the United Road. Inside the ground the build-up would throb with undiluted excitement in anticipation of watching this highly entertaining vintage of Red Devils. There were very few boring 90 minutes in the era that gave birth to the 'Theatre of Dreams'. It was a virtual guarantee that one of Bobby, George or Denis would produce a touch of magic to brighten even the bleakest winter's day and when a goal was scored a glow could be seen above the pitch and the wall of sound could be heard for miles around. Everyone who pulled on the red shirt was respected but the fans had their own particular favourite. Many revered Bobby Charlton for his non-stop foraging and thunderball shooting, while others idolised the glamour and genius of

George Best, but Denis Law seemed to be everybody's favourite player.

It might have been just as the former England manager Terry Venables said - Denis Law was loved for his personality as much as playing ability. He was a great character. He strode on to the pitch as if he owned it. He was cocky and confident, with his head always held high. He was a hell of a player to have on your side. I think it was his air of schoolboy mischievousness that endeared him to the crowds. That's a terrific assessment of what the Manchester United followers thought of one of their favourites. Denis was the King and he was fearlessly combative, a scourge of defences throughout the British Isles and Europe. He played up to the crowd and they were right behind him, especially once he retaliated against the shocking and often cynical physical abuse from defenders.

However Denis had a little distraction during his preparations for the new season. He became a proud father when his first child Gary was born in June. Yet all the talk before the first League game concerned United's prospects in the First Division title race. With a big grin Denis said: "Hope is my watchword for the new season," then went on to say that he never promised anything, knowing what a funny old game football could be. "Only a fool makes promises about football. Resolutions are ten a penny. How many of last year's resolutions did we keep? It's not the slightest use me oozing good resolutions over a nice plate of steak and chips. There is no steak and chips atmosphere when you are running as fast as you can for goal, or being brought down, or tackling or being tackled, or bumping into a defender or being bumped. But I can hope."

He said he wasn't being flippant, in fact he was being very serious when he mentioned that his month suspension during the last season was disastrous for him. "People might think that because I was born with fair hair, a face something like a cross between Danny Kaye's and Tommy Steele's, and a cocky sort of walk, that I'm incapable of getting down in the dumps. They don't know me." He said that he knew he deserved to be suspended and that made it worse still. He pointed out that after his suspension he was only booked once, which wasn't bad for him and had learnt the hard way.

He added that he was maturing: "It's no good me saying that I go into matches worrying how I shall behave. I can't play football unless I have full concentration on the job but the suspension curbed my impetuosity, at least I hope that's the case. My reputation means much to me. So does the reputation of Manchester United." He said that since taking over the captaincy from Noel Cantwell he had calmed down considerably: "But don't expect a gentle, docile Denis Law, who won't tackle, who won't play hard, who won't give and take a knock. That just wouldn't be me. I wouldn't be earning my wages. In fact, I'd be useless and right for dropping. And if you are expecting me to predict that Manchester United will win the League, the Cup, and the Inter-Cities Fairs Cup you've got the wrong man. Ask me again after Easter."

Ten toes, two legs, 24 muscles, 12 yards of blood vessels and 12 yards of nerves that were worth a fortune were receiving treatment at Old Trafford. The legs that had cost three football clubs £270,000 in transfer fees, brought immense joy to millions and made him a household name, were being toned for the big kick-off. And nowhere was the interest in Denis Law's spindly legs greater than at Old Trafford, where physiotherapist Ted Dalton was working to supply the answer to the one question worrying 50,000 United fans: Would Denis Law be fit for the big kick-off?

The golden boy of British football had strained his right groin playing in a warm-up game in Ireland a few days before. Denis had been having daily treatment at Old Trafford from 50-year-old Mr Dalton, who had been treating footballers' injured legs for over 29 years. Later, at his Chorlton home Denis told journalist Philip Finn: "I haven't gone full out in training all this week, but I've done some light ball work. I feel much brighter about the prospects of playing in our first League match next Saturday. The first match of any new season is always a terrific thrill before a home crowd as good as ours. I don't want to let them down." Ted Dalton, as always optimistic, added: "I have been giving Denis treatment every day. At the moment we are very hopeful that he will play and I would say that he has a very good chance."

Dalton, United's physio for over 25 years, was a grey-haired, obliging and friendly man, with a ready smile. His involvement with United began when he went to Old Trafford to buy a ticket for an England versus Ireland international being played at the ground. United's secretary, Walter Crickmer, saw him queuing and rushed out and invited Ted into the office. The club had purchased a machine for treating their injured players and asked Ted to help explain how it worked. The chairman, Mr J W Gibson, listened to what Dalton had to say and asked him if he would help the club. Ted accepted the appointment and over the next 25 years hundreds of players passed through his hands. He was also the physio for Lancashire County Cricket Club while many stars of stage, screen and radio regularly sought his advice and help. Denis came to know Ted over the years. They got on well and Denis liked the man's easy going nature while treating his injuries.

On a different note, Geoffrey Green wrote that when Denis and Paddy Crerand were acquired these two Scotsmen had "fire in their bellies, football in their blood and mercury in their veins and the magic formula was found." Indeed Paddy claimed that Denis was "the most spectacular footballer in the world...on and off the field", while to see him driving through Manchester in his flame-red Jaguar - often wearing a bright red jersey with his blonde hair waving behind him - Denis looked liked a Viking. "I often think Denis Law should have been one of them," said Paddy, who added, "of course he would have to be a chief. He couldn't be anything else. And I think this is how the fans see him. A warrior of the football field, with a fiery temper. A leader of lost causes. He's a laughing devil-may-care adventurer on the football scene."

Yet this wasn't the full picture: "Believe it or not the swashbuckling Law is the shyest professional footballer I have ever known! Tell me the man who has ever claimed to hear

Denis boasting about his ability and I will show you a liar. He has won the game's top honours, played for top clubs in England and Italy, seen hundreds of thousands of pounds change hands for his transfer, been acclaimed over and over again as 'the greatest'. But he is still only 24 years of age…and I repeat, a shy young man, the quietest member of any company." Continuing, Paddy said Denis liked a laugh, had a fondness for practical jokes but best of all he liked nothing better than to sit by the fire and chat. He said he counted himself lucky that it was his own fireside that Denis often chose and that Diana and his wife Noreen were good friends. He said there were handicaps to being a pal of Law's, such as, the need to always have the kettle on the boil. "Any time of the day he's liable to come bubbling through the door and the first shout is always, 'Have you got the kettle on?'"

Paddy said Denis hated gossip, he simply would not listen to nasty tales about other people. He would have no part of that, even as a listener. Paddy added that he had seen Denis walk out of company when the tongues have started to wag. Talking about the tag they stuck on Denis - 'Denis the Menace', Paddy said: "There's that temper that's landed him in trouble on the field a few times. There's that happy gesture of the upflung arms when he scores a goal. But these are spontaneous reactions. You've got to live and play with him to know the real Denis. I'll tell you something else. Folk in his native Scotland have no idea how wonderful a player this slim lad from Aberdeen really is. I'm not kidding. They've seen him have some good games and a couple of great ones at Hampden but to appreciate him properly you have to watch him week in and week out. Or, better still, play behind him all the time.

"I've told you part of what I think of Denis Law the man. Now I'll tell you what I think of him as a player. He is the greatest inside-forward in the world - bar none! That is, he is as good as anybody that ever lived, because nobody could have been greater! I'll add this. Without Law, the Scotland team were just an average international side. With Law, Scotland have a chance against any country in the world. Yes, even when he isn't at his best, because he has that knack of making a team play above itself. His presence alone is often enough."

What made Denis so great? Well in Paddy's opinion it was Law's 'fighting heart', his 'undoubted courage' and 'fantastic natural ability'. Then there was his incredible pace over a short distance and his amazingly fast and alert brain: "Denis thinks that fast that it's like mind reading. He's always a move ahead - which is one reason he is caught offside so often. On 15 April 1962, Scotland beat England at Hampden for the first time in 25 years. It was my biggest thrill. We won by two goals to nil, the scorers being Davie Wilson and Eric Caldow from a penalty and everybody in the team played well in my opinion. But I insist that the man who prodded us to victory was Denis Law. Denis the planner, the worker, the marksman, though he didn't get a goal, Denis kept us all going, especially the attack. I remember how we set a new tradition at Hampden afterwards by running that lap of honour. I can still hear the cheers rolling down on us, wave after wave. We loved it. We will never forget it and I think perhaps we deserved it. But if full justice had been done, Denis would have led the way."

Crerand recalled another match, Scotland versus Czechoslovakia at Hampden in the World Cup. On 26th September 1961, this was a match Scotland had to win if they were to stay in with a chance of qualification and they had already been hammered 4-0 in Czechoslovakia... without Law. "For me, too, this return affair was something special, because I'd been sent off in Bratislava. It was a memory I had to wipe out. Well we won 3-2. And I am almost tempted to say that Law won 3-2. This was Denis the magnificent. The man who could take hold of a match and transform it all by himself - yes, even against those great Czechs, some of them of the highest class. It wasn't just that Denis scored two great goals. His general play lifted inside-forwards' standards to a height that at that time, I did not think possible. There can have been few more dramatic matches than this one. Strangely enough, there were only 51,000 people at Hampden. Perhaps after the hiding we'd had in Bratislava most fans thought we had no chance. And it looked that way when Kvasnak - with whom I'd been sent off in the first game - put the Czechs one up after only seven minutes.

"But now we had Law on our side. And Denis just doesn't know what the word 'defeat' means. The fact that the Czechs had scored only put his back up. He stepped up the pace and on 22 minutes we were level. Davie Wilson sent over a cross, Denis jumped with the goalkeeper Schroif and the ball broke to Ian St John who headed in. However, those Czechs were hard to keep down. Six minutes after the interval, their inside-right Scherer, put them in front again. Denis just refused to accept the setback. Eleven minutes later, John White and Jim Baxter cut through the Czech defence, John crossed - and Law came in like a rocket to crack the ball in for our second equaliser. That set things up for the climax - and what a climax. We threw everything into attack. We hammered the Czechs with everything in the book and, with only six minutes left, we did it. Or rather Denis did it. White - a splendid player for us on this occasion, gave Law the ball. Denis flashed past one man, wriggled by another... then cracked a tremendous ball past the startled Schroif. What a wonderful moment that was, one of the memories that will never fade for me. After the game, a Czech official had an interpreter say to Denis, 'You are the world's greatest.' And that goes for me anytime."

Paddy explained that there were two reasons why Denis sometimes occasionally spoiled his image by losing his temper. "The first is because he can't stand losing! Never! Denis can never shrug off defeat. He believes it is his business to win - and if he and the team failed, he wanted to know why. The other reason was the abominable treatment he received in so many matches. You hear about Law being a tough tackler, which he is. You hear about him being sent off or ticked off. But you haven't sat beside him in a dressing room while he has peeled of his stockings to show legs scared from ankle to knees. Law is always a target and always having to take it. You will rarely hear Denis joke about football. For him it is a deadly serious business, his way of life. He respects the game; he believes he must never give it less than his best. He has told me often that if he escapes serious injury and retains his health he will play until he is 30 and then stop. He will not hang on. Even at the top. He wants to go when he is still at his own absolute peak."

He told another story that illustrated how deeply Denis felt about football: "During his suspension last season United had to play an FA Cup tie at Southampton without him. Denis travelled with the rest of the team to watch the match but in fact only watched the first five minutes, then went and sat in the dressing room. He just couldn't stand it any longer - and he could never watch a match in comfort." These were some of the many faces of Paddy's pal Denis Law. He could add a few more. He said Denis loves Italian food and good clothes and a game of golf. "And," added Paddy, "contrary to impressions you may have formed - he is liked enormously by the other players. He is, for instance, by far the most popular man at Old Trafford. And that goes not only for the other players, but groundsmen, cleaners, turnstile operators and everybody else around the place. He's 'Denis' to all of them. It's the way they like it...and the way he wants it."

*

At the season's outset supporters were full of optimism that the First Division title would be returning to Old Trafford. Reality though told a different tale. The Reds' first game at home to a unglamorous but effective West Brom side, was tinged with defensive uncertainty. Tony Brown gave West Brom a 13th minute lead before United fought back, a 25 yard strike from Bobby Charlton, following good work from debutant Connelly. A brilliant back-header from Denis following a Connelly cross put the Reds 2-1 up before shoddy work in defence allowed the visitors to score an equaliser - final score 2-2. The following two games, both away from Old Trafford, saw United lose to West Ham 3-1 and scrape a 2-2 draw at Leicester. In the return with West Ham at Old Trafford, the Reds reversed the score and won 3-1. However they lost their next game to Fulham at Craven Cottage (2-1) and from the first five games of the season United had secured just 4 points.

Denis' contribution looked good on paper - four goals in five appearances would satisfy most forwards but Denis felt the spectacular vigour of the previous season was missing as he explained: "I haven't been really fit all season, these two-games-a-week are killing once you get a knock. I no sooner get ready when I am kicked again and have to start recovering all over again."

The Fulham defeat could be put down to unfortunate circumstances. On the morning of the match Tony Dunne told Matt Busby he was not feeling well. Matt immediately phoned Old Trafford and Noel Cantwell was put on a London-bound train. British Rail was no more reliable then than it is today and because of delays he did not arrive at Craven Cottage until just after kick off so Dunne, though unwell, had to play the full game. Just before the team went out on the pitch Bobby Charlton and Paddy Crerand were heading a ball to each other when Pat bumped his head against a door and the blood poured from a deep gash. Matt Busby was beside himself. Luckily Paddy was a tough, big-hearted lad and as soon as the doctor stopped the bleeding he was out on the field in the thick of the action. It was little wonder that United lost though.

In September 1964 Matt Busby finally sold Albert Quixall to Third Division side Oldham Athletic for £7,000. The blond-haired 29-year-old had been a favourite at Old Trafford and many supporters were a little sad at his moving. Yet there was also an inevitability about his departure. Law's old manager from Manchester City, Leslie McDowall, was now managing Oldham and he had been trying to sign Albert for quite some time. Albert was a jovial lad but would be sick before every match. When United played well his ability had shone brightly yet when the team struggled he struggled - he averaged a goal every three games for the Reds. Quixall, though Sheffield born, remained in the Manchester area after his playing career ended and still lives there today.

After defeat at Fulham, United took on Everton at Goodison Park in a thrilling encounter that ended 3-3. Pat Dunne made his League debut for United in this game. In the fourth minute

John Connelly, who was proving a bargain buy, tore down the wing, beat Everton full-back Brown, centred and saw Denis swoop like an eagle to head the ball past Andy Rankin in the Everton goal. After half an hour it was Connelly who got the second but Fred Pickering scored two good goals for Everton. David Herd put United ahead again but Alex Young scored Everton's late equaliser.

Denis failed a late fitness test and missed the home game against Nottingham Forest, which United won 3-0 with goals from David Herd(2) and John Connelly. Denis was back for the winning return game against Everton at Old Trafford. He and George Best scored but he missed the game at Stoke, which the Reds won 2-1, Connelly and Herd the scorers and an Inter-Cities Fairs Cup game against Djurgardens of Stockholm that ended 1-1, Herd getting a late, face-saving equaliser.

Yet typically Denis was back for the glamour game against Tottenham at Old Trafford. It proved to be a little too one-sided to be called an epic game. Crerand gave United the lead after 17 minutes then Denis hit Spurs' crossbar with a riveting header. The game was played in a heavy rainstorm but it didn't stop Crerand putting United 2-0 in front. A few minutes later, Denis, limping badly from an earlier challenge, beat the offside trap and with the Spurs defenders screaming blue murder at the referee, Denis sped through and put the ball into the net. Robertson pulled one back for the Londoners before Law pounced again and made the final score 4-1 to United.

After the Spurs victory United hit championship form and went on a ten-game unbeaten run, winning nine and drawing just once - Denis getting nine goals. In a typical example of his form, against Wolves, Law reached a pinnacle in awareness. United won 4-2 at Molineux and Denis scored twice. In the 17th minute he ghosted into space before punting a centre from David Herd past Davies in the Wolves goal. It was a brilliant piece of jiggery-pokery from Law. He caused a stir just after the goal when like a greyhound out of its trap he raced on to a pass only to be flagged offside. Denis, a big smile on his face and a look of sheer innocence, walked down the touchline, congratulating the linesman. A few minutes later, Harris scored an own goal to put the Reds 2-0 in front but the Law complex continued to grip Wolves. Two defenders jumped with him to meet a corner kick only for all three to miss the ball and leave the unmarked Herd with a simple task: 3-0. Crawford scored for Wolves before Denis killed the game with his second goal. Crawford scored again just before the final whistle. This result typified a robust autumn run that made United look championship certainties.

Yet despite the team's new found success, rumours circulated around Manchester that Denis didn't get along with Bobby Charlton and many were convinced that they would not pass the ball to each other. This was utter rubbish. They might not have been close friends but both played for Manchester United and would never do anything as childish as refusing to pass to each other. One only has to look at United's form at the time to realise the folly of this argument. Also, over the proceeding years, both Denis and Bobby spoke highly about each other's ability. Bobby always praised the play of Law and never tired of telling the press about the bravery of his Scottish club colleague.

Yet it was a fact that there was a great deal of petty jealousy, bickering and disharmony at Old Trafford in those days. This became exacerbated in the 1970s when it was claimed that Bobby and George Best hardly passed to each other. In Leo McKinstry's excellent book *Jack and Bobby,* the story of the Charlton brothers, he writes that Noel Cantwell, talking about this period at Old Trafford, said: "It was a strange dressing room when you think about it. You'd be standing, stripping and talking to people every day, maybe five days a week, and half of them did not get on very well together." Cantwell said that Denis and Bobby never saw eye to eye with each other. But the former Manchester United captain also points out that there were other players who could not stand each other.

In his book *Denis Law's Book of Soccer No 2,* published in 1967, Denis dedicated a chapter to the Englishman - *Bobby Charlton: Soccer Crusader.* Denis said Bobby was a shining example to all young footballers. "You can take every attribute needed by a player who wants to get to the top and Bobby Charlton has them all. His temperament is unquestioned; his ability is world class; his modesty unimpaired," wrote Denis. He added that Bobby was a superb professional that other players and fans from all parts of the world respected. Bobby, said Denis, deserved his Footballer of the Year award in 1966. He praised Bobby for his brilliant season with United and for helping England win the World Cup in 1966. "Match after match he figured in some fantastic grafting partnerships with Pat Crerand, trying all the time to lay on goals for the rest of the forwards."

Denis also mentioned Charlton's friendship with Nobby Stiles and the late Shay Brennan. He commented on the fact that Bobby was self-conscious about his fame, adding that some players loved the limelight, the publicity, the recognition of the crowds. Adding: "To be honest, I rather enjoy it myself." People often asked Denis if he would have liked to have a temperament like Bobby's? Laughing, Denis replied: "I suppose the answer has to be 'Yes'. But we're built in different ways. I am a Scot and if anyone has a go at me I just have to get my response off my chest, be it verbal or physical. I've learned a great deal from his attitude and try to turn my back on an aggressor." So much for rumours of a rift.

'Is Denis Law Getting a Fair Deal?' This was the question Denis' loyal fans were asking. They wanted to know if there was a vendetta against him after seeing him injured in game after game. Most United fans, as well as many neutral observers, were convinced that some opposing players set out to get him, rile him and make him lose his temper. His sending off the previous season was still fresh in the fans' minds, and he had already been booked once this season and supporters believed that rival players were taking advantage of Denis' legendary temper. The previous season had seen Denis play in 30 of United's matches but miss 14 through injury or suspension. He had already missed five in this new season and for the games he had played there had been a frantic rush in the treatment room in order for him to take the field. He had suffered damage to his ankles, a groin and a thigh.

Yet Denis shrugged off supporters' claims of a vendetta. "I don't believe any professional ever goes out deliberately to hurt or maim another player," said Denis, "these things just happen, and I certainly don't bear any grudges toward players who have hurt me. Lots of things happen in the heat of a game, and they often look a lot worse from the terraces."

Paddy Crerand added: "There is no doubt that Denis suffers from close marking. In fact he must be the most closely marked player in Britain. But that's not unnatural because he is such a great performer and match winner." Crerand went on to explain that to some extent Denis invited injury because he was always in the thick of the action. "But," added Paddy emphatically, "I don't believe anybody really sets out to get Denis." Bobby Charlton agreed with Crerand's sentiments. "Denis is so quick that he is a sucker for the late tackle. It often looks a bad foul when in actual fact there is no intent." United centre-half, Bill Foulkes, no shrinking violet when it came to putting his foot in added: "If anyone really wanted to cripple Denis Law they could do it very easily. They could do it to any player. I know he gets more rough treatment than most but that is not part of a vendetta I'm sure." Yet despite these claim from his fellow professionals, the Old Trafford supporters were not convinced.

*

'Law is the Greatest' - this headline appeared in a Sunday newspaper the day after United had ravaged Aston Villa 7-0 at Old Trafford. Denis scored four fantastic goals and put on a super show for a surprisingly low Old Trafford turnout of just 36,000 spectators - and that meant thousands of United fans were kicking themselves that morning for missing the greatest sight in British football - Denis Law in four-goal form. '*The Greatest One-Man Show On Earth*' exclaimed another headline. This was United's biggest victory since March 1950... also at Old Trafford against poor old Aston Villa. This was just a picnic

romp for the surging Reds - and Denis pinched the jam. Villa never got a crumb as Denis conducted everything from start to finish. Without a doubt Denis proved a man of some substance on this memorable day. Without being biased, this man Law was in a super class of his own. He scored four fantastic goals and had a devastating part in two of the others. George Best was also in spectacular mood but no side could have held super Law in this mood.

After Herd had scored the opener, Denis dribbled along the edge of the area and the Villa defenders thought they had him boxed in but using those electric reflexes he spotted a gap and sent a searing shot into the roof of the net. Geoff Sidebottom, the Villa keeper, shook his head in amazement. In the 50th minute Nobby Stiles took a pass from George Best and moved towards the Villa goal. Just as the midfielder pondered his options a blur of light, Law, took the ball off his toe and from 20 yards banged it into the back of the net. John Connelly scored United's fourth. Then, in a great solo effort Denis completed his hat-tick. The Villa area was packed with players but Crerand found the torch-haired Denis, who dribbled round Sidebottom for a great goal. Herd got the sixth and with a minute to go Denis popped up again. Nobby Stiles crossed and Villa's massed defence, though prepared for the inevitable, were powerless to prevent Law out-jumping them all and adding a magnificent seventh to United's burgeoning total. It was a wonder show - no doubt about it and the United supporters gave Denis a standing ovation. At the final whistle, beleaguered defender Geoff Sidebottom managed a smile as he shook Law's hand and ruffled his hair. The ultimate tribute came from a man not known for uttering superlatives. Harold Hardman, United's chairman, had watched some of the greatest strikers in the game but was moved to comment: "I have seen none better than Law and I have not seen even Law play better than he did today."

Next came a tougher test in front of thousands of Liverpool supporters at Anfield, yet United pulverised the Champions 2-0. Denis didn't score in this game but was heavily involved in an often bad-tempered match. Crerand and Herd scored the goals but referee Jack Taylor was a busy man. Ron Yeats, the giant Liverpool centre-half and skipper, was involved in an ugly incident that saw David Herd on the floor. Later Herd, sporting a swollen nose, said: "I'm all right. Perhaps he should have been a boxer." Yeats denied any involvement: "What happened to Herd? He could have fallen down through exhaustion. He certainly did a lot of running around."

The second incident and big talking point concerned Denis. At one point the United captain raised both arms to the baying crowd in the manner of a matador accepting the plaudits of his fans. Referee Taylor rushed straight over to Denis and gave him a stern lecture. As the referee lectured Denis the Liverpool fans continued to scream abuse at him. Their outbursts were understandable and there was a touch of envy because deep down they respected him as a remarkable player. As Mr Taylor shook his finger at Denis the noise from the fans grew louder and louder but it was all so spontaneous as a huge Danny Kaye grin spread across Law's face and the referee stepped in and had words. "I didn't speak to Law about his showmanship," explained Mr Taylor, "I thought he looked towards my linesman and showed dissent." Yet another incident occurred when Nobby Stiles was down injured in United's goalmouth and, as he was receiving treatment, a hail of pennies rained down from the lovable Scousers on the Kop.

Nevertheless as big as Ron Yeats was, he held no fear for Law, who clashed with him on several occasions throughout the 90 minutes. Then, referee Taylor had to tell Denis and Ron Yeats to shake hands after another volatile clash. Yet in the end the Reds had gained two valuable and well-deserved points and silenced Liverpool's 'Spion Kop' as Law and his Scottish International team-mate Yeats shook hands and enjoyed a laugh as they left the pitch at the end of a tough baptism for United's championship ambitions.

It was in this period of the 1960s when football hooliganism had its genesis. As United's rivalry with Liverpool intensified so did the outrageous behaviour of both sets of supporters.

Football was becoming a rat-race and everyone agreed that Anfield on the Saturday that United beat Liverpool provided a nauseating example of a different and sinister influence on the struggle for success. Before the season had started various football journalists pleaded with the Anfield fans, the same fans that had roared their team to the title so joyfully the previous season, not to turn their champions into chumps. Nobody disputed that the paying customers had the right to criticise but the Liverpool supporters were going too far when they transformed Anfield into a bearpit, fit only for morons, by the senseless chanting of obscenities which were heard by every man, woman and child on the ground. Manchester United fans were becoming just as bad and the same trend was becoming more and more audible at Old Trafford. What was more upsetting about this farmyard behaviour was the players themselves were being affected by it, however strongly they might have denied it. Sadly this loutish behaviour continues to this day, although it almost certainly reached a peak in the seventies and eighties.

On Saturday 14th November 1964, Denis hit the newspaper, radio and television bulletins once again, but for all the wrong reasons. United were playing Blackpool at Bloomfield Road. Blackpool were a decent First Division club in those days and had some useful players in their line-up. Tony Waiters was an outstanding goalkeeper, Jimmy Armfield was England's right full-back and at centre-forward was big Ray Charnley to mention but three. In addition they had a new star, a flame-haired little inside-forward in Alan Ball who, many claimed, was England's answer to Denis Law. It would appear that the red-haired Ball had been given the job of making sure Law was kept quiet during the game. These two firebrands clashed several times.

The game had started quietly with the Reds seemingly strolling through it. As early as the fifth minute they scored a textbook goal when David Herd converted after a brilliant build up by Charlton and Crerand. Within ten minutes it should have been 2-0 as Denis soared high above the Seasiders' defence only to slam his header against the bar. But after 30 minutes Ball centred for Oates to net for the Tangerines and thirteen minutes later came the incident that ended the pure football in what had promised to develop into a classic contest between two well-matched teams.

Denis and Ball had what appeared to be a minor scuffle. The referee, Peter Rhodes of York, awarded a free kick to Blackpool for a foul by Denis on Ball. Denis obviously wasn't happy with the referee's decision and argued about it, with players from both sides congregating around the incident. There was a great deal of gesticulating and harsh words. Seconds later Mr Rhodes took out his notebook and ordered Denis back to the dressing room. Immediately trouble flared in the crowd as orange peel, cans and other objects were thrown onto the field. At half time extra police were rushed to the ground as angry United fans spent ten minutes demonstrating against Law's dismissal. Patrol cars and Black Marias were quickly on the scene. The police moved in among the crowd and four spectators were escorted out of the ground. Later Blackpool's Chief Constable, Stanley Parr, said the Manchester United fans were the worst behaved he had ever seen at a football match. Ironically, it was almost 12 months to the day since Denis had been sent off at Aston Villa by referee Jim Carr.

Four minutes into the second half John Connelly got the winner for ten-man United. After the game Matt Busby said: "It was a pity this should happen. The game was a great advert for football. There wasn't one dirty foul in the whole match. Naturally we are all upset about it. It could be a big blow to our ambitions." Denis was the 25th player to be sent off at that stage of the season. He was not the first League player to be ordered off twice in twelve months, it had also happened to two other Scottish Internationals, Bertie Auld of Birmingham City and Jimmy Scoular, Bradford's player-manager.

On a similar note Denis Follows, the Secretary of the Football Association, said that the ugly scenes of violence that had started to become more common both on and off the pitch had become one of the gravest crises to face the game.

On the subject of football violence, Professor John Cohen from Manchester University's Department of Psychology said that the number of players being sent off was worsening the situation. He asked: "Are the players themselves becoming increasingly ruthless?" He also asked if spectators were generally more ill-disciplined now than in the 1920s and 1930s? Talking about the violence on the football field the Professor said: "From time immemorial man has had to learn to curb his natural violence, for without such a curb social life would be impossible. The force of aggressiveness in a man is such that there is always a state of tension in the individual himself, as well as in society at large. This is a delicate balance which can easily be upset."

Professor Cohen said that two-thirds of footballers stemmed from bleak and drab backgrounds and often they had risen to fame and splendour from the back streets of industrial towns. "In some footballers, including the very best, the line between play and violence is very unstable," he said, "the superb Denis Law is an outstanding example. No one who knows him could possible accuse him of a deliberate foul. He is simply carried away by his ebullient temperament and the unfortunate incident is over before he realises the spot of trouble he has put himself in." This, said the Professor, was the price Denis paid for his dazzling success; his faults and his qualities are two sides of the same coin or as the professor put it: "Denis Law demonstrates how easy it is to relapse from the highest exercise of skill to the underlying crude impulse that animates it."

The following Monday morning Len Noad, a journalist friend of Jimmy Murphy's, and the man who paved the way for the Reds' eventual signing of Tommy Taylor from Barnsley in March 1953, visited a crestfallen Denis Law at Old Trafford before Denis and his club-mates left for a two-day golfing holiday at the Fairhaven course in Blackpool, of all places. "If only I could have explained," said Denis, shaking his head as he recalled the incident that led to his dismissal against Blackpool. "I'm terribly upset. I feel sick both for myself and the fans. It was such a good game and it was so well handled. I would have been a fool to address a remark to the referee. Pat Crerand said something to me and I turned and used a swear word to him." Before leaving for Blackpool, Matt Busby told his team that he didn't want any of his players discussing the incident. When Len Noad asked Busby for his reactions on the incident the manager wouldn't be drawn. Len asked him if the club would seek a personal hearing. "Until I know what the referee's version of the matter is I have nothing further to say." On the coach heading for Blackpool, Matt told Jimmy Murphy that when he did get the referee's report they would discuss the matter with Denis and the other players concerned. Only then, he said, would the club decide on the best course of action to take.

A few days later, Matt Busby announced that there would be a personal hearing. Reporters asked Denis if he was pleased, "Definitely," he replied, "I had given away a silly foul. I shouted at Pat [Crerand] after he had spoken to me. But the referee thought I was speaking to him. My remark was addressed to Pat and nobody else. I am terribly upset. I was sickened when the referee said: 'Go and get changed.' When I was sent off last year I was guilty and took my 28 days punishment without complaint, but I'm not guilty this time."

Paddy Crerand, the principal witness, said: "I back Denis to the hilt." Both Law, captain of Manchester United and Scotland, and Crerand believed that Peter Rhodes, the referee, was mistaken. They claimed that a remark by Denis was intended for Crerand and not the referee. "I was there. I heard what was said and who it was said to," added Crerand and a few days later told the press: "I'm to blame for Denis Law being sent off. I'd rather we lost two points than Denis." Denis was pleased about the personal hearing. He said he still felt terrible about the misunderstanding that led to him being ordered off and just wanted to explain the muddle surrounding his dismissal. "If I'd only kept my mouth shut this would never have happened," added Crerand, "I had a go at Denis about his foul on Alan Ball and he replied with a swear word, the kind you hear all the time. It wasn't meant for the referee. No player in his right mind would say a thing like that to a referee. If I could have explained it might have been different. I started to but Bobby Charlton brushed me aside because he thought I was starting a quarrel with the referee. This is a bitter blow for United and me personally. Denis has been a great captain and the team is playing magnificently. A suspension could hit us really hard. I hope they will listen to me when Denis gets a hearing. I'll go anywhere to try to help."

Yet Mr Rhodes was equally emphatic. "My report has gone to the FA and the Football League. There is certainly no misunderstanding in my mind." When he was asked if Law's remark could have been addressed to someone else he replied that it was "absolutely impossible". He then explained that when he approached Law he had no intention of even taking his name. "I just intended to speak to him," said Mr Rhodes. Alan Ball added: "I admit that I pulled Denis' shirt. Then he ran across me later. I heard Denis swear, but I didn't know who the remark was meant for. It was a pity because with no disrespects to Denis, Blackpool played better against 11 men than ten."

Many years later Alan Ball explained his admiration for the man he had clashed with that stormy day in Blackpool: "Denis Law was my idol when I was a young player, the one I tried to copy the most. The thing I admired most about Law was that he changed from being a great midfield player to become a striker and was even better at that. He was impossible to mark tightly and scored goals that took your breath away, particularly with his head. After I made my mark in English football during the 1966 World Cup I realised that, from then on, I would be a marked man. I knew that I would have to overcome this if I was to advance any further in the game. It was to Denis Law that I turned for advice on that subject. I watched film of him in action, noted the way he could put just that fraction of distance between himself and a defender without anyone really noticing and how he could sprint from a standing start with such speed that no-one could keep up with him. I learned enough to help me overcome the close markers but not quite enough to become as good at it as Law."

Meanwhile United's players wished Maurice Setters good luck as he left Old Trafford for Stoke City. Matt Busby had transferred the tough-tackling wing-half for £30,000. Setters had joined United in January 1960 and helped them win the FA Cup. On leaving he spoke of his affection for the club. "It is true that my leaving is tinged with sadness because I like the club, the players and manager, Matt Busby. I hope he achieves all his ambitions. I leave with no ill-feeling whatever on my part. In fact I hope United win the Championship which I think they will." He went on to say that he had to move if he was no longer wanted and that it was no secret that he did not want to leave the club: "My wife and I like the Manchester people and we have made many good friends. I am glad and so is she, that we will be staying in Manchester." He intended travelling to Stoke for training.

There was also a denial in the newspapers by George Best that he was leaving United to join Italian glamour club Juventus. It was reported that the crack Italian team had been watching his performances on United's left wing and had monitored him while he was in Switzerland for Northern Ireland's World Cup tie. "I'm flattered, of course," said George, adding, "which 18-year-old wouldn't be? But let me say right now, I'm not interested. Because I'm playing for the best club in Europe, and I'm earning at least £50 a week." George was due to play for Northern Ireland against Scotland at Hampden Park. His United team mate, Paddy Crerand, sent a message to his old Celtic pal, full-back Jimmy Kennedy, who would be marking Best. "This boy is better than Willie Henderson. He's the best winger I've ever seen," said Pat. There was no doubting that Best was attracting fans from every section of sport.

On a bitterly cold winter's day two years previously, Manchester United youth team coach Johnny Aston senior had had a quiet conversation with Leeds manager Don Revie. The talk got around to players in general and Johnny told the Leeds boss about one particular young player. "He's the greatest prospect I've ever seen," said Aston. He was of course referring to a slip of an Irish lad by the name of Georgie Best.

"At the time I thought that this was rather a sweeping statement to make about a lad who had not long left school," said Revie, "but then Johnny Aston has seen some truly great stars at Old Trafford like Duncan Edwards, Eddie Colman, Roger Byrne, and a host of others, who have carried United to great achievements at home and abroad and hadn't Johnny Aston himself played alongside many 'greats' in the 1940s such as Johnny Carey, Jack Rowley and Stan Pearson to name but three?"

Nevertheless Revie thought Aston's proclamation about Best was a bit of an exaggeration. "At least I thought so," said Revie, "that is until I saw George Best play for the first time last season. Since then I have watched him with great admiration on several occasions and now I confess to being of the same opinion as Johnny Aston." Revie added that he was not being wise after the event but Best, without a doubt, was going to be one of the world's greatest players, a star to be mentioned in the same breath as Di Stefano, Garrincha, Pele and Denis Law. "He's still only 18. Yet many critics of the game are now starting to put him on the same level as Stan Matthews and Tom Finney. I personally would not put him in that category just yet. But he is on the right track. The mind boggles when you think of him, Bobby Charlton and the phenomenal Denis Law in the same forward line."

So little was said by Denis to reporters because of his natural shyness that it was interesting to hear him voice an opinion on one of his club-mates. Talking about Best, Denis said that every so often football threw up a new young superstar that people romanced about. The youngster was a natural for the headline writers, an inestimable asset to his club and an immediate target for the press, television and radio. Everyone wanted to see him, interview him, photograph and be seen with him. "Such a richly endowed young man is my Old Trafford team-mate George Best," said Denis adding, "he is an immensely talented young Irishman. He first came into first team football in September 1963 and he has been right at the top as an international figure ever since." But when asked what it was like to play in the same team as Best, Law said: "how does he react to the intense pressures on the field? As his partner on so many epic occasions at home and abroad I enjoy the privilege of being able to answer such a question first hand. George has not changed since those first early days. He is a quiet boy, with little fuss and a gentle sense of humour. I remember him well when he gained his senior status at Old Trafford. All of us have butterflies in the tummy before a match but George seemed completely unperturbed. Obviously he would be expecting the same kind of emotion all of us feel before a match but he was like a seasoned professional. Those early days of his career were times of incredible promise by a youngster who, off the field, seemed like just another frail teenager who had stepped up from the junior ranks. Before his first team debut I had heard very little about him. Obviously I had not seen much of the reserve team and even less of the third and fourth teams but when George arrived on the scene I felt tempted to ask 'are there any more where you came from?' He is developing into a truly magnificent footballer."

A week after the fiasco in Blackpool it was back to action for League points. The Reds were at home to Blackburn Rovers. In a sparkling game Best and Connelly scored the first two goals and Herd added a third in a resounding 3-0 victory. Denis, perhaps not surprisingly, had a very quiet game but Bobby Charlton rose to great heights and was easily the best player on the pitch. The following game was against Arsenal at Highbury and it was a classic. United's attack gave the Arsenal defence a real hammering. They had a 3-0 lead after just 28 minutes and deserved every bit of their supremacy. In the opening minutes Bobby Charlton headed a ball down for Law to hammer the ball into the net off a post. In the 17th minute Connelly, having a storming game down the right, beat the Gunners' full-back McCullough and drove the ball past Burns, Arsenal's goalkeeper, into the net. Arsenal were shell-shocked and nine minutes later they felt knocked out as they went 3-0 down from another flash of Law genius. Charlton intercepted the ball in midfield and sent Best on a mazy run with a well-timed pass. The Irish wizard skinned Don Howe, the England full-back, and crossed a beautiful ball for Denis to volley first time into the net. This was brilliant, breathtaking football from the Red Devils. Nevertheless just before the interval Anderson scored for Arsenal and in the 74th minute George Eastham pulled another back for the Gunners. Yet United calmed their nerves and despite a Herd goal being mysteriously disallowed for offside, triumphed 3-2 at Highbury. However, the game ended strangely as, at the final whistle, over 50,000 Arsenal supporters stood roaring their approval, even though their team had lost.

Billy Wright, the Arsenal manager, was gushing in his praise for Denis after this thrilling game: "Law has just provided further proof that he is one of the great players of our time," said Wright. "Oh how I wish there were more players of his quality and class around today. Let's be frank, football drastically needs personalities, players of ability and artistry to lift a match to a rare peak of excitement." The former England and Wolves captain said that there were plenty of players who possessed this exceptional touch of genius before the war. "Don't rush to the conclusion that I am knocking modern-day footballers. The pre-war stars shone against a general background of mediocrity but the overall standard of play today is so high that only the truly great players earn wide recognition of their outstanding proficiency. Denis 'Goals Galore' Law climbs easily into this exclusive category." The Arsenal manager was posed the nagging problem that faced First Division managers at least twice that season - how to stop Law: "There is only one way to tame this master of soccer arts - mark him tightly, so tightly that there's not a single blade of grass on the pitch that he treads alone," answered Billy, "this is easier said than done."

The Aston Villa manager, Dick Taylor, spotlighted the great menace of Law when he told Billy how the Scot cracked four goals past them at Old Trafford. "We locked Law right out of the game for 20 minutes," said Mr Taylor, "then suddenly, he struck from out of nowhere. He scored with a magnificent 25-yard shot to turn the game completely in Manchester United's favour." Billy said that was typical of Law who could be having a really bad game, but defenders had to watch him every second because of this knack of doing the unexpected. "There are few inside-forwards in Britain today who can take command of a match with the same biting emphasis and authority as Law. Jimmy Greaves at his best and George Eastham are just two who easily come to mind as capable of similar feats. But I think it is fair to say that Law is the best all-rounder in the country. He can scheme, he can score, he can do so many other things. As I was saying, football could do with more like him."

The distinguished football writer, Laurie Pignon of the *Daily Sketch*, wrote an article that made for interesting reading and brought a few smirks from Law's colleagues and United supporters. He wrote: "Denis Law proved against Arsenal that he is one of the greatest footballers ever. He is also one of the most controversial, a victim of his own temperament. It all adds up to make him one of the outstanding personalities and performers of his time." Mr Pignon then went on to say that he had gone to Highbury to put Denis under the soccer microscope, which few players could have survived. Armed with a pocket tape recorder, stopwatch, binoculars and notebook, he marked and recorded every kick and move that Denis made. And the result was startling: Denis had the ball 47 times, 18 were single kicks or headers and in all they made an on-the-ball total of 126 seconds. He was offside twice and fouled three times. He scored twice and missed two more goals by inches and had a horizontal circus-act shot brilliantly saved before setting up an easy chance for Herd that was ruled offside. Spending most of the match as a spearhead he ran more than 20 yards with the ball on only four occasions. Twice he went into tough tackles and came away with the ball and twice was robbed of possession - once when Arsenal keeper Tony Burns dived at his feet. Although tightly but not always successfully marked, Denis did not commit one foul. He showed the speed of a hunted stag and the manners of Lord Fauntleroy. Once he ran 20 yards to collect a ball for Arsenal to take a free-kick and later ran 25 yards to quieten his own goalkeeper who was angry about a corner decision. "I had gone to Highbury to try and reduce greatness to facts and figures. In a way I failed. Pardon the pun...but Denis is a Law unto himself," wrote Mr Pignon. He said that Denis' movements off the ball were devastating: he could sprint from a standing start for 40 yards or he could produce a little shuffle that took two defenders out of position. He was a 90-minute danger man and 100 per cent entertainer.

The stage had been set for Law with a near 60,000 crowd - by far the biggest on another slumping Saturday - sending the adrenaline flowing through his Scottish veins like the floodgates of the tide. He loved every second of it and his spirit reflected the mood of a game that sent every fan home happy, even though 90 per cent had seen their own team, Arsenal, narrowly beaten 3-2 despite a tremendous second-half comeback. Law, whose temperament is the key to his success, as well as his slide to disaster, was playing under a dual cloud...but who would have guessed? On 10th December he was to appear before the FA's Disciplinary Committee for his dismissal against Blackpool. In Scotland there had been speculation that he would be dropped from the national team. "What rubbish," added Mr Pignon, "there isn't a World Cup manager who wouldn't include Law in his side. What a player...!"

*

Matt Busby was a very happy man as he sat in his office reading the rave notices acclaiming his club's run of 18 matches without defeat, including three in the Inter-Cities Fairs Cup. The previous night at Old Trafford he had watched his team mesmerise the German team Borussia Dortmund 4-1 (10-1 on aggregate.) Within 40 seconds of the game starting the Reds were 1-0 in front with a goal from Bobby Charlton that had Tilkowski, the German keeper, clutching at thin air. It was Bobby again in the 19th minute, when he did a Law and rose high above the defenders to head his second goal. The second half started off quietly but after Connelly made it 3-0 from a fierce drive Denis got on the scoresheet in the 63rd minute, pulling a goal out of the hat with an acrobatic overhead kick after a German defender had headed out a corner kick by Connelly. As the ball whistled into the net there was a hushed silence. It was if the crowd could not believe the unique movement they had just witnessed. It was by any stretch of the imagination superb!

Denis, Paddy Crerand, David Herd, manager Matt Busby and Cliff Lloyd, secretary of the Professional Footballers' Association, attended the FA hearing concerning Law's sending off at Blackpool. Crerand and Herd were going as witnesses to what occurred before referee Peter Rhodes sent off Law. After listening to all concerned the FA came down in favour of the referee and Law was suspended again for 28 days and fined £50. Cliff Lloyd said of the FA decision: "Under football law that is the end of it, because there is no appeal which I think is disgraceful. My association may have to look into the question of whether to make an appeal under the law of the land. It will be another costly Christmas for Denis. He could find himself out of pocket to the tune of £850 (a great deal of money in 1964) losing £120 a match for six games and the £50 fine plus the costs of the hearing - about £80." His ban would end on 10th January 1965 and he would miss the FA Cup third-round tie against Chester and three League games.

The referee, Peter Rhodes, the owner of a grocery business in York, said it was touch and go whether he attended the FA Disciplinary hearing because he had been ill. He had not refereed a game since sending Denis off, although the Saturday after the hearing he was expected to referee a match between Preston and Ipswich. In a newspaper article, he said: "I had to send Denis Law off the field, there was no alternative. He committed a foul and I warned him 'Don't do it again' or something like that. He then used two words in reply. You wouldn't expect to keep your job if you said those words to your boss. Law admitted using these words to me. He also admitted it in writing to the FA. Directly after using these words, Law said something else. He denied saying this to me at the Commission. He said he directed the words to his colleague, Pat Crerand. But Crerand's evidence was valueless as Law had admitted the first part anyway." Mr Rhodes said it wasn't a case of the Commission believing that a referee could do no wrong. Denis had admitted the first part and that was enough. He said he was really sorry but as a referee he had a job to do and it was no good shirking it. "I'm not a Sunday school teacher or anything like that but I take what I think is an intelligent view about swearing on the field. If a player stubs his foot in the centre circle and says a naughty word I'll let that go with a mild warning. But if, say, he does it out near the corner flag, then that man is on the trot for me." He said that football was a family entertainment and there were now many women and children attending matches. "If you jam your finger in the door near your boss and say something out of place it is different from going up to the boss and calling him a four-letter word. That's how you have to look at it," he said.

He said that he hoped this business would have a salutary effect on the others in regard to their language. "We referees aren't fools you know. I was on the line for four years before I became a referee in the middle. I've had 14 years now. We come up through the hardest school in the world." In another newspaper article Mr Rhodes said that he had been a referee for 25 years and in that time he had seen Wilf Mannion, Raich Carter and many other great inside-forwards but rated Denis Law above them all. However, he went on to say, "Law must learn that tantrums and temper don't mix with greatness. He's got ten years left to erase the bad memories and make himself one of soccer's immortals."

Not long after the hearing the FA called Mr Rhodes himself to appear before them. It was said that he had given one of the Sunday newspapers confidential information from the hearing regarding Denis. He was told in no uncertain terms that he must never repeat this sort of thing and bring the game into disrepute. Quite a few years later Denis and Diana were holidaying in Spain. At Barcelona airport Denis went to the toilet and as he was washing his hands he thought he recognised the person standing next to him but wasn't too sure. Imagine his surprise when he discovered that it was none other than Peter Rhodes himself. The referee obviously knew Denis straight away and spoke to him like a long lost friend and laughingly told Denis that he had collected £7,000 from stories he had passed on to the newspapers about Denis concerning the sending-off incident. If Mr Rhodes was expecting an endorsement from Law he was sadly mistaken. Denis was shocked at what he had just been told and could not understand the sheer audacity of the man to openly boast that he made £7,000 out of his own misfortune, not taking into account his own loss of income from the affair. Denis' normally cheerful disposition quickly changed to anger and without uttering a word to Rhodes he left the toilet and returned to Diana. He said the meeting with the former referee had spoiled his holiday.

On 12th December Denis played his final game, against West Brom at the Hawthorns, before commencing yet another 28-day suspension. Denis kept quiet about the episode but his wife Diana was upset and had a lot to say. She broke off from an afternoon washday at their smart semi-detached home in south Manchester, to tell reporters: "It's not fair. All Denis did was to say a few words to the referee in a heated moment. Anyone else would have got away with just a warning, or at the most a short suspension but Denis has got a reputation, and soccer officials are making sure he lives up to it. I don't usually interfere in Denis' professional career - but I've kept quiet long enough. We were just hoping and keeping our fingers crossed that for once the case would be judged on facts - not personalities. But that hasn't happened. I am sure Denis' soccer background has played a much greater part in the decision than the offence." Matt Busby said that the club was relieved to get the verdict 24 hours earlier than had been anticipated but he didn't want to comment on the outcome.

Diana was not the only one to speak out about the suspension. His club-mate Bill Foulkes was annoyed and said Denis was being made an example of because he was such a high-profile star. Foulkes believed that Law's suspension could be explained because he simply hated losing. "Denis gets into trouble with referees so frequently because when he loses the ball or is beaten in a tackle, he tries to retrieve it quickly. Denis can take chances that wouldn't be chances at all to inferior players. His reflexes are out of this world," said big Bill, who could speak from experience having tangled with Denis on the training ground. Bill also mentioned how Denis' amazing ability to outjump bigger defenders was a sign of his bravery as well as unique ability. "It is a shame that he has to pay such a heavy penalty for something done within a split second. Off the field he is a great lad, there are no airs or graces with him. He is a magnificent footballer and scores spectacular goals."

The match against West Bromwich was a characteristic farewell - marked with a goal and a flourish of the decanter that held his football skill. Amid pouring rain the fans were entertained and Denis never spoke to the referee or committed a foul. He scored a goal, saw West Brom equalise and at the end of the game the Albion players shook his hand and only then did a big grin crease his face. As the West Brom captain Graham Williams slapped Denis on the back there were shouts of "Good old Denis" from a large section of the 28,500 crowd - a record that season at the Hawthorns. Just before going into the dressing room a fan gave him a mysterious box that he graciously accepted. It was a Christmas present in advance for his young son Gary. Back inside he signed dozens of autograph books. "I naturally feel some sadness," said Denis, "it's like a bad dream but I have to take it and look to the future." He said he would obviously keep in training in readiness for his return. Joe Mercer, who was at the game said: "Just look at him…the best player in the world. And did you hear that crowd applauding him? They appreciate his greatness."

Matt Busby said that Denis must be pleased at the crowd's reaction to him. Midland football fans backed Denis to the hilt. This was surprising because after he was sent off a year ago at Aston Villa, following his tussle with Alan Deakin, he was regarded as a villain. Many Villa supporters were in the crowd at the Hawthorns but the old grievances were forgotten in a wave of sympathy. He was given a welcome roar from the terraces as he ran out at the start of the game and every Law touch was warmly applauded. His occasional mistakes drew sympathetic sighs, a week before they would have been jeered. And of course there was a special cheer for his 18th minute goal. Alf Hadley, of Quinton, Birmingham, a West Brom fan said: "I was standing with people who booed Denis Law last time he was here. Today we are all for him. You couldn't help feeling sorry for the way he's been treated. Why couldn't they just fine him the money they say he'll lose. That way neither the club nor the fans would have suffered."

Unlike his first suspension, when Denis was not allowed to use the facilities at Old Trafford to keep himself in shape, he was allowed to train at Old Trafford this time, although he would still not be paid. His club-mates decided to have a collection on his behalf. It was a well-meaning thing for them to do, but the FA officials were soon to put a stop to it when they heard about it in the newspapers.

*

There had been a great deal of speculation that Denis would be voted 'Footballer of the Year' for 1964 but again there was disappointment for him and the United followers as West Ham's Bobby Moore was given this honour with Charlie Hurley, the Sunderland centre-half, coming runner-up and Denis in third place. However, a week into his suspension a far greater honour was bestowed upon Denis as he was awarded the Golden Football as 'The European Footballer of the Year' for 1964. Denis was obviously thrilled at hearing this welcome news and felt deeply honoured. This was only the second time since the award was first made, in 1956, that a British player had been awarded this fabulous honour. Stanley Matthews, then with Blackpool, was the winner on that occasion but now the poll organised by France Football, the world's foremost weekly football magazine, asked correspondents in 21

European countries to nominate their top five European footballers in order of merit. For each first place vote a player received five points, for a second place four points and so on right down to a single point for a fifth place. The poll closed as follows:

1 Denis Law - 61 points

2 Luis Suarez (Inter Milan and Spain) - 43 points

3 Amancio (Real Madrid and Spain) - 38 points

4 Silva Ferreira Eusebio (Benfica and Portugal) - 31points

5 Paul Van Himst (Anderlecht and Belgium) - 28 points

Two other British players were mentioned in the voting: Jimmy Greaves came sixth with 19 points and Bobby Moore was among eight players receiving just one point. So Denis joined the 'Hall of Fame' along with Matthews (1956), Di Stefano (1957), Kopa (1958), Di Stefano (1959), Suarez (1960), Sivori (1961), Masopust (1962) and Yashin (1963). What a great milestone in the life of Europe's number one genius - Denis Law, the stormy petrel of English football. The honour was bestowed upon him as he began his second 28-day suspension. His first, in 1963, was for kicking an opponent. His second was for using bad language to the referee, Peter Rhodes. So while Denis was in the shadows of disgrace in Manchester, he was lifted into the glaring, glamorous spotlight by the sportswriters of Europe. This was so typical of Denis, a young man idolised by thousands of fans all over the world, tolerated by some, hated by others.

Dirty...Brutal...Temperamental. Those were just a few of the words used to describe him. However, none of them was true. The one word that was true and not mentioned was the simple term 'great' - used in its proper sense, not in the modern, over-used context. Denis Law was at that time a truly great player. He was thrilling, exciting and artistic. Who would have thought that the small, weedy, bag of bones that turned up in Andy Beattie's office in 1956 would have turned into this world-class demon of a player?

Wherever he played crowds flocked to see him. At Old Trafford he was idolised, he had raised the gate to well over

40,000 and the enthusiasm he brought to the Reds was such that United's reserve team gates in the 1963/64 season were not far below those of Manchester City's first team! It was no wonder that an Arsenal supporter, after watching Law tear his team to pieces when United beat them at Old Trafford, was heard to say: "Matt Busby should be locked up for robbery, because he stole Law for £115,000."

Only jealous people doubted Law's great talents. He could play a midfield role, lie upfield as a striker, or he could double up and do both jobs. He feared no opponent, they all came alike to Denis. He was a natural born footballer, an all-round player. He could tackle as hard and as effectively as any full-back or wing-half, he could dribble superbly, his passing was a model of accuracy and he could shoot with devastating power. But the aspect of his play that delighted spectators more than anything was his heading ability. He wasn't a tall man but what he lacked in inches he made up for with almost perfect timing. Spectators would watch Denis go up for those high balls and the other players would be on their way up as he made his move. Then, instinctively, he would soar into the air like a guided missile and nine times out of ten you could guarantee that it would be his blond head that got to the ball first. When he scored a goal a huge smile would light up his face as he took the crowd's cheers with both arms raised high above his head. He celebrated and expected and received the applause of thousands of fans. Even his walk had an arrogant air about it.

Denis Law had the temperament, eccentric at times, of a true artist. It was this temperament that got him into trouble with referees every now and again. He suffered an awful lot of fouls and unfair play by cynical defenders and there were times when he retaliated. Authority would then make an example of him. After all, it was far better to do this to the fabulous Denis Law than poor, simple Joe Bloggs, who wouldn't even rate a line in the newspapers. When Denis retaliated it was headline news, usually front page. Denis also had a quick tongue which again got him into trouble on the football field.

But here again Denis was an artist. Football wasn't just a job to him. It was his life. He treated every goal scored against Manchester United as a personal insult. There was no doubting that Denis had his critics. There were pompous folk who didn't tolerate his antics on the field, who did not want their football tinged with excitement. But when they made Denis Law they threw away the mould which was a great pity, because it is the Denis Laws who add spice to football, who get the spectators clambering through the turnstiles. For all his faults, Denis was one of the greatest discoveries to have happened in British football. He was an artist and a genius. Now he was deservedly known as Europe's Number One.

Friday 15th January 1965 was a bright and breezy day and Old Trafford was buzzing as the sun shone brightly through the windows at the back of the Stretford End. And it wasn't only the weather. Denis was gloriously happy and getting ready to make his return to duty the following day in an away game against Nottingham Forest at the City Ground. There were dozens of reporters hanging around the ground hoping to get a story. As he made his way past the office, Denis shouted: "Come on, Mrs Burgess. Where's my cup of tea, love?"

In his absence the team had won once and drawn twice but a player of Law's calibre was an added bonus for any team. Would he be ready for first team action? That was a question many reporters were asking Matt Busby. He had no doubts whatsoever. He said that Denis had been fortunate in that he never carried any extra weight so would be fit enough. Matt also said that some people had the wrong impression of Denis. "A man came to the ground recently," said the manager, "and while he was here he met Denis. Later, he told me: 'What a mistaken impression you can have sometimes from the tittle-tattle of other people, sometimes for no reason at all. Any wrong impression I had about Law has now been removed forever.'" Matt went on to say that although Denis was still only 25, he was maturing with age and experience.

Saturday 16th January 1965 would surely be a day that Forest goalkeeper, Peter Grummitt, would remember for the rest of his life. Why? Well it was the day that Denis came back into football with a bang. Nobody expected Denis to be at his sharpest after his suspension but he surprised even his own team-mates. He slipped into top form from the first whistle. His distribution was superb and he gave the kind of display that had everyone agreeing that he was back to his best. United, wearing blue shirts to avoid a colour clash, were given a rapturous reception. After just three minutes the 43,009 fans were stunned as the Law man announced his return with a goal that had all the majesty and power of the king of football. In atrocious conditions and with the heavens sending down bucketfuls of rain, he wriggled his way through a tight defence to put the ball into the net before turning to the crowd, a big grin across his face and with both arms reaching skywards to acclaim his return. Forest got an equaliser through Hinton and after nearly half-an-hour went in front when Hinton got his second but this day belonged to Law. He scored the equalising goal from a rebound off Peter Grummitt after the keeper had blocked a rocket from David Herd. Later Denis thought he had scored the winner, as did referee Mr Grundy, only for a linesman to flag for an offence.

Henry Newton, Nottingham Forest's tough-as-nails half-back, had been detailed to stick as close to Denis as his blue shirt. "It was an exhilarating experience and a valuable milestone in my football education," said Newton, "I discovered just why Law is more than merely a first class player; why he is in a category of his own. He has superb ball control, timing and accuracy. He's dangerous in the air and with either foot but those attributes alone don't make a world-beater. Plenty of other players in the First Division have those qualifications. I think Law's finest asset, the one that puts him above everyone else, is his knack of kidding you that he's temporarily out of the game." Newton went on to say that for long spells Denis was content to stand in an offside position which tempted a defender to think there was no danger from him there but at the last moment he would suddenly slip back so he was onside and ready to pounce on any balls coming through. His other great weapon, said Newton, was Denis' instinctive positioning for the unexpected chance. "I'd like to play against him more often, but not every week. The human body can only stand so much."

Ken Jones, one of the best sports writers in the world and a close friend of Jimmy Murphy, was at the match reporting for the *Daily Mirror*. Years later Ken recalled this game: "It took Denis Law just three minutes, yes three minutes, to stamp his genius on this match. He moved through a packed Nottingham Forest penalty area like a greyhound and scored a goal. It was done so quickly I had to replay the move in my mind. The goal brought forth a deafening chant from the Manchester fans of 'Denis Law - Denis Law.' Later on they used the old Al Jolson number 'Mammy' to sing a song about Denis. 'I'd walk a million miles for one of your goals my Den-is' they sang loud and clear. He did score again and although he wasn't as sharp as normal, because this was his first game since his suspension, he took his goals with the same impish style. Jimmy [Murphy] raved about Denis and I can understand why. On his day there were few better inside- forwards than him. He was a character and a world-class player."

After his two-goal comeback Denis and United had a three game marathon with Stoke City. These games appealed to the Reds' fans because Stoke had virtually become a United old boys' association. Former club captain Dennis Viollet had left Old Trafford three years before after a distinguished career with the Reds during which he had set the club goalscoring record which he still holds. The first game was a League match played at Old Trafford and it ended in a 1-1 draw with Denis Law getting the goal. Maurice Setters, back on his old ground, relished the job of marking Denis. The fans of both teams expected an all-action, no-holds barred clash between these two friends. They had a mutual respect for each other, that was until the referee blew his whistle to start the game and then the friendship stopped and the action began. They didn't disappoint the fans expecting fireworks and clashed on several occasions, although Maurice had extra help when Stoke manager, Tony Waddington, selected wing-half Eric Skeels to play inside-forward but with orders to stay close to Denis, explaining: "With players like Charlton and Law against us, I had to provide extra cover."

The next game was an FA Cup tie at Stoke's Victoria Ground that ended scoreless. The match was dour and personal feuds erupted between Law and Setters, Ritchie and Pat Dunne, and Crerand and McIlroy. Denis and Setters had a real old set-to, they gave each other a good pounding. After one lecture from the referee, Mr Callaghan of Merythr Tydfill, they threw their arms around each other - cherubs with dirty faces. The replay at Old Trafford was watched by over 50,000 and ended in a narrow 1-0 victory for the Reds, with a David Herd goal. Once again Denis and Setters clashed throughout the game and the referee was a busy man indeed.

However, there was more exciting news for the newspapers to headline as United had now set an unenviable record of having nine players sent off in 18 months. Harry Gregg and club captain Noel Cantwell had received their marching orders while playing for the reserves against Burnley at Turf Moor. Cantwell was sent off after he had been earlier booked for a foul on Burnley centre-forward Colin Blant and when another flare-up ensued he was ordered off. Harry Gregg was dismissed after words with the referee. It was five minutes, however, before either player left the field as the United players carried on a private war with the angry crowd. There was an incredible scene as the United players hurled back pennies, divots and soil which had been thrown at them by fans. Order was only restored when the police intervened. The referee, Mr Ackroyd, also had to tell Wilf McGuinness, United's coach, to leave the field.

Back at Old Trafford after the weekend's escapades, there was a great deal of 'mickey-taking' by the players to Cantwell, Gregg and McGuinness, but not by Matt Busby. Why? Because football had been rocked to its foundations when ten current and former professional footballers were found guilty of 'fixing' matches and all of them had been given custodial sentences at Nottingham Assizes. Tony Kay and Peter Swan, two

England internationals, were among those sent to prison and banned from football for life. The newspapers were pointing the finger at so-called over-paid heroes who, they said, were leading a cushy life while they cheated the supporters who paid their inflated wages.

After the Cup action it was back to picking up points in the League. It was February and the Reds were going for the treble of League, FA Cup and Inter-Cities Fairs Cup. This was asking a great deal from the players. In the fifth round FA Cup tie against Burnley, at Old Trafford, the Reds were trailing 1-0 from a Andy Lochhead goal with less than ten minutes left. The United fans were feeling dejected and the prospect of a place in the sixth round draw looked extremely remote but the old saying that a game is never won or lost until the referee blows the final whistle held true. Just as the Old Trafford crowd were beginning to accept defeat, the Law man came to the rescue. He had his back to the Burnley goal with players from both sides shoving and pushing each other as George Best centred - the ball dropped to Denis and within seconds he became a contortionist genius. He seemed to do a backward summersault, the crowd held its breath and with a scissor kick, he had the ball into the back of Burnley's goal with goalkeeper Adam Blacklaw an astounded spectator. But just as the fans were acclaiming this truly phenomenal goal Paddy Crerand scored the winner. The Burnley fans said the Reds were lucky to score twice in the last 10 minutes but they could only admire the audacity of Law's unbelievable goal that set up the game's decisive moments.

After disposing of Burnley, United were drawn against Wolves in the sixth round while they had also reached the quarter final of the Inter-Cities Fairs Cup by beating Everton 3-2 on aggregate over two legs. They were drawn against R C Strasbourg, the first leg to be played on 12th May. Meanwhile United hammered Wolves at Molineux 5-3 in a typical cup-tie full of thrills, spills and bags of entertainment, lapped up by the capacity crowd. Wolves had the audacity to take a 2-0 lead within 15 minutes but the Reds fought back with tremendous spirit and scored five times before Wolves got their third, a consolation, near the end of the match. At one point Denis was kicked in the head and had to be helped from the field by trainer Jack Crompton. After treatment he was back in action and helped the Reds pull a goal back just before the interval. Connelly took a corner kick, a Wolves defender headed it but Law raced forward and rammed a header into the net. Six minutes after half time David Herd equalised and then George Best put them in front. Paddy Crerand made it 4-2 before Denis sealed the game with a fifth. United were through to a semi-final showdown against Leeds United.

*

Writing in *The Book of Soccer*, edited by the late Bobby Moore, Denis said that from his own personal point of view, being a member of a team that won the World Cup was a professional footballer's greatest ambition. He went on say that it would make winning leagues and cups seem less important. He asked what British football would have to do in order to become a permanent power on the lines of Brazil. In his opinion, and he had no doubt, he firmly believed that English league football was the best in the world. Week after week football followers in England could watch fast, entertaining, open football with the minimum importance placed on tight defensive play that made watching most foreign league football dreary. It was like digging gardens, Denis' idea of hard labour. He mentioned his year in Italian football and said that he was not exaggerating when he described the ordinary league football that the Italians had developed. Eight men, he said guard each goal and a handful of forwards make occasional raids, while he explained that the constant obstruction and shirt-pulling could only lead to neutral spectators becoming bored. "That," he said, "is my idea of Italian football."

However for all that it was that kind of football that seemed to bring results in the winning of European competitions. Denis said that people were saying that British teams must follow suit if we hoped to win the World Cup. He mentioned that league games were tough, all-action matches with plenty of goals, 'end-to-end' play and 'incidents'. "All the great, exciting stuff which British fans watch on Saturday afternoons from August to April." He admitted he liked playing in those games and was of the opinion that although all football fans wanted their own teams to win more than anything else, the fact was that they were good entertainment. If English players were asked to change to the slow, short-passing, safe style used by the continentals, they would go out of the game. "Believe me," said Denis, "football in Italy isn't fun. They eliminate scoring chances, the Italians play a brand of football that I would hate to see being played in England."

Denis also spoke about the punishment for dirty play in Italy: "The penalty is more severe there and because of this the Italian defenders have virtually cut out the heavy tackling that caused so much trouble - they're too anxious to tackle. Instead they rely on obstruction - not tackling but shirt pulling rather than shoulder charges. Contrast that with the atmosphere at Old Trafford, Goodison Park or Anfield, where 22 players give everything and both teams go all-out to score goals as players give and receive the physical challenge as part of the basic appeal of football." Denis added that coming to England following a season in Italy was like "coming out of a hothouse into a spring breeze. Wonderful!"

He concluded by saying that in England there was an ideal balance between natural enthusiasm and theoretical planning. In other countries they tended, in his view, to put too much value on the theory. In fact, he believed that it was possible for the home countries to beat the continentals by improving our own styles and abilities. "We needn't go overboard on military-style planning and we could keep the life in our Saturday afternoons, watching the most exciting league football in the world."

In April 1965 Nobby Stiles, who had only secured a regular first team position that season, was selected by Alf Ramsey for England's annual match against Scotland. This had been a fairy-tale season for the popular Stiles. He was awarded an

Under 23 cap and in the opinion of many was in the running for the Footballer of the Year award which Leeds' Bobby Collins eventually won. Nobby had represented England at every level and was overjoyed to be playing in his first international match.

As a result of Stiles' selection, the England - Scotland game at Wembley became the focus of discussion at the Cliff training ground, between Denis, Paddy Crerand, Bobby Charlton, Nobby and John Connelly, who was a reserve. It was all friendly and high-spirited with not a touch of animosity. However, in the tunnel as both teams lined up to walk out onto the Wembley sward, Nobby spotted Denis and with a big, melon-sized grin held his hand out to shake Denis' hand.

"I greeted Denis warmly," recalled Nobby, "after all, we were team-mates at Old Trafford. I was shocked when he just blanked me. I foolishly thought he hadn't heard me so I shouted 'Denis!' and then he looked at me, without a smile or friendly gesture he looked down at my feet and up to my head without breaking his expression." Denis takes up the story: "It was the worst thing I could have done because Nobby kicked me up and down that Wembley pitch. He had a great game and he blossomed into a great wing-half for Manchester United and England." In the event Law scored for Scotland in a 2-2 draw.

In later years when he was asked what he thought of Denis Law, Nobby grinned, then spoke in glowing terms of the Lawman. "I am not being nostalgic in saying that Denis was one of the best players in the world, because without a doubt he was one of the best ever. If he was playing today he would be sensational. What price would Denis Law be worth in the twenty-first century? Priceless I would say. With the media coverage players receive today, he would never be off the television or front pages. I'm not sure he would have liked that, because he avoided that sort of publicity in his prime. Denis was a special type of player, a forward who never feared to go in where Angels fear to tread. And no matter how big, rough or tough the defenders were Denis would clash with them if he had to in order to go for goal. He had fantastic balance and coordination. He was unique really. From a standing position he could move like a whippet. But he could weigh up situations in an instant and this helped his team. On the field he displayed all his emotions and fans either loved or hated him, but never ignored him. He was more than one of the best ever goalscorers, he was also a wonderfully gifted footballer."

*

In this period Leeds, under Don Revie, were one of the teams of the era yet they were perceived as a rough, tough, niggly and cynical side. For example, in November they had played Everton at Goodison Park in a First Division game. In a bitterly fought match both sides were going at each other hammer and tongs. So competitive did the game become that the referee ordered both teams to the dressing room for a cooling-off period. In their promotion season, Leeds virtually battled their way out of the Second Division. There were reports of ruthlessness and cynicism but it was thought that once they reached the First Division they would calm down. However, this was wishful thinking because if anything they became a team more determined to win at any cost. Other teams didn't relish playing the Leeds team of this era. It seemed to players from other clubs that Leeds went out of their way to intimidate and stamp their mark on games and certain players. Their methods saw them lose a great deal of support outside Leeds. They hated being beaten. Who doesn't? Yet they played the game as if it were a war. Nevertheless they had some skilful players like Eddie Gray, Peter Lorimer and a black South African left-winger called Albert Johanneson along with United old boy Johnny Giles, little Bobby Collins, the fiery Billy Bremner, Jack Charlton and Norman Hunter.

Jack Charlton, the elder brother of United's Bobby, was known as the Giraffe by opposing fans because of his long neck and tall 6 foot 3 inch frame. He gained a reputation for speaking his mind and caused a minor sensation when he appeared in a one-to-one interview on Tyne-Tees Television. In the interview Jack revealed that he kept a little black book and in it were the names of five players who he was going to sort out on the field before he ended his football career as a player. "I mentioned that if a player did something nasty or unnecessary to me, I wouldn't forget it. His name would go down in my black book. If the chance of retaliation came, I'd tackle him as hard as I could. I'd kick him five yards over the touchline if I had the opportunity. But I'd do it within the laws of the game, when the ball was there to be played."

Jack was the ideal pivot in that defensively-minded Leeds team under Revie. Jack used a ploy at corner kicks which brought howls of protest from opposing players and fans, yet proved very successful for his team. He would stand with his back to the opposing goalkeeper, completely blocking the keeper's view of the ball. No matter where the goalkeeper positioned himself Jack would stand in front of him. Of course this caused a great deal of friction and pushing and shoving, but it paid off for Leeds.

Many people throughout the British Isles, upon hearing Charlton's proclamation regarding the five names in his little black book, believed that Denis was top of Jack's list because of an incident that took place in the FA Cup semi-final between United and Leeds at Hillsborough. From the start Leeds were the better team, they were calm and played good football with Paul Reaney holding George Best in a tight grip. However, it was the Reds from Manchester who looked the more likely to score. Yet as the game wore on it soon descended in to acrimony as tempers became frayed. The Leeds defence looked impregnable. The game was like a volcano ready to erupt. Then in the 58th minute all hell let loose.

One national newspaper reporter wrote: "The referee needed a bucket of ice-cold water to throw over men who became mad dogs in a snarling, clawing, spitting, punching, kicking mob." The incident that led to the big flare-up was between Denis and Jack Charlton. The referee, Dick Windle, was very tolerant indeed. Denis seemed to chase after the Leeds centre-half, caught up with him and then obstructed him. The two men tore into each other and Denis ended up with his red jersey torn to shreds. As this battle was in full flow, players from both sides rushed over and more pandemonium broke out. Paddy Crerand and Billy Bremner had a rare old set-to and Nobby Stiles and Norman Hunter had to be parted. It was like a full-scale punch up in a public house. FIFA president Sir Stanley Rous commented: "Had I been the referee, I would have watched the boxing match just as he did. It was tough and good play was spoiled." Denis and Nobby Stiles were booked. George Brown, Minister for Economic Affairs, who sat watching, was quoted as saying: "The referee was jolly tolerant." The tally of fouls: 22 against United to only nine against Leeds. Oh, and the game ended goalless.

The return was played four days later at Nottingham Forest's ground where Billy Bremner shot Leeds into their first Cup Final with a goal scored barely two minutes from the final whistle. The feuding that had taken place on the Saturday was forgotten as both teams played delightful football. At the end of the match a young hooligan struck the referee, Mr Windle, and he collapsed in a heap, motionless on the ground. United had several clear-cut chances to have sealed the game up but scorned them.

Jack Charlton wrote in his autobiography: "A lot of people thought Denis Law topped the list in my black book, but that wasn't the case. In fact he's always been a good pal of mine. I've got two or three of Denis' shirts at home that I ripped off his back. The first semi-final at Hillsborough, was a bad-tempered game. I had a number of clashes in the penalty area with Denis Law, nearly pulling the shirt off his back on more than one occasion. You had to hang on to Denis, because he was so sharp and so good in the air. I used to hate playing against him, though I've always regarded him as a good pal of mine. Denis was a great competitor. I'll never forget going for a cross at Elland Road, and as I went to volley the ball, suddenly Denis was diving over me and heading it into the net. I kicked Denis right in the mouth, I really walloped him - not deliberately, of course, it was an accident. Anyway, I remember Denis lying on his back, and there's blood and everything coming out of his mouth and nose and the trainer was sponging him down. I was standing over him as he started to come to. He looked up at me and smiled, and he asked, 'Did I score, big fella?'"

After the teak-tough semi-final duels with Leeds, it was back to League action and Leeds were also going all out to become champions and get the double of FA Cup and First Division championship. United's form since Christmas had been patchy, the Reds winning five, drawing three and losing three of their games before April.

The next seven games would prove vital for the Red Devils. In the first fixture Blackburn Rovers were well and truly walloped 5-0 at Ewood Park as Bobby Charlton took the game by the scruff of the neck, scoring a brilliant hat-trick with John Connelly and David Herd joining in the scoring spree with a goal apiece. Charlton, in particular, and United in general were simply magnificent. "On this form I cannot see how Leeds or Chelsea can prevent Manchester United from taking the League title," said Blackburn skipper Ronnie Clayton.

Next up Leicester were beaten 1-0 at Old Trafford by a David Herd goal before the championship showdown proper against deadly Yorkshire rivals Leeds at Elland Road. There were more than 52,000 present for the game that was destined to decide the title. It was a clash of styles: The Red Devils, apostles of attacking football, against Leeds' seemingly impregnable, cast-iron defence. Match of the season is a title often given loosely, but never could it have been more apt than for this clash. In the three games the two teams had played against each other that season, the Reds had not scored a single goal while Leeds were enjoying a 25-match unbeaten run.

Yet it took just 14 minutes of this match after precisely four hours and forty-four minutes of frustrated, scoreless action, for the Reds to score. It turned out to be a golden goal scored by John Connelly. George Best sent over a cross, Denis headed it back and Connelly sent the ball smartly just inside the post out of the reach of Gary Sprake's left hand. Forced to attack Leeds were repelled as Nobby Stiles and Bill Foulkes stood firm in United's rearguard and were heroes on this occasion. United had a firm grip on the title now and two days later they beat Birmingham 4-2 at St Andrews - Best with two, Cantwell and Charlton getting one apiece. This was certainly Championship form from United.

However, another big test was awaiting them in their next match at Old Trafford as champions Liverpool visited. Before the game Noel Cantwell told reporters: "You'll be seeing the First Division champions today," and with almost 56,000 packed into the ground the Red Devils set about Liverpool and just before half time Denis scored. After the interval United surged forward: Best and Cantwell had goals disallowed for offside and Charlton hit the post before Denis and John Connelly got the Reds' second and third goals. Denis was injured in the process of scoring his second and left the field for 15 minutes to have seven stitches inserted in his right knee. After the game he was receiving treatment in the dressing room when Matt Busby, looking a little forlorn, saw Denis wincing as the doctor and Jack Compton worked on his injured knee. 'So near, yet it could be so far', was the thought that might have been going through Matt's mind as he contemplated the following game. The coming games were so important that he would need his best team in action if he were to secure his first First Division championship since Munich. He knew he would need Law!

Just forty-eight hours later, on a drizzly grey Monday night, the Reds were at home to Arsenal. United were still a point behind Leeds with a game in hand but with a superior goal average. Leeds last fixture of the season was on the same night so it was imperative that United won and 51,000 turned out to see if they could keep the momentum going. Denis should never have played in this game because of his badly gashed knee from the Liverpool match. Matt Busby had said the day after the Liverpool game that when he saw Denis in the medical room at Old Trafford he was shocked. "His knee was a terrible sight," said Busby, "I told Denis that it was impossible for him to play, but Denis replied, 'I won't give up, boss…I'll try again later on.'" According to the manager Denis went back to

Old Trafford later on that afternoon and was told it really was impossible for him to play the following night. "I shook my head," said Matt, "you can't play like that. But Denis said 'I think I will have a try. I am sure I can make it.' This was one of the biggest gambles I have ever made - backed by the courage of Denis."

However, according to Denis in his 1979 autobiography, he said he wasn't expected to play because of his injured knee. But after going into Old Trafford for treatment on the Monday lunchtime he was on his way out of the ground when Matt Busby shouted him into a room for the team talk. Denis was surprised and explained that because he had six or seven stitches in his knee he didn't think he would be considered fit to play. Matt told him he would be all right, and Ted Dalton and Jack Crompton strapped his knee up tightly and he played.

Leeds also had a game that same night. It was their final League fixture and they were away to Birmingham. It was a nail-biting occasion and the Reds were jittery. After seven minutes Denis justified himself and Matt Busby by laying the ball on for George Best to open the scoring. In the 59th minute there was a shattering noise from the crowd, many holding tiny transistor radios, when they heard that Leeds were 3-0 down to Birmingham. The incredible Law seemed to want to get in on the celebrations. He had switched to the left wing because of his injury but he did it again. This time Stiles took a free kick, Herd headed against the Arsenal bar and Denis, the ace goal poacher, was there as needed - slotting in the rebound for United's second goal. However, the hearts of fans and players were pounding as Arsenal got a penalty that George Eastham took. His first shot was saved by Dunne but following up, Eastham put the ball into the net.

Five minutes from time, with the tension mounting, Denis came to the rescue again when from a Best corner he stabbed the ball past Furnell in the Arsenal goal to give United a 3-1 victory. It was the moment of truth for Manchester United...the sweet, sweet taste of success. The roar of the crowd was deafening as the fans proclaimed that the Red Devils were back. At the final whistle the supporters went crazy with delight and there was a pitch invasion. The players escaped with the help of the police. It was all good humoured with the fans draped in red and white scarves and banners, persistently shouting: "We want Matt [Busby] and Denis [Law]". After ten minutes Denis appeared but there was pandemonium.

Meanwhile Leeds had fought back for a 3-3 draw and both teams had ended the season level on 61 points. Leeds had completed their fixtures but United had one game in hand and to lose the title Aston Villa would have to beat them 19-0 in their last game.

"You can safely say that will never happen," said a delighted George Best. To all intents and purposes the Red Devils of Manchester were First Division champions again. They had scored 88 goals and conceded just 37. Thanks to the defence of Dunne; Brennan, Dunne; Crerand, Foulkes and Stiles. By comparison, Leeds' figures were: 83 for, 52 against. Two days later United went to Aston Villa and lost 2-1. Nevertheless this was United's fourth First Division Championship since the war and their sixth in all. Matt Busby and Jimmy Murphy were dancing with joy - they were on top again. The scenes of pandemonium and delight inside and outside Old Trafford will never be forgotten. Many tears were shed that night.

Back in the sanctuary of the dressing room the Moet champagne was opened in celebration. All the Old Trafford backroom staff were there joining in the celebrations. George Best and Paddy Crerand were first in the bath. Matt Busby embraced vice-chairman Louis Edwards. "I am proud of these lads who have won the Championship for Manchester United - every single one of them," said a delighted but emotional Matt Busby. Real Madrid stars Alfredo Di Stefano and Puskas joined in the congratulations, while out on the pitch the police struggled to hold back an estimated 35,000 wildly excited Mancunians who were calling for another appearance by their heroes. Busby led his players out to salute the United faithful but they had to scamper back down the tunnel in double quick time as the hordes besieged them. Three players lost their shirts in the melee.

Denis was having his knee tended as he swigged a glass of bubbly. To play with an injury as he had done showed his fortitude and courage. The stitches were almost in the centre of his right knee. He was in terrible pain. When the players were dressed they went into the boardroom for a drink - George Best, sipping lemonade said: "I felt it was going to be our night once Denis Law gave me that great pass for that first goal. But it was difficult to concentrate on the game in the tense atmosphere, particularly with the news coming from the Birmingham versus Leeds game. What a night and what a way to round off the season." News came through that Shay Brennan, although born and bred in Manchester of Irish parents, had been selected under a new FIFA rule to play for the Republic of Ireland. Shay, one of the most popular players at Old Trafford, was toasted and congratulated.

Leaving the celebrations aside for a moment. Many people were unaware that for Denis to play with an injured knee was something extraordinary. Harry Gregg wrote in his excellent autobiography *Harry's Game* : "Denis was a quiet lad at heart, more of a thinker than his extrovert alter ego would suggest. He was always his own man, even at United, where Matt Busby was the archetypal authoritarian. If Denis made up his mind about something, nothing, and I mean nothing in God's earth, could shift him. Take injuries. The rest of us might have been easy to talk into playing if we were carrying a knock. Not Denis." Harry said that if Matt was in the dressing room most of the players who were injured would be swayed into trying out their fitness. But this tactic never worked with Denis. Harry said that Matt Busby would ask him to try out his injury. Denis would get changed into his kit, walk onto the pitch have a little jog and walk back to the dressing room, get changed and leave without saying a word.

Denis himself had mentioned his time at Huddersfield and of Bill Shankly's behaviour towards him or any other injured player. Apparently Shankly would totally ignore you if you were injured and unavailable to play. "Shanks couldn't stand players getting injured," said Denis, "if you were injured you were no good to him and he didn't want to know you. He would never ask about your injury or how it was responding to treatment. Before a game he would tell me I was the greatest player in the world but if he saw me coming out of the treatment room he would walk right pass me without saying a word."

It seemed that a number of managers were like Busby and Shankly when it came to injuries. The late, great Tommy Taylor, who died tragically at Munich, suffered terrible agonies with an injured ankle and was constantly on the treatment table at Old Trafford. He was told: "It's all in your mind, son," and it was only after he had an operation that his complaints were taken seriously. David Gaskell, United's goalkeeper in the 1963 FA Cup final, speaking on a BBC documentary, said that once his arm was in plaster and as Harry Gregg was also injured that left only teenage novice keeper Ronnie Briggs. Sadly, Briggs had conceded a number of goals while playing in the first team and Gaskell said Matt Busby called him into his office and explained that if he could not play then he [Busby], would have to sign another keeper. Eddie Hopkinson, the Bolton Wanderers goalkeeper was mentioned. David added that the indication was that when Gregg was fit again, he [Gaskell] would be third in contention for the first team position. The plaster was removed!

'What A Night For Busby' roared the headlines in *The Sun*, while the *Daily Express* proclaimed in huge bold headlines '*Busby's Night*'. '*Law Clinches It*' was a later headline in the *Daily Express*. '*Manchester United Champs*' was the banner headline in the *Daily Mirror*. '*Manchester United are Champions*' was the *Daily Telegraph* headline.

Real Madrid icon Alfredo Di Stefano believed that the player ideally suited to replace him when he retired was the blond-haired Denis Law. It was a wonderful gesture on the part of the truly great Di Stefano to mention Denis as his replacement. Happily for the future welfare of Manchester United and British football, already devoid of personalities of the immediate pre-and post-war variety, it was unlikely that Denis would again be tempted away from Britain. Denis had long decided that his one-year stay with Torino was experience enough for a lifetime. Besides, he and Diana were settled in Manchester and extremely happy.

Soccer connoisseurs, reared on such artisocratic inside-forwards as Wilf Mannion, Jimmy Hagan, Billy Steele and Len Shackleton had had a lean time over the past few years. There were of course good players, international players... but none to compare with the classy stylists who so delighted the crowds after the war. Until Denis. He alone among contemporary exponents stood in a comparable class. He was a great player already and who could honestly say how significant a contribution he would make to the future fortunes of his club and country?

Seven years after the Munich disaster that robbed the Reds of some of the greatest players in the history of the club, Matt Busby and Jimmy Murphy, along with their loyal backroom staff, had resurrected Manchester United and led them to the Championship of the First Division again. It was a miracle. This great club had risen from the ashes of that snowbound runway at Munich like a Phoenix. Now they could look forward to more glorious nights and enjoy the honours that seemed certain to come their way. They were also back in the prestigious European Cup and determined to emulate, and hopefully better, the achievements of Tottenham Hotspur and West Ham United. Spurs won the European Cup Winners' Cup in 1962/63 and West Ham won the same trophy in 1964/65. Busby's dream was that an English football team composed of British players could prove to be as good as any club team in Europe.

The club had had a fabulous season. Besides winning the Championship they had been FA Cup semi-finalists and were still in the quarter-finals of the Inter-Cities Fairs Cup. Just over a week after their final League game, United played the French team Racing Club Strasbourg in France and won 5-0, Denis getting two headed goals with Connelly, Charlton and Herd also scoring. In the seven Fairs Cup games they had played that season United had scored 25 goals. The second leg was played at Old Trafford on 19th May. The players were tired and weary after a long hard season, but there was a party atmosphere in the ground despite a mere 34,188 paying to see the game. Before the start Denis, as captain, was presented with the Championship trophy from the president of the Football League, Mr Joe Richards. The team did a lap of honour around the ground and were cheered to the echo. Then, a golden moment for Denis as Max Urbini, the editor of *France Football,* presented him with the golden bauble for being voted European Footballer of the Year 1964. However the football failed to match the celebrations, the Reds drawing 0-0 in a disappointing game.

Yet instead of going on holiday United had to play Ferencvaros of Hungary in the semi-finals in June. This turned into another mammoth encounter with the teams having to play three games. United eventually, and extremely unfortunately, went out 2-1 in a play-off. The Reds won the first game at Old Trafford 3-2, Herd two and Law the scorers. Then came the long, tiring trip to Budapest for the return in the Nep Stadium. After a horrendous journey the Reds lost 1-0 in a game in which Crerand was dismissed along with Pal Orosz, with the Hungarians' goal coming from a hotly-disputed penalty. But with the tie at 3-3 on aggregate (this in an era before the away goals rule had been introduced), armed police formed quickly at the end of the match to surround the United players who left with the jeers of the 50,000 crowd ringing in their ears. Ten minutes later the Reds lost the toss for the choice of ground and saw the Hungarians win the right to play the third game at their own ground. They won 2-1, with Connelly getting United's only goal.

"I have a message for Manchester United fans which must not go unheeded," wrote Terrence Elliott of the *Daily Express.* "Hide the disappointment of your team's defeat and go along and salute 11 heroes when they return from this Inter-City Fairs Cup semi-final play-off. That's the least they deserve. To say they went out with honour would be an understatement. Better to say, in all fairness, they should never have lost this game at all." Ferencvaros went on to beat Juventus 1-0 in the final.

The season was finally over. Denis had played in 36 League games and scored 28 goals. In six FA Cup games he had scored three times while in the Inter-City Fairs Cup he had played ten times, scoring eight goals.

10. European Law

Denis Law's contribution to Manchester United's championship season had been immense. In this period Denis was the greatest footballer in Britain and possibly the finest inside-forward in the world. Pele of Brazil vied with him for this honour while Eusebio and Greaves couldn't quite match up to the phenomenal standard of individuality the Lawman set. Denis could take a game by the throat, shake it up and leave it lying with his imprint clearly marked on its passing. He was the Danny Kaye of football: a puckish, whimsical, taunting, mocking, irrepressible clown who kept a crowd roaring with good humour. At other times he was a fiery, furious, devastating beanpole of energy, infuriating everyone around him. But a star he certainly was. And in his case no one can dispute the application of Genius. Denis was a Red Devil from the top of his blond head to the tips of his feet, and that was no mistake.

He had perfect ball control. It was lovely to watch him step on the ball and, with his foot on it, wait for an opponent to 'dare' tackle him - dare because, if the opponent dared, he would be made to look foolish. His dribbling skills and his use of open space was artistic. He covered more ground in the course of a game than half-a-dozen workmanlike players, he was a sort of footballing Scarlet Pimpernel that his opponents sought here, there and everywhere without ever quite catching him. He was difficult to mark, and almost impossible to subdue, sometimes he strolled through a game at walking pace for long periods and then he would suddenly flash into incandescent brilliance like a shooting star lighting up the dull skies around it. He had his poor games, which player didn't but a lacklustre Denis Law was rare indeed. He always seemed too nervously high-tensioned, too dynamically all elbows, knees and darting irregularity for that.

Perhaps, as many London fans went to great pains to tell Old Trafford fans, he lacked the clinical deadly finishing of Jimmy Greaves. Although they had obviously not checked his goalscoring record with the Reds carefully. In his first three seasons back in English football with Manchester United he scored 81 times in 104 games. Other critics claimed Denis didn't have the terrific power of shooting that his colleague Bobby Charlton possessed. But despite these faults Denis was still, with the attributes he had, the greatest controller of a game of football at that time. He could change the course of a match with one flash of unexpected genius. He could ghost into unmarked space, round a couple of defenders quickly and slip the ball into the net before anyone could stop to think what was happening. He thought twice as quickly as the average footballer. His brain was quicksilver, his reactions lightning fast and his footwork magical. When he was in the mood he bounded about all over the pitch panicking the opposition. He shook his body, twisted his frail-looking shoulders, waggled his spindly legs and in a flash - he was off, dashing for goal.

He looked frail, but he needed some stopping. He was as tough as old boots and as hard as steel, and as difficult to dispossess of the ball as a lion its prey. In the air there was none better. He had been accused by the press and opposition supporters of being hot-tempered, malicious and spiteful. The truth was that his heart was so much in winning that he hated losing! Going back to rectify his own mistakes was Denis' undoing, because it often led to him fouling his opponent. He was quick to retaliate when victimised, and often paid the penalty. He found it hard enough to turn one cheek, let alone the other!

Denis must have known that he was following in the footsteps of football's martyrs. Who can ever forget the great Hughie Gallagher was almost driven out of football by the deliberate provocation he had to endure. No one liked being made a fool. Stanley Matthews did it like a gentleman. Jimmy

Greaves did it neatly and moved away. But Denis taunted. His pose was all arrogance and his body language seemed loaded with a 'come-on-I-dare-you' conceit that riled the opposition. When they inevitably fouled him he would retaliate and that brought trouble! Denis couldn't change the way he played. Matt Busby and the United supporters did not want him to lose the devil in his play that made him such a great player and competitor, and lifted him above the ordinary and made spectators never tire of him. But he would have to learn to take it as long as he played the way he did. Being Denis Law was the penalty of greatness.

Before the start of the new season the United players knew they would be in for some physically hard games. The new champions always are, as other teams pull out all the stops against them. Denis missed the opening two matches with a hip injury sustained in a pre-season friendly in Nuremberg. It proved to be a season in which Denis missed quite a few games. The manner in which he performed meant that he was bound to pick up more than his fair share of injuries which was the case with most spearheads and goalscorers while the treatment of players' injuries was fairly basic in this period. United though, had their own hospital in Whalley Range, which was not too far from Old Trafford. Well, to put it into proper perspective, many people thought it belonged to United, but in reality St Joseph's Hospital belonged to a Catholic order. Any players requiring operations or surgery were sent there by Busby.

The 1965/66 season proved to be an indifferent one for the Reds. Inconsistency in the League saw Liverpool win the championship again. Evidence of their form came in the first eight games out of which United won just twice, drawing four and losing twice. Denis scored just once in this spell. Yet in the ninth league game of the season, against Tommy Docherty's Chelsea at Old Trafford, Denis scored a pulsating 17-minute hat-trick of brilliant headers. First John Connelly crossed into the box and Denis beat Ken Shillito to the high ball to put United one up. The second came from another Connelly cross and there was Denis the Menace, leaping high to glance the ball past Peter Bonetti. The third followed a Paddy Crerand cross, McCreadie challenged this time but Law was king of the air again and his hat-trick was in the bag. Bobby Charlton also scored to make the final score 4-1. In the next game, away to Arsenal, they came down to earth with a bump as they were gunned down 4-2. John Aston junior, who had taken over the left wing position after George Best had been dropped, scored, as did Bobby Charlton.

In September Denis was responsible for Bobby Charlton receiving the one and only booking in his long and illustrious career. Nobby Stiles takes up the story: "Bobby, without a shadow of a doubt, was looked upon as a model player by other footballers and referees. But when he received the only booking of his career it proved just how loved and respected he was in the game. It happened in September 1965, during our 1-1 draw against Newcastle United.

"You see Denis Law was speaking to the referee and Bobby turned to Denis and said, 'Never mind it Denis, come on. Let's get on with the game' and I can only assume that the ref thought Bobby was addressing his remarks to him."

The incident soon rose to national prominence. Players from both teams were stunned and angry when Bobby was booked by referee Ken Stokes. And as both sets of players surrounded the referee he claimed that he was booking the England great "as an example. Perhaps it will shock you all sufficiently to quieten you down." Afterwards the Mr Stokes said that the United players were "yapping around me. There were two or three of them. I had to stop them. Charlton was the last to speak, so he suffered. In fact," said the referee, "I feel sorry for him."

Nobby continued: "You can imagine the stick Denis took about this incident from the lads. However, that was not the end of the matter. In fact Bobby ended his career with a clean record. Thousands of letters were sent to the Football Association from people throughout the British Isles. Both United and Newcastle players wrote to the FA and as a result the FA checked with Mr Stokes, who told them that he had not cautioned Bobby and did not intend reporting the matter." The referee admitted later that technically he had made a mistake. "Even referees are human," he said.

United's form appeared to improve at the start of October as, with Best once again back in the first team after a two match demotion, United thrashed Liverpool 2-0 at Old Trafford. In the following week Denis played for Scotland in a World Cup qualifier against Poland at Hampden Park. Scotland were eager to go through as the World Cup was being staged in England the following summer. However, during the game Denis received a painful kick on his right kneecap that would have repercussions for the rest of his playing career. To make matters worse, Scotland lost 2-1 and later failed to qualify for the World Cup. The following morning Denis missed an early flight back to Manchester. The club rule was that injured players had to report as quickly as possible in order to receive treatment. Being young and impetuous Denis thought the two-day rest would see the knee feeling much better.

Before the next game against Tottenham at White Hart Lane Matt Busby was given a wonderful surprise by his players as a tribute to his 20 years in charge of Manchester United. The players had bought a beautiful, unique cut-glass vase hand-made in Czechoslovakia. As captain, Denis was expected to make the presentation and make a little speech. Many couldn't believe that this simple task for the cocky, confident player who seemed to prance on the field would prove a problem. However as we've seen, off the field Denis was very quiet and on this occasion he was embarrassed and extremely shy, so he turned to Bill Foulkes and said: "You do it. You've been here longer than the rest of us. Besides, knowing me I would only drop it."

Despite his injury Denis played against Spurs and suffered agonies. At half time he obviously could not continue. Substitutes were now allowed and John Fitzpatrick replaced him, becoming the first-ever substitute for Manchester United in a league game. In the event Denis might have been glad to have missed the second half as United were trounced 5-1 by an in-form Spurs outfit. The kneecap injury meant that Denis missed the next few games as the season took a topsy-turvy course for the champions. United now embarked on a 10-game unbeaten League run which included a 5-1 win in the return against Spurs in December, Denis getting two.

Yet the focus of the players, fans and management was the growing sense of destiny being attached to Matt Busby's search for the Holy Grail - the European Cup. In the preliminary round first leg the Reds played HJK Helsinki away and took things a little too easily, but nevertheless prevailed 3-2 after Herd and Connelly had scored in the first 15 minutes. John Fitzpatrick, another Aberdonian, played in place of Crerand, while young John Aston took the injured George Best's place on the left wing. Denis added a typically opportunist goal. The return at Old Trafford for the second leg saw United romp into the first round 6-0, Connelly getting a well-merited hat-trick, with Best (2) and Charlton also on the scoresheet.

In November, United were drawn to play East German champions ASK Vorwaerts. In the first leg in Berlin, a 2-0 away win was achieved with Denis and John Connelly the scorers. Law's goal was magical: he lost Unger, his German marker, before hovering in the air to head a truly phenomenal goal. Denis also made the opening for John Connelly's goal, drawing Weiss out of his goal with brilliant balance and footwork before rolling the ball for John to finish. In the return United won 3-1 with David Herd netting a well-deserved hat-trick. Denis had another good game and although he didn't score on this occasion he hit the German crossbar with an acrobatic header. Vorwaerts could not subdue him when the high balls were pumped into their penalty box, but they cynically tried to hack him down whenever he rose to get his head to the ball. After this victory the Reds could relax because the quarter-final was not scheduled until the following February.

However Denis came in for a considerable amount of leg-pulling. "It's near Christmas, Denis," were the words he heard in the dressing room and during training sessions at the Cliff, a reference to Law's perceived propensity for lengthy suspensions during Yuletide. As Christmas drew closer he was often asked by laughing team-mates: "Well, what's happening?" They all wanted to know whether he had made any plans to go back to Scotland for the holidays.

United drew Benfica in the last eight of the European Cup, a tie that was sure to be the highlight of the season for everyone connected to the club. The Eagles of Lisbon had overtaken the invincibles of Real Madrid as the premier team in European football, having won the tournament in 1961, 1962 and featured in the finals of 1963 and 1965. The city of Manchester and its surrounds were gripped by the magnitude of these two games for weeks before the first leg at Old Trafford on 2nd February 1966. Compared to the grey, dour Germans, Benfica were vivacious and glamorous, fifteen of their squad were Portuguese internationals while in the great Eusebio they possessed a forward of rare pedigree - the scorer of 31 European Cup goals, he was chasing Alfredo Di Stefano's record of 49 in the competition.

Bela Guttmann was Benfica's tactically astute manager and any fears the Old Trafford crowd might have had that he might scheme his team into an early lead were proved well-founded as Jose Augusto headed the pride of Portugal ahead from a corner. Yet with the Stretford Enders roaring United on, David Herd scored the equaliser. Later, Bobby Charlton centred and Denis, with lightning reactions, headed the ball past the keeper and when Bill Foulkes headed in from a free kick, his third goal in 14 seasons of League and Cup football with United, it seemed that United might have a sufficient lead for the notoriously tough return at the Stadium of Light. But a typical piece of genius by Eusebio made sure that it would be a tricky return for the Reds as goalkeeper Harry Gregg explained: "Eusebio was on the byeline and I had come a little way off my line expecting a centre. Instead he swerved the ball fiercely between me and the near post. All I could do was dive backwards and push the ball out. It hit Torres' knee and went in. Few could have spotted the opening and I think only

Eusebio could have created a goal from it."

Perhaps not surprisingly the Portuguese felt that they had done the hard part and at the final whistle their smiles rang with confidence as they walked to the dressing-room. Few now believed that one goal would be enough to carry the Reds through to the semi-finals. Naturally, the Portuguese newspapers claimed that United had no chance in the Stadium of Light, the beautiful but intimidating home of Benfica, and would go back to Manchester chastised. Benfica were indeed a superb team who, on their own ground, were near invincible. As mentioned they were the natural successors to Real Madrid's crown and offered the most formidable and frightening opposition for any away team on their own ground. Since 1960 they had played 18 home matches in the European Cup on their own ground and won them all, scoring 78 goals while conceding a mere 13. Yet United had reason to be confident in their own ability. With superstars like Bobby Charlton, George Best and Denis Law they were quite capable of beating any kind of opposition on any given night, at least that was what United fans kept telling themselves.

The atmosphere in Lisbon leading up to the kick-off was almost an event in itself. The tension was unbearable with the roads leading to the stadium packed solid with fans blowing horns, ringing bells, blowing whistles, chanting and singing. The referee was an Italian, Mr Lo Bello. He had found it difficult to get into the stadium and the match was delayed for over twenty minutes. Then the Reds had to wait anxiously while a presentation was made to Eusebio in honour of him becoming European Footballer of the Year 1965 - all this performed on the pitch before over 80,000 passionate spectators. Denis, being a little superstitious, had arrived at the ground wearing an old shirt, his lucky shirt he claimed. Yet any charm emanating from this looked to have been smashed when Paddy Crerand cracked a mirror while kicking a ball about in the dressing room. The looks of disgust he received from his team-mates said it all.

It is now folklore that in his team talk Matt Busby told his team to play it tight for the first half hour or so. But with Best heading in Tony Dunne's cross after just six minutes Busby just couldn't believe what he was watching and neither could Benfica. A few minutes later Best dummied three defenders and tapped the ball into the net past the despairing hands of Pereira. In the 15th minute Connelly added a third after excellent play from Charlton and Law. Nobody could believe what they were watching. Mancunians thought they were dreaming. Then Shay Brennan scored, but much to his dismay, it was in his own net. He took some stick for that later.

By now Nobby Stiles' battle with the powerful Eusebio was no contest - he was tackling and out-thinking him, anticipating passes meant for the Benfica forward. He played what Jimmy Murphy later called a 'blinder'. In the second half, Law delivered an inch-perfect through ball for Crerand to score and a few seconds later Charlton, in magical form, swerved past three defenders and made it 5-1 to United. This was the ultimate peak of United's potential, they produced a fantastic display of awesome, breathtaking football and would have beaten any team on that form. The name on everyone's lips, though, was George Best. Still only 19, he had one of those flawless, fabulous, unforgettable games where everything he tried came off. From the moment he landed back in Manchester wearing a huge sombrero, George Best's life changed forever. "This was our finest hour," said a delighted Matt Busby and with the 5-0 beating his team had suffered two years earlier against Sporting Club of Lisbon in the forefront of his mind the great man added, "tonight makes up for that."

The newspapers now gushed with praise for the Red Devils. *The Sun*: 'Benfica...were more than just beaten, they were pulverised'. *The Daily Telegraph* said: 'If they can play like this in the semi-final and again in the final no one, not even Inter Milan, can feel safe from them'. *The Daily Mirror* added: 'If United continue to play like this I doubt if there is a club side in the world to match them, never mind beat them', *The Daily Mail:* 'This was not only United's greatest-ever display in Europe; it will rank as one of the gala occasions as England's contribution to the world game'. *The Daily Express:* 'I have never seen a British team abroad play with such spirit and with such brilliance'. *The Guardian:* 'If they reproduce the play they gave us last night they will prove they are without doubt the finest club side in Europe'. Even the European press praised them. 'The myth of Benfica collapsed in 14 minutes, destroyed by the powerful, irresistible Manchester. Manchester showed themselves as the great stars of European soccer, worthy rivals to Internazionale of Milan for the European Cup' said *Corriere dello Sport* in Rome.

The only hint of derision predictably came from the Portuguese: 'A notable exhibition by Manchester. But after all, wasn't it the English who invented football' said *Secuulo,* Lisbon. Nevertheless Benfica never recovered from this pummeling, their season swiftly fell apart as Guttman was sacked as manager and rivals Sporting won the championship.

Yet the contrast between United's opponents in the last eight and last four couldn't have been more pronounced. The Reds now drew Partizan Belgrade with the first leg in Yugoslavia. Partizan were a strong, robust and well-disciplined team. They had a few internationals: Milan Galic was a quality centre forward, Vasovic a wonderful defender and Soskic a dependable goalkeeper. Nevertheless, United were confident of success.

George Best should not have played in the first leg because he had suffered a cartilage injury following United's 3-1 victory in a sixth round FA Cup tie against Preston. In the event, Matt Busby took a chance on George that sadly went wrong as the Irishman broke down in the first half - he was forced to undergo a cartilage operation upon his return.

Meanwhile Denis was still suffering from the knee injury he picked up while playing for Scotland against Poland and missed a sitter early in the first leg when he hit the crossbar. Nevertheless the game was scoreless at half time and most reckoned United had the game well within their reach. Yet mistakes at the back cost the Reds and with the confidence flowing from a two goal lead, the Yugoslavs were bound to be hard to breakdown in the second leg at Old Trafford.

Stan Liversedge, a sports journalist, was a friend of Busby's who wrote for the *Sunday People*. He was in Belgrade for the semi-final and after the game he and Sam Leitch, another prominent journalist, tried to get a taxi back to their hotel. After failing to get a taxi the two journalists flagged the driver of a milk float. Once back in the hotel, Stan was supposed to meet Paddy Crerand, who wrote a regular column for the *Sunday People* - Stan was his ghost writer. He was standing in the foyer of the hotel as the United team came in looking far from happy after their shock defeat. Paddy and Denis were together when Stan walked over to them to ask if he could give him a few minutes of his time. Stan realised that under the circumstances, with the Reds losing 2-0, this might not really be the right time but nevertheless, he needed to get something down on paper from Paddy, who was of course being paid for the article. Denis said they were going out. Stan told Denis that it would take only ten minutes or so and he would then gladly put Paddy into a taxi and pay for wherever Denis was going. Denis, no doubt fed up with way the trip was going, wanted Paddy to go out with him.

"Paddy was caught in the crossfire of the argument," said Stan, who wasn't best pleased, "he didn't know whether to stay and do the article or go with Denis. Eventually Denis won." Annoyed, Stan reasoned that there would be time on the way home to get Crerand's story. At the airport the following day Denis was sitting reading as Stan passed him. Denis looked up at him and smiling cheekily asked if he was all right. Stan, still annoyed at Denis, briefly acknowledged him and walked past. He eventually got the material he needed from Paddy before the team arrived back in England.

In the second leg, Partizan came to Old Trafford determined to hang on to their 2-0 lead and though Nobby Stiles scored for the Reds they lost 2-1 on aggregate. This was extremely upsetting and disappointing after the way the Reds had played against Benfica. Denis had not played well, but neither had any of the other forwards. Willie Anderson came into the side in place of the injured George Best but the loss of the Irish wizard almost certainly upset United's balance.

Afterwards Matt Busby was visibly upset. He knew that his team could have beaten Real Madrid, who beat Partizan in the final. It was his lasting ambition to lift the European trophy as a tribute to the people who had perished at Munich in 1958. He was secretly distraught. Denis, like many in the team, believed that the Reds should have won it in 1966. He was upset, but realised that the injuries George Best and himself were carrying proved too big a handicap.

Three days after their disastrous European exit, United faced Everton in an FA Cup semi-final. With any prospect of winning the league now gone this represented United's only chance of silverware.

In the third round United had drawn Derby County at the Baseball Ground and in a really thrilling match United triumphed 5-2, Denis getting a brace of goals, as did George Best, with David Herd scoring the other. The fourth round saw them draw 0-0 with lowly Rotherham in a surprising turn-up at Old Trafford but win the replay 1-0 after extra time, thanks to a John Connelly goal. Wolves were their opponents in the next round for the second year running. Molineux was packed solid with 53,000 as the Reds romped home 4-2. Denis was again in form, scoring twice, with one each for Herd and Best while the quarter-finals paired the Reds with Preston North End at Deepdale. In a hard-fought game, David Herd saved United's blushes when he scored in a 1-1 draw - former United favourite Alex Dawson scoring for Preston.

The replay at Old Trafford saw 60,433 pack the ground and with just three minutes left, and the game 1-1, the Reds were dreading extra time. Then John Aston took a corner and Foulkes headed the ball on to Stiles who guided it goalwards, when out of nowhere Law pounced to win the game. Earlier Law had put United in the lead as early as the 30th minute when he forced Howard Kendall into a mistake. Tony Singleton had equalised for North End while John Connelly added another in the dying minutes to make it 3-1. United's victory equalled an 89-year-old Cup record. The only previous side to reach the semi-final in five consecutive seasons had been Oxford University between 1873-77. The semi-final was to be played at Bolton's Burnden Park ground and Everton were the opponents. Yet in a rather dull and unexciting game United's cup run ended in a whimper with a 1-0 defeat.

In the space of three days United's season had hit the depths of despair. There was little doubt that Busby mourned the loss of the European Cup the greater. Amid the criticism, many now blamed Matt's tactical naivety and old-fashioned methods. It was clear to the Manchester public that to have taken apart the finest team in Europe in front of their own spectators only to lose to the unknowns of Partizan defied logic. There was little doubt either that United were now the best team in Europe despite Real Madrid's eventual triumph in the competition.

The semi-final defeats nevertheless pushed Matt Busby closer to retirement. On the Monday after the FA Cup semi-final Matt was pondering his future when he stopped his car at a crossing near the blind school. "I saw seven little children with white sticks being led across the road. I just sat in the car and thought, 'Matt, what problems have you got? You've got no problems' and in a way that did me a lot of good."

*

George Best told reporters that Denis Law was the sort of player who wanted to play in every match. "He almost has to be told when he is injured, because he doesn't know the meaning of 'crying off'. With the nationalistic fervour that seems to belong to the Scots, Irish and Welsh, he is the kind of player who will fight on longer in pursuit of a cause that many an Englishman might well have given up for lost long before," said George. George went on to say that Denis was the sort of player who, by his own style, could so often mean the difference between victory and defeat. "I well remember recalling, with my friend David Sadler, when we both played a match against Burnley, about Denis' influence in that particular match.

"Of course, his great potential is around the goalmouth, but even in midfield he used to create attacks out of nothing. Burnley had lots to remember him for, not least the most amazing overhead scissors kick he made against them in one important game. Arsenal, too, can vouch for his skill because he demolished them with a backheeled goal that everyone else felt sure was passing harmlessly over the line for a goal kick. I remember seeing him against Chelsea at Old Trafford on one occasion when I had been dropped early in my career and though I tried not to be hurt by being left out of the team, I was interested to see how the lads got on without me. Well, Denis scored three of the most fantastic goals I have ever seen and United strolled to a 4-1 victory. That show of Denis' made me think that United could do without me completely from there on. He certainly made me determined to go out and win back my place so that I would never lose it again. Denis' performance didn't do much for the youngsters of Chelsea but it certainly helped me appreciate that there was a lot more in the game to learn about."

Like the rest of his team-mates Denis was not too happy with United's trophyless season. Because of injuries Law had managed just 33 League games and scored 'only' 15 goals, his lowest tally since joining the Reds in 1962. In the FA Cup he played in seven games and scored six times and in the European Cup he made eight appearances, scoring three times. Yet his overriding disappointment was at seeing three trophies slip away, one after the other. In addition there would be no European competition at Old Trafford the following season as United missed out on the precursor of the UEFA Cup, the Inter-Cities Fairs Cup.

To add to Denis' woe, Scotland failed in their World Cup qualification bid. Earlier in the season, in April 1966 to be exact, England had beaten Scotland 4-3 on their own patch at Hampden Park and, although he scored, Denis was seething, having wanted to beat the 'auld enemy' more than anything before England took part in the World Cup a short time later.

Law loathed England. The story that Denis purposely played

golf with his friend John Hogan at Chorlton-cum-Hardy on the afternoon of the World Cup final between England and West Germany is part of folklore in and around Manchester. There was always a fierce rivalry between Scottish players and their English counterparts. It is a fact that Scottish players loved nothing more than beating their English counterparts when they encountered each other, a pathetic state of affairs but nonetheless that's how it was. The Scots seemed to play with a great deal more zeal, aggression and passion against England than they did when playing any other team. On his own admission Denis, for obvious reasons, did not want to watch the England players try and win the World Cup, despite two of his Manchester United colleagues, Nobby Stiles and Bobby Charlton playing in the England team, and John Connelly being in the squad. He decided to play his friend on that particular day when, after winning a particular bet, they had agreed sometime earlier to play the game anytime and anywhere. Mancunians, like the rest of England, were glued to their television sets or with their ears pressed against radios hoping and praying for an England victory. Denis and his friend were the only two on the course that afternoon, while other golfers were at the clubhouse celebrating England's great victory as Denis finished his game. England had won. "It was the blackest day of my life," wrote Denis in his 1979 autobiography.

11. The Ultimatum

During the close season Denis decided to rest. He and Diana and his young son travelled back to Aberdeen for the summer. However, before leaving his home in Manchester and heading north he wrote a personal letter to Matt Busby, who was on holiday in Ireland. Denis' contract was up for renewal before the start of the coming season and, in the contents of his letter to the manager, he outlined certain points that he wanted clarifying before he would re-sign with Manchester United.

He asked for a signing-on fee and an increase in his salary from the present one. The biggest surprise, though, was that he stated that if he did not get what he was asking for, then he would leave Manchester United for another club. Denis waited patiently for the reaction to his ultimatum and quite some time passed before Denis heard anything regarding his letter to the manager. It was a surprise that he had indicated that he would leave United if he didn't get what he was demanding, because he truly loved Manchester and his family were settled, happy and comfortable.

When Matt Busby read the letter from Denis he was upset and annoyed but acted swiftly and decisively. He immediately called a press conference at Old Trafford and dropped the bombshell that he had put Denis Law on the transfer list. "Manchester United are bigger than any individual, no matter how famous they might be." After answering Law's ultimatum, the United manager then left Manchester for Portugal for a UEFA meeting. The news came as a shock to everyone, especially Law's loyal subjects, the Manchester United supporters. Everyone in Manchester waited with baited breath as they speculated about the outcome. Meanwhile, Denis was still in Aberdeen. When he heard the news he was shocked rigid. Diana was expecting their second child and Denis did not want her worrying unduly, but with newspaper reporters and photographers converging on Aberdeen in droves, he moved away for a couple of days.

In addition to the shock in Manchester there were many more throughout Britain who blamed Law's greed for Busby's announcement. Alan Hardaker, the gruff, blunt-speaking secretary of the Football League, not known for his love of highly publicised players like Denis, was one who believed that Denis was wrong in what he had done. It was fair to say that Mr Hardaker might not have been a member of the Denis Law fan club. He had in the past expressed his dislike for the way players like Denis celebrated scoring a goal by raising their fists skywards.

In reality what had happened had been a lesson Matt Busby had patiently waited to play in order to warn Denis and any other star players of the consequences of their demands. He most definitely did not want Law to leave Old Trafford. Indeed, he would never have considered this happening. He knew the Laws were quite happy and content in Manchester but he needed to show that nobody was bigger than the club, and he was right in this respect. Once Denis flew back to Manchester and met his manager everything was resolved amicably. Busby had already got a press statement ready to hand out to waiting journalists in which Denis publicly apologised to Matt and the club. It was a masterful exhibition of Public Relations by the canny Busby. Money, however, is a great motivating factor in professional football and nobody could blame Law for trying to get as much of it as he could for his future and that of his family. And, in those days, it was a well-known fact that the Manchester United players were by no means the highest earners in the old First Division. Unlike today, where the Premier League is a billion-pound industry and half the clubs are paying out more than 70 per cent of their income in wages, in the football world of the time many a renowned player existed on a pittance.

For example, Billy Wright played 21 seasons for

Wolverhampton Wanderers and 13 years for England, he captained both club and country and was the first player in the world to win 100 international caps and was never booked in 541 League and Cup games for his club. Yet the plain fact is that David Beckham earns more in one week more than Billy Wright earned as a player throughout his entire career.

It was around this period that Matt Busby made enquiries about Geoff Hurst, now Sir Geoff, from West Ham but Ron Greenwood turned his offer down flat. This would have been a wonderful signing for Manchester United: Best, Charlton, Hurst and Law, what a forward line! There were one or two other players he would have liked at Old Trafford. Players like Jim McCalliog (who later joined the Reds under Tommy Docherty) and Bobby Tambling.

The reason for Busby's interest in the transfer market was the continued criticism of David Herd by a section of the press and United supporters. This criticism was unfair and totally unjust to a loyal, honest player who never claimed to have the skills of a Law, Charlton or Best, but helped the Reds achieve success in this period.

As an example of Herd's reputation in this period, a gag doing the rounds in the pubs and clubs of Manchester went something like this: A policeman stopped David Herd for speeding - the policeman flagged him down and then walked in that majestic way that only policemen have up to where David was sitting at the wheel of the vehicle. "What's your name?" asked the constable. "David Herd," replied David. "Oh," said the policeman, "you mean David Herd the footballer?" "Yes," answered David. "Well," said the policeman, "I can see you can't drive either!"

Denis went to great lengths to defend his striking partner. He believed that the stick Herd took was unjustified and when things did not go right for the Reds, poor Herd was blamed and had to carry the can. He also said that he knew he himself was a bit of a 'show-off', especially after scoring a goal, but said no matter what play-acting he did during a game he hoped that the fans never saw him showing anything more than disappointment with his playing colleagues. He went on to explain that David Herd was playing in one of the most exposed positions on the field and was reliant on the service of his team-mates. "David is a very important player for Manchester United," added Denis, "facts speak for themselves, and they clearly show David's value to United. In the year we won the League Championship I was fortunate enough to be our leading scorer with 28 goals. David scored 20, a wonderful contribution. He also got 20 goals the season before, and 19 the season before that. That's a good strike rate. Where would we have been without David's goalscoring? Forwards like him who can get their team 20 goals a season are much appreciated by their team-mates."

*

The end of the stand-off over Law's contract brought a tangible sense of relief among supporters. With their idol back in the fold the Stretford Enders could finally look forward to the coming season. The club, its players and followers, wanted a repeat of the First Division Championship achieved in 1965. The winning of it was not only an end in itself but a further opportunity for a crack at the prize Busby had craved throughout his managerial career - the European Cup.

The previous season had been a terrible disappointment, more especially because following the destruction of Benfica in Lisbon, United appeared to have the world at their feet. To have subsequently lost to the dour Yugoslavs of Partizan Belgrade provided more evidence of United's quixotic nature - mercurially brilliant at times, desperately poor at others. Nevertheless with Bobby Charlton now a world champion and hailed as the finest midfield player in the world, playing consistently well in midfield and George Best producing ever more magical performances on the wing, there seemed to be less of a burden on the frequently injured Law.

In contrast to the previous season's all-conquering close season tour, United had a disastrous outing this time as far as results went. They lost 4-1 to both Celtic and Bayern Munich while FK Austria Vienna thrashed them 5-2. United's problem seemed to be in goal. Poor Harry Gregg was suffering agonies with the shoulder that he had injured a couple of seasons before while Pat Dunne, the goalkeeper who had starred in the previous Championship winning side, was out for the opening League game of the season against West Bromwich at Old Trafford. So it was David Gaskell who returned to the first team, keeping his place for the first five games.

Clearly the uncertainty regarding United's rearguard wasn't helping the normally reliable defence. Thus it was with some relief to all concerned when Busby and Murphy travelled to London and signed Alex Stepney for £50,000 from Chelsea. As a result Harry Gregg managed just two more appearances before he was sold to Stoke City while, later, Gaskell would also move to another club. Both Gregg and Gaskell had served United well during their time, yet both had been unlucky with injuries at vital times of their careers. The United followers would always have a special affection for these goalkeepers.

It was a beautiful sunny day at Old Trafford on the opening day of the season as the players formed a guard of honour to applaud the club's World Cup winners; Bobby Charlton, Nobby Stiles and John Connelly as the 41,343 spectators gave them a standing ovation. Being the patriotic Scotsman that he is, Denis led the clapping with clenched teeth. Later, there was a presentation of a silver tea service and cutlery to Jimmy Murphy for his 20 years service to the club as Matt Busby's right-hand man. Bobby Charlton also received the same presentation for becoming 'Footballer of the Year'. Amid these celebrations it might have been easy for the team to lose focus on the football, yet United made it a memorable day as they played exquisitely in winning 5-3. Denis got off the mark with two goals, while George Best, David Herd and Nobby Stiles added a goal apiece.

But United's problem still seemed to be at the back. Out of the opening seven league games they won four (against West Brom, Everton twice and Newcastle) but lost to Leeds, Stoke and Tottenham, scoring 14 and conceeding 12 in the process.

So with the season just a month old the Reds played Blackpool in the League Cup at Bloomfield Road. This was only the second time United had played in this competition since its inception in the 1960/61 season. Pat Dunne made his last senior appearance for the club in goal. Denis and new signing Alex Stepney watched the game. Denis, as has been mentioned, hated watching his team-mates. He would rather play than watch and soon left his seat and went down to the dressing room. But what went through Stepney's mind as he watched his new colleagues get hammered 5-1? Within a short time of joining the Reds, Alex had seen his three main rivals leave the club.

After playing in the opening six games of the season and just two months after playing in England's World Cup squad, John Connelly was surprisingly sold to Blackburn Rovers for £40,000. Denis was surprised at this move because he rated Connelly highly and thought he was a good acquisition for the Reds. John had given the Reds sterling service and in 112 appearances had scored 35 goals and helped to make countless others. He would go on to play for Bury, his fourth Lancashire club, and finish with a career total of 567 matches for all his four clubs, scoring 179 times. What a winger!

The young George Best was now a regular in the first team. He was brilliant to watch and fans all around the country would pack grounds to see the magic of the 'The Holy Trinity' of the Law-Best-Charlton trio. Yet there were many who firmly believed that because of Best's penchant for holding on to the ball and his love of dribbling past defenders, he prevented the electric-heeled Law from scoring more goals than usual. Denis loved playing the quick one-two pass and running into position for the return but often when he attempted this ploy with George he would discover that the ball would not arrive as he watched George dribbling past bemused defenders. It annoyed him and he would have words with his young team-mate, telling him in no uncertain terms to deliver the ball more quickly.

With Connelly's departure, Busby introduced John Aston to

the left wing and moved the Irish wonderboy onto the right
flank. A section of the Manchester United fans shamelessly
berated young Aston's style of play. It was so unfair the way he
was criticised. He was not in the George Best mould and in
fairness he never claimed to be: he was a more direct winger.
He scarcely wasted a ball and would run all day long in the
cause of the team and through his unselfish efforts the team
often scored important goals.

David Sadler was another youngster who had played quite
regularly throughout this season. The former bank clerk from
Yalding in Kent had joined the Reds as a centre-half. After
making his debut at 17 he made 12 appearances before losing
his place. For the following two seasons he made only a handful
of first team appearances while it was thought that he could
eventually replace Bill Foulkes at centre-half. Indeed so
accomplished did he look at the back that he was capped by
England in this position. However, David provided a stark
contrast to big Bill and often partnered the veteran in the heart
of United's defence. He was later switched to midfield and later
to inside-forward. David proved a loyal clubman.

In October 1966, Denis was on the treatment table with his
damaged calf at Old Trafford when his friend, journalist Peter
Slingsby, came in. Denis had scored eleven times in the
opening ten First Division games. The talk got around to
Dennis Viollet's record feat in the 1959/60 season when, from
36 League matches he scored 32 goals.

"Will this be a record season for Denis Law?" Peter asked.
Denis himself modestly disclaimed any interest in trying to beat
Dennis Viollet's record. "I'm just delighted to see the ball go
into the opposition net," he said, "records don't really matter
as long as we can stay on the winning track and, basically, that's
all I'm concerned with. Goals and glory count for very little if
the team is not doing well and all the boys are determined to
get some tangible reward for the club this season, especially
after last winter's disappointments."

Denis was now wearing the number eight jersey but the
numbers on the back of the jerseys meant nothing to United's

forwards because they regularly interchanged positions. Denis looked fit and razor-sharp as the team reorganised after the departures of Dunne, Gaskell, Gregg and Connelly. He returned to the team against Blackpool at Bloomfield Road, and scored twice in United's 2-1 victory. He scored in the following game against Chelsea, which ended in a 1-1 draw at Old Trafford, and also helped the Reds beat Arsenal 1-0 with a David Sadler goal at Old Trafford before missing the 3-1 away victory at Chelsea as United embarked on a six-match winning streak. His swift return from injury allowed him to play in the following five games, of which the Reds won four and lost one, Denis scoring twice in the process. He missed the subsequent 2-2 draw with Liverpool at Old Trafford but was back for the away game against West Brom, which ended in a fantastic 4-3 win with David Herd netting a hat-trick and Denis adding one. He played in three more games before being out of action again.

Despite his frequent absences United were now functioning like champions-elect. An unbeaten run following a 2-1 Boxing Day defeat at Sheffield United meant that by Spring 1967 they were clear at the top of the table. On Friday 3rd March 1967 United made history when their game against Arsenal at Highbury was screened 'live' on closed-circuit TV at Old Trafford. It was the first time that this type of transmission had been used to show United. It was also the first First Division football match to be televised on closed-circuit television. Nothing ventured, nothing gained, was Matt Busby's view of the event. A crowd of 28,423 helped to make it a historic occasion as they watched their heroes battling it out with the Gunners over 180 miles away. Watching the Reds on the giant screens was a little strange but overall the fans who attended enjoyed watching United's 1-1 draw. For the first half hour the Reds were hardly in the game and the fans back at Old Trafford were quiet. But the spontaneous thunder roar that greeted United's equaliser and the sustained chanting as the team went all out to win the game was almost deafening.

On 18th March 1967, before the home game against

Leicester, Bobby Charlton was presented with two awards from the Editor-in-chief of *France Football*, Max Urbini. The first was the European Player of the Year trophy, the second for being the outstanding player of the 1966 World Cup finals. He received a tremendous reception from the crowd, and the Reds stormed to a 5-2 victory. However, there was a rather sad note to the victory celebrations because it was in this game that Denis lost his strike partner, the much-maligned and underestimated David Herd.

Herd broke his left leg in the act of scoring against Leicester City at Old Trafford. Herd took a pass from Denis and cut inside, finishing as Leicester defender Graham Cross crashed into him. As he fell to the ground Denis rushed over to him. "Get Jack [Crompton], I've broken my leg," Herd told Law. Denis and the staff at Old Trafford were saddened by this injury to the big-hearted centre-forward who had averaged 20 goals a season over the previous five years. He had scored 16 before his injury and was well on his way to maintaining his average. Although not too popular with a section of the Old Trafford fans, Herd was well respected and liked immensely by the United playing and coaching staff. He was a quiet, affable man who just got on with his job of scoring goals. Denis had defended his club-mate on several occasions when he was being unfairly criticised. Although he was born in Hamilton, Scotland, the son of Alec, a former team-mate and friend of Matt Busby, David was raised in Moss Side, Manchester, and played football on the cobbled streets of south Manchester. He was a close friend of another player who would go on to become a Manchester United legend, Dennis Viollet. When he signed for the Reds in July 1961 David cost £35,000. It would prove one of the bargains of Busby's reign because in 262 first team games for the club he scored 144 goals before joining Stoke City in July 1968. Denis always praised the lethal shooting of Herd - it was estimated that he could shoot with a velocity of 72 mph.

Another sad blow for the Reds was the car crash in which Bobby Noble was badly injured. Denis was of the opinion that

Noble was the best young player to emerge from the Reds' youth system for a long while. Bobby had captained United's FA Youth Cup winning team of 1964 and played for England's Youth team. He seemed destined for every honour. He had greyhound speed, could tackle, had an abundance of skill, used the ball magnificently and had that spirit that all great players possessed.

After making his first team debut against Leicester in April 1966 at left full-back, Bobby had kept his place in the first team. But on April 22nd 1967, United had played a scoreless draw with Sunderland at Roker Park. Later that night, after the team coach had dropped the players off at Old Trafford to pick up their cars, Bobby was involved in an accident near his home in Sale. Bobby was critically ill for a while and unconscious for a few days - he was still only 21 but his glittering career had disappeared in an instant. After a long stint in hospital he attempted a comeback but two years after his accident he was advised by the FA Medical Board to retire from professional football. He was just 23 and had made a total of 33 first team appearances.

"I think Bobby Noble would have taken over the England left full-back position from Ray Wilson," said Denis. "Bobby had a little bit of a chip on his shoulder, and was inclined to be a bit naughty. Bobby and I had several heated tussles in five-a-side matches in training. Bobby would tackle as if his life depended on the outcome even in those five-a-side games. He would get stuck into players no matter who they were. He had no respect for anyone's reputation. When he came into the team he slotted in very smoothly. He read the game well and used the ball intelligently. For me, Ray Wilson was the best left-back I ever saw and yet Bobby Noble might have been better. He had a little nasty streak which is essential in a defensive player, and great confidence. What a tragedy that his career was cut short."

Manchester United ended the season unbeaten following defeat at Sheffield United. In time-honoured fashion they drew their away games and won at home so that their final record, though unspectacular was nonetheless impressive - United winning 24, drawing 12 and losing six for a total of 60 points.

Symptomatic of the Reds' confidence was the manner of their victory at Upton Park to clinch the title. West Ham, with World Cup heroes Moore, Hurst and Peters aboard, were breathtakingly annihilated 6-1. Indeed so keen were United to ensure victory that Matt Busby, having been delayed in the dressing room, reached his seat in the dug-out in time to watch Best score United's third! The following Saturday fans gathered at Old Trafford to crown their heroes as Champions again. Denis didn't play in this final game of the season but nevertheless led the team out at the start to a rapturous response from the loyal support. Despite niggling injuries Denis had still played in 36 League games, scoring 23 goals. In the FA Cup, during which United had surprisingly fallen to Norwich City in the fourth round, Law scored twice.

*

At the end of the season Denis joined his club-mates on a five-week summer tour to America, New Zealand and Australia. The senior players were buoyant, as champions again they felt on top of the world. Joining the senior players on the tour were youngsters John Aston, David Sadler, Jimmy Rimmer, Francis Burns and Collyhurst-born Brian Kidd. Busby and Murphy knew these youngsters were knocking on the first team door and they would get their chance on this tour. Matt was pleased with what he saw of his youngsters. Earlier in the season, just before the transfer deadline, after weighing up the consequences of Denis Law's knee injury, it was rumoured that Busby had made enquiries about six players in order to strengthen his squad. The brilliant, flamboyant Celtic winger Jimmy Johnstone was his top priority. However, nothing came of any of the six targets and he turned once again to his youngsters rather than the transfer market as Wilf McGuinness and John Aston senior had done a wonderful job coaching the latest crop of Busby Babes.

Jimmy Murphy liked to tell of an amusing little incident

concerning himself and Denis. It took place in the team hotel in Australia. While on tour, Jimmy liked his breakfast in bed. In the team hotel they left a breakfast card on the back of the room doors. If you wanted to order breakfast and have it brought to your room then all you had to do was fill in the form with your requirements. The staff would collect the card during the night and at the requested time the following morning deliver your order to your room. One night, after Denis watched Jimmy going up to bed, he filled in such a card. He ordered eggs, bacon, sausages, baked beans, fried bread, mushrooms, toast, marmalade and whatever else was on the menu. When Denis was certain Jimmy was fast asleep he crept to his door, removed the card Jimmy had filled in with his light breakfast and replaced it with his.

Sure enough Jimmy was awoken by a knock at the door. Getting out of bed and rubbing the sleep from his eyes he opened the door to met by two waiters loaded down with his vast breakfast order. "Who the devil ordered this lot?" shouted an irate Murphy, asking what time it was. "6am sir," said one of the waiters. Needless to say Jimmy later saw the funny side of Denis' prank. Later on he prowled around the table where the team were having breakfast looking to see if he could finger the culprit. "I might have known it was that scallywag Law," recalled a laughing Jimmy.

The tour went well except for one ugly incident which, surprisingly, Denis failed to mention in his autobiography. Law was sent off while on the tour Down Under. The incident took place on Tuesday 27th June 1967 as Denis received his marching orders during the Reds' 7-0 win against Western Australia. There were over 18,000 people present and they sat stunned as they watched the referee, Roy Stedman, known over there as the 'Iron Man' because he stood for no nonsense from players (he had apparently sent off three players during a two-week spell and booked 12 others) ordered Denis off for what was reported in some newspapers as 'rough play' after only 33 minutes. As Law walked from the field to the dressing room many of the crowd showed their disapproval of the referee's decision. It was Denis who had started the Reds' spree when he opened the scoring in the 21st minute, then George Best added two more before Brian Kidd gave United a 4-0 half-time lead.

'*5,300-mile Phone Link Lets Law Off The Hook*' was the headline in the *Manchester Evening News*. Manchester United feared the worst when their explosive Scot was sent off for swearing at the referee. It appeared that their final match in the garden city of Perth would spoil United's triumphant tour of Australia. If the Australian Football Federation had sent a report to the English FA then Denis would have been in big trouble and in all probability he would have been suspended again and would likely miss the start of the new season.

But things were about to change for the better as Matt Busby got busy with the local football officials regarding the sending-off. He called on Sir William Walkey, the president of the Australian Football Federation, to deal with the case in the few hours remaining before United returned home. Sir William ordered an immediate tribunal to be set up in Perth, as the Federation officials from four state capitals joined in an inter-state telephone hook-up to deal with Denis Law's case.

The result was that Law escaped with a A$50 (£20) fine and was free to kick off the new season in England. An additional charge of using foul and abusive language was dismissed. A relieved Denis paid the fine in Australian dollars out of his own pocket immediately the result was announced. The tribunal lasted 90 minutes and the Federation heard phone evidence in Sydney, Adelaide and Hobart. The Australians felt under an obligation on two counts, first they had already made a £50,000 profit from having the Reds in Australia, which had been an unqualified success in terms of attendances. Secondly they thought the referee, Roy Stedman, who was originally from England, was much too harsh. The Australian officials took the view that in a country noted for its colourful language it would have been ironic if one outburst had landed the English champions in trouble and deprived them of Law's services at the start of the new season.

As a precursor to the new season someone replied to a letter in the *Manchester Evening News* Soapbox, which was edited by Jack McNamara. A few days after the Law incident, a Mr E Worthington, of Fazakerley, Liverpool wrote: "So one of your young readers wants to clean Denis Law's boots, does he? Good for him. Please ask him to tie his laces together as well before United play Everton next season." Jack McNamara replied: "Not the most charitable of pre-season thoughts, one might say. Ah, well, United know where they stand on Merseyside."

*

In the 1967 FA Charity Shield game United played Spurs and, as champions, the game was played at Old Trafford. It was the day that Matt Busby introduced Brian Kidd, the tall, eager youngster from Collyhurst in north Manchester, to the first team. It wasn't a great game by any means, ending in a 3-3 draw. The match was notable for two remarkable goals. The first went down as one of the greatest 'What Happened Next?' moments in television history when Spurs keeper Pat Jennings' length of the pitch goal kick bounced over both Foulkes and Stepney and into an unguarded net.

The highlight of the match though was a wonder goal scored by Denis. It was a fascinating goal which, had the referee allowed it, would surely have gone down in the Football Hall of Fame. Spinning beneath a centre lofted in from Spurs' left wing, and with a wrench of his muscles, Denis propelled himself upwards, his legs criss-crossing into a bicycle volley which drove the ball into the roof of the goal. For a fraction of a second the whole ground fell silent. It was the Stretford End which reacted first with an explosion of acclaim as Law, bounding up from the floor, turned to them, his right arm raised in a familiar, imperious Roman salute, as the rest of the ground erupted into a cauldron of deafening noise at Law's unforgettable effort. Thousands in the stands leaped to their feet, and the roar that erupted from their throats shook window panes in the streets around Old Trafford. Then Denis was lost beneath the bodies of his congratulating colleagues.

They had grown used to great goals from the man but this goal was something extra special to put in the memory bank. Suddenly there was silence as the referee disallowed the goal. No one knew why but the referee had robbed a superb player of a goal they were fortunate to see scored perhaps once in a lifetime. It would have no place in the record books, but would never be erased from the memories of those lucky enough to have seen it. Denis threw his head back in disgust and then turned to the crowd, arms out, the palms of his hands raised in a gesture of total disbelief. There had been no more effective protest. But the referee stood firm.

The new season started with a visit to Everton in the opening league game. Goodison Park was packed with almost 62,000 fans waiting with baited breath for a feast of entertaining football. Thousands had made the trip from Manchester and Salford down the East Lancs Road, but they were disappointed, seeing their favourites hammered 3-1 by a rejuvenated Everton side. Denis remained captain and played in the opening three games of the season before he missed the next two matches with yet more injuries - in his absence the team won one and drew one. Denis came back for the away match with Sheffield Wednesday in which the Reds scraped a 1-1 draw. He played in the following six League games, of which United won five and lost once, but Denis scored only twice. However, during those six games he found himself in serious trouble once again with a referee and the football authorities. It was perfectly true that everything that happened to Denis during this time, good or bad, was always blown out of all proportion, as we shall see. It's easy to do anything if you are victorious. It's in the bad times that a man reveals himself.

On 7th October 1967 the Reds were at home to Arsenal, coached by future United manager Dave Sexton. There were over 60,000 spectators inside the ground for one of the glamour fixtures of the English game. The Gunners had their big-money signing: the craggy-faced, blond-haired Scottish International centre-half Ian Ure marking Denis and what a battle this confrontation turned out to be between two players who had cost their clubs a grand total of £240,000. The busiest man on the field was referee George McCabe. It was a tough and, at times, exciting game with Ure giving Denis no opportunity. As soon as Law had the ball the big, long-legged Ure would be challenging him for possession. The two players exchanged kicks, pushes and other physical contact in front of irate, yelling fans. Passions were boiling over and things got a bit heated during the first half as the Scottish internationals clashed several times and referee McCabe booked both for fighting.

It's fair to say that Ure could possibly have been given his marching orders in the first half for some of his challenges on Law. In the second half the feud showed no sign of abating and the referee had little option but to send both players off after they were involved in another punch-up, with the crowd baying noisily. United eventually won 1-0 with a goal from John Aston. Four days later Law and Ure were re-united as colleagues for Scotland against Ireland. It had been an horrendous and disappointing start to the season. Aside from the dismissal that wasn't in Australia, Denis had only been booked twice over the previous three years. There was a great deal of newspaper coverage about the way 'star' players like Law were being singled out for special treatment by opposing defenders. It was felt that referees should clamp down quicker on the defenders who were over-aggressive in their method of tackling.

A couple of days later in the *Manchester Evening News*, Mr Alan Wales, from Manchester 10, wrote: "Who has the most cautions and 'sendings off' in football, Denis Law or Billy Bremner?" The paper answered: "Since joining United, Law had been sent off four times and received ten bookings. Bremner had been sent off twice, and booked 19 times". However, it was no laughing matter when, on 27th October, both Denis and Ian Ure received six week suspensions. Their bans were the longest for on the field offences for more than 20 years. As the controversy raged many people in football were asking where Manchester United stood on this latest early bath of Law's? After all, they pointed out, this was Law's fourth dismissal in as many years.

Would he remain as captain of Manchester United? Another question hanging over 'The King' was whether Denis would face disciplinary action from the club in addition to his suspension. Many thought Matt Busby was being too soft with his players as United had had 14 players dismissed in just four seasons. Admittedly these 14 dismissals included players from all five of United's teams. In response, Busby retorted that he had no intention of washing the club's dirty linen in public and that whatever action he and the club took against Denis would remain inside the club. In an attempt to ease his selection worries Busby later asked the FA to release Denis to allow him to play in the European Cup against Sarajevo, but the FA refused point blank.

"Whenever I got into trouble on the field it always seemed to be as a result of retaliation," Denis later explained, "there were only eight minutes left of the game against Arsenal when Ian Ure clattered me for the umpteenth time and then gave me a kick as I was lying on the floor. It was the last straw. I had come to the end of my tether. I got up and took a wild swing at him which actually missed the target but the referee turned round at the crucial moment - no doubt attracted by the shout which went up from the crowd and saw my fist flying. The incident undoubtedly looked bad and yet once again it was the retaliation that had caught the eye. Although I do admit that I wasn't entirely innocent, once again it was a case of a referee giving a forward player inadequate protection."

"Denis Law has extraordinarily rapid reflexes, which not only makes him the great goalscorer he is, but also land him in trouble," said Jimmy Murphy after Denis' latest sending-off. Jimmy was apoplectic about the FA's ruling and went on to say that it was easy to point an accusing finger at Denis because he had been sent off four times. Jimmy said it was easy to ask: "Why doesn't Law control himself?" but that, according to Jimmy, the circumstances of his dismissals all boiled down to the same thing. "He has the reflexes of a cat; because he has a blaze of brilliance, a smouldering temper. Have they ever thought what it's like to move with the lightning speed of Denis Law and in the act of creating some flash of brilliance be cynically chopped down from behind by a malicious defender?"

"These defenders," said Murphy, "will have been told that if they missed the ball not to worry if they catch Law on the ankle. Both Matt and I have told Denis to try and curb his temperament when he is being goaded beyond his endurance. But out on the pitch players like Denis, moving with the speed of a sprinter, were being kicked and hacked, chopped and pushed just when their mind and muscles were geared to performing some act of creative or dazzling brilliance, then bang - the player is sprawled out on the floor. The referee blows his whistle, the player picks himself up with rage and pain flashing messages to his brain and a move which could have thrilled thousands of fans is stopped for an innocuous free kick. This is Denis Law's problem, just as it is a problem for other great players once they invade the danger area near goal where defenders are grouped en masse - each with one thought: 'Thou Shalt Not Pass'." Jimmy went on to say that this was nothing new to Denis, but because he was a huge personality in an era where there are hardly any, he was the player whose name was in the headlines because he retaliated.

There were rumours flying around Manchester that Denis's career was hanging in the balance because of his dodgy knee. He had lost his place in the Scotland team to play England in the Nations Cup and he wasn't his usual confident self. Jimmy Murphy explained: "Denis needs to be 100 per cent fit, less than that affects his game. People don't understand that Denis is so brave, but he has to be right. His injury occurred because he was too courageous."

12. The End of an Era

During his enforced lay-off for suspension and injury, Denis watched his team-mates continue their championship form of the previous season. Before Christmas, United suffered just three defeats, yet by the start of 1968 Denis was still suffering with his knee and rumours abounded that a razor-sharp Law was now a thing of the past. Certainly by this time Law had passed his absolute peak. Whether this diminished ability to take games by the scruff of the neck could be put down to the injuries he had sustained throughout his glittering career or whether it was merely a case of a natural decline due to age rather than ability was anyone's guess but 1967/68 would prove to be Denis' worst season since he joined the Reds in 1962. He played just 23 League matches, scoring a mere seven goals, while in the FA Cup he played a solitary game - a 2-2 draw with Spurs in the third round at Old Trafford which the Reds lost 1-0 after extra time in the replay, while his meagre contribution to the European Cup run was a mere two goals from three games.

Law was worried and understandably so. After all, this was his career and his livelihood and in those days players did not receive the huge salaries of present-day players. Over the previous couple of seasons he had played for the club when he really should not have been on the pitch. Yet he put Manchester United's cause first and played through the pain. The machismo of playing on despite injury was very much the trend in English football and remained the case until very recently. Denis did not have access to the kind of specialist treatment modern day stars are used to. The long-term effects remain for many players from this era, many are debilitated by injuries that were exaggerated by the use of cortisone injections used to numb the pain. The long list of casualties from this era is too exhaustive to mention here but the hard-tackling stars of the sixties and seventies cut a grim figure today.

As mentioned, Denis Law had played in the first two European Cup games against Hibernians of Malta in September 1967 - scoring twice in the Reds' 4-0 victory in the first leg at Old Trafford. The Maltese team was managed by a priest, Reverend Father Hilary Tagliaferro. Denis, described as 'Demon Denis' by Derek Hodgson in the *Daily Express,* was at his sharpest. David Sadler had scored an early goal before Denis struck in the 43rd minute with an unstoppable shot that the Maltese keeper, Alfred Mizzi, couldn't hold. In the second half Denis terrorised the opposition defence with his aerial ability. Sadler got another goal and Denis completed the scoring in the 61st minute. In the return game played in 80 degree heat on a rock hard sandy pitch in the Gzira Stadium, United could only draw 0-0. Denis was quiet in this game because he was suffering with a bruised toe.

In the FA Cup the Reds had two third round matches against Tottenham. At Old Trafford, it ended in a 2-2 draw. Best and Charlton scoring the goals. In the replay at White Hart Lane, the Reds went down 1-0 after extra time. After their exit from the FA Cup to Spurs Denis played spasmodically for the rest of the season, in fact he played just once more and did not get on the scoresheet.

He was clearly in terrible pain from his knee injury and tried every remedy known to man until he finally spoke to Matt Busby, who sent him to see one of Harley Street's finest, Mr Osmond-Clarke. Denis had been examined by other specialists but had never felt confident that they could solve his knee problem. The usually cheerful Denis was looking rather pensive when he was examined by Mr Osmond-Clarke. The surgeon wrote a letter to the club with his findings, which stated in short that Denis' knee was in such bad condition that he didn't believe it would last much more than a couple of seasons at the most. The contents of the letter were never shown or divulged to Denis.

In his 1979 autobiography Denis talked about the letter from Mr Osmond-Clarke, explaining that he did not actually see the report until many years later when his career as a player was finished and it would have certainly not been what the 28-year-old player wanted to read. Could you imagine that sort of thing happening today and the repercussions that would follow? The specialist suggested an exploratory operation and then, once he had diagnosed the problem, a remedial operation. At the time, though Denis was obviously worried, he also felt a sense of relief that the specialist had at last confirmed that he did genuinely have a very serious knee problem, which was career- threatening and could affect his livelihood.

Meanwhile, his club mates were on course for a double of League and European Cup yet despite his enforced inactivity the Old Trafford fans never once criticised Denis. They knew that he was struggling but, just as United fans still serenade a certain Frenchman despite his absence, to sixties fans Denis was 'The King'!

In the event United's season turned on a poor run of form in March during which they lost to Chelsea, Coventry and eventual champions Manchester City. The derby defeat was particularly galling for United as, with a victory, they would have gone four points clear at the top. But United were stretched to breaking point with the European Cup run taking priority and their defeats had followed tough ties in Europe. The Reds eventually finished runners-up to Manchester City (United finishing with 56 points, City 58), the loss of the title confirmed by a demoralising 2-1 defeat at home to Sunderland on the final day of the season. Yet to finish runners-up was no bad achievement when one considers that they had started the season without Bobby Noble and David Herd, while Nobby Stiles was also out for quite some time after a cartilage operation and of course Denis had been absent for nearly the entire season.

The European Cup was, as mentioned, the priority and all else was sidelined to concentrate on it. United had followed their victory against Hibernians of Malta with a narrow and hard-fought 2-1 win over Yugoslav champions Sarajevo. The Yugoslavs were, according to Paddy Crerand: "A vicious side, they really did kick lumps out of us. Our trainer Jack Crompton was on the field so often that most of the crowd thought he was playing." After a goalless draw in Yugoslavia, the second leg saw United grind out a 2-1 win thanks to goals from Aston and Best, the latter getting unneccessarily involved with the Yugoslav goalkeeper during an incident in the tunnel.

Next up in the quarter-finals came Polish champions Gornik Zabrze. Without Law, who failed a fitness test on the morning of the match, the mantle of main goalscorer now fell to George Best. And it was Best's deflected shot that gave United the lead following a defence-splitting dribble that left the Poles floundering. In the last minute United added a vital second when a scramble in the area saw Kidd get a vital touch.

United arrived for the return in Poland to discover the pitch covered in snow and despite Busby's vain attempts to get the match postponed, the game went ahead under blizzard like conditions. A 1-0 defeat proved enough for United to advance to the last four and the relief for Busby was audible when he was heard singing 'I belong to Glasgow' in the hotel after the game.

Yet surprisingly, after such a long absence, Law played in the first leg of a momentous European Cup semi-final at Old Trafford against Real Madrid. It was the clubs' first meeting in Europe for 11 years and represented a long-awaited opportunity for revenge. Bobby Charlton, Bill Foulkes and Gento were the only survivors from the clubs' previous meeting.

On a beautiful April evening, before a 63,000 capacity crowd, Denis, captain of United, and Gento, captain of Madrid, led their teams out onto the Old Trafford pitch. Roared on by the crowd Denis appeared to lack that vital zip that made him such a formidable opponent and though he tried, nothing seemed to go right for him. In the event the game was disappointing but the Reds took a slim 1-0 advantage into the second leg following a stunning first-time strike from Best.

Denis went to Spain for the return leg as a tactical manoeuvre only; there was no chance of him playing. Meanwhile in the Bernebeu Stadium United faced long odds to reach the final. To make matters worse, by half time they looked out of the competition - they were 3-1 down and could be considered lucky to have scored following a mis-directed clearance by Zoco that beat his own keeper. In truth, United could have been five or six goals down at half time but now, forced to attack, the game took on a different complexion. With 20 minutes left a free kick landed at the feet of centre-half David Sadler who tapped the ball into the net. Then, eight minutes later, Best tore down the wing and laid the ball into Bill Foulkes' path. Centre-half Foulkes, survivor of Munich and United's longest-serving player, calmly side-footed the ball past Betancourt in the Real goal. United were through to the final and the tears flowed from Busby's eyes once more. Yet already Denis knew he would play no part in it.

*

Throughout the trip and for most of the season Denis had been creased with pain and it was decided that he would have to undergo the operation Mr Osmond-Clarke had recommended. Matt Busby suggested that Denis delay the operation until after the European Cup final. Denis, though, thanked his manager but said he would prefer to have the operation as soon as possible so that he could train throughout the summer and be ready for the new season. Busby agreed and, as his Old Trafford colleagues played at Wembley on the greatest occasion in the club's history, Denis was in bed in St Joseph's Hospital, Whalley Range.

As the hordes of Manchester United supporters flocked into London for the big occasion, Denis Law was in almost all of their thoughts. They were, of course, disappointed that their 'King' was missing on this night of all nights but they were eagerly anticipating his return to something close to his sharp-shooting best for the new season.

Denis' reluctance to appear on television came to the fore

again when the BBC's David Coleman wanted to bring the cameras into the hospital to film Law's reaction and get his views on the game. Matt Busby said he had no objection but it was up to Denis to decide if he wanted to do it. St Joseph's raised no objection. However, Denis politely said 'No' and that was the end of that idea.

So how did Denis spend his time on the most important night in Manchester United's history? In his excellent book, *Reliving The Dream* about the 1968 European Cup triumph, the author, Derick Allsop, interviewed Denis. Denis, by now the father of five children, told Derick that three days before the European Cup final the surgeon at St Joseph's Hospital removed one-and-a-half inches of cartilage. "It took a load off my mind," Denis told him. He explained that he had arranged for a few friends to join him in his hospital room to watch the match, but he had not bargained for the enthusiasm of the nuns who ran the hospital.

"At six o'clock on the morning of the game one of the nuns, a nurse, came into my room to see if I was alright and she was wearing a huge red rosette," said a laughing Denis. He went on to say that although he was upset and obviously disappointed at missing the greatest occasion in both his own and United's life, he was hoping and praying that his club-mates would beat Benfica for Matt Busby's sake. "I was extremely nervous as the game got underway, especially when Eusebio broke through a few minutes from time. I thought: 'That's it, we're never going to win this thing', but somehow either Alex Stepney saved his blockbuster of a shot or it hit him. I think Eusebio saw the morning headlines because he tried to blast the ball into the net. If he could have had that chance again I'm sure he would have side-footed it. If Jimmy Greaves had been on the end of that chance we would have lost. But we deserved to win because we went at them throughout the game."

United took the lead after 52 minutes through a rarity, a Bobby Charlton header. Sadler had a chance to put United 2-0 up before Benfica equalised through Graca. Talking about the European Cup triumph, Paddy Crerand said that when

Eusebio had the ball at his feet and was only about ten or twelve yards away from putting the ball past Alex Stepney he felt anxious and worried. He said he knew there were only a few minutes left before the referee blew his whistle to end the game. "This didn't look like the kind of chance Eusebio, the Black Prince of Portugal, would miss," said Paddy, "my heart sank as the powerful figure of Eusebio raced through preparing to score and put Benfica 2-1 in the lead and end United's dream of lifting the European Cup but what a relief when I saw him blast the ball, it was like a thunderbolt, straight at Alex Stepney, who made a brilliant save. Later, while analysing that moment, I realised that there would have been no celebrations for us if Eusebio had not been an incurable exhibitionist! If Bobby Charlton, George Best, or certainly Denis Law had been in Eusebio's boots at that moment it would have been a goal." Why was he so certain? "Because they wouldn't have been thinking about the crowd. Their only concern would have been to put the ball in the net by the easiest method. But then, they didn't have ego trouble like Mr Eusebio!"

United had made it through to extra time and in the short period between the end of normal time and the restart, United were revitalised, so much so that they scored three goals in the first seven minutes of extra time. First Best latched onto a Kidd flick, beat Jacinto and side-footed the ball past a sprawling keeper, then Kidd scored after his shot had been blocked before Charlton finished a fine cross from Kidd with a side-foot volley. 4-1 to United and Busby had achieved his dream.

After the game all the United players phoned Denis, who was enjoying the victory celebrations with friends and a few beers. "I think I was the only one in bed that night!" he said later. The television cameras came into the hospital to film Denis' reaction to United's wonderful victory but they decided not to film Denis because he was too "emotionally disturbed". The following day the entire United party called into the hospital with the European trophy, a lovely gesture by Matt Busby and the team. They wanted to let Denis know that he had played a big part in securing it.

Shortly after winning the European Cup, Matt Busby was knighted by the Queen. It was a great honour not only for Matt but for the club as well. George Best was also in the honours list, being voted European Footballer of the Year for 1968. This was also a wonderful honour for Manchester United because George Best was the third player from Old Trafford to win this much coveted and prestigious award, following Denis and Bobby Charlton.

*

Pre-season tours are often misleading guides to form. So when, during the 1968 close season, the newly crowned European champions beat Hamburg 2-0 in Germany thanks to goals from Bobby Charlton and George Best and a Drumcondra Select XI 2-1 in Ireland with Denis on the scoresheet - hopes were high that United could pick up where they left off the previous season. By now Manchester United were the most respected team in England but, as this season was to prove, significant members of the side were showing signs of wear and tear.

The return of Denis boosted the Old Trafford fans, and considerably boosted the Reds' chances of more success in the coming season. Everyone, including Denis himself, knew that during the previous season he had been a mere shadow of the world-class player he had been and while many felt confident that Denis' operation had put his long absences through injury behind him, the man himself knew he had a long way to go before he could match the kind of performances that his adoring public expected of him.

During the summer Matt Busby, now Sir Matt, had strengthened his team, buying Willie Morgan, a right-winger, from Burnley for £100,000 in August. Several newspapers referred to him as another George Best, which was stupid really because nobody could be another George Best. Morgan was a good player and was capped by Scotland but really there was simply no comparison between Best and the former Burnley winger - Best was a genius, a truly magnificent world-class player.

In the first match of the season the new European champions were at home to Everton.

Hopes were high that the team could gather more success, defend the European Cup successfully and win the First Division title again. There was a massive 61,311 crowd inside Old Trafford to give the Reds a fantastic welcome. United won 2-1 with goals by Best and Charlton. In their second game of the season, away against West Bromwich, the Reds were disappointing and lost 3-1, Charlton getting United's only goal. Denis missed the following three games.

And while before the season started, fans, players and management were highly optimistic that following his operation Denis would return to his brilliant best, sadly it was to be. His knee was beyond repair. It's not the length of a footballer's career that wears a player out. It's the number of hard tackles he takes and Denis had taken far too many - even at this stage his playing days were numbered.

Nevertheless there are thousands of Reds who speak in glowing terms about a game they describe as the greatest League game this great sixties side ever played. It proved to be a swansong, the beginning of the end of a beautiful era. The match took place on the last day of August 1968 at Hillsborough, Sheffield. In the first half both forward lines gave an exhibition of speed, goals, excitement, and attacking play that would have put even the great Real Madrid in the shade. Seven goals were scored in that first 45 minutes and the spectators were in a frenzy of excitement. This was football at its sparkling best. Wednesday took the lead after only 90 seconds, the Reds however, roared on by their loyal fans, started stoking the ball around and one player stood out...Denis Law! He was the dynamite Law of old; confident, sharp, super-skilled and eager for the ball. The Stretford Enders were chanting that the 'The King' was back and he certainly looked to have discovered his old flair. Denis was hunted by the Wednesday defenders but avoided their crude challenges with all the grace and subtlety of old. The United forward line looked awesome with Denis in this mood.

George Best got the equaliser and then Denis added another to put the Reds into a 2-1 lead. This was the first League goal of the season for Denis and what appropriate timing because this was his 200th League appearance for the Reds. The cheering and noise showed no signs of abating as the thrills came thick and fast. The Yorkshire team pulled back on level terms. Then the graceful, gazelle-like Bobby Charlton started moving like the world star he was and United were buzzing again. Bobby roamed all over the field looking for gaps in the Wednesday defence and sent a string of accurate passes to his forwards. 'The Three Musketeers', Charlton-Law-Best, were at their most compelling, gelling together brilliantly. Two more goals saw United take the lead again when Denis and Bobby notched a couple of goals to make it 4-2. Denis' second goal was his 128th goal in League matches. What a day, what a game! The Old Trafford team looked set to beat their Hillsborough bogey as the roar echoed around Yorkshire from United fans singing 'Give us a goal Denis Law' continuing with, 'I'd walk a million miles, for one of your goals, my Den-is' to the old Al Jolson 'Mammy' song. The chanting and singing got louder and louder from the United faithful. United certainly gave the fans something to please them, this was more like the Red Devils of old and the Denis Law loved and respected.

But, as if in anticipation of the team's decline, United surrendered their two-goal advantage. The Reds later pointed to an injury to Tony Dunne as an excuse but there was no hiding United's leaky defence, Wednesday went on to register a 5-4 win in a game long remembered for beautiful, exciting football and goals galore.

*

From the start of their managerial careers with Manchester United both Sir Matt Busby and Jimmy Murphy were revolutionaries as far as football was concerned. They had watched spellbound as the Magical Magyars slaughtered England in 1953 giving an unbelievable exhibition of football.

In fact it was Matt who defied the powerful and autocratic football authorities in the British Isles and entered United in the European Cup of 1956. So when, following the Reds' European Champions Cup victory in 1968 United were invited to play in the World Club championship against the champions of South America, Estudiantes of Buenos Aires, Busby had little hesitation in accepting. However by the end of the two leg play-off the newly-knighted manager must have regretted his decision.

The first leg was due to be played in Argentina on 25th August 1968, yet right from the moment Sir Matt agreed to take part there was an air of foreboding and unpleasantness associated with the game. The previous year in this competition Celtic, the 1967 European champions, had played Racing Club of Argentina at Hampden Park. Celtic won 1-0 but the game was littered with fouls and intimidation. The Argentine players kicked and fouled their way through the game. The return in Argentina was even worse. Racing Club won and a third game had to be played during which five players were sent off by the referee. It was a nasty, vicious brawl. Two years previously, when England had defeated Argentina in the quarter-finals of the World Cup, the game had descended into farce and the after effects left a sour taste in the mouth. It seemed that Argentine anger at the outcome of that game was clouding their games with all British clubs - English and Scottish.

From the time United landed in Argentina the Manchester United party were subject to intimidation while the match itself, played in Boca Juniors Stadium, was a disgrace to football and sportsmanship. The pitch was surrounded by steel-helmeted riot police carrying truncheons and tear-gas and when the teams ran out a huge firework hit the night air like an explosion followed by clouds of red smoke - and that was just the start of the trouble.

Denis, who had done his share of travelling with United and Scotland, stood hands on hips as he looked up at the smoke and fireworks. At that moment he understood the scale of the opposition. Charlton, Law and Best were singled out for special marking and poor Nobby Stiles bore the brunt of the cynical Argentineans. The Benfica manager Otto Gloria should have been ashamed of himself for the article he wrote in the official match programme. It was inflammatory and totally unfair to Stiles, who was labelled 'El Assassin' by the local press. The Benfica manager said Nobby was brutal, bad intentioned and a bad sportsman. During the game, Nobby was butted in the face, spat at, kicked and elbowed and then sent off for being offside. Bobby Charlton was fouled and received a nasty gash on his leg. In fact, there wasn't a United player who wasn't fouled, kicked or spat at throughout the game. The refereeing seemed non-existent. Estudiantes won 1-0 but hardly any of the English contingent cared or were interested after this excuse for legalised mayhem. Denis said that in all his travels he had never experienced anything like that which he and his club-mates had been through. Sir Matt commented: "Any of our players who held the ball during that game put their lives in danger."

The return at Old Trafford on 16th October 1968 was little better. Mr Gustav Wiederkehr, the President of UEFA, made an appeal in the programme for the United supporters to uphold the traditions of English sportsmanship. "I hope to see a fine match played in a sporting atmosphere," he said. Matt Busby had also asked the fans to co-operate in making the game a sporting occasion. Yet George Best and the Argentine Jose Medina were both sent off after Best retaliated against a foul by Medina. "He hit me on the lip first of all and I retaliated," said Best, "the moment I did it I knew it was wrong but it is human nature to defend yourself." George Best was far from a coward - next to Denis Law he was probably the most marked man in football, fouled regularly by less skilled defenders. He said if he didn't even try for 70-30 balls in his favour then something was drastically wrong. The Argentines used scything tackles, blatant fouls and were guilty of play-acting and time wasting.

After about twenty minutes their goalkeeper blatantly flew into Denis feet first and he had to be carried off. "The keeper dived at me with his studs up and ripped a big gash down my right shin," said Denis adding, "I wish the referee had blown for full time after about ten minutes because there was no way we were going to be allowed to play any kind of football." The Reds lost 2-1 on aggregate but nobody really cared because most had been sickened by the nasty, cynical behaviour of the Estudiantes team.

The season would prove to be unlucky for a number of United's senior players. Aside from Law's injuries, John Aston junior was a frequent visitor to the treatment table. John had played a 'blinder' in the European Cup final and the new season promised much for this quiet, likeable young winger. But in only the third game of the new campaign John broke his leg at Maine Road in an historic Manchester derby which featured the champions of Europe and the champions of England. Poor John was out of action for over seven months. Bobby Charlton also missed quite a number of games with strained knee ligaments, his longest spell out of action for six years. Francis Burns was also out with cartilage trouble, having already gone through two cartilage operations before this latest setback. Left-back Tony Dunne broke his jaw in two places toward the end of the season and missed the two important European Cup games against AC Milan. With Shay Brennan also sidelined with a pulled thigh muscle it meant the Reds had to play their two terrier wing-halves Nobby Stiles and John Fitzpatrick at full-back.

Law's decline through injury and age was symptomatic of his team's waning power. In the League, United practised the art of inconsistency. Where the 1967 championship had been won by good defence, there now appeared to be a profligacy explained perhaps by injury but also by the sense that the team's ambitions had been fulfilled in May. In addition to the 5-4 reverse at Hillsborough there was a 4-0 defeat away to a strong Chelsea outfit, as well as heavy defeats at championship contenders Leeds, Liverpool and Arsenal. In truth the team never stood a chance in the League; Busby had always played the game to win through attractive, old-fashioned methods.

Now the new breed of footballer was having his day and the title challengers were far too hungry to allow the aesthetics of the game to prevent them from ultimate victory. In the event Leeds won the 1968-69 league title by a street from Liverpool. Don Revie and Bill Shankly were following in Busby's footsteps, yet in doing so they displayed a hunger missing from United's game.

*

Yet there's no doubt that over the shorter course United and Law still had the propensity to dazzle and where better to do it than in defence of the European Cup. Denis, eager for a second bite at the cherry having missed May's final, played in the Reds' first round tie with Irish champions Waterford. The first match was played at Lansdowne Road, Dublin, because the tiny Waterford ground would not have been big enough to accomodate the number of spectators wanting to see the game. Over 48,000 tickets had been sold for this match but thousands gatecrashed and it was estimated that the attendance was nearer 50,000. There were incredible scenes: George Best was besieged by female fans wanting his autograph while referee Bill Mullan had to wait until the girls were removed from the pitch before starting the game. There were frequent pitch invasions and at one stage the referee threatened to abandon the game if fans did not stop coming on. There was nothing cynical or violent about these incursions onto the grass, just a natural over-enthusiasm on the part of the United-mad (and Best-mad) Irish.

In between interruptions Denis displayed a hint of the old Law by scoring all three in a 3-1 win. He scored his first after George Best had laid on a simple chance and the huge crowd went ballistic after half an hour when Denis scored his second. The game came to a standstill as exuberant fans invaded the playing area once more - Brian Kidd had centred from the left and Denis rose skywards, head and shoulders above everyone, arched his back and his neck muscles before punching the ball powerfully into the net. It was a brilliantly executed goal. He got his third a few minutes after the interval and hit a post with a penalty as the Reds won 3-1.

The return was a mere formality. Nobby Stiles scored the first, then Bobby Charlton unleashed a thunderball of a shot from 35 yards that Waterford keeper Thomas parried to Law who nipped in and scored. Later, Bobby Charlton beat a defender, dummied the keeper and passed to Denis who nonchalantly slotted the ball into the goal. He completed his second hat-trick against the Irish when he nodded in a Crerand cross. Later Francis Burns scored but the loudest cheer greeted Waterford's goal scored by Al Casey. Denis scored his fourth and United's sixth in the 72nd minute after David Sadler's shot broke loose from the goalkeeper. Bobby Charlton completed the rout when he thundered a shot that hit the net like a rocket to complete a 7-1 rout at Old Trafford. The United fans were gloriously happy, chanting Law's name all the way home.

Despite a seven-star performance against Waterford, Law was aware that the true test of his recovery from injury would come against tougher opposition. A two-goal performance against Anderlecht in the next round played before 51,000 at Old Trafford was another step in the right direction and saw him claim another cup record. Up to this point Denis had scored 14 goals in the European Cup while Dennis Viollet had scored 13 in the same competition.

However, Denis' goals tally would have been much higher had he not missed two penalties in the competition - one against Waterford in Dublin and another at the start of this game against Anderlecht. Over the previous twelve months he had missed four out of six from the spot. It was true to say that the old Law would have dispatched all six penalties safely. After the set back of a missed penalty, Brian Kidd opened the scoring against the Belgian champions and the Reds were aware that they needed at least a two-goal lead to take to Brussels. Then, after 70 minutes, Charlton crossed and Denis flicked a delicate header past a startled Anderlecht goalkeeper. Eight minutes later he stuck again to make the tie safe when Carlo Sartori, one Collyhurst lad, shot straight at the keeper as another

Collyhurst kid, Brian Kidd, dived in and following a brief melée, Denis kept calm and lashed the rebound into the goal to round off a 3-0 victory. Kidd gave United an early lead in the return but the Reds ended up hanging on to a 1-3 defeat and a 4-3 aggregate victory.

Another sad blow for the Reds had come in early February 1969 with the death of Ted Dalton. Ted was a much-respected and much-loved friend of Busby, Murphy and every player and official at Manchester United. Busby said Ted was a member of United's 'happy family'. "He was a personal friend," said Matt, "he was a true friend and an able counsellor." During his 33 years as the Reds' physiotherapist he became famous. He had a private practice on St John Street in the city centre and also had connections with St Joseph's Hospital where he was closely linked with its organisation and charitable work. The chapel in St Joseph's was packed with United players and representatives from the cricket, business and newspaper worlds for his funeral. Ted was a sad loss!

In the quarter-final in March 1969, United faced Rapid Vienna. The first leg, again at Old Trafford, saw the Reds win 3-0. Denis played in this game but did not score and United's triumph was largely down to a superb performance from George Best who scored twice, his second a breath-taking individual effort. Willie Morgan scored the other while Denis had two goals disallowed, both of which seemed harsh decisions to say the least. Nevertheless, despite tight marking Law played well and when United battled to a goalless draw in the return they were through to the semi-finals again.

Arthur Walmsley, a prominent journalist for *The Sun* was a close friend of United's management team. Arthur was discussing Denis and said that he believed he was back to his best after his injuries. "I have known Denis Law for several years, both on and off the field. Although his enthusiasm for the game has never been in doubt I have never before seen him with such a fanatical urge to play, it's almost as if he were trying to compensate in time for the matches he was forced to miss because of his injured knee." Shortly after Denis' return

Arthur asked him how he felt: "Great, just great," replied Denis enthusiastically. Arthur said that Law, the brilliant showman on the field, shed his flamboyance once he came off the pitch. "To hear him confirming his fitness in such an unqualified manner convinced me we were in for something special now that he was back. Law quickly proved my conviction was right."

In the European Cup semi-final, against the Italian champions AC Milan, who had defeated Celtic in the quarter-finals, the Reds could count themselves extremely unfortunate. There are still, to this day, many supporters and players (Denis included) who believe that United were eliminated from the competition through a refereeing mistake. It was the fifth occasion that the club had reached the semi-final of this most worthy and prestigious competition and the first game was played in Italy in front of 80,000 boisterous Milanese at the fabulous and intimidating San Siro. The visitors were so popular indeed that this game produced gate receipts of 206 million lire - an Italian record at the time.

The game was beamed back to fans at Old Trafford who could not afford to travel to Italy. Nobby Stiles, who was the Reds man-of-the-match, was carried off with a knee injury after having a magnificent game despite no little provocation from the Milan players and fans. Matt Busby detailed Denis to stay with Milan's danger man, Gianni Rivera. Law did a good job, and the Milan player was taken off in disgust having failed to get into the game. In one particularly ugly incident John Fitzpatrick was punched in the face by Kurt Hamrin, Milan's Swedish-born winger and the Czech referee amazingly failed to give him a warning. But when John retaliated by kicking Hamrin he was given his marching orders 15 minutes before the end. By then United were two down thanks to Sormani and Hamrin and though the Reds battled manfully it was near impossible for British teams to get any kind of a result there - up to that period no British side had ever won there. In Milan, United's forwards were held in the firm grip of the Italians' catenaccio defence. They applied their usual tricks: shirt tugging, tripping, spitting, over-physical challenges and to

British eyes the referee appeared to acquiesce in these kind of tactics.

But as United licked their wounds and prepared for the second leg at Old Trafford on 15th May, there seemed to be a genuine belief that the deficit could be turned round. United were quietly confident and most of the 63,103 fans who saw the tie went home believing that the Reds had been robbed of a certain goal by a weak referee.

Old Trafford was like a mad house as the crowd urged United to victory. The Milan players employed the same tactics as in the first leg and Denis was tightly marked by his former Torino club colleague, Roberto Rosato. The Italian intended to take no prisoners and tackled Denis with venom. Several times Denis found himself on the grass, courtesy of Rosato's robust play and the Stretford End's rage as they watched the Italians get away with this kind of play led to missiles being thrown onto the pitch at one stage. The French referee, M Machin, declined to take action and Denis and his former club-mate had several verbal arguments. Denis, using the little Italian lingo he had picked up in his year with Torino, warned Rosato that if he did not stop fouling then he would take his own action. The Italian shrugged his shoulders and held his hands out as if he did not understand what Denis was saying to him. Then, when the referee was not looking, Rosato was suddenly on the floor holding his face and the Italian players were waving their hands about, shouting excitingly and pointing towards Denis.

After the shenanigans had died down Bobby Charlton scored in the 70th minute after a great run by George Best, who for once eluded the tight grip in an otherwise faultless man-marking display by Milan's Anquilletti. A few minutes later Paddy Crerand delivered a beautiful ball into the goalmouth and there were bodies flying all over the place but it was Denis who got a touch and sent the ball rolling toward the Milan net for what appeared to be a perfectly taken opportunist goal. Suddenly the Italian substitute Santin booted the ball from what appeared to be a good foot behind the line. The crowd and the United players bellowed 'Goal!' as one but referee

Machin, who had a perfect view of the incident, waved the protests away. The howls of derision could be heard all around Lancashire. Later, television and newspaper photographs appeared to support United's view that the ball was over the line. The Reds had been denied a certain equaliser.

Denis always claimed that, had his goal counted, the Reds would have gone on to win either on the night or in a replay in Brussels. "A single controversial disallowed goal cost us our European crown," said Denis. So what proved to be United's last game in the competition for 24 years was also Denis' last European club match - he had a quite remarkable goal scoring record. In the European Champions Cup he played 18 games and scored 14 goals - a club record he held until Andy Cole's Champions League exploits. The European Cup Winners' Cup saw him play in five games and score six times while in the Inter-Cities Fairs Cup, Law played ten games, scoring eight goals.

The inquest on the Reds' failure to hold on to the European trophy appeared in every newspaper and football magazine. What was never taken into account were the horrific injuries the team had suffered that season. With players such as Bobby Charlton missing for nine weeks, Francis Burns, who had twice been in hospital for cartilage operations, Nobby Stiles, Tony Dunne and poor John Aston it was no wonder the Reds struggled. Yet the general consensus of opinion in the media was that the Reds were a team in decline and some of their stars were past their best and needed replacing. It was a fact that Sir Matt, before standing down as manager, had tried to sign a young striker named Allan Clarke who later joined Leeds United and became known as 'Sniffer' because of his goal-poaching exploits.

This was United's most disappointing season for half a decade; finishing a lowly 11th in the League and going out of the FA Cup in the quarter-finals to Everton. Yet though the Reds had failed to win honours it couldn't be called a season of complete failure. In fact, they met with bad luck in their semi-final games against the crack Italian team, A.C Milan. For

Denis it had been a fair season by his own recent standards. He had played in 30 League games scoring 14 times while in the European Cup he had had perhaps his best season, scoring nine times in seven matches. And then there was that agonising 'goal that wasn't' in the semi-final. In the FA Cup, United reached the sixth round and Denis played in six games, including replays against Watford and Birmingham, scoring seven goals. In contrast to the physical pain of the previous season, Denis had at least contributed meaningfully to United's ultimately fruitless European campaign. Nevertheless, two days after United's Milanese misery the fans went through entirely different emotions - Sir Matt Busby retired as manager.

13. Decline and Fall

The final whistle at Old Trafford on 17th May 1969 ended an unprecedented and remarkable era for Manchester United. Following a 3-2 win over Leicester City at Old Trafford the faithful turned to the stand where Sir Matt Busby was sitting and a deafening din of applause, chanting and noise could be heard for miles around. They were saluting Sir Matt for everything he had done in the cause of this great club for he had officially announced his retirement as manager. It was the end of an often wonderful, sometimes sad but never-to-be-forgotten era. Like many present that day, Denis had known Busby since he was a teenager and respected him immensely. Things would never be the same for him again at Old Trafford.

His successor, Wilf McGuinness, was a north Manchester lad. Like Nobby Stiles, Brian Kidd, Carlo Sartori and Laurie Cassidy, he was born in Collyhurst before his family moved to the Blackley district of north Manchester. Now 31, Wilf had been with United since the early 1950s when, along with Bobby Charlton, he had joined the club straight from school. He had played and captained Manchester, Lancashire and England Schoolboys and served the Reds faithfully until, in December 1959, he broke his leg while playing for United's Central League side. Wilf was only 22 and his career as a player was virtually over.

He became a coach at the club, managed the Reds' youth team and trained the England youth team. He helped produce several youngsters for United and was also involved in Sir Alf Ramsey's successful World Cup campaign in 1966. His pedigree was good and he was regarded as one of the brightest coaches in Britain. However, in taking over the United team he wasn't much older than players like Bobby Charlton and others. In

A Champion at Last!
Denis played the star role in United's 1964/65 championship campaign contributing 28 goals in 36 league games. His heroic final appearance, despite a serious knee injury, against Arsenal in the decisive game proved his worth. He scored twice, his first (right) following a Stiles free kick that hit the bar.

United Let Their Hair Down
For Busby the new champions were proof that he had a team capable of challenging at the very highest level - some achievement just seven years after the Munich Air Disaster. It also gave him a crack at the club's Holy Grail - the European Cup.

Raise The Law!
Denis' contribution to the club's first league title for seven years is recognised by his team-mates as he raises the famous old trophy.

Changing of the Guard

The 1964 European Footballer of the Year presents the 1965 European Footballer of the Year with his prize before United's European Cup Quarter-final Second Leg in Lisbon on March 13th 1966.

It's fair to say that the newly crowned King of Europe, Eusebio, was not smiling at the end of 90 minutes as United ran riot, winning 5-1 in what Denis later described as the team's greatest-ever performance.

Following victory in the quarter-finals, the Reds subsequently lost to semi-final opponents Partizan Belgrade and despite this rare Nobby Stiles goal (inset) United went out 2-1 on aggregate and exited a competition they were overwhelming favourites to win.

A Good Walk Spoiled

The story of Denis' whereabouts on the afternoon of England's World Cup Final against West Germany is the stuff of legend. Denis was such a committed Scot that he refused to watch the match, calling in a long-standing bet with his friend John Logan to play golf at Chorlton on what Denis later described as 'the blackest day of my life'.

Hat-tricks

No one has scored more hat-tricks for Manchester United than Law. His first came (above) against Ipswich on 11th November 1962 - here scoring his second. Denis went on to score 3 goals or more on 18 occasions for the Reds.

Headers

Although not the tallest of strikers Denis was unbelievable in the air, outjumping centre-halves six inches taller than himself.
Chelsea's defence attested to his prolific leaping ability in 1965 when he scored a remarkable hat-trick of headers.

Right Place, Right Time

Denis scored his fair share of tap-ins, as typified by this effort against Fulham in 1968.

Overhead kicks

Denis perfected the art of the overhead. His ability to turn even the most unpresentable of chances into a goal became a source of frustration to teams the length of Britain. Here he demonstrates the poacher's art against Burnley.

Spellbound
The denizens of United's Stretford End were held in thrall by Law's acrobatics. Although many dismissed Denis' season in Italy as a dead loss, there's little doubt that his confidence to attempt 'continental' tricks such as the overhead kick came from his spell with Torino. As such the Stretford Enders were the first British crowd to witness these kind of exotic skills on a weekly basis.

Photo - finish
By the mid-60s Denis was the biggest star in English football. His face dominated Boys' soccer annuals of the time, a typical example being this excerpt - his exuberant and aggresive style ushered in a new era for the game in England.

LAUGHTER

PROTEST

DESPAIR

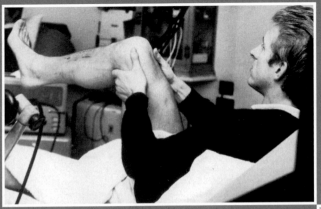

Treatment Table
Denis suffered a great deal for his all-action style. A mysterious knee injury remained unresolved for two years from 1966 and it took one of Harley Street's finest to diagnose a cartilage injury in 1968, caused by a botched operation he'd had as a Huddersfield player.

The Auld Enemy
One of Law's greatest days as a footballer came on April 15th 1967 when he played a starring role, alongside Jim Baxter, in Scotland's 3-2 defeat of then World Champions England. Right: Law celebrates with an ecstatic foot soldier of the Tartan Army.

Despite injury, Denis remained one of the most feared strikers in the league, demonstrating his ability to convert the toughest chance (left) against Spurs in 1967. It was this ability that helped United to their second title in three years (bottom).

No Goal!

Denis missed the 1968 European Cup Final but returned the following season determined to make amends. However this incident ended United's interest in the tournament. Denis claims to this day that the ball was a good two feet over the line but French referee Machin thought otherwise and United had played their last European Champions' Cup game for 25 years.

Old Foes

The early seventies saw Denis in the the twilight of his career, yet he could still produce the goods - scoring (top left) against Spurs at White Hart Lane in 1970; while (top right) Bobby Moore knew enough about Law to make sure he was closely marked at corner kicks; (bottom left) he makes a trademark run for goal against Reading and (bottom right) outjumps Moore at Hampden.

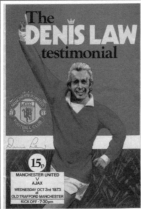

Surplus to Requirements
With the arrival of Denis' former international team-mate Tommy Docherty came a surprise as 'The King' was given a free transfer despite a previous offer of a coaching position. A short while later he was snapped up by Manchester City. (Top) the cover of the programme for his testimonial against Ajax in September 1973 (second down) he greets George Best before the match. Denis missed the game through injury.

A Citizen Again
Denis experienced something of a revival during his final spell with City: so good was his form that a recall to the Scotland squad for a vital World-Cup qualifier against Czechoslovakia quickly followed - victory guaranteeing qualification. Bottom left: Denis poses in the blue of city Below: Denis gets up to meet a cross against Leeds - Colin Bell waits for the ball to drop.

The Moment Time Stood Still

Denis' backheel in the 82nd minute of United's do-or-die relegation crunch match in the 1974 Old Trafford derby has gone down as one of City fans' most cherished memories. Yet for the man himself his last goal in competitive football was not a matter for celebration he later said, "I have seldom felt so depressed in my life as I did that weekend".

An Ambition Fulfilled

Denis' main acheivement during his time at Maine Road was his return to international football. Having helped the Scots to qualify, Denis headed to West Germany for the 1974 Finals. Unfortunately he only managed one game (against Zaire, right) before the Scots' premature exit at the hands of Brazil and Yugoslavia.

The King

Denis remains a regular at Old Trafford. In 2001 a statue of him was unveiled, appropriately, at the Stretford End. His moniker 'King of Old Trafford' remains virtually unchallenged (the odd Frenchman aside) while his reputation as the club's greatest-ever striker has only recently been challenged by Ruud van Nistelrooy's stunning strike-rate. For older fans though, his dare-devil antics are the stuff of legend - to them he remains 'The King'.

hindsight, and Denis Law agreed with this assessment, it would have been more sensible if the club had appointed Jimmy Murphy as Wilf's right-hand man during his early tenure in charge of team affairs. Jimmy's vast knowledge and experience would undoubtedly have helped Wilf immensely. If only! There is no doubt that with any other club, Wilf McGuinness would have been a success but with United he was doomed to failure from the start.

If ever a manager needed a bit of luck it was McGuinness. With the weight of history and expectation on his shoulders, Wilf needed instant success to make a break from the Busby era. In actual fact the reverse happened and in his first season McGuinness's United were extremely unlucky. The team reached the FA Cup and League Cup semi-finals. In the FA Cup they went out 1-0 to Leeds United but only after a three game marathon. In the League Cup they lost to neighbours Manchester City after the first leg ended 2-1 to City following a very debatable last minute penalty. This was the game where George Best was sent off for knocking the ball out of referee Jack Taylor's hands. They managed only a 2-2 draw in the second leg. In the League, United finished eighth yet McGuinness tried to initiate new ideas at the club. He looked around and saw how football was changing and how other clubs were becoming more astute in their planning and training methods. He saw the impact Malcolm Allison had made at Maine Road and he wanted United to adopt these methods. His heart and soul was in the job. He planned defensive strategies and other tactics, something which some of the more senior players didn't appreciate. He was young and ambitious and clearly wanted to make the Reds a more organised and disciplined team. But far from joining in with their manager's enthusiasm, the Cliff training ground soon became a sea of gloomy faces.

Denis played in the opening three League games that garnered a draw and two defeats, including a 4-1 lashing by Southampton. After this embarassment a thunderbolt hit the club. On 19th August 1969 Denis was sensationally dropped, along with Bobby Charlton, goalkeeper Jimmy Rimmer, veteran Shay Brennan, and Bill Foulkes before United's match against Everton. This was the first time in his long and illustrious career that the charismatic Law had been dropped. It was not a happy position. Later, Bill Foulkes retired to help coach the club's youngsters while Law's old sparring partner Ian Ure was signed from Arsenal.

Following a 3-0 defeat to Everton, Denis and Bobby were swiftly restored to the first team and drew the next game at Wolves 0-0. It was Ian Ure's debut and the team went a further seven games without defeat. However, during the drawn game with Wolves, Denis injured his groin and was out of action for two months. Sadly, this would prove to be another season of frustration for Denis as he played in only ten League games, scoring just twice. Meanwhile in the Football League Cup, a competition in which United managed to reach the semi-final, Denis played in three of the eight matches and scored twice. In the team's run to the FA Cup semi-final, Law played just twice and then as a substitute for young Carlo Sartori in both semi-final replays. It seemed that the magic touch had finally deserted Law and he typically failed to register in the competition.

Despite all this gloom one good piece of news for United came with the announcement that Bobby Charlton was to receive the 'Football Sword of Honour 1969' for distinguished service to British football. This honour was presented by the *International Football Book.* "Bobby will be remembered as the jewel of them all," said Geoffrey Green, of *The Times.* It was a wonderful honour for Bobby and Manchester United. In winning this prestigious honour Bobby joined Sir Matt Busby, Sir Stanley Matthews, Pele, Dr Willy Meisl, and Jock Stein CBE as previous honourees.

There was little secret in the fact that Denis and other senior players were far from happy with the new set-up. It's a truism to say that everyone is entitled to an opinion and the senior players at Old Trafford certainly voiced theirs. They were less than satisfied with McGuinness's tactics and didn't believe they suited them personally. They were so used to Sir Matt's easy-going, calming influence and attacking policy that the defensive formations Wilf wanted to impose on the team were met with derision. There were several rows and flare-ups at the Cliff and in the dressing-room at Old Trafford. To make matters worse, at the end of the season the Reds surprised the supporters, the Stretford End in particular, when they placed Denis on the transfer list at £60,000. To say that many people were shocked at the club's decision to sell 'The King' was putting it mildly. Nonetheless, it was clear that injuries were taking their toll on Denis and he was now far from the razor-sharp, high-jumping star of a couple of seasons earlier. Law's loyal followers still believed that if he could sort out his injuries he could be as good as ever. Sir Matt Busby told the press that although Denis had been a superb player for the club, it was in the best interests of Denis and United if they now parted company because he had been plagued by injuries and found it hard to regain his top form. "It would be better for Denis to have a fresh start somewhere else because of all the changes and pressure that the club are going through." So, after a seven-year reign, it appeared that the King was abdicating. He remained United's most revered goalscorer and would always be remembered as a great player who set the passions and imagination on fire.

Clearly the reign of the 'holy trinity' was coming to an end. What a threesome they had been! Football will never see their like again. Bobby Charlton was a thoroughbred of a player who was highly respected by fans and officials alike. Bobby had started the 1969-70 season having scored more goals than any other contemporary player at Old Trafford - a total of 179 league goals. However, he scored these goals having played 488 games. George Best, up to the end of the previous season, had netted 94 League goals from 250 appearances while Denis had scored a remarkable 142 League goals from 236 matches. Incredible! That was not all - in the cup competitions Denis was out on his own. Four years before he had surpassed Blackpool's Stanley Mortensen, West Brom's Ronnie Allen and

Bristol's John Atyeo as the top post-war goalscorers in the competition with 31 goals. He also surpassed Jack Rowley's United record of 28 FA Cup goals. By 1970 he had maintained a goal-a-game average of 34 goals from 34 ties, another magnificent record. This included spells at Huddersfield and Manchester City. In the European Cup, Denis had scored 14 goals for the Reds, beating Dennis Viollet by a single goal. He had been a truly unique player for the Reds and many fans now resigned themselves to wishing him well at a new club.

Yet despite fevered speculation during the summer months, transfer talk died and the issue was forgotten for the time being. In any case, Denis was determined to get himself in the best possible shape. He had set up his own training programme and stuck to it diligently throughout the summer break, ensuring that he was as fit as ever. Yet from the start of the 1970/71 season, Denis didn't feature in the first team. No longer an automatic choice, he certainly didn't appreciate his demotion but vowed to regain his place. Indeed, until Boxing Day 1970 Denis made just 15 League appearances at inside-left, inside-right and outside-right scoring seven times.

There was one particular game during Wilf's reign that stays in the memory. United played Tottenham in a league game at White Hart Lane and with the Reds struggling on and off the field, Spurs were expected to hammer them. Wilf had brought his own players into the team, lads like goalkeeper Jimmy Rimmer, David Sadler, Brian Kidd, Johnny Aston, John Fitzpatrick and Steve James. Denis wore the number seven shirt, which was unusual for him. Soon after the game began in wet and muddy conditions, David Sadler looked to have scored the opening goal, yet the referee disallowed it, claiming the ball had not crossed the goal line. The pressure was beginning to tell on Wilf and he needed a bit of luck - he jumped from the dugout and walked around the pitch cursing the official.

Meanwhile, out on the pitch, tempers were becoming frayed. Alan Mullery and Mike England were driving Spurs forward, while their strike force of Alan Gilzean and Martin Chivers looked dangerous. Then, out of character with the rest of United's performance, Bobby Charlton gave a lovely pass to young John Aston who had moved out to the right wing. Aston beat Cyril Knowles, Spurs' experienced right-back and delivered the ball to Brian Kidd. Kidd saw Denis moving forward and instantly passed the ball into his path. Whoosh! Like a bolt of lightning Denis accelerated away from the defence and shot past Pat Jennings' right hand. Vintage Law! The goal was brilliant in its execution and finish - it was not just vintage Law but vintage United. The late Brian Moore, commentating on the match for ITV, bellowed: "Would you believe it. For thirty minutes they [United] were outclassed and then in a flash Law has put United in front. What an astonishing turnabout, but what a superb piece of opportunism by Denis Law. Nobody could doubt that Denis Law's eight seasons at Manchester United had been eight of the most exciting seasons for all who have watched him."

In the second half, George Best added another brilliant goal after a fine build-up between Kidd and Fitzpatrick. The Reds looked rampant and destined for victory but once Martin Peters pulled one back for Spurs with a slick header it all went wrong. It was bad defending from the Reds and they were now very jittery and it was no surprise when Gilzean headed Spurs level. The United players seemed to be arguing among themselves by now and from looking confident they were now struggling. Spurs were now going all out for victory and looked certain winners. But as Jimmy Rimmer prepared to take a goal kick, drama was unfolding on the right side of the pitch. "There's a United player down injured," said Brian Moore, then suddenly he shouted: "Steve James, Fitzpatrick and Law, there's a fight in fact between the United players on the field." What had happened?

It seems that an argument had broken out between Law and Fitzpatrick and the two fiery Aberdonians clashed. Steve James attempted to calm things down between them and he pushed 'Fitz' and then Denis pushed his hand out towards Fitzpatrick's face. Denis and his young team-mate continued arguing. For a few brief seconds things looked quite ugly and they had to be separated both by their own team-mates and the Tottenham players. Alan Mullery, acting as peacemaker, put his arm around 'Fitz' and walked him away from the argument. Martin Chivers stood close to the confrontation, smiled and looked bemused by the incident between the Scottish team-mates. It was bedlam with the noise of the supporters splitting the air.

Whatever went through Law's and Fitzpatrick's minds only they knew but suddenly Denis, with a smile on his face, gently back heeled his fellow Aberdonian up the backside. Then, as if realising that as a senior professional he should have shown restraint he flung his arms around his young colleague and embraced him. It all ended peacefully and Denis and John remained firm friends. Denis was saddened to hear in 1973 that Fitz had been advised by specialists to retire from football. He was only 26. United lost a wonderful young player who looked destined for certain stardom. Yet the incident, and indeed the match, underlined the pressures Wilf was forced to work under. Caught between the rival camps of old players on the wane who demanded a say in tactics and youngsters who needed firm guidance Wilf didn't stand much of a chance.

In the end, the killer blow came in the form of a a 4-1 home derby defeat followed swiftly by a League Cup semi-final defeat to Third Division Aston Villa. Just after Christmas, Wilf McGuinness was dismissed as manager of Manchester United. He was broken-hearted. His brief reign had brought some success: two League Cup semi-finals and one FA Cup semi-final which they lost narrowly to the best team in the country, Leeds. So Wilf resumed his job as coach to the club's reserve team, along with Bill Foulkes but that didn't work out either and he eventually left the club in June 1971 before Frank O'Farrell was appointed the new United manager.

Sir Matt Busby came out of retirement to steady the ship after Wilf's demotion. Under their old boss the senior players became noticeably happier and in the following 19 matches the team managed to finish 8th in the First Division, the same position as the previous season. Denis played in 13 of these games and notched eight goals for a total of 15 goals from 28

League games over the season - a definite improvement on last term. In the FA Cup he played in the two third round games against Middlesbrough, a 0-0 draw at Old Trafford and the replay which United lost 2-1, but he didn't score. In the League Cup, in which the Reds reached the semi-final again, Denis had four games, coming on as a substitute and scoring in the fourth-round 2-1 victory over Chelsea.

*

On 17th April 1971, Denis scored a hat-trick for the Reds at Crystal Palace. It was his first hat-trick for more than two years and, sadly, it would be his last for the club he loved and adored. But whether he liked to admit it or not, the days of Denis the Menace, the great goal predator, were well and truly over. His injured knee had robbed him of his greatest asset - his speed and confidence - and robbed his legions of followers of Law's goal poaching exploits. Denis had been injured in a 1-0 home victory over Wolves, Brian Kidd coming on as substitute for Denis and he also missed the next game, a 2-1 defeat at Coventry, because of a badly bruised shin. Again Kidd replaced him. However, when Denis was declared fit to play against Crystal Palace, Sir Matt Busby immediately restored him to the first team and dropped Kidd, playing him in the reserves against Blackburn Rovers in a Central League match at Old Trafford.

Upon hearing he had been dropped from the first team Kidd was upset. "What is he trying to do, humiliate me altogether?" Brian asked in a *Daily Mail* article referring to the Manchester United manager. "Does Sir Matt think he can trample all over me until a new manager takes over? I've got my pride. This is the *coup de grace*. Everybody must know now that he doesn't want me at Old Trafford. I only wish he would come clean and say it." *The Daily Mail* also reported that Kidd had now put in a written transfer request that he had made verbally a few days previously to Sir Matt. Kidd had been a loyal and dedicated club man for the Reds and should have gone on to become one of the foundations for the 1970s Manchester

United coaching staff to build on. These were sad times for the Old Trafford establishment: the club was going through turmoil, a point underlined by Kidd's willingness to talk to the press - something unheard of at Old Trafford.

In the match in which Kidd feels he should have played, a terrible display of football from the Reds saw them two down to a very ordinary Crystal Palace side. Yet United came back and eventually emerged victorious 5-3. Denis got his hat-trick, his second goal being a spectacular scissors kick. Prominent football writer Jeff Powell said: "The truth of United's extraordinary 5-3 victory is so bad that Palace were kidded into believing they could beat them without trying." Meanwhile Kidd scored in the reserves' 5-0 victory over Blackburn Rovers. Kidd eventually left United in August 1974 for Arsenal. During his United career he played a total of 255 senior games, scoring 70 goals. He later returned as junior coach and was appointed assistant manager to Alex Ferguson.

The last League game of the season saw the Reds play Manchester City at Maine Road. This was definitely Sir Matt Busby's final game in charge of the team. At City, Sir Matt's old friend Joe Mercer and the volatile Malcolm Allison had revived the Blues fortunes. They were First Division champions in 1968, FA Cup winners in 1969 and European Cup Winners' Cup winners in 1970. Since their crucial victory at Old Trafford in 1968 that proved the catalyst for their Championship victory, the Blues were unbeaten in derby games and had already beaten United 4-1 at Old Trafford in December.

Yet in Busby's final farewell the Reds from Old Trafford put on a vintage performance and won 4-3. Denis scored, along with Bobby Charlton and George Best, who scored twice. Denis later admitted that Busby's return had rejuvenated him, while it also made a few of the other senior players more happy and relaxed. He also believed that Sir Matt had saved the club from relegation by returning.

Yet throughout the summer the guessing game continued as to the identity of the new United manager. Don Revie, Jock Stein and Dave Sexton were among the names mentioned as a likely successor to Sir Matt. Denis, however, wasn't bothered in the slightest. He was feeling good and continued his private gym and fitness sessions in readiness for the new season.

When it was finally announced the name of the new manager surprised a lot of people. Frank O'Farrell was the nice, genial, quietly-spoken former manager of Leicester City. The Irishman had guided Leicester up from the Second Division and led them to the 1969 FA Cup Final which they lost 1-0 to Manchester City. Frank had played for West Ham United and Preston North End as a cultured wing-half. His appointment, in June 1971 led many to claim that because of his experience, he instantly gain the respect of the Manchester United team, although hardly any of the United players knew much about him.

O'Farrell brought his coach, Malcolm Musgrove, another former West Ham player, to Old Trafford with him and if Denis and the other senior players at Old Trafford thought Wilf McGuinness' training techniques were hard, then Musgrove's Royal Marines schedules were harder still. Meanwhile set-pieces, free kicks and marking were practised at the Cliff in readiness for the coming season. Yet during pre-season training it became noticeable that Frank O'Farrell hardly ever took part. Malcolm Musgrove generally took charge and Denis and the other senior players didn't seem to bother at first but as the weeks went by they began making jokes about their invisible manager. But O'Farrell soon realised he had inherited an ailing team that had several different cliques pulling in separate directions - yet this team of individuals surprised the football world with their early season form.

What a start the Reds made to the season. Away at Derby County they drew 2-2, Denis scoring United's first goal of the new campaign and Alan Gowling grabbing the other. The football they played was near faultless. Having slung off the defensive yoke designed by McGuinness, O'Farrell's United resorted to the beautiful attacking football reminiscent of their glory years. For the whole of the autumn and half the winter they looked and played like champions. George Best was brilliant - before the end of November he had scored 14 goals, including two hat-tricks while also Denis enjoyed life under the new manager, scoring 11 goals in 18 games. By Christmas 1971, having won 14, drawn six and lost just twice, scoring 45 goals and conceeding 25 in the process, the Reds were five points clear at the top on 30 points.

*

Because of his popularity Denis was always in demand to attend various functions but being a rather private individual he rarely accepted the offers. It wasn't because he wanted payment, as many scandal mongers were quick to say, he just wasn't interested in the majority of invitations. However, Denis made an exception when he agreed to attend an amateur boxing tournament staged by Collyhurst Lads Club at St Edmunds Social Club on Monsall Street, Collyhurst. Paddy Crerand and Carlo Sartori also attended and the players agreed to present the trophies to the kids after each contest. In previous years, Nobby Stiles and Brian Kidd had been regular guests of the Lads Club at these functions. Collyhurst were boxing a team from Waterford in Southern Ireland. The club was packed to capacity with nearly a thousand people squashed into the venue. Denis and Paddy received a hero's welcome by the boisterous, but good-natured crowd. Paddy and Denis sat up on the stage and really enjoyed themselves as the Collyhurst and Irish youngsters battled it out. Denis was feeling good: "When you keep winning, you feel like you can't lose," he said presenting a prize to one youth, "it's like when you are scoring goals regularly, you feel you can score every time you run out onto the field." Because of Denis and Paddy's involvement the tournament was a huge success and at the end of the evening they were cheered and clapped all the way to their car.

At the start of the season United had to play their first two homes games on neutral grounds because of crowd problems the previous season when a knife was thrown onto the pitch. Anfield was chosen for their first such game as United thrashed Arsenal 3-1. The next 'home' game was played on Stoke City's

Victoria Ground and ended in another 3-1 victory. The Football League Cup saw the Reds play six games before going out 2-1 to Stoke City in a fifth round second replay. Denis played only twice in these ties and failed to score. Yet United's illusory five-point lead at the top at Christmas swiftly evaporated as United's Indian summer turned into reality. From New Year's Day to 4th March 1972 United lost seven games in a row before a scoreless draw with Everton on March 8th provided solace. The run put an end to idle talk of a return to glory for the 'Holy Trinity' and while many supporters liked to believe that the six matches in the abortive League Cup campaign were to blame, most saw the decline of United for what it really was.

From United's New Year's Day drubbing at West Ham any title momentum was stopped dead in its tracks and while they defeated Southampton, Preston and Middlesbrough in the FA Cup, they eventually left the competition at the hands of Stoke who won 2-1 in a replay. Denis played in all seven FA Cup matches but failed to get on the score sheet.

In March 1972, O'Farrell realised he needed new players and bought Ian Storey-Moore from Nottingham Forest, after Brian Clough had cheekily paraded him around the Baseball Ground as his new signing. Derby were subsequently fined £5,000 and reprimanded for this piece of Clough showmanship. In normal circumstances this would have been applauded as a masterstroke signing but Storey-Moore, a fast, powerful, well-built player who had scored more than 100 goals for Forest, saw his United career cruelly cut short. He was regarded as the best winger of this period and scored on his debut against Huddersfield Town, helping the Reds to their first victory for more than three months. Unfortunately, an ankle injury restricted him to just 23 first team appearances from which he scored 12 goals and in December 1973 he retired from football on medical grounds. Another case of O'Farrell's bad luck as United manager.

One of O'Farrell's best signings was undoubtedly the excellent Martin Buchan, who arrived in March 1972. Buchan had captained Aberdeen aged just 20 and went on to become United and Scotland captain playing a total of 455 games, scoring four goals before his departure in 1983 for Oldham Athletic. Buchan also lifted the 1977 FA Cup and later replaced Denis Law as the pride, if not the King, of Old Trafford.

Sammy McIlroy, another youngster from United's academy, made his debut under O'Farrell. Then, in September 1972, Frank paid a record £200,000 for Third Division Bournemouth's Ted McDougall. A prolific lower league goalscorer, Ted was reckoned to be the long-term replacement for Denis. Law knew his number was up, well almost. By the end of the season he had managed 32 League games and scored just 13 times, yet he was still the second highest scorer behind George Best who had played 40 games and scored 18 times. But rumours persisted about O'Farrell's management and it wasn't long before the knives were being sharpened again.

*

The summer of 1972 saw Denis in Brazil following a recall by Scotland's new manager Tommy Docherty. Denis' international career had been in suspension since 1969, his last competitive appearance coming in a 1-1 draw with West Germany at Hampden. Yet in April 1972, following United's brief resurgence under Frank O'Farrell, Law was recalled for a friendly against Peru at Hampden, scoring in this game and a subsequent Home International against Northern Ireland.

Before his recall Scotland had become, in Denis' words, "something of a joke", losing to Belgium, Portugal, Northern Ireland, England, Denmark and Russia and drawing with Wales. Law's return was partly responsible for a resurgence in fortunes north of the border and he was even made captain. Law appreciated The Doc's easy-going attitude was popular with players, particularly during the summer tour to Brazil where his flexibility about training times endeared him to the squad.

So Denis' loyal followers on the Stretford End had good

reason to expect the spiky-haired striker to be back to something near his best. Yet the hard, relentless battle to get fit and stay fit was now such a large part of his football life that fans could never imagine the pain he went through. He had suffered badly with his knee injuries and that summer was similar to previous ones in that he punished himself on a daily basis in preparation for August.

Obviously the 1970s version of the Lawman was a completely different person to the ultra confident player of the 1960s. He was a curious mixture; fun and wisecracking in the company of his team-mates but to them he also seemed something of a loner. As Harry Gregg has explained, off the field Denis was a completely different person to the one who displayed such fire, passion and bravery on the field and despite all the talk of him being put up for transfer again, Manchester United was where Denis was happiest. After all it was where he had been most successful. It was here that the Old Trafford fans still called him 'The King'. And why not? After all, he had scored more than 300 goals in top-class football, played a big part in the Reds' sixties success and had been named European Footballer of the Year a decade before. Nevertheless most commentators believed that these glories would remain in the past and only the optimists on the Stretford End envisaged a return to his pomp.

Indeed the 1972-73 season would be his last as King of Old Trafford. Denis played in only nine league games, appearing twice as substitute and managing just one goal. He even played wing-half in the Reds' only FA Cup game of the season, a 1-0 defeat to Wolves. In the League Cup, United had four games, Denis scoring against Oxford in a 2-2 draw, before winning the replay 3-1. He missed the next two League Cup ties that ended in a 2-1 exit at home to Bristol Rovers.

In contrast to his first season in charge, O'Farrell and United suffered a harrowing start to the new term during which United took until late September to register a league win (albeit against champions Derby County). In their next 11 games they managed a further three wins and nine days before

Christmas 1972, following an embarassing 5-0 defeat at Crystal Palace, Frank O'Farrell's number was well and truly up.

At half-time Tommy Docherty, who was at the game to check on players for his Scotland team, was approached by a Manchester United official. He took Docherty to one side and asked him if he was interested in becoming the new manager. The Doc told the official: "I'd walk from Scotland to Old Trafford for the job," and so a few days later he became manager of the club he said he it was his destiny to manage.

Of O'Farrell's departure Denis caustically said: "He came as a stranger and left a stranger." Tommy Docherty, the eager, joke-cracking and flamboyant character took charge. It had been Denis, along with Willie Morgan, who had recommended Docherty to Sir Matt Busby. The 'Doc' had played in Denis' first international match for Scotland. Law, although only a teenager at the time, remembered the confident, cocky Doc, and over the following years they became quite friendly. Doc joined United at a time when the club was on its knees: team spirit was non-existent, and morale at an all-time low. An air of desperation and apathy surrounded the club.

14. An Ambition Fulfilled

Tommy Docherty soon changed all the doom and gloom at Old Trafford. He had everyone laughing and joking as he wisecracked his way through Old Trafford and the Cliff. The United supporters immediately took to his brashness and joviality. He intended to change things at the club and as quickly as possible. He worked with the players on the training ground and motivated them. The younger players were charmed by him and hung on to his every word and for his first game in charge at Old Trafford, against Leeds, he brought Denis back into the team at right-half. Denis had made only one first team appearance over the previous two months while he had come on as substitute in the last two games. Ted McDougall gave the rejuvenated Reds the lead and Denis was substituted before Leeds scored a late equaliser. It was a pity because United had tried hard and put plenty of effort into their play, yet Denis wasn't selected for the next game, a 3-1 defeat to Derby County.

The Doc was seething about the nature of United's performance and it brought home to him the task he now faced. "Some of the players thought Old Trafford was a holiday camp," said Docherty of his early months in charge, "they were taking big money out of the club but giving nothing in return." He went on to say that he believed there was a certain clique who thought they were running the club. He also believed that some of the players had got Frank O'Farrell the sack. "There were some household names at Old Trafford that were coming towards the end of their careers at the top and obviously they didn't like being told so." He said that some of the star players were more interested in how long they played for, rather than how well they played. "It is a club riddled with cancer," said the

Doc. He was also reported as saying the old players, or 'skivers' as he termed them, were more concerned with getting rid of the next manager than their performance. He added that this older element had lost their edge and were preventing the youngsters coming through. Tommy Cavanagh, who the Doc had brought from Hull to take charge of training and coaching, added that Docherty was never given the credit he deserved for rebuilding United.

In a television documentary about Manchester United, many years after his departure from Old Trafford, it was said that Docherty had been brought to the club to bring the 'good times' back and have a clearout. The Doc said that Sir Matt Busby was a great man and a great manager, but had held on to some of the older players like Denis for too long.

One of the toughest decisions the Doc faced was how he was going to handle the likes of Denis, Bobby Charlton, George Best, Willie Morgan and Alex Stepney. He knew the tittle-tattle and backbiting that went on between certain players and Matt Busby. "Bobby Charlton was the club's biggest star name and was a shinning example of sportsmanship and good sense. Bobby came to me one day and told me he had decided to retire from playing. He asked if I would mind if he informed the chairman and directors. It was a marvellous gesture from a magnificent servant of the club," said the Doc, adding, "I wish some of his team-mates had behaved as he did. But then, Bobby was man enough to accept the situation as it was." Bobby Charlton played his last game for Manchester United in April 1973 against Chelsea at Stamford Bridge.

Always a ducker and diver in the transfer market, the Doc got busy. George Graham was signed from the Gunners for £120,000 in December 1972 while full-back Alex Forsyth came from Partick Thistle for £100,000. Docherty also brought Denis back into the first team for the next two matches: a 3-1 defeat at Arsenal and a 2-2 draw at home to West Ham.

By this time Paddy Crerand had become Docherty's assistant and Tommy Cavanagh was brought in as coach but United were bottom of the First Division. To his credit, the Doc kept up his banter and cheerful disposition yet he remained a volatile character not averse to bust-ups with players and it wasn't long before Ted McDougall was on his way out of Old Trafford. The honeymoon period was well and truly over for many star players at Old Trafford.

In January 1973 Docherty signed Lou Macari from Glasgow Celtic for £200,000, a record fee for a Scottish player at the time. Big Jim Holton of Shrewsbury was signed at the same time for £80,000. There was a great deal of coming and going at Old Trafford and after the West Ham game on the 20th January 1973, Denis wasn't selected again for the first team until the 7th April home game against Norwich City, which would prove to be the last of his 393 games for the clubs. Denis failed to add to his amazing tally of 296 goals.

By now Docherty regarded Law as a spent force and he told the Manchester United directors that he should be given a free transfer. However, initially Sir Matt did not agree with this assessment and the Tommy Docherty - Denis Law friendship came to an abrupt end when, just before the end of the season, Docherty called Denis into his office at the Cliff. When Denis walked in the Doc told him that he had been given a free transfer! Denis was stunned! This was all news to him. He had, of course, known that his automatic selection for United's first team was now a thing of the past but he was under the impression that once his actual playing days were over he was to be given a job on the club's coaching staff.

Who had promised him this position? Denis claimed it was Docherty himself. Later, Docherty denied this of course. Denis felt badly let down and he was upset at the whole rotten outcome. Docherty assured Law that his testimonial with the crack Dutch side, Ajax, a game that had been arranged for the start of the following season, would still go ahead. His mind was in complete turmoil at the news Docherty had given him. Away from the club he could think much more clearly and he believed he still had a couple of seasons left in him. The idea of moving to another club, perhaps away from Manchester, didn't fill him with enthusiasm. After all, his wife was expecting another child and his family were settled and comfortable in the area. Another big factor was his reluctance to drop down into the lower divisions of football. After discussing the situation with friends and family he decided that after his testimonial match he would announce his retirement from football. He told Docherty of his plan and the Doc said he was in full agreement.

Denis then left Manchester with his children and headed for Aberdeen while Diana stayed behind because she was pregnant. Imagine the way he must have felt when one lunch-time in Aberdeen, while having a quiet drink with friends, news came through via the television that Denis, along with Tony Dunne, had been given free transfers by Manchester United. He was shocked, very embarrassed and deeply hurt and humiliated. He rushed back to Manchester with his children in case Diana had been bothered by newspaper reporters. It was a messy affair and certainly no way for Denis to have been treated after his sterling service for the club. But these were not happy times at Manchester United.

In his book *The Manchester United Story,* Derek Hodgson writes: "Denis' departure should not be, but is, a shock. The news that Manchester United have given him a free transfer is a practical, logical step for the club and player. He had insisted that he wanted to play nowhere else. He is, says manager Tommy Docherty, no longer regarded as a first team player. There has been a financial settlement and he is to be given a testimonial match." The author went on to say that the break was abrupt and cold for a player who "in a puff of red smoke became the Demon King, the most explosive and lethal player in and around the penalty box in the world. He was, and always will be, the terrace favourite, because he was in style and wit and character, the street Arab who really made it."

It was a sad parting but times were changing. George Best had retired and made several comebacks. Bobby Charlton had retired gracefully, and now Denis was leaving Old Trafford. Best - Charlton - Law. No other club could boast of three such great forwards who all played together in the same team and now they had gone their separate ways.

Yet this was not the end of Denis Law's dealings with Tommy Docherty. In 1977, while Docherty was still manager of Manchester United, former Manchester United player and captain Willie Morgan appeared on a Granada television programme. During his interview he said that Docherty was about the worst manager he had ever played under. Docherty was advised to take legal action against Morgan and Granada TV. He decided that he would. It was a mistake.

In November 1978 his libel action finally reached the High Court and by then the Doc was manager of Derby County. He had been dismissed by United in July 1977 after an affair with Mary Brown, the wife of United physio Laurie Brown. After three days in court, Docherty dropped the libel action and withdrew all allegations against Morgan and Granada. He admitted under cross-examination that he had told lies over the free transfer of Denis Law from United. Denis was going to be called as a witness for Willie Morgan. He didn't really want to be involved and was secretly pleased that he wouldn't be called to give evidence after all. This, however, wasn't the end of the whole shoddy episode, because Docherty now had to appear at the Old Bailey to answer charges of 'lying on oath' appertaining to the libel case. There was the possibility that if found guilty, Docherty could face prison. The Old Bailey trial lasted a week. The two counts against him alleged that he falsely swore on oath during the High Court case that when he spoke to Denis about his free transfer, Denis didn't seem disturbed or surprised. The jury acquitted him on both counts by unanimous verdicts. He told the court he hadn't deliberately lied but was 'hopelessly confused' by the high pressure of the cross-examination he had undergone. The sorry saga was over.

*

At the Football Writers' Annual Dinner in London, Denis was in conversation with Manchester City's new manager Johnny Hart. During their conversation the City manager offered

Denis the opportunity to play for the Blues. Denis was surprised - he never in his wildest dreams believed that he would end up playing for City again. But the move certainly suited Denis' family circumstances and his desire to stay at the highest level.

For the most part United's fans wished Denis every success, as did his former team-mates. Denis rejoined the Blues in July 1973. Denis' new manager Johnny Hart commented: "What United have decided to do with Law is nothing to do with me, nor am I entitled to comment on it. I feel that a player who was capable of being captain for Scotland 15 months ago with the competitive streak which Denis has never lost, would have something to offer. I wouldn't like to think that one of my players could go absolutely sour in such a short period."

Others believed however that what City had done, offering Denis a contract, was no more than a PR job on the club's behalf. Yet Denis seemed rejuvenated at Maine Road as the coming season would prove. Denis started pre-season training with the Blues and played in their opening game of the season, scoring twice in a 3-1 home victory over Birmingham City and then in the 1-1 draw at Stoke City.

A few weeks into the season Denis celebrated two wonderful events: firstly Diana presented him with their fifth child, a girl - Denis and Diana now had four boys and a girl. Secondly, and perhaps a bigger shock than his new daughter was a recall to the international team by Willie Ormond.

On the international front Scotland had discovered their form and Ormond professed his admiration for Law after watching him in City's 1-0 home win against Coventry City telling reporters: "It's the best centre-forward display I have seen this season." Law would partner Kenny Dalglish in attack for the vital forthcoming World Cup qualifier against Czechoslovakia at Hampden.

Scotland were in a three-team group that, besides the Czechs, featured a Denmark team that Scotland had already defeated twice under Docherty while the Czechs had dropped a point in Copenhagen. This slim advantage meant that a victory at Hampden would send Scotland to their first World Cup Finals since 1958.

On 26th September 1973, there were 95,786 Scots on hand to roar their team to triumph, but the atmosphere disappeared in an instant once Nehoda gave the Czechs an early, unexpected lead. Yet the Scots fought on and, following a 40th minute equaliser through Jim Holton and a 78th minute Jordan header, Scotland and Law were through to the World Cup Finals. The plaudits poured in for Scotland's elder statesman. Many north of the border claimed that Law's calming influence had had an immediate effect upon the Scottish team, while Denis admitted: "I have never been happier. After all these years in the wilderness Scotland can now make the rest of the world sit up and take notice in West Germany next summer. We can start playing an established and successful pattern."

What made the victory all the sweeter for Denis was England's absence from the finals following a draw with Poland at Wembley a month later. Denis, whose career seemed all but over in Spring 1973, had staged a remarkable comeback as he now anticipated a magnificent swansong - a valedictory performance against the best in the world the following summer.

*

On Wednesday 3rd October 1973, three months after he had been given a free transfer from Manchester United, Denis had his testimonial match against Dutch European Cup holders Ajax at Old Trafford. A crowd of over 45,000 turned out for this friendly game, a testimony to what his loyal supporters thought of him, even though he was now playing for United's deadly rivals. Ajax, World club champions and winners of the European Cup over the previous three years, came to Old Trafford to salute Denis Law, a player who was one of the World's greatest players in the 1960s. The committee for this testimonial had done wonders to secure the services of this fascinating club side. A quick look at their record took your breath away. 16 times Dutch champions; six times Dutch Cup winners; three times European Champions' Cup winners; Inter-Continental Cup winners. They had that summer sold their superstar Johan Cruyff to Barcelona for £922,300, an astronomical sum in those days.

Denis couldn't play in his own testimonial because he was ruled out of City's game in the League Cup against Walsall. Johnny Hart, the City manager commented: "Because Denis injured himself in training yesterday it also means he must miss his testimonial match. I am afraid we have to get our priorities right. We have to get him fit for Saturday."

Denis had been set to make a one-game comeback for United against the European champions when asked how he felt about missing the game replied: "You can't imagine how sick I feel." Denis, who the previous week had helped Scotland in a World Cup triumph over Czechoslovakia and then a few days later celebrated the birth of his first daughter added: "I don't know whether to laugh or cry! I could probably go on and stroll around a bit tomorrow but I can fully understand Johnny Hart's decision." Denis had already missed five games for City that season, which was just a few weeks old. He said he injured his groin the previous day. He had only just recovered from a thigh injury in time to play for Scotland. When asked to comment on the testimonial he said, "Most people tend to regard testimonial games as a bit of a stroll but I want Manchester United to win this match. We need to be competitive if we are to take part in European competitions in the future."

His testimonial programme included contributions from David Meek, the *Manchester Evening News* reporter. David covered the United scene and had seen Denis arrive at the club. "The King lives again," wrote David. "He is back in the blue shirt of Manchester City but with his mane of lion-coloured hair still flying in the goalmouths, his spring-heeled menace still stalking the grounds of the First Division." Meek went on to say that United supporters would be indebted to him for ever. Whatever he might achieve for City could not wipe out the memories of his brilliance for the Reds. "He was one of a special trinity...Charlton, Law and Best. Their names trip of the tongue like a football litany. Now alas two have departed from Old Trafford but the image of the Law man's fire and flair in the penalty area will never fade." A sentiment echoed by all United followers. Derek Potter of the *Daily Express* wrote: "Every generation has 'buzz' players. They catch on with the crowd. They are busybodies, always in the action, eager for the fight, crowd pullers. He is the sharpest blend of mind and muscle - that was Demon Denis."

Steve Richards wrote that it was the sons of Denis Law who had his sympathy. "I mean... how, in this case, do they ever follow their Dad? They could be quick, I suppose, if we are to witness a repeat of such quickness in the penalty area. They could be as uncomplicated in his skills. They could be as abrasive. As impudent. As daring. As scornful or as demonstrative. But never, surely, are we destined to witness all the attributes (and the odd failing) in one such lean frame ever again. The perfect player?" Richards went on to say that Denis was not perfect, and pointed out the imperfections in the Denis Law of the 1960s period that provoked enough confrontations with referees to make "Billy Bremner seem like a saint and Alan Ball fairy-like. He seldom walked, it appeared, without one foot in the football gutter and the memories of Law being sent off at Blackpool for swearing at referee Peter Rhodes and at Villa Park for threatening to kick Alan Deakin are no less sad with the passing of time." He went on to say that headlines in those days were burying him alive. He mentioned that Denis could seldom walk away from trouble like Bobby Charlton or Tom Finney, although, said Steve, he was kicked far more than Bobby if not more than Tom. "His opponents readily used his easily-ignited nerves as a piano to play their artful tunes. Perhaps he was never artful enough himself. When he was kicked he just kicked back."

Jim Rodger of the *Scottish Daily Express*, reckoned that Denis would go down in the history books as one of Scotland's all-time greats as a result of his international feats for his country.

"Although his senior football has all been in England and Italy, his is a household name in Scotland. His brilliant performances in the Dark Blue jersey have thrilled everyone in Scotland - who are proud of the Aberdeen boy who gained world fame." Mr Rodger said that he and Denis had been close friends throughout Denis' career. He said he remembered the night the young Law went to Glasgow to join the Scottish squad. "Bringing him North was another Scottish international, Tommy Docherty. And right away it was evident to everyone that Scotland had another Great Scot." He said that although Denis was capped 49 times for his country, he would have played for nothing, since he considered it his greatest honour. "He had that will to win, possessed the pride that Scotland was a great football nation."

Peter Slingsby also contributed to Denis's programme. He spoke of his many personal memories of Denis. "Like the day he arrived in Manchester to join Manchester City in March 1960 and I took him to a darts competition final sponsored by the old *Evening Chronicle,* Denis impressed at once as a 'nice guy', who preferred a cup of tea to anything stronger." Peter said that he was delighted to help Denis stage his 21st birthday party and, on his return from Italy, he drove him to Old Trafford to sign for United because Denis told him he had no idea where Old Trafford was and thought there would be less fuss if he arrived in Peter's car. Peter also divulged that both he and his family shared in his engagement party and his marriage, while Denis's kindness and consideration helped Peter to overcome a personal tragedy, although he knew that Denis hated the thought of hospital visits and the heartache his friends had to endure.

"We shared, too, his many successes on the field at club and international level. We regretted his brushes with authority, but like few other stars in the sports spotlight, Denis has succeeded completely in divorcing his private life from his public one." He said that there were, of course, many headlines but none related to his life outside football, a life, said Peter, with a solid base of the happiest of marriages and many real friends who would always hold him in the highest esteem. "To all who knew him intimately, Denis Law is the same now as he was when it all began so many years ago...a thoroughly nice guy."

The referee for the game was Roger Kirkpatrick from the Midlands and his linesmen were John H Yates from Redditch, and J R Griffith from Manchester. Mr Kirkpatrick looked a Dickens type of character, he had just a bit of hair around his head, a round, red face, a bubbling personality with gesticulations and always left an impression on a game.

Denis received a shock when his testimonial committee told him he would have to pay out a British record guarantee of £18,000 for Ajax's visit to Old Trafford. But he was expected to make £30,000. As the 45,000 loyal fans clapped and cheered the proceedings before the game kicked off it was sad in a way. It was a final farewell to a great player...Denis, but a warm welcome home to another...George Best. The crowd gave Denis a magnificent tribute with no bitterness for joining their 'arch enemy' from Maine Road. The supporters appreciated the wonderful match-winning games the golden-haired forward had achieved for the Reds in his never-to-be-forgotten career at Old Trafford. They also gave Best, playing his first game at Old Trafford for ten months, a morale boost by cheering him to the echo. George looked extremely nervous, he almost fell over the ball the first time he received it! The game was played fairly competitively with United winning 1-0 when full-back Alex Forsyth took a free kick and scored with a thunderous shot.

At about this time Tony Dunne, Manchester United's long-serving and popular full back, had also been promised a testimonial game, in fact the two testimonials were played within a short time of each other. This caused a certain amount of grievance because Tony felt that Matt Busby had reneged on the arrangements over his testimonial however he didn't blame Denis in any way for what eventually happened. Suffice to say that Tony only made £7,500 from his game, and paid out £1,500 in expenses.

Things were about to change for Denis at Maine Road. Johnny Hart stepped down as manager due to ill health in November 1973 and Denis was sad to see him leave, as were the other City players. Ron Saunders became the new manager. Saunders had formerly been with Norwich City and was known as a stern character and he soon stamped his authority on the players and changed the tactics of the team. Denis had seen it all before and didn't particularly like it. He played in the reserve team for a few games but was back in the first team by the time that City took on Wolves at Wembley in the League Cup final. Sadly for Denis, the Blues were beaten 2-1 in a very disappointing match and a week later, after a particularly poor 1-0 defeat by Leeds, Denis, along with Francis Lee and Rodney Marsh, was dropped by Saunders. City were now uncomfortably near the wrong end of the table, the Blues only comfort being the sight of United a few places and points below them.

In March 1974 City were due to play United and Denis was looking forward to the game but was extremely disappointed to be told he would not be playing. He wasn't alone, Francis Lee and Rodney Marsh were also out. The match ended in a 0-0 draw but with tempers raised throughout the game. Mike Doyle and Lou Macari were dismissed and several others booked, both teams were ordered back to the changing-room for ten minutes in order to cool down. A little later Denis learned that Saunders was trying to sell him to a Fourth Division club - something that would surely scupper his World Cup hopes. Fortunately, a short time later, Ron Saunders was sacked as the manager of Manchester City. His assistant, City stalwart Tony Book, took over as the new manager following a 3-0 defeat in April at QPR.

On a nicer note one of the soccer sensations of the early 70s, Arsenal Double-winner Charlie George, paid Denis a lovely compliment when he told newspapers that as a child in the playground, he and his school chums would play an Arsenal versus Tottenham match with the agony and full intensity of a real live game: "I always saw myself as Denis Law. He was the only footballer ever to influence or impress me as a player. For me he was always the 'complete' footballer. And it wasn't just a question of ability. He had a unique style, a tremendous arrogance born of a wonderful talent, and a confident authority that would leave me breathless with admiration."

*

What an ending for Denis Law's playing career - yet it was certainly not the ending Denis had envisaged. The Saturday that shook United to its very foundations drew together a former hero and arch-rivals Manchester City in an epic drama of relegation. After 36 unbroken years of First Division history United suffered humiliation in a momentous Old Trafford derby that supporters would never forget. Saturday 27th April 1974 saw the most famous backheel in British football history consign United to the Second Division. A goal scored for their detested rivals Manchester City by a former Old Trafford idol. The glorious reign of Best, Law and Charlton had come to an end. Charlton had retired and Best's career had finished following a brief comeback under Docherty. Once Denis had been given a free transfer nobody could have predicted the bizarre drama that followed as Denis travelled the two miles across from Old Trafford to Maine Road. The crunch match was fraught with emotion as City, with the former King of Old Trafford in their forward line, had secured their First Division future the previous Saturday with a 2-1 home win against West Ham.

It was a cold yet sunny April day when Manchester City came to Old Trafford on the last weekend of the season. Denis later admitted that he didn't really want to play in this game but agreed with his manager's assessment that, as a professional, he had to play. United had managed to win just ten games all season and looked doomed for relegation while City had fared only slightly better. A crowd of 56,996 packed into Old Trafford, anticipating a rousing, exciting game and hoping against hope that a United victory and a defeat for either of their relegation rivals (Birmingham and Southampton) would see them safe. Yet, perhaps understandably, the game turned out to be a very tough and scrappy affair with little good football but plenty of incidents and excitement. The Reds were desperate for the points and attacked relentlessly but in doing so they left themselves exposed at the back. With just eight minutes left and the score 0-0, City were on the attack and Denis was lurking about in the penalty box, not looking particularly dangerous, when all of a sudden Lee passed him the ball. His last touch in league football saw the man who had thrilled so many at Old Trafford consign them to the Second Division with an impudent, instinctive backheel.

Immediately, there was a tremendous roar from the Blues supporters and absolute silence from the Red faithful - City players swarmed all over Denis but he was in no mood for celebration. He looked the picture of dejection. As he later explained: "The ball came into the box with a few minutes to go and I just backheeled it in. I hadn't got a clue where the goal was, but it went in. It was a fluke really."

Tony Book immediately brought Law off the field and within seconds of him heading back into the dressing room the pitch was invaded by irate United fans. As he left, many fans shouted out to Denis that he was still 'The King' and a red-and-white scarf was draped around his neck. The match was abandoned but the score stood, City had won 1-0 and United were consigned to the Second Division. Denis left the buoyant, noisy City dressing-room, headed home, excused himself to Diana and his children, lay on the bed and as he fell deep into his thoughts he saw the faces of his Manchester United connections and shed a few tears.

Back at the stadium Alex Stepney explained his view of the incident: "There seemed to be that split second of silence when Denis scored. When Denis realised what he had done I don't think he wanted to be the person to put United down. As I moved across to my right Denis put his foot out and the ball went back across to my left. I was wrong footed and it looked a horrible goal to me."

Mike Summerbee recalled: "When the ball came to Denis it

was just an instinctive thing he did. I don't think he knew exactly where he was when he backheeled the ball I think he might have thought he was at the side of the goal. When the team got back into the dressing-room I sat next to Denis. He was upset and he threw his boots in the corner and I knew he was never going to put them on again."

"I felt absolutely terrible and disgusted and I felt even more disgusted because Denis Law had scored the goal," recalled Tommy Docherty. "He came back and haunted me that day. Good luck to him, it was great for him. I was as sick as a parrot obviously."

"To me it was the worst moment of my career," recalled United captain, Willie Morgan. "To get relegated was terrible, because it had never happened to me it was a nightmare. To be the United captain and get relegated was bad enough but to get relegated playing against Manchester City made it even worse. But daft as it was, we got relegated but I felt sorry for Denis, because when he walked off he was heartbroken."

Denis managed to put the disappointment of that goal behind him in order to concentrate on fulfilling his life's ambition, to appear in the 1974 World Cup finals. Selected to face Northern Ireland at Hampden Park in the Home Championship, a poor team performance and a 1-0 defeat meant he was dropped for the other games in the tournament against Wales and England. Yet despite fears he might be left out he discovered to his delight that Ormond had chosen Law, along with all the players who took part in the Home Championship, as part of his World Cup squad.

Playing in the tournament was, according to Denis, "the greatest thrill of my football life". Although Scotland remained unbeaten in their three matches they failed to qualify for the next stage, and unfortunately for Denis, he played only once, against Zaire in a 2-0 victory. Disappointed at being left out of Scotland's games drawn games against Brazil (0-0) and Yugoslavia (1-1) there was little doubt that a razor-sharp Law might have made all the difference. What a great pity Scotland never qualified for the World Cup in the 1960s when Law was in his prime. It would have been a magnificent setting for this world-class player. Still, he could always tell his grandchildren that he played in the World Cup. But it proved to be his last association with the Scotland team for whom he had played 55 times and scored 30 goals, which remained a record for Scottish International football for many years.

Back home, Denis still had a year on his contract left with City and, after coming back from West Germany, he took the family on holiday and afterwards prepared for the 1974/75 season. But Tony Book explained to Denis that he wouldn't be required for the first team, although he could play in the Central League if he wished. This, however, was not what Denis wanted to do. He discussed the situation with the City manager and the outcome was that Denis reluctantly announced his retirement on August Bank Holiday Monday. There was no falling out with anyone at Maine Road. City had to think of the future and so Denis ended his playing career on the World Cup stage. It certainly was not the way he intended his career to end but at least he went out at the top. He could, if he had wanted, have joined the exodus of British players going over to America. He received offers to join the likes of Pele, Cruyff, Beckenbauer, Best and Moore in the States. He has since regretted not giving the States a try and admitted that he possibly hung up his boots too soon. He was also offered contracts with lower League clubs in the British Isles, but he didn't fancy that. His family: wife Diana, sons Gary, Andrew, Robert and Iain, and his daughter, Diana, were paramount in his thinking and he wouldn't change his mind.

15. The Legend Lives On

Denis Law was still a young man and in the years following his retirement he tried several ventures in business and was also asked by the BBC to act as a radio summariser with Peter Jones. He later appeared on television with Alan Parry and Jim Rosenthal. Not bad for someone who as a player hardly ever gave interviews to either radio or television. He enjoyed this work and travelled around the world covering important games. It kept him involved in the game to which he devoted his professional life. He was inundated with requests to make guest appearances in testimonial games and other charitable games. At one stage a pro-celebrity team begged him to play for them and he made a couple of appearances in these matches, but in one particular game he was scythed down in full flow by an over-eager player out to make a name for himself and after this Denis decided that as he didn't like getting kicked when he was getting well paid for it, he certainly had no intention of being flattened and kicked for the fun of it. And so, apart from an occasional cameo role in a benefit game for former colleagues, he hung up his boots for good.

In 1989 he and George Best went on a tour to Australia, and did quite a lot of after-dinner functions. Best had become a close friend and Denis had introduced George to his agent Ken Stanley when the Irishman first broke into the Manchester United first team. Talking about Denis's trip to Australia, Sir Stanley Matthews told a story about the time Denis and George did a spot of coaching with youngsters. Sir Stanley said that all the local kids wanted to be coached by the two former Manchester United greats, however there were far too many youngsters in Denis and George's group, so when the other youngsters were put into another group that was being coached by a rather paunchy, overweight chap the kids were naturally disappointed and were not slow to show it. The kids seemed to lack respect for this heavy-jowled coach and smirked at his attempts to organise them. By noon, they were paying no attention whatsoever to their coach and he was unable to hold their attention. In short, his session had been a disaster.

Denis and George's group of youngsters had finished their session and they were all deliriously happy as they broke up for lunch. As the two former team-mates walked towards the changing rooms they noticed what was going on on the other pitch and made their way over to the group where they were immediately surrounded by kids. Denis and George quickly restored order in no time at all and the kids didn't take their eyes off them as they spoke.

"You could hear a pin drop," said Sir Stanley, "without saying a word George placed ten balls on the pitch about 20 yards from goal. He then asked the kids how many times they thought that their coach could hit the crossbar? After a great deal of banter and various numbers being called out, one lad shouted: 'None'. His reason being that the coach would not be able to see the balls because of his large belly. What a shock was in store for those mocking, unknowing youngsters! George asked the coach if he would commence the drill. As the first five balls hit the cross bar with precision the kids looked on with disbelief on their faces, absolutely dumbstruck. The coach continued and as the ninth one hit the target they were ashen-faced. But as they watched him flick the tenth ball up in the air, catch it on his forehead, flick it onto his left shoulder, then let the ball drop to the heel of his left boot before flicking it into the air and volleying it perfectly, almost breaking the crossbar in two, the kids were astonished. Ten out of ten!

"The kids gave him a rapturous ovation, cheering and yelling. Denis and George smiled and headed toward the clubhouse as the youngsters gathered around their coach requesting that he show them the technique he had so majestically just displayed. One little urchin shouted out: 'What's ya name, mate?' Upon hearing this George turned around sharply and said: 'To you, son, he's Mister Puskas!'"

Yet in the years following his retirement Denis admitted that he missed the day-to-day involvement with the game. "It took me three years to get over the fact that I was no longer a player. I missed the lads more than anything, all the laughing and joking. If I had my time as a player again I'd probably enjoy it a bit more," said Denis, "I didn't fancy being a football club manager. You need a hard streak in you to do that job. You've got to be good and cruel, and if you've not got it you'll be out."

Another job which Denis took on after his playing days were finished was working as a salesman for a friend's carpet firm. At this time the late Brian Moore, one of football's best-known commentators, picked seven of his 'All-Time Greats'. They were Bert Trautmann, Sir Tom Finney, Sir Stanley Matthews, and four Manchester United players; the great, irreplaceable Duncan Edwards, Sir Bobby Charlton, George Best and Denis. Talking about Denis, Brian Moore paid the former player a wonderful tribute when he said: "Somewhere today Denis Law is selling carpets. I'm glad I'm not in competition with him because winning meant so much to Denis." Brian continued his tribute which summed up Denis precisely: "Whether it was kicking a ball or, I suspect, selling a length of Axminister, Denis just hates being a loser."

In more recent years Denis has become a regular at Old Trafford on match days and the many functions that take place at the club. He still has a full head of hair, looks slim and full of energy, darting about all over the place. He is first and foremost a family man and quite naturally they mean everything to him, he comes across as extremely happy and contented.

*

Over the proceeding years any animosity which may have existed from their playing days between Denis and Bobby Charlton seemed to have been forgotten. Denis appeared with Sir Bobby on a football programme on Sky television, which was hosted by Dickie Davies. Denis and Bobby watched a few of

Manchester United's games from the 1960s. They weren't bosom pals, but they had a mutual respect for each other and enjoyed a laugh watching an England versus Scotland match. In fact both players and George Best were often brought together for some function or other at Old Trafford. With the passing of time all three had mellowed and rightly so. After all, the three of them were instrumental in that wonderful period for Manchester United in the 1960s that culminated with the club winning the European Cup.

Denis always said his favourite player was Alfredo Di Stefano, of whom there is more in an earlier chapter. Yet his number two selection was Dave Mackay. Denis was a big admirer of his former Scottish international colleague, explaining: "What makes him a 'great' is his fanatical will to win and this also made him the best captain I've ever played under. He makes you want to win however forlorn the battle. He is the only player I tremble to play against." His number three candidate was Russia's great goalkeeper Lev Yashin. Denis played with the great man for the Rest of the World against England in the 1963/64 season. Denis said he could never forget the nonchalant way he punched away a Jimmy Greaves special. "The ball almost went to the halfway line," said Denis, who said that Yashin didn't go in for spectacular diving about because "his positional play was planned out to the inch."

At number four Denis made no apologies for mentioning the greatest goalscorer of all, Ferenc Puskas. The 'Galloping Major' left a deep impression on Denis when he first saw him score a goal in a film of the England versus Hungary game from 1953. "He seemed completely blocked in, but he coolly rolled the ball back with the sole of his boot, twisted to make an angle - and fired the ball home," said Denis. Puskas was such an accurate placer of the ball that when he watched him take a penalty in the classic European Cup Final for Real Madrid against Eintracht at Hampden Park in 1960, Di Stefano was so confident that by the time Puskas's shot was being taken, Alfredo was already standing in the centre circle for the restart. His fifth choice was Tom Finney. "Tom was such a complete player he could play in any forward position," said Denis, "he could dribble, shoot, use either foot and what many people forget, he was equally good with his head." Finney, like Di Stefano was as quick as greyhound for speed over a few yards.

In the early 1980s a football magazine ran an article entitled *The Art Of Goalscoring - Past and Present.* Denis was mentioned as one of the greatest goalscorers ever. It was a very flattering article. In this period Denis had exchanged his football boots for a microphone as a radio commentator. Denis was of the opinion that the role of a goalscorer, or striker to use the modern terminology, had changed dramatically from the days when he was playing. He said that he would feel like a fish out of water if he had to play for a club at that time. "In my day a striker had to be good in the air, brave and always ready to snap up the half chances around goal," said Denis, "we had to develop a good understanding with our goalscoring partner. There were always at least two of us, and we could count on a regular service from both our wingers. Yes, wingers. Remember them?" He mentioned how, in his opinion, the ability of the current players to head the ball as hard as some players could kick it was a thing of the past. He also said that there were only a few players who possessed the courage to go in where it really hurts in the penalty area, although he mentioned Andy Gray, now Sky TV's leading soccer analyst, as a notable exception. Denis said that in modern football it was criminal to see so many half chances go begging. He bemoaned the fact that coaching saw mediocre teams cutting out the supply of passes to the forwards.

Yet Denis wasn't criticising modern day strikers. "In fact," he said, "I feel sorry for them. I'll let you into a little secret," he said Denis laughing, "believe it or not - I hated being a striker! Yes, I was always a reluctant front man. I never felt playing as a striker was my best position. I loved scoring goals - but hated the lack of involvement. I was always an old-fashioned inside-forward in my early days at Huddersfield Town and Manchester City and loved collecting the ball from my own defenders to run at opposing defences. That is the way I love to play. I saw a lot of the ball and always felt involved in the game. When I moved to Italy I was forced to play as an out-and-out striker and it was awful. The Italian defenders marked me so closely that I thought they were going to follow me back to our dressing room at full time."

He then recalled his return to England and Manchester United. He said that Sir Matt Busby had a problem, a shortage of goalscorers in the squad. Busby, he said, had no one else to score goals so he agreed to play up front. That was why he said he had sympathy with modern strikers. He maintained that the likes of Trevor Francis, who had recently joined Nottingham Forest from Birmingham City for over a million pounds, was a reluctant striker. He also accurately predicted that Diego Maradona, a typical inside-forward, would at some stage of his career be turned into another reluctant striker.

Of the strikers Denis admired in his later years he admitted that Ted McDougall, who Frank O' Farrell had bought to replace him during his reign at Old Trafford, Bob Hatton and Malcolm Poskett were three strikers he admired a great deal from that period. Steve Archibald and Kenny Dalglish were another two strikers whom he thought were exceptional. The partnership of Ipswich Town's Alan Brazil, who would also join Manchester United and Paul Mariner also impressed the Law Man.

He finished by defending players from his own era. "It's said by a lot of modern 'experts' that players from the 1960s would never survive in the football of the 1980s. They say that modern football would prove too fast for my contemporaries. Well my reply to that is…Nonsense! Who could be faster than the great Real Madrid left-winger Gento? Who could control a ball quicker than Puskas? Who is swifter off the mark than Di Stefano? Every age breeds its own stars and it's a complete waste of time comparing one era with another."

Another little story that illustrates the real Denis Law is told by the late Jimmy Murphy's son, Jim. "My dad thought Denis was one of the greatest forwards he had ever seen, and over the years he had coached and watched a great many. I have personally met Denis many times but this story which I think sums up his personality." Jim was invited to the Manchester United Grand Reunion Charity Dinner which was held in the palatial London Marriot Hotel, in Grosvenor Square, on Thursday 28th May 1998. This occasion was organised by the London Branch of Manchester United Supporters' Club and the only people invited from the club were the eleven players who played in the 1968 European Cup Final, plus Denis Law, who as we know watched the final from his hospital bed. Also invited would have been the manager Sir Matt Busby, assistant manager Jimmy Murphy and trainer Jack Crompton. In the event Sir Matt was represented by his son Sandy and daughter Sheena, Jimmy Murphy by Jimmy junior and his wife Pam while Jack Crompton and his wife Sheila also attended. All the players from that famous occasion were there except Sir Bobby Charlton and Tony Dunne.

The party travelled from Old Trafford by luxury coach but Denis could not attend because of television work in Scotland, however his wife Diana was with the official party. After a very enjoyable evening, the following morning the party set off for the journey back to Manchester. After travelling on the motorway for an hour or so a tea trolley was pushed up the aisle. Tea, coffee and biscuits were served to all the passengers on the coach. But who was this cheerful 'trolley dolly?' Only the 1964 European Footballer of the Year, Denis Law. This was how Jimmy Murphy junior remembered Denis the player: "A cheeky chappie with plenty of charm and completely unfazed by his fame. Ready with a smile and some flattery for the ladies; a laugh and some banter with the men. I was twenty when Denis joined United and watched him in many, many games. He was a wonderful player to watch. Plenty of skill, fast and committed, quick reflexes and a joy to have in your team in the penalty area. I have seen many great strikers play for and against United and obviously on television that gives a worldwide view now. If I had to use one word to describe Denis Law, it would be...Lightning!"

*

At this point I would like to give the reader my own personal opinion of Denis Law as a Manchester United forward and I will try and compare him to past Manchester United forwards who were my particular favourites. However, briefly I would like to digress and give my opinion, for what it's worth, on a question always being asked whenever United followers get together and discuss past United teams. Here goes: During Denis Law's career with the Reds the question was always being asked: "Which was the best team? The brilliantly gifted 1948 team, the United of the Busby Babes era, or the United of Charlton, Law and Best?" It is a similar question to the one that is often asked about Sir Alex Ferguson's brilliant 1990s teams. Unfortunately, this is a question that can never be answered. Everybody has their own opinion but one thing I can honestly say on that question and that is, in my humble opinion, Denis Law would have been found a place in any of United's past teams, of that I have no doubt whatsoever.

I was fortunate enough to see in action the team that is referred to as the great Manchester United 1948 FA Cup winning team, who went on to win the First Division Championship in 1952. Although only a schoolkid I couldn't help but admire and idolise players such as the cannon-ball shooting of Jack 'The Gunner' Rowley. Wow, what a player! Rowley was a ferocious forward with a quick temper. He scored 208 goals in over 400 first team games for the Reds. Jack scored fantastic goals with his head and feet. Then there was Stan Pearson. What an intelligent inside-forward! He was beautiful to watch, with immaculate ball control and a superb passer of the ball. Beside being the linkman, Stan could score plenty of goals, as his record of 149 goals from 345 first team matches attests. He made the other players play well.

Then there was the matchstick-thin, quicksilver Dennis Viollet. Dennis and Tommy Taylor had perhaps the best partnership in British football. They could read each other's thoughts and the goals they scored were phenomenal. Dennis scored 178 goals from 291 appearances, while big Tommy got

128 goals from 189 first team games. Tommy was the first player who celebrated a goal with a huge, melon-sized smile on his handsome face and both his arms pushed skywards like a matador. (In those days a player who scored a goal would usually just run back to the centre circle, accept a handshake or a pat on the back and a 'well done' comment from team-mates.) Billy Whelan, the quiet Irishman, had sublime skills and scored 52 goals in his 96 first team appearances. I will include Sir Bobby Charlton in this list because at the start of his career he was a dynamic goalscorer. He made 752 appearances in United's first team and scored 247 times. In his first four seasons in the Reds' first team (149 games) he scored 86 goals, before moving out to the left-wing. And then there was the vastly underrated, old-fashioned centre-forward of the late 1950s and early 60s Alex Dawson, who plundered 54 goals from 93 first team games.

All these Manchester United players had that special knack of being able to put the ball into the back of the net with regularity. The memories of those goalscorers will live with me forever. They were all brilliant, exciting and special players. However, I must confess that the player who gave me a rare kind of pride was Denis Law. At Old Trafford he found his spiritual home and his goals gave untold pleasure to thousands of people. Denis scored goals that you would never, ever expect other forwards to score. He was a flash of lightning in the penalty area - 'whoosh!' - it was a goal. Denis was unselfish in setting up goals for his team-mates, yet inside the six-yard box he had the killer instinct. His blond hair and one arm salute helped to make him a legend. He regularly scored goals from impossible angles and the crowds would rise to him as he would smile, raise one arm in the air - the King of Old Trafford.

Perhaps Derek Hodgson of the *Daily Express*, described Denis best when he wrote: "A player who, in a puff of red smoke, became the Demon King, the most explosive and lethal player in and around the penalty box in the world. He was, and always will be, the terrace favourite because he was in style and wit and character, the street Arab who really made it." Hodgson said fans couldn't love George Best because he wore mod clothes and entertained girls that they couldn't afford. Speaking of Bobby Charlton, the journalist said Bobby was cool and aristocratic in his play and too distant in his personality and marked for the prefecture from his first appearance. Bobby was respected. "But," he said, "Denis had the panache they coveted. He ran like fire, scored spectacular goals with either foot or head, exchanged blow for blow and curse for curse with opponents, quarrelled with linesmen and referees." The journalist said there were times when Denis would claim the ball was his and would walk off home with it. He mentioned an incident at Old Trafford, when a zealous linesman repeatedly flagged him offside. Denis waited and then, when a long ball came his way, and knowing himself onside, feinted as if to chase it. Up went the flag and there was Denis, who had not moved an inch, pointing a mocking finger and grinning at the red-faced linesman. Enough said!

*

In 2002, a bronze statue of Denis was unveiled in the Stretford End of Old Trafford. This was unusual to say the least. Previously only Sir Matt Busby's statue had been commissioned and erected outside the main entrance to the ground. The United fanzine *Red Issue* had an audience with the King and Denis Law professed surprise at the statue because those things didn't usually happen until the recipient has passed away, saying: "Yes, I wondered if they knew something that I didn't!" Apparently, 18 months before, Martin Edwards had asked Denis if he would give his permission. He thought it was an excellent honour and was delighted. He laughed when he said his first reaction was: "I wonder what Bestie and Bobby would think?" He had no idea why the club selected him to have a statue erected, "perhaps its because I live nearest! No seriously, I haven't got a clue."

He then spoke about the current team. Asked about Ruud Van Nistelrooy, Denis said he thought he was a great player, as good as any seen at Old Trafford. "He's got a bit of everything, he's a fighter, a battler and you need that anyway if you are going to play up front. He's a good header of the ball, has good feet and most importantly he scores goals. He has also got the players to supply him with the right service." Denis admitted that he rarely goes to watch matches, adding that he was never a great 'watcher'. When told that George Best had confessed that Law would have scored more goals if he had passed the ball to him more often, Denis laughed heartily and said: "Tell Bestie 'thanks'." When told that they were surprised to read that Denis had slightly dodgy vision when he was younger, Denis replied: "I was never able to see out of my right eye since I was a young boy. My eye was in the corner for 10 years until I had an operation when I was 15. I can see you out of my right eye, but it's blurry."

He was then asked if that was the secret to goal scoring - was it a case of goalscorers being instinctive and knowing where the goal was without looking? Denis said: "Nobody can teach goal scoring - it is something you have either got or you haven't", and added that you can tell when you watch some players going through for a goal and you think 'they're not going to score'. And then you can see another player go through, like Greavsie in my time and you knew you could forget it, he'd score."

When asked about his disapointment upon missing the European Cup final in 1968, Denis said that he understood how Roy Keane and Paul Scholes felt when they missed out on European Cup glory but said that he was more disappointed in 1966 when United should have won it. He emphasised that the team had a few injuries: "Bestie wasn't too clever and I think it was Nobby Stiles, we all had knee injuries. Against Milan in 1969 I scored a 'goal' that was about two foot over the line and would have been the equaliser but the referee disallowed it. I can assure you it was about two foot over the line and if that was given we would have beaten them then. And we would definitely have beaten the team Milan comfortably beat in the final, Ajax. At that time Holland were not yet producing the teams they did a few years later that were some of the best Europe has ever seen."

He was asked if it irritated him to see his record as the club's European top scorer overtaken because the strikers have so many games in which to score now? He laughed loudly and replied: "Not at all. Records mean something to me, but records are there to be beaten, the same as whoever's record I beat, you know? It doesn't bother me at all."

It was also mentioned that some had said he deliberately got sent off and suspended over the Christmas and New Year period, and was reminded of the time the team had a whip round for him because the wages were not what they are today! He told them that it was true there was a whip round, because anybody suspended never got paid. He pointed out that it was against the Treaty of Rome in relation to working conditions but said it only lasted a year because they couldn't confiscate people's wages. "Times change," he said, "wages change. And I gave too much thought to it." When asked which era would he have preferred to have played in if he had the choice? Straight away Law answered: "Being Scottish? Now!! I don't even have to think about it."

He said he didn't think it was right for him to choose his best-ever performance in a United shirt but admitted enjoying the 1963 FA Cup final. "Playing in a Cup Final is every player's dream and playing in that final at Wembley and to be on the winning side and scoring a goal, that was very nice." He ended by saying that he was honoured to play for Scotland. When asked what the future held for Denis Law he said laughingly, that he works for his family, doing odd jobs for them. He spoke lovingly about his wife and family and said he was very fortunate that he had a lovely family. "They are more like pals," he said. "They go for a drink together and have meals together and cook for each other." He praised his wife's influence: "She's a Glasgow girl and she's kept us all on the ground. If we can all be happy that's the most important thing for me."

After the interview Denis thanked everyone concerned. The interviewer watched from the window as Denis strode across the car park, nodding hello to the people who recognised him. You could see them nudge each other after he passed, and you just knew that they were saying to each other: "That was Denis Law -The King!"

Appendix 1:
Tributes

NOEL CANTWELL

Noel Cantwell was a former monastery schoolboy who became captain of his country, the Republic of Ireland and Manchester United. It was said of Noel that he had kissed the Blarney Stone. As captain of Manchester's Red Devils he was the coaxing, soothing and sometimes shouting 'boss' of the brilliant Manchester United team of the 1960s.

"Denis Law...Denis the Menace...The Lawman - a veritable soccer genius and, say some, an ace trouble-shooter. As Denis' ex-skipper at Old Trafford, and as his pal, too, I can tell you a heck of a lot about the lad. And although millions of words have already been spilled out about Law, I know that soccer fans - and even the uninitiated - never tire of hearing about the blond-haired phenomenon. For that's exactly what Denis is. Later we saw a new Law on the field; a more mature, controlled player. And there's not much doubt that one of the things that cooled him a little, if that's the word, were those famous - or infamous - suspensions he got after being sent off against Aston Villa, Blackpool and Arsenal. There's no doubt about it, and not just because he was a club-mate who does a powerful lot, as you know, to help us win games. Denis was a truly great player. If I had to choose an inside forward from all over Europe - and that includes all the top clubs, Real Madrid, Benfica, you name them and I wouldn't hesitate to choose Denis Law. Some called him a big head. He isn't. He simply has a slightly cocky confidence in his own ability. I admire his courage. You never saw Law shirk a hard tackle. He would go for that ball regardless, whether he ran the risk of bumping into Maurice Norman, Charley Hurley, and Jack Charlton ... or Goliath. Who can mistake the Law gimmicks, the Law flair and cheeky-kid Law showmanship? He was a great club man. And he had a great, almost father-like, respect for the Boss, Matt Busby. Denis was an ideal club-mate; he likes a bit of fun and can take it as well as give it. A magnificent player in every respect!"

Jimmy Greaves

Jimmy Greaves was a goalscorer supreme. One of the greatest ever! Greaves played for Chelsea, AC Milan, Tottenham Hotspur and West Ham United. Greaves' final goal tally was a marvellous 357 goals in 517 League matches. Quite remarkable, because he scored them all in the First Division. He played 57 times for England, scoring 44 goals.

"It is a pity that I have such a high opinion of Denis Law. No one but a lunatic would leave him out of any side in contemporary football. Yet I would dearly have liked to fill my inside-right position in my best British XI with my late friend, John White. However, taking everything into consideration, I must still give the vote to the incomparable Denis Law. Football fans can talk all night about their ideas of the greatest living players, but Denis is the only man that players and managers alike, without exception, single out as being on top of the list. Controversy followed Denis everywhere. With his great talent and his golden locks, it was difficult for him to escape attention. Denis is an explosive character. Everyone knows that and some of his team-mates have told me that he is like a Spanish matador in temperament. He's like a coiled spring of nervous energy, which unleashes itself on the field. In the dressing room he is a knot of tension as he paces up and down. Somehow he is unlike a footballer or any kind of athlete, simply a nervous youth waiting for a stiff examination. But everything changed once he ran out onto the field. The roar of the crowd and the challenge of the opposition are to him what a fix is to an addict. Suddenly he became 10 feet tall. It is in this context that one most judge the man..."

BRIAN MOORE

The late Brian Moore was one of television's best-known football commentators.

"I've been lucky to see most of the world's greatest football stars in the past years. But, on his day, I've seen none that excited me as much as Denis Law. He started his career with Huddersfield Town, moved to Manchester, not to United, but their rivals Manchester City. From there he tried Italian football for a season with Torino, before coming back home and joining Manchester United. It was Matt Busby and Manchester United that saw the vintage Denis Law. After over a decade in the limelight with the Red Devils he was revered by the thousands of Old Trafford fans. He scored some never-to-be-forgotten goals and was part of that astonishing threesome of Law, Best and Charlton. In the evening of his career he rejoined Manchester City, but his heart was still with United. And there was no more poignant moment than when Denis returned to Old Trafford with Manchester City at the end of the 1973/74 season and scored the goal that made it certain that his old club would slide into the Second Division. Throughout his career he scored some astonishing goals and plenty of brave ones. But most of them were snapped up from rebounds off the post or goalkeeper simply because his wits were tuned that fraction finer. Then we'd see that right arm raised in a scoring salute. We'd often see a flash of temperament quelled by a wicked smile; the shirt floppily outside the shorts; but most of all we should thank him for the decision to get out of the game before the memories became blurred by performances below his high standards. And what memories they are!"

PADDY CRERAND

Pat Crerand is a close friend of Denis Law. A former Celtic player and Scottish international, he joined Manchester United in 1963. United fans said that 'when Crerand played well United played well.' He was a fantastic wing-half and a beautiful accurate passer of the ball. Denis Law himself often praised Crerand for helping him score a vast number of his goals. He was a great character and well respected by his club mates. After his playing career ended he briefly became assistant manager to Tommy Docherty at Old Trafford. Today he is a radio pundit on United's games.

The first time I saw Denis Law play I thought he was the most arrogant so-and-so I had ever seen on a football field. He didn't just act as if it was his ball. He acted as if it was his stadium. And even when he scored a goal he made you wonder if anyone had ever scored a goal before. I thought to myself: 'What a big-headed so-and-so this bloke must be.' I met Denis for the first time we played in a Scottish Under 23 international. We got to know each other better and became quite friendly, and still are. There are two sides to Denis. There is the Denis Law you saw on the field, all gestures and genius. And there is the Denis Law his public wouldn't even recognise. The Law the press boys wrote about since he hit the sporting headlines. The blond bombshell that was a football wonder-boy in his teens and one of the most controversial characters the game ever saw. His timing in the air was fantastic. His reflexes on the ground uncanny. His reading of the game brilliant. So how good was Denis Law? I'll tell you. 'He was the greatest player in the world.'

TREVOR BROOKING

Trevor Brooking, the former West Ham and England midfield player and now a respected commentator on the game with BBC television, is idolised by West Ham supporters. Football followers appreciated him all over the world. He was a quiet, dignified person. Trevor, in his 17-year career, was selected for England 47 times. He was booked a mere five times and never sent off. He wrote this tribute to Denis in his book 100 Great British Footballers.

"Denis Law was one of the great strikers and characters in the modern game. He had grace, flair and magnetism and, of course, played for Manchester United when they were most probably the most glamorous team in Europe. He was a skinny, pale young Scot with glasses when Andy Beattie signed him for Huddersfield Town in 1955, but he developed into one of the most dangerous and athletic strikers of the 1960s. He spent three years at Huddersfield before Manchester City signed him. He spent one season at Maine Road, scoring 21 goals in 44 League games and attracting the attention of Torino. By this time he had already shown an astonishing instinct in front of goal and in one FA Cup tie against Luton Town he scored six times. Unfortunately, the match was abandoned and Luton won the replayed game. He had only one season in Italy and returned to Manchester with United in 1962. It was at Old Trafford, alongside players like Bobby Charlton and George Best, that he enjoyed his most magical years, winning two League titles and an FA Cup winner's medal. He was a brave, wiry, determined striker with terrific reflexes, blistering pace and the ability to out-jump taller defenders. He liked to play with his shirt hanging loose over his shorts and the shirt cuffs bunched in his fists. His blond hair and the one arm raised to salute a goal helped establish the Law legend. His ability to snap up half chances in the turmoil of the penalty area and score with spectacular overhead kicks made him one of the game's most exciting strikers in one of the game's most attractive teams.

The transition to the international stage frequently brought the best out of Denis and in 55 games for Scotland he scored 30 goals. Nothing motivated him quite as powerfully as the England-Scotland clashes and on the day that the rest of the football fraternity was watching England's 1966 World Cup triumph he was playing golf, and on hearing the result is supposed to have said: 'That's really spoiled my day.' But the biggest disappointment of his career must have been missing Manchester United's 1968 European Cup Final triumph over Benfica because of injury. In 10 years at Old Trafford he scored 171 goals in 300 League games and in 1973 returned to Manchester City for one last season in an illustrious career. He scored nine goals in his final 22 games with City and one of them was laced with bitter irony. With a typical, cheeky piece of improvisation, he back-heeled the goal in the local derby with United that sent his old team down into the Second Division. There was no arm raised in triumph on that occasion. Of all the goals he scored that was the one that gave him the least pleasure."

GORDON BANKS

Gordon Banks said he could look back almost lovingly at the men who were in the firing squad facing him for all those years he had been in professional football. He had an action picture file in his memory of all of them, the long, the short and the tall. Long like Portugal's beanpole centre-forward Jose Torres, who even Jack 'The Giraffe' Charlton had to look up to; short like West Germany's Gerd Muller, who could turn a half-chance into a goal before you had time to blink. After hours of agonising, Gordon came up with the following Top Ten list of strikers from the gallery of goalscorers that he was privileged to play against during his brilliant career. In Gordon's list there are three Manchester United players, all playing colleagues. His full list was the following: Pele, Jimmy Greaves, Gerd Muller, Denis Law, George Best, Bobby Charlton, Eusebio, Johan Cruyff, Jairzinho, and a tie between Geoff Hurst and Roger Hunt. About Denis he had the following to say.

"The Press often referred to Denis as the Electric Eel. I think Electric Heel would have been more appropriate. He had such fast reactions in the penalty box that it was as if he was plugged into the mains. I will always remember with mixed feelings his remarkable performance for Manchester United against us in the 1963 FA Cup Final. He produced one of the greatest forward displays ever seen at Wembley and inspired United to a 3-1 victory. Denis, a menace if ever there was one, scored one goal and was jumping in celebration of another when his header struck the bar. I turned expecting to see the ball in the back of the net and gratefully received the rebound into my arms. Denis, always a marvellous showman, threw both arms in the air and collapsed to his knees. He could be arrogant, precocious, evil-tempered, hilariously funny and simply brilliant all in the space of a few minutes. Often when the pressure of a match was at its peak, Denis brought a smile to my face with a sudden aside. That was at club level. When he was playing for Scotland, he didn't have a good thing to say to any of us Sassenachs. He was a great competitor, a great player."

JIMMY HILL

"Looking back at the ability of Denis Law, the two words that come to anybody's mind are 'electric' and 'quicksilver'. Denis was an electronic, or even bionic, player, a devastating piece of goalscoring equipment beautifully designed to reach the ball before any other player and produce whatever movement was necessary to get it into the net. But dashing Denis was a long way from being just a piece of machinery. Football fans the world over, and particularly those north of the English border, adored the handsome, arrogant, Scotsman. He had the looks of Danny Kaye, and there was something of the clown in him, too. He was always ready, whatever the excitement or the stress, to break into a magnetic smile. Denis could never be described as one of the world's great ball artists. I remember filming him for television when, because of the pressure and the excitement of the camera rolling, he had some difficulty in just keeping the ball up on his feet. Yet part of his superb ability was that he never made two movements when one would do. So many of his best goals were scored with just one touch of the head or a flick with the foot with defenders wondering just where he had come from.

Law was very precise in his passing. I can see in my mind's eye now the picture of him concentrating on laying the ball back perfectly for a colleague. He was also one of those players who did everything twice as quickly and twice as accurately in places where it mattered. And for him that was in the opposition's goalmouth. Law had one other supreme attribute. With him in the side no cause was ever lost. He was a picture of optimism to those off the field and the same influence was exerted on the field for every team in which he played. He could be rated the perfect competitor, ever aware, ever determined, ever inventive, and never beaten. More than that, to relax when Denis was around was asking for trouble. Seldom did he give defenders a second chance. Law's first chance came in the middle 1950s when he was sent down from the family home in Aberdeen to join Huddersfield, a teenager wearing steel-rimmed spectacles. By the time he was 16 the super-confident Law was in the club's first team, directing players twice his age. He got away with it because he was that good, good enough for Matt Busby to offer £10,000 for him when he was still eligible for Huddersfield's youth team. Busby was to make Law Scotland's youngest international at 18 years and seven months when he played him against Wales in 1958. Law was to go on until the 1974 World Cup, winning 55 caps and deserving many more.

"Bill Shankly, then assistant-manager at Huddersfield, had an expression for the young Law. It was simply: 'The greatest thing on two feet.'"

"Eventually, Huddersfield had to sell Law. Busby had the chance to buy but Dennis Viollet and Bobby Charlton were playing so well at inside forward at Old Trafford that Law was not approached. It was Manchester City who handed over

£55,000 in March 1960, with City boss Les McDowall reckoning that he had signed another Raich Carter. Law spent less than two seasons at Maine Road and was away again. Nobody could ever accuse Law of not knowing his own worth and there was a lot of lire to be made out of Italian soccer in 1961. But the disciplines of Italian club life were not for Law. A year of frustration ended when Busby paid out yet another record fee, this time £115,000, to take Law to Old Trafford, where he could have gone five years earlier. Within a few matches, the Stretford End fans had christened him 'The King,' and the title survived the challenge of George Best and stayed with him until 1973, when United let him go for a second spell with Manchester City. He was over the hill, anyway, they thought at Old Trafford. But he did enough at Maine Road to win back his Scotland place. Those were the real glory days, through the 1960s at Old Trafford where he won First Division championship medals in 1964/65 and 1966/67, an FA Cup winner's medal in 1963 and the honour of being European Footballer of The Year in 1964. Always a victim of injuries because of the furious style and pace at which he played, he was out of the side when Manchester United achieved their greatest triumph, the European Cup success in 1968. But Law needs no medals to confirm his magic. All those who saw him will never forget that fiery packet of unique skills. Law is among Matt Busby's all-time greats. That should be good enough for most people."

RAY WILSON

Ray Wilson played for Huddersfield Town, Everton, Oldham Athletic, and Bradford City. Ray was a compact figure, small and tough. He played for England in the 1966 World Cup Final against West Germany. In all he represented his country on 63 occasions. He is regarded as one of the best left full-backs to ever grace the game. He was a playing colleague of Law's at Huddersfield Town in the 1950s.

"Having to some extent grown up with the lad, I have varied

feelings about Denis Law. As a player I would say he had everything. As a personality he had something extra - something that makes it a bit frightening to play against him. Not many players would admit to be frightened of facing Denis, but I'm sure they were. If I thought I had to be up against him in a match I would spend the whole week thinking about it. Because of his reputation I know that everyone expects him to do something out of the ordinary and it would be silly to pretend that you're not worried by the prospect of having to cover a man like that. It's psychological warfare really - a defender can never afford to play his normal game against a razor-sharp goalscorer like Denis. If you beat a normal forward you don't think twice about moving forward 20 or 30 yards, but with Denis you have this idea that it's dangerous ever to leave him at all. So a wing-half or full-back who marks Denis never plays his normal game, because you have this nagging feeling at the back of your mind that if you make the slightest mistake he's going to turn it into a goal against you. It seems funny to think that the little lad who came to my digs in 1955 with his two big brothers is the same man who has all defenders on edge…"

KENNETH WOLSTENHOLME

The late Kenneth Wolstenholme was one of the best-known commentators of football matches in Britain. In the course of his career, he had visited every European country, the United States, and most of South America. During the war he was a bomber pilot in the RAF, was one of the original 'Pathfinders' pilots and was awarded the Distinguished Flying Cross and Bar. Kenneth penned this tribute to 'The King' in 1968.

"Everybody has told Denis Law to calm down, to play his football at a more even pace. But they are wasting their breath. Denis Law has no intention of calming down. The authority for that statement is Law himself, who has said quite definitely, 'If

I calm down I shall lose all my assets.' So now we know. In the future we are going to see the same Denis Law, and although it will worry some referees and administrators, it is mighty good news for the millions of football fans who pay their hard-earned money to see players like Law, combining character and a sense of showmanship with their high degree of skill. Even today, when the game is reputed to be so organised that the successful teams are those that work as one unit and plan everything, these players stand out. You can plan all you like, but you will never stifle them - the Laws, the Charltons, the Bests, the Alberts, the Peles and the rest. If they are ever stifled, then football is stifled too. Denis Law is a Jekyll and Hyde. Off the field he is quiet and reserved. He has a friendly smile for everyone. If you met him casually at a reception or a party, you would never think that you were meeting a man who becomes a firebrand once he walks onto the football field. But you would be doing just that. The moment Denis Law leaves the dressing room he is a changed man. In the dressing room he is just as he is off the field - kindly and jovial. If there is a dressing room joke or prank, then you can bet that Denis Law is the culprit. He leads the banter. He engineers the fun. That, though, is before the game. Once the game starts, Law becomes a demon. As he himself puts it: 'As soon as the game starts, people cease to exist. There just aren't any people any more. Just situations.'

"Situations, Law thrived on them. He acknowledges that managers have to plan their strategy, but he still insists that the successful teams are those with players who can meet any situation and know what to do instinctively. Football is not a game you can rehearse. Things just happen on the spur of the moment and you have got to have the right reaction. Denis Law is a player of reaction. A situation is created and he gets hold of it, takes advantage of it and has thereby established for himself a reputation of being one of the game's finest match winners. The 1963 FA Cup Final, for instance. Manchester United, believe it or not, were a struggling League side that season and were nearly relegated, played Leicester City, and for half an hour it was, as the cliché has it, anyone's game. Then Law plucked a goal out of nothing, and United never looked back. Only a truly great player would have scored the goal. He was running forward at the time the ball was passed to him, but Pat Crerand, who made the pass, had been forced into parting with the ball hurriedly and his aim had gone astray. The ball moved quickly towards a point well behind Law. Somehow or other, Law managed to check his forward stride, go back, trap the ball on the instep of his left foot, turn a complete circle anti-clockwise and although seemingly hemmed in by two defenders, hit a glorious right-foot shot low into the corner of the net. It was the goal of a master, a goal that could never have been rehearsed.

"Great goals are food and drink to Denis Law. He has scored them with his right foot, his left foot and with his head, and it is his heading ability that has thrilled most people. The game has had brilliant headers of the ball in the past - players like 'Dixie' Dean and Sandor Kocis - but no one has been better at the art than Law. He is not a tall man, but what he lacks in inches he makes up with his expert timing. The other players are all well on the way up towards a high ball before Law moves. Then suddenly he takes off, rises head and shoulders above the defence, gets his blond head above the ball, and another thrilling Law header rolls off the assembly line. He produced one special one in that 1963 FA Cup Final. He soared to the ball with all the grace of a ballet dancer. He hit it just right of the right-hand post. Gordon Banks, in the Leicester City goal, was helpless. He could only stand and watch as the ball sped towards the net at incredible speed. But this time Law's aim was an inch wrong. The ball hit the upright and rebounded straight into the arms of the astonished but grateful Banks. Simultaneously, Law landed on his toes, sank to his knees, covered his head in his hands and beat it against the turf. Another Law gesture had rolled off the assembly line."

Appendix 2:
Career Record: 1956-57 to 1973-74

Born Woodside, Aberdeen - 24th February 1940

<u>FOOTBALL CAREER</u>

Joined Huddersfield Town groundstaff April 1955, signing professional forms on 25th February 1957

<u>TRANSFERS</u>

> **15th March 1960** - Huddersfield Town to Manchester City
> £55,000 - a new British record
> **9th June 1961** - Manchester City to Torino
> £110,000 - a record between British and Italian clubs
> **12th July 1962** - Torino to Manchester United
> £115,000 - a new British record transfer fee
> **2nd July 1973** Manchester United to Manchester City
> free transfer
> Retired **August 1974**

INTERNATIONAL RECORD

OPPOSITION	DATE	TOURNAMENT	VENUE	FT	GLS
Wales	18/10/1958	British Champ	Cardiff	3-0	1
N Ireland	05/11/1958	British Champ	Hampden Park	2-2	-
Netherlands	27/05/1959	Friendly	Amsterdam	1-2	-
Portugal	03/06/1959	Friendly	Lisbon	0-1	-
N Ireland	03/10/1959	British Champ	Belfast	4-0	-
Wales	04/11/1959	British Champ	Hampden Park	1-1	-
England	09/04/1960	British Champ	Hampden Park	1-1	-
Poland	04/05/1960	Friendly	Hampden Park	2-3	1
Austria	29/05/1960	Friendly	Vienna	1-4	-
N Ireland	09/11/1960	British Champ	Hampden Park	5-2	1
England	15/04/1961	British Champ	Wembley	3-9	-
Czech	26/09/1961	W Cup Qual	Hampden Park	3-2	2
Czech	29/11/1961	W C Play-off	Brussels	2-4	-
England	14/04/1962	British Champ	Hampden Park	2-0	-
Wales	20/10/1962	British Champ	Cardiff	3-2	1
N Ireland	07/11/1962	British Champ	Hampden Park	5-1	4
England	06/04/1963	British Champ	Wembley	2-1	-
Austria	08/05/1963	Friendly	Hampden Park	4-1	2
Norway	04/06/1963	Friendly	Oslo	4-3	3
Eire	09/06/1963	Friendly	Dublin	0-1	-
Spain	13/06/1963	Friendly	Madrid	6-2	1
Norway	07/11/1963	Friendly	Hampden Park	6-1	4
Wales	20/11/1963	British Champ	Hampden Park	2-1	1
England	11/04/1964	British Champ	Hampden Park	1-0	-
W Germany	12/05/1964	Friendly	Hanover	2-2	-
Wales	03/10/1964	British Champ	Cardiff	3-2	-
Finland	21/10/1964	W Cup Qual	Hampden Park	3-1	1
N Ireland	25/11/1964	British Champ	Hampden Park	3-2	-
England	10/04/1965	British Champ	Wembley	2-2	1
Spain	08/05/1965	Friendly	Hampden Park	0-0	-
Poland	23/05/1965	W Cup Qual	Chorzow	1-1	1
Finland	27/05/1965	W Cup Qual	Helsinki	2-1	-
N Ireland	02/10/1965	British Champ	Belfast	3-2	-
Poland	13/10/1965	W Cup Qual	Hampden Park	1-2	-
England	02/04/1966	British Champ	Hampden Park	3-4	1

Opposition	Date	Tournament	Venue	FT	Gls
Wales	22/10/1966	Euro Qualifier	Cardiff	1-1	1
England	15/04/1967	Euro Qualifier	Wembley	3-2	1
USSR	10/05/1967	Friendly	Hampden Park	0-2	-
N Ireland	21/10/1967	Euro Qualifier	Belfast	0-1	-
Austria	06/11/1968	W Cup Qual	Hampden Park	2-1	1
W Germany	16/04/1969	W Cup Qual	Hampden Park	1-1	-
N Ireland	06/05/1969	British Champ	Hampden Park	1-1	-
Peru	26/04/1972	Friendly	Hampden Park	2-0	1
N Ireland	20/05/1972	British Champ	Hampden Park	2-0	1
Wales	24/05/1972	British Champ	Hampden Park	1-0	-
England	27/05/1972	British Champ	Hampden Park	0-1	-
Yugoslavia	29/06/1972	Indep Cup	Belo Horizonte	2-2	-
Czech	02/07/1972	Indep Cup	Porto Alegre	0-0	-
Brazil	05/07/1972	Indep Cup	Rio de Janeiro	0-1	-
Czech	26/09/1973	W Cup Qual	Hampden Park	2-1	-
Czech	17/10/1973	W Cup Qual	Bratislava	0-1	-
W Germany	14/11/1973	Friendly	Hampden Park	1-1	-
W Germany	27/03/1974	Friendly	Frankfurt	1-2	-
N Ireland	11/05/1974	British Champ	Hampden Park	0-1	-
Zaire	14/06/1974	World Cup	Dortmund	2-0	-

Total 55 appearances, 30 goals

CLUB RECORD

League debut: 24th December 1956 **Huddersfield Town** v Notts County (A)

First goal: 26th December 1956 **Huddersfield Town** v Notts County (H)

Last Appearance and goal: 27th April 1974 **Manchester City** v Manchester United (A)

SEASON	LEAGUE		FA CUP		EUROPE		LEAGUE CUP	
	APPS	GLS	APPS	GLS	APPS	GLS	APPS	GLS
HUDDERSFIELD TOWN								
1956-57	13	2	5	1	-	-	NA	NA
1957-58	18	5	2	1	-	-	NA	NA
1958-59	26	2	-	-	-	-	NA	NA
1959-60	24	7	3	1	-	-	NA	NA
MANCHESTER CITY								
1959-60	7	2	-	-	-	-	NA	NA
1960-61	37	19	4	2*	-	-	2	-
TORINO								
1961-62	27	10	NA	NA	-	-	-	-
MANCHESTER UNITED								
1962-63	38	23	6	6	-	-	-	-
1963-64+	30	30	6	10	5	6	-	-
1964-65#	36	28	6	3	10	8	-	-
1965-66	33	15	7	6	8	3	-	-
1966-67	36	23	2	2	-	-	-	-
1967-68	23	7	1	0	3	2	-	-
1968-69	30	14	6	7	7	9	-	-
1969-70	10	2	-	-	-	-	3	1
1970-71	28	15	2	0	4	1	4	1
1971-72	32	13	7	0	-	-	2	0
1972-73	9	1	1	0	-	-	2	2
MANCHESTER CITY								
1973-74	22	9	1	2	-	-	3	1
TOTALS	**479**	**227**	**59**	**41***	**37**	**30**	**16**	**5**

+ *In Cup Winners' Cup; # in Inter-Cities Fairs Cup;* **Years in Bold in European Champions Cup**

* *Figures do not include six goals scored in abandoned cup-tie against Luton Town*

HONOURS AT MANCHESTER UNITED

FA CUP: 1962/63
LEAGUE CHAMPIONS: 1964/65, 1966/67
EUROPEAN CHAMPIONS CUP WINNERS: 1967/68

SCORING FEATS

FOUR IN A MATCH

Opposition	Venue	Date	Competition	Score
Ipswich Town	A	03/11/62	Div 1	5-3
Stoke City	H	07/12/64	Div 1	5-2
Aston Villa	H	24/10/64	Div 1	7-0
Waterford	H	02/10/68	ECCup	7-1

HAT-TRICKS

Huddersfield	H	04/03/63	FAC	5-0
Leicester City	A	16/04/63	Div 1	3-4
Ipswich Town	A	03/09/63	Div 1	7-2
Willem II	H	15/10/63	ECWC	6-1
Tottenham H	H	09/11/63	Div 1	4-1
Bristol Rovers	H	25/01/64	FAC	4-1
Sport Lisbon	H	26/02/64	ECWC	4-1
Sunderland	N	09/03/64	FAC	5-1
Djurgardens	H	27/10/64	Fairs	6-1
Chelsea	H	18/09/65	Div 1	4-1
Waterford	A	18/09/68	ECCup	3-1
Sunderland	H	18/01/69	Div 1	4-1
Birmingham C	H	24/02/69	FAC	6-2
Crystal Palace	A	17/04/71	Div 1	5-3

Statistics courtesy of www.stretfordend.co.uk

Appendix 3: Bibliography

Books

Allsop, Derick: Reliving The Dream
(Mainstream Publishing 1998)
Banks, Gordon: Banks Of England
(Arthur Baker Ltd 1980)
Bellers, Lance: The Unseen Archives of Manchester United
(Parragon 1999)
Best, George: Blessed the Autobiography.
(Ebury Press 2001)
Cantwell, Noel: United We Stand (Stanley Paul 1965)
Clark, Brian: Docherty (Kingswood Press 1991)
Crerand, Pat: On Top With United (Stanley Paul 1969)
Green, Geoffrey: There's Only One United
(Hodder and Stoughton)
James, Gary: The Pride of Manchester
(Polar Publishing 1990)
James, Gary: Manchester, the Greatest City
(Polar Publishing 2002)
Law, Denis: An Autobiography
(Macdonald and Jane's Publishers Ltd 1979)
Law, Denis: Denis Law's Book of Soccer
(Pelham Books 1967)
Liversedge, Stan: Busby - Epitaph To A Legend
(Soccer Book Publishing Ltd 1994)
McKinstry, Leo: Jack and Bobby (Collins Willow)
Gregg, Harry with Anderson, Roger: Harry's Game
(Mainstream Publishing 2002)

Mackay, Dave: Soccer My Spur. (Stanley Paul 1961)
Matthews, Sir Stanley: The Way It Was
(Headline Book Publishing Ltd 2000)
Motson John: The European Cup 1955 - 1980
(Queen Anne Press 1980)

NEWSPAPERS

The Manchester Evening News
The Daily Mail
The Daily Express
The Daily Mirror
The Daily Sketch

Index

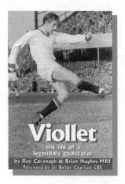

Sir Alex, United & Me
A Tale of Footballing Obsession
by Andy Pacino
Foreword by Sir Alex Ferguson
£8.99 - Paperback

Sir Alex Ferguson is one of the most respected and successful characters in British sport today but were it not for the support of die-hard supporters like Andy Pacino he may have been lost to United before he had a chance to weave his managerial magic.

Roger Byrne
Captain of the Busby Babes
by Iain McCartney
£16.95 - Hardback

"A good old-fashioned book about a good old-fashioned player" Daily Telegraph

Morrissey's Manchester
the essential Smiths Tour
by Phill Gatenby
Foreword by Mick Middles
£5.99 - Paperback
"A tour of the people and places that influenced the most influential of bands"

Bobby Murdoch, Different Class
by David Potter
Foreword by Billy McNeill
Available August 2003

'Bobby was an enormous presence with the Lions... his delight in playing for his beloved Celtic always showed in his happy expression on the field and he certainly did not hold back in celebrating our share of victories.'
Billy McNeill

To order call 0161 273 7007
or send a cheque (payable to Empire Publications) to
1 Newton St., Manchester M1 1HW